T0392274

A LABOR OF LOVE,

Volume 1

UNDERSTANDING HERCULES

ANNA D. ARAPAKOS

WESTBOW
PRESS®
A DIVISION OF THOMAS NELSON
& ZONDERVAN

WestBow Press books may be ordered through booksellers or by contacting:

WestBow Press
A Division of Thomas Nelson & Zondervan
1663 Liberty Drive
Bloomington, IN 47403
www.westbowpress.com
844-714-3454

ISBN: 979-8-3850-3351-5 (sc)
ISBN: 979-8-3850-3352-2 (e)

Library of Congress Control Number: 2024919401

Print information available on the last page.

WestBow Press rev. date: 09/28/2024

Any similarity to real persons, living or dead, is coincidental and not intended by the author.

Books Available by This Author:

- *Connecting the Dots: An Unanticipated Journey of Finding Faith* (written under the pseudonym Dimitria Christakis)

- *Living Stones: 52 Love Letters* (written under the pseudonym Dimitria Christakis)

- *Labor of Love, Volume 1: Understanding Hercules: An Introduction to the Greek Hero, A Primer on Huntington's Disease, Including Genetics and Neurology, and a Background on My Father's Life Up To When HD First Manifested Itself in Him*

- *Labor of Love, Volume 2: Helping Hercules: Caretaking My Father As Huntington's Disease Progressed in Him, Using the 12 Herculean Labors as a Framework*

This book is dedicated to all caretakers of those with Huntington's disease. May you find strength, courage, and support here.

I also commend this book to my nieces and nephews who never got to know their grandfather as well as they might have. May his memory be eternal now in you.

"Old man, take a look at my life
I'm a lot like you.
I need someone to love me
The whole day through.
Ah, one look in my eyes
And you can tell that's true."
— From "Old Man," by Neil Young,
emphasis mine (1972)

²"I *am* the LORD your God, ⁶ showing mercy to … those who love Me and *keep My commandments...* ¹²**<u>Honor your father and your mother</u>**, that your days may be long upon the land which the LORD your God is giving you."
— Exodus 20:2, 6, and 12 (NKJV), emphasis mine

Contents

---

*Author's Note: Huntington's disease and Huntington's Disease (HD) are both acceptable and will be used interchangeably throughout both volumes of *A Labor of Love*.

The Foreword for *Both* Volumes of
A Labor of Love: Understanding and Helping Hercules

Congratulations! You hold the <u>*first*</u> of two volumes of one giant love story in your hands! In essence, this story is about my father and how I came to care for him when he was elderly; this phenomenon is a universal experience we all will share or witness in one capacity or another.

I want to give you options about how to go about reading this two-volume account: if you have a passion for probing into the hows and whys — the science behind Huntington's disease (HD), you will appreciate the information I share in the *first* volume. There, you'll also learn about my father's socio-historical background from birth until age sixty through carefully chosen family stories that bring to life the historical facts that shaped his outlook and foundational life experiences. That way, you will have a baseline to see how HD will impact and distort certain inherent features, ways, and tendencies of his. We will cover genetics, neurology, and critical characteristics of this rare and progressive disease; you will be able to distinguish it from other neurodegenerative diseases. If I don't share this with you, you won't be prepared to understand how and why changes will occur at every level — intellectual, physical, psycho-emotional, and spiritual. Despite the damage this disease leaves in its wake, the essence of one's personality and soul remains. My father was his core self to his dying breath.

If you love a good story full of triumphs and agonies, highs and lows, one serious in tenor with touches of humor, all leading to a job well done, then the second volume is for you! There is no more popular Greek myth about a hero than Hercules, and while you may not know my father or me, by the time I superimpose my father's story onto the labors of Hercules, you will! Think of it like getting a fantastic review of the Herculean labors with my story piggybacked atop it. You will learn so much, and my overarching aim is for you and your parents to benefit from what I tell you. Hercules and I had much in common, and we wanted to help make things right despite going against many odds, and we were both victorious.

In **Volume 1, *my father is Hercules*,** and the portion of the myth I share in this volume is everything in Hercules' life *before* he undertakes the labors for which he has become so well-known. Here also is where I recount my father's cultural-historical background and the essentials of Huntington's disease, including its features, the genetic backdrop, its impact on the brain, and much more. Then, I make appropriate analogies between Hercules and my father during the formative years; this book stops at the point when my dad retires and his disease really "kicks in."

In <u>Volume 2</u>, the roles reverse, and *you will find me taking on the part of Hercules* as I perform *my* adaptation of the twelve "Herculean Labors" to care for my father when HD began making a pronounced mark on his life and person. I retell each labor Hercules undertook before I made parallels to what I did for my father. *Think of it like a guidebook for caretaking your loved one with HD* (or any other neurological disorder). You can read these two volumes independently, but I hope you'll read them *both*. Even the order is not obligatory. I am confident his *and* my story will move you. Then, the circle of love will continue through *your* actions and a better-informed mind and heart-set for *your* loved one in need.

The Preface for *Both* Volumes of
A Labor of Love: Understanding and Helping Hercules

"*The steps of a man are established by the LORD,*
And He delights in his way.
When he falls, he will *not* be hurled headlong because
the LORD is the One who holds his hand."
— Psalm 37:23-25 (emphasis mine)

"Your eyes have seen my unformed substance;
And *in Your book were all written the days that were ordained
for me*, when as yet there was not one of them."
— Psalm 139:16 (emphasis mine)

Here it is mere months after *Living Stones* has been published, and we are still in the middle of the global pandemic COVID-19. Its end is not yet in sight. I thought I would be done with writing for a while, but every morning after *Living Stones'* release, I woke up, and the singular chapter I wrote on my dad while I was writing *Connecting the Dots...* haunted me, goaded me, and drove me to make itself known in its own right! You wouldn't know this, but back when I was dictating into my phone much of *Connecting the Dots...* as I would drive to and from school, at one point, I got sidetracked and waylaid on a massive tangent of a side story. I found myself delving into the details of what happened during an incredibly intense trial I underwent: caring for my Huntington's disease-afflicted father over the last seven years — mainly the final two — of his life. At the time, I made the practical decision to put that Greek frying pan on the back burner, realizing that this was an entirely different topic, one I might feel compelled to explore later. Sure enough, I did and do now; it has beckoned me with a vengeance to share.

The two selected Biblical epigraphs above get down to brass tacks and remind us that we each and all have a slated time of life, not one day, more or less. I tell you that when I pray over my purpose and offer Him my life, I sometimes literally extend my hand and imagine the Lord "holding [my] hand" during the "days [He has] ordained for me." I am in *His* book of life! Perhaps writing the last two books was His way of preparing me to write this one for *you*! Maybe He knew I'd need experience writing before He set me to scribe *this* arduous journey. In any event, I accept His divine nudge and return to expand upon and flesh out the epoch of taking care of my dad in his final years. More importantly, it is with great hope and enthusiasm that I can offer *you* some practical advice to help *you* when that time comes in your life, and it will. None are exempt.

Perhaps you might not be the primary caretaker of your mother and/ or father; it could be a sibling or your spouse or their spouse; nonetheless, their need will impact you, too. Ah, it is a messy affair that exhausts, expends, and extols. Your parent's time of dying likely won't go down like it did for my dad; perhaps nature will take its course and gently bring them to their eternal rest without your having to do anything special or even at all! Like me, many will find it necessary to provide a broad safety net and comfort measures. We *all* hope for an easier, softer way to die with grace and dignity; no one wants to contend with or endure pain or disease. To die peacefully in one's sleep seems more of the exception than the rule. It seems to me that we weren't ever psychologically equipped to deal with death and dying, and the absence of our loved one will strike us as somehow *unnatural*. Platitudes of comfort do not soothe. And as we, the living, gaze at the infirm or elderly, I would venture to guess that we all are like my sister, who staunchly vowed that she "doesn't *ever* want to become a burden to *her* children." I replied, "Who does??" No one gets a crystal ball to know how it will all go down, but I reassured her then — and you now — that it doesn't matter if this were to happen! Part of loving others means being there for each other when we are down and out, *especially* on our way out.

It may be the case that *you* are getting up in years. I get that, too. When your body begins to break down in the middle years, the immanence of death comin' 'round the bend makes itself known with every new ache and spot and wrinkle. I am no exception and have started to experience this myself. When I feel an unexpected or inexplicable pain, wake up to spy a few more grey hairs, or silently fret when I can't easily recall a name or word or forget what I went for downstairs, I get reminded that *my own expiration* is coming. Although I happily maintain a Mediterranean diet and try to keep my mind, body, and spirit fit and actively engaged, it doesn't change the stark fact that one day I will perish. *We weren't born knowing how to handle death*, but if you should get a heads-up that life just *might* be cut short, oh, don't tarry in the love you show! Even though I can sometimes be impatient, as a believer, I *do* dwell in a deeper calm, possessing the truth and knowledge that "while we are at home in the body, we are absent from the Lord — for we walk by faith, not by sight — [*I am*] *of good courage...*" (2 Cor. 5:6–7). *Why* am I of good courage? This isn't the end, and I will see my father again. How do I know? We are told that "what is mortal will be swallowed up *by life*" (2 Cor. 5:4). This means there's even *more* life *after* this one, one far vaster than we can imagine or comprehend. Do I miss my dad? *Terribly*, yes, I *still* do, even if the pain has receded. Also, flesh contests and makes me protest, "Don't get me wrong; I'm not trying to rush things!" Even if I try to honor the temple with good health and spiritual habits, I am also keenly aware that He numbers my and *all* our days. Therefore, the clock is ticking, and I still have much fruit to bear for Him while I am on His watch. Steady is the keel and course of us who focus on giving ourselves away for His gain and glory.

Writing *Living Stones* was a testament to seizing that day to acknowledge and pour love on my precious ones *through my words*. **This book will focus on loving and caring for my father as he hobbled towards and took his last breath.** From this first-hand account, you will read that this would require so much of me. I agreed to get on that rollercoaster ride, which sometimes felt like I was on a runaway train wreck going in slow motion. In the end, though, even while I was grieving behind the scenes, I experienced the sweetest of satisfaction knowing *I had done all I could for him*, and it was good in His eyes. Looking back, I realize I have been blessed with one of the richest experiences of my life. The Lord has such mercy!

Reflecting on the care I gave my father came only *after* completing his affairs, and all was in order. As I mentioned, the *first* time I thought to capture this occurred as I was writing *Connecting the Dots…: An Unanticipated Journey of Finding Faith*, and it briefly recurred when I was penning *Living Stones*. In abiding by my own ground rules of writing love letters to the *living*, my father was automatically <u>ex</u>cluded from that list. Neither of these books was the right time or place to delve into his contending with Huntington's disease. **The longing to share my father's quirky and rich life story overlapped with and blended into a portion of mine, and ours grew into a larger-than-life dance. I *chose* to join in! How could I not? I look upon the labor of love to care for one's aging parent as a gift; recounting it here for you is a calling. If you accept the job someday, be forewarned that it will require energy beyond your mustering and volition; it will come from a love beyond measure.**

Know that such a sacrifice is also an act of obedience to God. Before you know it, He will have *you* walking through tense moments like some tightrope walker, like one breaking into a bank vault, trying to crack the code and find the best way to handle your aged person with kid gloves. All the while, you try to avoid the laser beams of their detection, which, if they ferreted out your taking the reins, they would feel raw, robbed, if not rageful. Caretaking my dad had me juggling *many* tasks and duties, so much so that it became apparent to outsiders. <u>One time, a colleague and friend noticed that I was squeezing in phone calls about my dad between</u>

school classes. She quipped, "It looks like you are performing the labors of Hercules." Even then, her analogy struck me as apt, and I never forgot it even though I couldn't recount all the labors at the time. A decade or so later, as I look back now, the comparison still rings true, thus the impetus for choosing the book's title. I never really thought of what I was doing as "my duty" or even "honoring" him, though at times, it certainly felt like I had a second job, but there was never a doubt in my mind that this surely was a labor of love.

Won't you join me now as I tell you about the days and ways I served as my father's caretaker? I can assure you that you will learn more than you ever expected! Such an experience as mine may one day forecast a version of yours to come. May I pray here together with you and ask God to "teach us to number our days, that *we may apply our hearts unto wisdom*" (from Psalm 90:12)? Let's put our wisdom into kind action and good works by loving on our mother and father in their *final* days, too.

Introduction to Volume 1

"Will you still need me, will you still feed me
When I'm sixty-four?"
— The Beatles, from *Sgt. Pepper's Lonely Hearts Club Band* (1967)

"Do not fear those who kill the body but are unable to kill the soul;
but *rather fear Him who is able to destroy both soul and body...*
Not one sparrow will fall to the ground apart from your
Father... *The very hairs of your head are all numbered, ... [but]* <u>do
not fear; **you are more valuable than many sparrows**</u>."
— from Matthew 10:28–31, emphasis mine

Everyone loves a good story, and boy, have I got one for you! Søren Kierkegaard once said, "Life can only be understood backward, but it must be lived forwards." I'm going to do both for you right now. As I peel back the skin of this zesty orange, you can look at my father's life, starting some eighty years ago in the boulders of southern Greece, which led to his voyage to America and subsequent successes. He made his mark and way along an odd and twisted path that drew to an unanticipated demise. As the one who chose to take the reins to make the end just a little easier for my dad (and curb the insanity along the way), I pass my experience, strength, and hope to *you* now. I have no doubt my tale can be a part of your story. For all I know, you may be helping ease your parent(s) toward that tender night.

Before I'd picked out a title for this book, I was compelled to explore the biblical principle of "<u>honoring</u>" our parents; *this* would be the book's bedrock and one of a personal nature. Considering the subject of showing what it looks like to walk in full-throttle caretaking mode, you will discover that with each step *I* took, just how intense and arduous it can be to do all that needs to be done in "honoring" one's elderly parent. It can bring you to your knees — if not break you — if you don't keep yourself fortified. I hadn't thought about what it would look like to help my father; he was fiercely independent! Such a plighted path came to be mine before I realized I was already on it. As I reviewed the Ten Commandments, I was struck by its internal order. What do I mean by this? The first four are of obvious importance: they inform us of *God's* priority above *all,* and the deference due Him, but of the remaining six biggies that follow, the *first* of them is to "honor thy father and thy mother." Have you ever noticed or thought about this? I see its ranking or prioritization as hardly accidental, random, or happenstance. To anyone young, this may sound like some patronizing edict to "mind your elders *because I said so*," but it turns out God's imperative involves so much in its value and scope than you could ever imagine.

Plainly put, *minding* your folks who nurtured you when you were young at some point *ought* to turn into *tending to* your folks when they are old. It's about loving them exactly when they are most likely to be dismissed, discounted, discarded, or even left for dead by the rest of us in the land of the living. Ironically, the elderly often turn on the very ones caring for them and treat them like the enemy, snarling at and biting the hand feeding *them*. Caring for them can be exhausting or exasperating to feel like you are being treated as public enemy number one. They'll likely forget or distort what you've said or done. Jesus gives us encouragement and unexpected advice when we get hit on the cheek or spit upon: we are to offer the *other* cheek also (Luke 6:29). Why? It is one of life's hardest lessons to be generous to and patient with loved ones who are confused or upset with you for every *and* no good reason. Your frail, furious, or fraught parents will forget the golden rule, but even a toothless lion likes to roar. Oh, but you are not casting your pearls before swine! This is how lavishing love can look like in their later years. Do quietly carry on, Christian soldier!

Jesus challenges our motives and maturity by asking us, "If you do good to those who do good to you, what credit is *that* to you?... Love your enemies, do good, and lend, *expecting nothing in return* (Luke 6:32 and 35, emphasis mine). No, your parent is not your "enemy," but let ye know they might treat *you* as one during their dying time, and that's *if* they remember you. Completing the circle of life necessitates closing the loop with love; sometimes, we need someone to hold *our* hand as their end approaches. God saw to it in His Top Ten to remind us to give back to the ones who gave their life to us when *we* were in a state of dependency. That's why the fifth commandment ranks as number one down here. Tag, you're it! To encourage us of our *real* purpose in life, that is, to *love others as ourselves*, God stacks His commandments as He sees fit and slates in the topmost order of His directives for human relationships the one to honor our parents. It is number one. Anyhow, He used *them* to bring *you* into being, or, if they were not the ones who birthed you, He matched them up to be the ones who sought and raised *you* in love.

I can hear the protestations and counterclaims: "My mom wasn't there for me, never *really* loved me." "My father abandoned us." "My stepmom was cruel." "My dad abused me." I know there are harsh realities out there, and they deserve attention! Do know Jesus can help heal and liberate *you* from shame and inner pain! He's a chain breaker and healer like no other! To be fair to you, dealing with such emotional scars goes beyond the scope of this book, but do let me say right here and now that if this was the case for you, *I am so sorry* that this happened! If you come to forgive, you will get a double blessing. That decision is your call. Jesus chose to forgive us *all* transgressions and *died* to make our restitution and restoration complete forever. If you come to believe in this — in *Him*, you won't *ever* lose your life, die though we all must. The long and the short of it is, if you take a look in the mirror, it oughtn't take you long to recognize and acknowledge that "there is none righteous, no, not one" (Romans 3:10)" and that includes us both. Why? "All have sinned and fallen short of the glory of God" (Romans 3:23). Nonetheless, despite our flaws, when you come to saving faith, you are summoned "to be perfect as your heavenly Father is perfect" (Matthew 5:48). I know. That's an impossibly tall order, but ought we not at least try? Those who choose to follow Him are nonetheless still sinners, but hopefully, we who do are working out our salvation "with fear and trembling" (Philippians 2:12).

At the time, what this looked like for me meant was to do the right thing *for my father* in his time of trouble. Life got interrupted when he began his slow descent into a form of madness; he was spared only by another unexpected blow. You'll see. I took one step after another, and often, it felt like I was scrambling. I certainly didn't *seek* to bear a burden such as caretaking, but I couldn't look the other way. I don't judge you if you can't do this because I certainly haven't taken up my cross for all my calls to duty. Should *you* be in the position to help your aging parent, all the more so when they reach a dependent state, have you thought about or discussed with others how to respond? I know; it's a *lot* to consider, let alone take on. This book is for those who decide to say *yes* to helping these decrepit elder babes, for those who become the parent to *their* parents. Not all can, and frankly, that's the norm, but should you be in the position and find your inner voice (or, more likely, your siblings') urging you to accept this unique challenge, let me be there for you right now: *I cheer you on!* You have less to lose than others do to gain. For me, it may as well have been God as the Beatles who asked me on behalf of my dad: "*Will you still need me, will you still feed me when I'm sixty-four*?"

You may tell me that although those who are advanced in their years might need special care, they are a *far* cry from tending to infants! You would be correct. It's easy to love babies! Caress their soft newborn skin, smell their little necks, or look into their innocent eyes, so full of wonder as they follow you around, recording millions of fresh, new impressions! In fact, the title I chose for my book, *Labor of Love*, is one more typically used for books advising parents-to-be! But what about those in their winter season of life? The husk deteriorates, systems break down, and sicknesses set in, regardless of whether we have put our best foot forward to avert, avoid aging, *or* live like there's no tomorrow! I don't mean to be morbid, but it *is* coming. You get little reminders of this stark fact. At four, my nephew looked at my middle-aged, veiny hands and asked, "Why do you have worms under your skin?" Spots, wrinkles, aches, and pains may not yet have made their debut in *you*, but they are coming.

Like you, I am one hungry for life! I try to gulp in all those good-to-the-last drops to the point that sometimes, I feel like I'm burning the candle at both ends! Quotes abound that say something to the effect that "getting old isn't for sissies," but an even harsher truth is for those *watching*: there will be some elderly family members who will not recognize family members. The sands seem to fall faster the further down the hourglass, but "ashes to ashes, we all fall down." I challenge you to consider whether those in the advanced years are *also* "even the least of these" (Matthew 25:40) worthy of our care and attention. What I experienced while I was caretaking my dad didn't have me thinking I was "honoring" him. That came later, much later! This experience proved to be one of *the most daunting and fulfilling challenges* of my life. I learned early, hard, and fast *not* to expect gratitude from him. I came to expect the opposite: much like tots in their "terrible twos," older people can be ornery, oppositional, and headstrong. Like babes at the other end of life's spectrum, they can and will get fussy, cranky, and petty. And then, with some, you can also add descriptors like "accusatory," "suspicious," or "hostile." Some turn more simplistic, if not sweet and angelic, as if the emotional edges have been smoothed away, others, even catatonic. I do not pretend to say that what I underwent with my father is anywhere near what some have gone through! Some expend every last resource and exhaust themselves to the point of getting sick while they care for their aging or dying parent. Nonetheless, what I underwent was no cakewalk either.

Unlike babes and wee ones, whom we know how long it takes before they reach their teens and the various stages in between, we cannot predict how long (or brief) the years of independent living before *your* senior reaches a state of fragility or dependency. Many causes contribute and play a role. We can also factor in a person's essential nature, including their temperament, personality, and genetic makeup (at least, the part we can be made aware of). A sunny disposition and good genes surely don't hurt, but these are not the be-all, end-all factors to longevity. One's nurturing plays a hefty role, too, including those learned behaviors and habits, not to mention the impact of your physical environment, life choices, and lifestyle. And how can we neglect to mention our outlook on life? How else could those who have survived incomprehensible and horrific ordeals do so but through faith *and* chosen optimism? I have also learned that being vibrantly connected to family and community plays an even more significant role than our health habits and genetic factors. However, this is no book on longevity; there are scads of books on that. My dad had a monkey wrench thrown in his system, and the disease threw us all for a loop; it was something no one could have known or predicted.

These arguments notwithstanding, I quickly volley forth two biblical truths that trump any nature-versus-nurture argument. My aim is not to serve you common clichés but beacons of hope and bright opportunity. First, we each *are* on a fixed timecard; we *have an expiration date,* just not one tattooed on our skin's surface. You may think you can read the proverbial writing on the wall, but that doesn't make it accurate or true! The consequence of our disobedience to God *still* remains and steers us: "The wages of sin is death, but the gift of God is eternal life in Christ Jesus our Lord" (Romans 6:23). I *have* accepted that gift, so I have this assurance that I will never die even though *my physical body* cannot sustain itself forever. Observing others whose lives *appear* to have been cut short — *including my father's* — I can't help but gasp at "how fleeting ... life is" (Psalm 39:4 NIV), but God has known it all along. Speaking of fleeting, those who are well in their seventies, eighties, or beyond will either retreat quietly into their woodwork *or* reach out and try and stay plugged into life. There is an end-zone, a shade of gray — pun intended — *before* your parents become dependent; typically, it is a couple of decades since they retired (or the like) and are living on the outer rim of independence. You haven't yet gotten that phone call that says they have fallen and can't get up. *This* is the time to honor them so that they don't feel irrelevant, alone, or unimportant, even if they aren't a part of the hustle and bustle of your days. Double this sense if they happen to be a widow or widower. Triple it if they are sick or injured. If you don't take the time, then you may lose your chance. Preemptively strike against future regrets; you won't be sorry! Recently, I spoke with a dear friend of mine who is my mother's age, and she complimented her son, who heeded the words of his dying father, "*Look after your mother.*" Should *you* find yourself in this position, I implore you to reach out and make a start, renew, or increase regular contact. It often gets harder to say goodbye when they sense they are rounding the final lap.

Let's now get to the underbelly of my dad's unique story. I want to share this volume's master plan with you so you can more easily invest in what's in store. It will help you better appreciate a journey you may someday travel. Know that I will be selective in my father's biography;

this is no tell-all book! Here in Volume 1, my father's life, starting with his literal conception up to the point of his divorce at around age fifty, will be compared to the fate and fortunes of Hercules. This volume concludes with my father's retirement. You may be curious as to why I would start with Dad's conception. That is precisely when the die was cast, and he inherited the disfiguring Huntingtin gene that would set his life on a trajectory leading to his disfigurement and an early demise. It was like watching him turn into some contorted cartoon creature, a scarecrow, a stick figure of the man I knew and loved. The love never stopped for either of us. I will familiarize you with this disease, starting with a small dose of describing what Huntington's disease (HD) is. Frankly, it's too much to read in one fell swoop, and that's not all this story is about by a long shot! I am aware that most didn't pick up this book solely to learn about this deadly disease, let alone hear what happened during the Greek Civil War as it blurred alongside World War II; however, these are the building blocks of my father's life that make his narrative rich and unique. I want to honor him and his memory by bringing them to life here for you.

I will introduce you to my father's formative years in Greece from 1935 to 1945, during WWII *and* a part of the Greek Civil War, followed by his subsequent life in America. In this volume of the book, <u>my dad will be our modern-day Hercules</u>. The comparisons I make to Hercules here will be limited and relegated to Hercules' experience *before* he performed the labors for which he became famous. You will not find a blow-by-blow biographical account but rather *carefully selected snapshots*; his story is not so much linear as parabolic. I want you to become familiar with the environmental "fish tank" into which my father was born. Cultural norms, societal expectations, historical events, and a nation's values are imbued in the individual from birth through youth, so you will learn what was going on in the land in which my father was born and lived for the first decade or so of his life. Who my dad was at his core would be shaped by factors as influential as his biogenetic foundation. There will be historical events you will learn of in greater detail. Still, not all of my revisited recollections will be as accurate as if published by the Associated Press or detailed in the *Encyclopedia Britannica*. I am no historian; nonetheless, this will be a real account. I will compress time and bend his formative years to take you through vital moments of his adult life. Along the way, I add daubs of pertinent Greek history and, yes, simplified neurology as it relates to Huntington's disease.

To that end, Volume 1 is where you will learn all about what Huntington's disease is — and what it is *not*. You'll find our study of genetics and the parts of the brain adversely impacted by this disease fascinating. To do this account of my father justice, you must understand what was happening to him *before* we get to the point of no return, as in when the decline begins. Pockets and patches of himself got distorted, but you will know why. By the end of this first volume, *you will know my father to his core*, and by that, I mean his native personality, intelligence, and soul's essence. Thus, you will be prepared for Volume 2 when the turning point occurs, and his decline is undeniable. Proportionately speaking, *this* book will cover three-fourths of his life. After the first chapter, each subsequent chapter covers (1) Greek history, (2) genetics, parts of the brain affected by Huntington's disease, and features of the disease itself, and (3) my father's background before we knew he had HD. That's a lot in a short amount of space! Let's now begin with a tiny primer on what HD is — and what it isn't to know what would be in store for my father.

Chapter 1

A Background on What Huntington's Disease Is and What It *Isn't*

⁶"All flesh is grass, and all its loveliness is like the flower of the field.
⁷ *The grass withers, the flower fades,*
When the breath of the LORD blows upon it;
Surely, the people are grass…
[Only] the word of our God stands forever.
— From Isaiah 40:6-8, emphasis mine

"Hey, Woody Guthrie, but I know that you know
All the things that I'm a-sayin' and a-many times more
I'm a-singin' you the song, but *I can't sing enough*
'Cause there's not many men that done the things that you've done."
— From "*Song* to Woody," by *Bob Dylan*, on his debut
album, *Bob Dylan*, 1962, emphasis mine

"I have lived to see **strange days**."
— From J. R. R. Tolkien's *The Two Towers*

Allow me to establish a baseline foundation and tell you what Huntington's disease is and how it differs from other diseases you are familiar with that malign both body and brain. You, too, will see glimpses of the "strange days" I allude to above. I have read many articles and books on this disease because that's what my dad had, so naturally, I took a personal interest in it. This disease wrecked my dad, impacted our family, and made steep demands of me. Sure, some scientific information on HD *can* be dry and arcane, but when you see how it wreaks its havoc in the actual person — my dad — you, too, will feel the weight of the destruction it left in its wake. I promise not to overwhelm you with too much information, but at this point, the *least* I can do is to differentiate it from other types of dementia with which you *are* familiar. "Huntington's disease? What's *that*?" you may well ask. For me, it all began when we noticed my father's right shoulder would twitch upward for no rhyme, reason, or regularity, as if he'd argued with himself and quickly shrugged the thought away. We had no name for it because we did not know what was happening to him. We just thought it was our quirky dad whose Greek side was spilling out in some weird way.

It is unlikely that you've even heard of Huntington's disease, but if you have, you may possess a few vague notions about it. Huntington's disease (**HD**) is an extremely rare disease affecting only up to 7 people in 100,000 people of Western European descent and ten times less than those of Asian and African descent. In the United States alone, it is estimated that more persons per 100,000 live with the disorder.[1] This disease has no cure yet, and treatments can relieve or reduce only some symptoms.[2] Based on Huntington's disease statistics, this disorder affects about around 30,000 people in the United States.[3] My dad unknowingly drew the (un)lucky straw.

Technically speaking, Huntington's disease is what's known as an "**autosomal dominant, neurodegenerative disorder**." Let me translate: if one of your parents has the marker for it in their genetic code and *if* the gene gets passed onto you, you *will* get it; thus, each child will have a 50-50 chance of inheriting it. (In the even less likely scenario that *both* have this code, it would be an absolute *certainty* for their children.) If the child inherits the gene, they <u>will</u> get the disease; it will 100% happen. If *you* have it, you already know that it affects the mind, mood, *and* body, and it will steadily worsen as the years pass until the death knell tolls. You won't see it coming because there is no definitive moment when "it" starts. How this disease impacts a person is different than just the aging process, where systems falter and fail due to normal wear and tear on the system. Here, I mainly focus on mental processes or losses due to dementia. If you are the one who inherits HD, it's usually in the late middle years when it makes its inauspicious first appearance, which only later, in retrospect, you may look back and speculate, "Hmm, *that* must have been when it started." In a sense, any such "starting point" is inaccurate because HD is inherited, so technically, there never was a day when you didn't have it. There are no firm and steadfast rules as to its onset, expression, rate of progress, or method of striking death. Often, those in the most advanced stage of HD die from choking or asphyxiation.

The impact of HD on the person who inherits the disease is devastatingly complete — holistic even, and fascinatingly, *no two persons with HD express identical symptoms or manifestations*, though similarities surely exist. Jagged edges of the soul and personality remain firmly fixed, but the body's movements degenerate into a tragi-comic, herky-lurchy perversion of the former self. It's like watching Charlie Chaplin in one of his silent flicks; only he's gone berserk. Can you see it? Unfortunately, since it shows up later in life, the behavioral and cognitive problems that ensue because the person is not of sound mind are a tragic bonus to what you must deal with when treating the *person*. What do I mean? First, they can feel lost and frightened but don't know what's happening or how to communicate it.

Further, troubles with the law and society, finances, and independent living skills can crop up at the drop of a hat. *Life* will put you on the clue train when prompt action and proper care for the person with HD become undeniable and imperative. Manifestations of the changes that will occur are likely to pop up anywhere in them, yet because these changes happen so gradually, you almost imperceptibly get accustomed to the dance with no name. Maybe that's why this disease is also called <u>Huntington's **chorea**</u>; the term "chorea" is derived from the Ancient Greek "χορεία," as the "quick movements of the feet or hands are comparable to dancing."[4] Outsiders can see it; there may be whispers, but hopefully, they will lovingly and tactfully confront you about it.

At this point, you may be speculating, "Well, isn't that like Alzheimer's? Is HD kind of like that? What about Parkinson's or Lou Gehrig's disease?" First, let me quickly clarify and dispense with the chief differences between Huntington's and other diseases that impact the brain. Unlike Parkinson's disease, where the movements are predictable, somewhat automated, and of a similar degree manifested throughout the frame, HD, called initially "St. Vitas' dance," after the patron saint of dancing, is "sporadic, idiosyncratic, and <u>unpredictable</u>"; <u>it is manifested uniquely in each person who has it</u>.[5] You'll quickly notice that something ain't right, but you won't be able to put your finger on it. Unlike Parkinson's, the person with HD *also* has cognitive and emotional disturbances that only increase with time. This "progressive" part of its nature makes its effect devastating to all who experience or deal with it. In a sense, you can compare it to muscular dystrophy in its slow and steady march to dominion over a person's muscle control, but you would need to add a spray of buckshot to the mental functions, too. Yes, it is like Alzheimer's in that there *is* a component of memory loss, but it is nowhere near as severe. The way I depict what the HD does to the mind in comparison to Alzheimer's is that eventually, Alzheimer's brings about a t.k.o. to the memory. Sometimes, everything and everyone will disappear into the abyss. Not so with HD: specific portions of the brain become pock-marked and ravaged, making it look like it is turning into Swiss cheese. You can observe the brain riddled with twisting and cavernous tunnels deep within. The part of the brain that preserves memories is *not* wholly molested. For example, my dad could recall in great detail how silk is produced. He had observed this as a young lad in charge of feeding the worms their yummy mulberry leaves. In his last days, he might not have been able to remember if he had taken his vitamins, but certain older memories remained crystal clear and sparkling, and newer ones that were connected to his emotions were sharp. He certainly did forget if he was mad at me! Other executive functions such as deductive and inductive reasoning, holding one's temper, controlling impulses and obsessive thoughts, would t-totally fly out the window. He had *no* control over the in**v**oluntary *fluidity* of his motor skills.

At this point, some might wonder if HD is like Tourette's syndrome or general dementia, and the answer is "Well, sort of, but more." Yes, you would notice some bizarre antisocial behavior, agitation, and a lack of empathy, similar to what you would find in a person with Tourette's. Still, HD does not diminish with age; instead, the opposite occurs. TS usually begins in childhood, yet frequently, the facial and vocal tics have waned by adulthood. This is *not* the case with HD. Depending on the severity of the case, which one is born with, but wouldn't know for sure unless he got tested — and that wouldn't be a thought to do unless the weird symptoms began and trouble followed — likely, you wouldn't notice the odd movements or moodiness until middle age. What about muscular dystrophy? Is HD like that? Perhaps you have seen the tragic writhing and twisted movements of one whose muscles are twisting and atrophying in the unique way that MS afflicts the brain and body, and insofar as how HD impacts the physical frame, you absolutely *can* make a comparison to the unintended and out-of-control contortions and gyrations of frame and limb. Still, it would help if you also figured in HD doing that to *thought and mood.*

Let's speak more on Parkinson's disease and a few others. We've all seen those in their golden years whose hands tremble; maybe it is also the head or whole frame, be it ever-so-slightly or disturbingly. Yes, as the Huntington's Disease Society of America slogan states, "*We Move,*" but the way HD impacts the body can make it seem more like a tic or two or ten gone haywire. Nothing is anticipatory, regulated, or remotely rhythmic as Parkinson's disease is in its way. We can make one final comparison to ASL or Lou Gehrig's disease, which, like HD, is a progressive disease that weakens the whole physical frame. The difference is that while ASL is more rapid in its progression, it does *not* have the bizarre behavioral changes HD does. Fun times. When we found out my father had HD, I could hear my sister quietly gasp as she swiftly made the mental association with Woodie Guthrie, who, like his mother before him, died from it, albeit in an insane asylum and not their burned-down home. The degenerative nature of the disease compounds with interest when you experience it for yourself, watching your loved one jostled by its whim. You will learn how it impacts motor, cognitive, and behavioral functions so that by the time we get to its most pronounced manifestation here in my *father*, you will be by my side as I start caring for my dear and demented dad. I hope my tale will leave your soul "panting for God" (Psalm 42:1), and though, at the time, my burden hardly seemed light to me, I did have Christ's yoke, which gave me holy stamina. This book is hardly intended to be a case study or some manual, just a very personal guide, one I hope can benefit *you* in the future as I honor my dad now and again this way.

Chapter 2

The Mark of Destiny

For You formed my inward parts;
You wove me in my mother's womb.
I will give thanks to You, for *I am fearfully and wonderfully made…*
My frame was not hidden from You,
When I was made in secret,…
Your eyes have seen my unformed substance;
And in Your book were all written
The days that were ordained for me,
When as yet there was not one of them.
— Taken from Psalm 139:13–16
****

so much depends
upon

a red wheel
barrow

glazed with rain
water

beside the white
chickens

— William Carlos Williams, "The Red Wheelbarrow," 1923

Myth, Man, and Maker

Every year, when I teach William Carlos Williams' "So much depends" to my juniors, their initial response is always the same: "*I could have written that when I was* five!" they boast. They are incredulous as to how something so seemingly simplistic could make it into the annals of our text. I gently push back and counter *them* with a question: could they name some building blocks that impact how they function on a basic level, things *they* are likely to take for granted? Then, we discuss the poet's choice of primary colors and interpret his seeming happenstance choices and images; we always come back around to the first line: "*So* much depends..." *So much depends on your genetics, the time and place of birth, family, culture, and value system of which you become a living part.* Ultimately, if we go all the way to the source of life, matter, and existence, every aspect of you depends upon how our Heavenly Father fashioned you. He thought of you and purposed you to exist well before you were conceived and born! With this macroscopic lens, I examine the environment and family into which my father was born. Throughout his story, for your ease and entertainment, I will segue from retelling the story of a hero you all know to the fiery man my father was. Let us begin before he began to see the writing already on the wall.

"*The greatest hero of Greece was Hercules.*" So penned Edith Hamilton in her renowned classic, *Mythology.* I can't think of any child who *hasn't* heard of Hercules' exploits, and we still wonder about his strength and cleverness. In a short mythology unit I teach, hands down, for more than any other movie I show, my sophomores beg to watch *anything* about him. Beyond their awareness, a familiar timber and temper exist in his character from which we can still learn lessons. We will visit and consider his more complicated impulses later on, but for now, let's briefly look at Hercules's origins, which contributed to his becoming the unique hero we all admire. In a sense, through no fault of his own and before his mother had birthed him, we could argue that Hercules was a victim of circumstances and destined for difficulties. His is a story for those who feel like they were born with one strike against them and yet have found a way to succeed spectacularly. In this capacity, the mythical hero Hercules and my mortal father share a common bond.

The ancient Greeks would look beyond the here and now and sense and self to speculate about the origins of mankind and the world. Through myth, they came up with stories that transcended time and space and, in the bargain, truly tapped into what they intuited was beyond them: the divine. Of course, the Greeks are hardly unique as mythmakers, but they grasped at the straws as to the meaning of the human condition — our mortality — and tried to make sense of seemingly random forces of nature and life. At the time, these Greeks couldn't fathom that what they were grasping for were not animated gods but the living *God.* God would stir in their hearts and minds to prepare them to know Him — *His Son* — later on; mortals conceiving of gods was the magnificent prequel of God coming to man! Greeks took the raw potential and pathos of man's nature and parceled them as attributes among the gods. They were also marred by familiar flaws and character defects, which gave them dimension and pathos. In short, we have the best and worst aspects of a man projected onto a host of gods, and as you know, *the* most powerful of them all, as well as their topmost ruler, was

Zeus. Zeus was also infamous for his escapades, infidelities, and deceptions; we are concerned here only with one of his affairs.

Hercules' Parentage

One of the mortal women Zeus was attracted to and beguiled to bed was a woman named Alcmene. To ensure his seduction would be a success, he assumed the appearance of her husband so that she wouldn't know any better, and they slept together. The result of this night's union was that Hercules was conceived, so, yes, technically, he was half god and half man. (And may I take a moment to insert here that this is neither the same thing as *our* being made in God's *image*, nor is this comparable to Jesus being both fully God and fully man.) When Alcmene's actual husband came back the next night, you can imagine his surprise when she was less than receptive to his amorous advances, all the more so since he came back victorious from having avenged her brothers' deaths, a stipulation she set forth before she would give herself to him. The angle Zeus chose to use to seduce Alcmene was not only by coming to her in the appearance of being her husband but also by bragging to her of his exploits and victory. Zeus was the exuberant husband returning home from battle in a grand mood with good news. In short, his wooing began with moving her mind; he did not take her by force, and she would be the last mortal he slept with. Already knowing this would be his final affair, it was Zeus's intention the whole time to beget a son "powerful enough to protect both gods and men against destruction."[6]

That next night, when Alcmene's husband came home and despite his wife's lukewarm reception, they united, and the result was the conception of a *second* child, Hercules' half-brother and fraternal twin, who lay next to him in the womb. The soothsayer Tiresias cleared up the mystery for Alcmene's spurned husband and foretold him of Hercules' future glories and destined greatness, so he left Hercules alone. Meanwhile, having returned to Olympus, Zeus bragged that He would have a son. He had the audacity and the foresight to quell his wife's renowned jealousy by naming his son after her, "Hercules," which ironically means "Glory of Hera." He had great hopes and plans for his son to be a ruler of nobility. All of this meant nothing to Hera, so she looked for a way to punish her husband by vowing to kill Hercules when he and his half-brother were born. Not only that, but Hera made her husband promise that if his son were born *before* midnight, he would be that high king. Zeus swore an oath in agreement to this condition, and right away, Hera set to working on nullifying the possibility.

The long and the short of it is that Hera successfully worked her magic:

the boy's birth was delayed, and Zeus lost the bet. Hercules would *not* rule the House of Perseus. However, Zeus *did* find a way to elevate his son's stature by offering Hera *another* proposal to which she agreed. The result was that after he died, Zeus's son Hercules would gain immortal status and become a god, ennobling and enabling him to remain with his father on Mount Olympus forever. Not a bad consolation prize. The particular proposition Zeus proffered to his wronged wife was that Hercules would have to perform twelve exceedingly difficult and protracted labors thought up by a king who was a lesser man than his son. This satisfied Hera, and she agreed; nevertheless, she never stopped trying to find a way to kill Hercules.

I tell you the backstory to Hercules because I want you to see that long before Hercules was ever born, the die was cast such that during his lifetime, there would be a price to pay for a transgression that did not even start with him, and it was a punishment that he alone would have to bear. I should also like to insert here that this is *not* the same notion as Old Testament references to the iniquities of the father visiting the children; we are *not* talking about generational sin or consequences due to our disobedience to or disrespect of God. Hercules had no idea what lay in store for him. Although *technically* he was no longer paying for the transgression of Zeus — as that was taken care of by his no longer getting to be the ruler his father had initially intended — he *would* commit heinous crimes of his own, and the conditions that would lead Hercules down this arduous path were specially concocted by Hera. It is said that no other man ever suffered or paid the price for atrocities committed as much as Hercules did, yes, even though he did what he did while not in his right mind.

Our hero never pled innocent by reason of insanity — though if he had committed his misdeed today, his appointed defense attorney would have told him to plea just that. He accepted responsibility for his unintended, unconscious crime. After completing these impossible tasks and thus fulfilling his sentence, no mortal ever attained the heroic status Hercules did: immortality. This feature sets Hercules apart from all the other heroes; my father, too, would have something better in store for him after all his suffering ceased. As we return to the day of the birth of Alcmene's twins, you should know that *neither* of her sons was named after her husband, and Hera, *still* discontent, would search relentlessly for a way to terminate Hercules. Indeed, it wasn't too long after the boys were born that the troubles soon began. It is reported in ancient texts that Hercules' birthday is celebrated on the fourth day of every month, even though according to zodiac descriptors, all signs point to the tenth month.[7]

Greek History Tied to Family Stories

Ages later, light years past Hercules' fictitious beginnings, my father was born on a dark winter's day in the Peloponnesian port town of Gythion; the date was December 4, but in this case, it was the *day* — not the month of my dad's birth that was to be in some dispute for years. Was it the third, as we'd always been told? Was it the fifth like we heard decades later? His own mother couldn't seem to remember. Greeks celebrate their name day in a grand fashion more than the day of their birth; the saint after whom one is named bears greater significance on a person's identity than the date of their arrival. I came to learn of the actual date of my father's birth when I saw a copy of his birth certificate some two years after his death. It was fascinating for me to behold that alongside the right portion of this document was his baptismal certificate — a two-for-one — as if man needed God's seal of approval for authentication. My father was named after the Apostle Paul and *not* after his father, let alone any other male relative. This is both an uncommon name and an unorthodox occurrence in Greece. I was told he was named after the family doctor; perhaps this man showed my grandmother no small kindness when she felt isolated and alone during the war. After all, this was her third son and last child, and she had not forgotten that she was snatched from her happy home and family.

Some of the early years of her marriage were spent with her in-laws, and her mother-in-law, in particular, lived up to the stereotype of being an exacting and unaffectionate woman. This woman even swept out the dirt floor of their house, so *"just so"* was she. Not only that, but her husband, my grandfather, was no warm Zorba either. He was a reserved and quiet man who expected formality to be shown toward him. He has been described to me as *stern*, hardly a quality sought by a young bride, and he *expected* respect. Perhaps he permitted his bride to name their third son as she wished; I'll never know. The first went according to custom, meaning their eldest was named after the *paternal* grandfather. The second *ought* to have been named after his father, but instead, he was named after my *grandmother's brother* (and *not* her father, with whom she was likely to have held a grudge). Instead, all three sons bore my grandfather's first name as their *middle*. As was the case for Hercules, who was *not* named after his earthly father (or Zeus, who sired him), my dad's naming and identity started in an atypical manner.

It is not uncommon for many little girls to idolize their fathers, and I was such a one. One particular way I respect my dad here and now is to share key events that transpired before he was born and continued not too far into his youth. Why is this? You need to understand the world into which he was born. My dad's first cousin, Vivian, told me the following family history, who, in good humor, would tease my dad that "*she* would always be the younger one," even if by only one year. They grew up close together in those early years. She is my source for what you find quoted in the following account of his youth. As it turns out, my father shares other similarities with Hercules, and these got their start before either was born. Let's first take a look at their mothers. My dad's mother was betrothed to a man some seventeen years her senior; she was twenty-three, and he was pushing forty. Though born and raised in Greece, he came to America for work as a youngster at the turn of the century. At this time, there was a considerable influx of Greeks, Italians, Jews, Slavs, and other Europeans from non-W.A.S.P. origins who emigrated to the States.

In those days in Greece, marriages were arranged between the father of the bride and the groom's father, and favorable factors were based on compatible backgrounds and mutually benefitting attributes, *not* on fickle feelings founded on attraction. According to Vivian, there was no love between my grandparents when they married. In fact, she rolled her eyes at the mere suggestion but added that their love *came later*. At this point, Vivian's husband said my grandfather was already referred to as "papou" or "grandpa" because he was so much older than her and was already balding. It would come as no surprise that as a young woman with prospects of furthering her education, something she had been excited about, my grandmother would have been disappointed at best and turned off at worst by such a prospect.

Looking at it from my grandmother's perspective at the time and pointing out another similarity within our story to that of Hercules, I would imagine that my then-young grandmother, who, although unlike Alcmena, was *not* tricked into infidelity, certainly would have felt like she was sleeping with a stranger. I am told my grandmother was grateful for her older brother stepping in and trying to come to her defense beforehand, but their father dismissed him and curtly said, "These are not women's affairs." In short, the marriage contract was more like a business arrangement: my grandmother's father *paid* my grandfather's father, Nikola. In turn (and probably on stipulation), he bought land in Gythion, where *she* was from and where all his grandsons would be born. Having received the dowry and with his young family started and all now stable, my grandfather returned to America to begin his business, but I get ahead of myself here. That was to come closer to when my father was about five.

The long and short of it was that my grandparents made a family in less than five years and produced three sons. When my papou left behind his young wife and children to return to America, he did so with the intent and expressed purpose of sending back every available red cent to *his* father so that his dad, in turn, could buy property in *their* nearby home village of Agios Nikolaou, located in the Taygetos Mountains way up and back from the coastal port of Gythion. This his father did. It's just a 40-minute drive by car today, and I have been there now five times. All my grandfather wanted to do was buy land and build a house for his wife and sons through the sweat of his brow and on his home turf. My grandfather could never have imagined that his father ended up putting the house in his *own* name and later passed it on to his *other* son's children. What deceit and treachery! In fact, with the property bought and the house built, my grandfather's father even put his daughter-in-law and her three young sons out of the house, at which point they had to return to *her* family in Gythion. I would have been relieved, but I am told that she put up a fight. Later, during the war, they were "allowed" to come back and stay in a portion of this house. That's why, decades later, my dad's oldest brother, my godfather, and Uncle Kolya would have remembered this injustice with sizzling gall and refused to return to the village of Agios Nikolaou.

Life in America and an Unanticipated Genetic Destiny

Meanwhile, from across the ocean, you can imagine my grandfather would have been steaming hot at such a betrayal. Only much later did my grandfather forgive his father because, during the war, he took care of his daughter-in-law and grandsons in this home in the village. You may ask, why didn't my grandfather return to Greece straightaway to take care of this matter? Trans-Atlantic travel, a six-week voyage across the ocean to return to Greece, would have been disallowed for civilians during the mid-1940s in the thick of WWII. Greece was then in a state of acute distress, as I will tell you about later on. I learned from my father that my great grandfather's rationale for re-appropriating this money was because his *other* son, Kostas, also working in America with my grandfather, as it turned out, had a penchant for gambling; precious funds were squandered. Therefore, it was decided that he should be *shipped back to Greece and married to a village girl* to keep him out of financial dire straits (or worse) in America. This Kostas came back and had five children.

I find myself returning to the mindset of my grandmother, who, as a young bride and mother, *had* to have been lonely and resentful, all the more so with her husband absent. Understandably, she would have been all the more clingy to her sons. This would have a most profound impact on her eldest son, who, for better and worse, *never* left home. The second son bowed up in pent-up rage against his controlling mother and would, as an adult, choose to live in another continent rather than be too near his mother. My father, the youngest and most carefree, the one his oldest brothers nicknamed "*bou*ffoss," which in Greek means something akin to "dunce," a name he carried through adulthood, flew the coop. My dad became the renegade among the bunch, a modern-day iconoclast in his family. He left their orbit, became a scientist, and married a non-Greek, breaking *centuries* of Hellenic history, culture, and tradition, not to mention an all-Greek bloodline with his defection. In this sense, it is *I* who, like Hercules, am half and half. I was told later that as infants, my grandparents referred to us as "misbegotten," but it is not for the reason you might think. It was not for a so-called tainted bloodline, but because my parents did not legitimize their marriage by getting wed in the Greek Church (and therefore sanctioned by God), a wish my father surely had but one my mother would never make come true. We will make further comparisons to Hercules in the upcoming chapters. When it's all said and done, my dad chose to make a life of his casting, founded on freedom, the most primal of all Greek impulses.

Man, god, and God

Like Hercules, who eventually had bad fortune coming his way since Hera was bent on retribution, my father had the deck stacked against him by being born with a disease that would impair him later on in life. No one volitionally *caused* it. Thus, both Hercules and my father entered the world with an aberration established in their frames, which would beset them with many problems later on; they just didn't know it yet. However, *unlike* Hercules, my father's future issues would *not* result from anything he had *done* for which to be punished. My father had no more notion that he was born with a disease than Hercules could have been aware that who he *thought* was his dad, Amphitryon, the husband of his mother's Alcmene, was *not* actually his biological father. As it turned out, both Hercules and my father would have terrible tempers, resulting in unintended consequences. Hercules' crimes were far worse, but there would be hell for each of us to pay. Please keep in mind the sense of eventuality or inevitability for both men having to bear a cross in their futures as a result of something that happened *to* them before they were born. If you recall, Zeus, in hopes of appeasing his wife, Hera, *would permit* an extreme hardship to take place in his son's *future*.

My dad wasn't "punished" by God, but because of the tainted state of humanity brought on by the transgression of one man, one such extrapolation of our defected world got manifested in a corrupted code in my dad's genetic makeup. It would be well into adulthood before Hercules would have to pay penance for his wrongdoing; likewise, it would not be until my father's sixth decade that his disease would present itself and launch a plethora of problems. Hercules *did* something that warranted punishment; my dad did *not*, but in his acquiring the disease, he did odd things that he might not have had he not had the disease. At the end, whether each was a passive victim, an active agent, or a combination of both, eventually, posthumously and ultimately, matters turned out victoriously for both Hercules and my father. Meanwhile, in real life, each man in his own right would have to endure torment for a flaw imposed upon them, like some ghost or kink in the machine. Such would result in unforeseen and horrific consequences: Hercules' was moral in nature; my father's, genetic; both were tragic.

Myth explores and expresses universal situations that are present in real life, but what you *see* is never the primary source or cause of the apparent problem or harm. While possessing impressive powers, their host of imaginary gods was capricious and selfish. On the other hand, the living God in all His holiness can never give rise to that which is imperfect: the presence of pain, harm, hurt, or evil. Disease, death, and dying are all byproducts of man's original sin, his disobedience. We are not the only ones who cry and crave for things to be better and feel woe every time we turn on the news! In fact, *"the whole creation* groans and suffers the pains..., and [all] waiting eagerly for...the redemption of our body" (from Rom. 8:22–23). Couldn't this truism also be extrapolated to the *molecular* level? Couldn't our very *cells* be silently screaming for restoration? Oh, I think they do! That said, we who believe and know Jesus has already justified and reconciled us to our Heavenly Father still scrap and scrape and fight the good fight to live a better life than we did yesterday. Paul, the apostle to the Gentiles after whom my father was ultimately named, informs us that "just as through one man sin entered into the world, and death through sin... the gift by the grace of the one Man, Jesus Christ, abound to the many...so that, grace would reign through righteousness to eternal life..." (from Romans 5:13–14 and 21).

In the final curtain call, neither my father nor I, nor any believer, is a slave to genetics, history, or any wrongful action or predicament. We who believe in Christ Jesus have righteousness *imputed* on us from God. What does that mean? <u>God didn't *cause* my dad to get bad genes that went haywire</u>. Still, He did permit the situation to occur, knowing that my father, His son, in the end, ultimately came to Him and that maybe, just maybe, this event would lead to his daughter becoming a part of "all [those] things [that] work together for good to those who love God, to those who are called according to His purpose" (Rom. 8:28). My father's faith served as a balm to him in later years. Still, there's no denying the imposition and impact of history and genetics are potent and apparent, so now I turn to Greece and the socio-historical milieu into which my father was born and was soaking up its sap during his first decade, here and now mere months before he was born.

Pre-1935 Greek History in a Nutshell

I begin with the months closest to my dad's *conception* because it is at this junction that his disease became a part of his system as much as would his limbs and bones and blood; there is no myth or fiction here. When researching this particular period in Greece, I realized that it was incumbent upon me to set the stage properly and mention other high points worthy of acknowledgment. All gets stitched into a person's subconscious and outlook, the prism through which they perceive their surroundings. There are many points I could tell you, but I will be selective; therefore, I will hit the high points as if I were making a greatest hits package for you of that which became part of my dad's collective consciousness. For starters, how can I not give a nod to the fall of the Ottoman Empire on March 25, 1821? Let's zoom back four hundred years from *that* to provide this date its full due and respect. Americans may be familiar with the year 149**2** because that is when "Columbus sailed the ocean blue," but the year 145**3** is etched in every Greek's memory because this is the year when Constantinople fell and, with it, the collapse of the mighty Byzantine Empire, and with *that*, the vastness of Greece's glorious outreach.

It is no spoiler alert to say that Greece never regained her glory or stature from the days before the fall of Constantinople, that is, the "Golden age" of the fifth century B.C., where we find all of Greece's powerhouse philosophers whose ideas we still herald today. While Greeks can, did, and do rise and band together like nobody's business to fight a *common* enemy, say the Persians in 490 B.C., another equally historical truth is how brutally and viciously Greeks can turn on and fight one another. Greeks love to discuss politics and the meaning of life, and, for sure, they are one of the most closely-knit groups of people where family unity is concerned, but they will stab their brother in the guts or back in a heartbeat if he proves to be a rat or a fink. You need to know this fact and tuck it away because it will happen repeatedly — even in our family. Let's return closer to when Greeks were being moved from one zone to another, like unwitting chess pieces, a reality my father would also be subjected to.

What other facts from Greece's "modern" history do I handpick to reveal what goes into forming the core identity of this nation and the nature of Pavlos? I return to the nineteenth century, right after this momentous liberation. Things quickly began to unravel and got twisted up in knots. My dad, too, would live through one of Greece's most violent and anguishing periods of history, which I am leading up to right now. From 1827 to 1832, Greece became a republic for five short years, with her capital briefly moving from Athens to the Peloponnesian city of Nafplio; then, in 1832, Greece became a monarchy. For most of the remaining part of the nineteenth century, Greece went about the quiet and steady business of expanding her borders and gaining new territory. However, this was also the last century when kings ruled their countries, and Greece was no exception. Revolutions in England and France in the eighteenth century gave rise to the common man's demands for equality and power. With it, institutions became founded on principles of egalitarianism, which is nothing short of an updated and more vivid expression of the ancient Greek ideal of democracy.

It's odd to think that Greece had a Bavarian King named Otto in the mid-1800s, but during this new epoch of expansion under him, while little Greece was making her territorial gains, doughty nations like England and France would soon effectively neutralize and snuff out these advances, and to his and the country's disgrace, Greece's King Otto surrendered in 1862. I sweep through the next fifty years in a few short sentences to inch us closer to our decade of focus; the following events impacted millions of lives. Afterward, King Otto came to King George I, who reigned for fifty years, the longest stretch in modern Greek history.[8] I learned more about the Balkan Wars and the territories hard won by the Greeks during his reign. Moving on to the outbreak of World War I in 1914, we find Greece with a new king, Constantine I, who, although was an admirer of Germany, thankfully, had a Prime Minister by the name of <u>Eleftherios Venizelos</u> who called for neutrality and encouraged Greece to join the Allies. If you ever go to Greece, you'll learn that the airport's name in Athens is Eleftherios Venizelos, which should indicate his stature. At about this time, events and leaders *really* began to get intertwined and convoluted, so I had to stay on the straight and narrow path to avoid getting tied up in the knots of twentieth-century history in Greece. My father and his family nearly got choked off in one such entanglement. It was inevitable for the Greek royalty and those *actually* in charge of Greece to butt heads and determine who the top dog was.

When the monarchy and Eleftherios Venizelos went head-to-head and toe-to-toe to determine who had the authority to make decisions, *warfare resulted in Greece.* Two byproducts of this "<u>National Schism</u>," as this conflict of 1915–1917 was called, came about: first, this brought about a sharp reduction of the stature and power of Greek kings. You will see evidence of this diminishment because the kings would *not* remain in Greece for fear of losing their lives, not to mention the crown. Self-preservation trumped ruling their subjects; many would call it cowardice. The net psychological effect of this was that although the monarchy was a source of continuity and pride for Greeks, Greeks *had* to have felt abandoned and would have become jaded. The net effect was that the Greeks got used to being led by more powerful prime ministers who displayed a strong force of personality, competence, and aptitude in the international arena. Meanwhile, my family would have been a part of the southern stream of Greeks, far removed from politics in Athens and still adhering to the uninterrupted ways of centuries-old traditions. I've even stayed in a hotel in Kardamyli where rich portraits of Greek kings from an era long gone hung, like whistling "Dixie" down south in the States.

For Greece, the end of WWI bled right into the <u>Greco-Turkish War of 1919-1922</u>. The second significant result capitulated: the Greeks lost the Ottoman City of Smyrna, and vast pockets of Greek and Turkish populations were forced to swap places based on religion as if people could be moved as easily as puzzle pieces. Genocide is an appellation *not* to be relegated solely to one particular people. The term "**diaspora**" is particularly relevant for me because my own family was *not* among the nearly one million Greek and Armenian Christians who left Turkey in a murderous exchange for about *half* that number of Turkish Muslims from Greece in the blink between 1914 and 1923, <u>less than fifteen years later, *another* wave of Greeks left Greece, and my dad was among them</u>. This exodus altered the direction of my Greek side of the family forever. My father, his two older brothers, and his mother were forced to flee their ancient homestead to survive. They rejoined their father, who was already making a new life for them in the young mishmash land of the free and home of the brave. We are not ready for that part of our story yet.

Political pragmatism would trump religious affinities and created a vacuum during the days that my dad was a boy. Civil War combusted in that vacuum. The social parity that the Soviets fought and died for in *their* socialist evolution is not the same as the inchoate desire for democracy and fairness that abides in the Greek's breast. The Soviet brand of communism, with its heavy-handed and imposed egalitarianism, would eventually appeal to certain Greeks who got sick and tired of feeling duped, disappointed, and disenfranchised by lackluster or inept leadership. Time and again, the combination of the king's waffling or hesitating would contrast sharply with the swift decisiveness of military generals-turned-prime ministers. Community leaders were left scrambling to pick up the pieces; eventually, they gained much power and authority in their own right. When all else failed and others floundered, many local Greeks became members of the communist party to take decisive action and concrete steps to unscramble the chaos and muck in their backyards. At its best, it was the Greek Communist Party, the KKE, that would become *the* most formidable opponent to fascism during WWII; at its worst, it would be the most insidious and ruthless player in Greece's fratricidal war. During WWII, in trusting naïveté, the Greek Communists would naturally have looked up to and expected support from *their* "big brother," the Soviet Union, but I get ahead of myself. That never happened. You should know that my grandmother's brother, my great uncle Gerasim, would become a member of the KKE, so the role of the communists in Greece is brought even closer to home and thus begs I speak to this situation in some detail; it will come in its own due time. So much is interrelated, and I want to prepare you as we delve into my father's fate.

Greek History at the Outset of My Father's Birth in 1935

I will briefly return to Prime Minister Eleftherios Venizelos and King Constantine I. You should know that Venizelos was an aristocrat from Crete, who, although he is credited with being "the maker of modern Greece,"[9] from what I can glean, he was a bit of a snob and, ironically, thought of most Greeks as cretins. Keep in mind that with the spoils won in the Balkan Wars, which contributed to the near *doubling* of the total area of Greece, the friction between the monarchy and the prime minister governing the republic was growing, all the more so as evidenced by Venizelos being elected eight times! During his leadership, we find the so-called "Megali [Great] Idea," a popular and romantic notion of reviving the Byzantine Empire amidst the truculent times with the Turks. In actuality, Venizelos was more pro-Ally than he was pro-Greek king, and as a result, he would soon find himself in a situation where he would become unpopular with Greeks. There were even a couple of assassination attempts on his life, the second one occurring in June of 1933.[10] There is a now second major player you need to know; there was a man who worked under Venizelos for a while, and he was pro-royalist with a penchant for liking all things authoritarian and German.

This key player is vital to our story because he was in power in Greece for the first five years of my father's life. His name was Iannis Metaxas; you may recognize his surname because it is the name of the brand of Greece's famous liquor; that aside, the bottom line is that he was a dictator. My father's final trip to Greece in 2006 had him attempting to bring home five bottles of Metaxa, and he chose the five-star black-labeled brandy for his Greek friends at his home church. Most of those bottles were shattered due to my dad's careless and haphazard packing, which left his clothes smelling like a Greek taverna for weeks. Contrastingly, *his* father neatly sipped Metaxa from a conservative tumbler every evening before taking his meal as if quietly taking private communion. Maybe there were things in his past that he hoped would fade. One final fact from Greece's past I wish to leave you with will serve as a summary and bridge as we peer into the crucible when my father lived in Greece. A decade before his birth, between 1924 and 1935, "there were *twenty-three* changes of government, a <u>dictatorship</u>, and thirteen *coups d'etat* in Greece..."[11] I find it all the more shocking to imagine a country that is only slightly smaller than the state of Alabama having to bear these changes. In short, during the decade of my father's life in Greece, we find a shifting, cracking foundation while little Greece marched, hobbled, and survived a dizzying array of overlapping subplots, dramatic political turmoil, and its war-beleaguered people during two nearly simultaneous and cataclysmic events. You know them simply as WWII and the Greek Civil War. Seventy-two years later, my father's own body would wage war against itself, and he would be the casualty of its murderous mayhem. However, it's almost time for him to make his debut.

One month *before* my father was born on 3 November 1935, the tide had turned, and the overwhelming majority of Greeks supported the restoration of the monarchy. Therefore, the Greek king at the time, King George II, returned to the throne at the *end* of that month. Tucked in between the brief stint of King George II's return and Metaxas' installation, by August one year later, when my dad would be a tot of one and a half, King George endorsed the establishment of a government led by a veteran army officer by the name of <u>Ioannis Metaxas</u>. King George II went into exile right after the <u>German invasion of Greece on April 6, 1941</u>,[12] <u>when my dad was but five years old</u>, and the king did not return to the throne until the fall of 1946. By then, my father and the rest of the family would have crossed the ocean to join my grandfather; my dad would have been three months shy of turning eleven. Greek history would be mirrored in my family's life: for those five years that king was safely harbored away in another country, my father's father would be on distant shores earning money for his family. I am sure this made little sense to a young son: he just missed his pop. I will never forget my dad's telling us that "*his father was nothing but a picture on the wall*" during that five-year absence. By the time the king returned in September of 1946, my father and his family would have already crossed the ocean for more hopeful days in America.

That September, the king came back to a wreck of a country, and outside help was desperately needed to revitalize Greece, but our story does not concern itself with this part of history. In short, when <u>my dad entered the world in December 1935, his homeland was run by a bonafide dictator</u>. Metaxas was taking all measures to whiff out anything he considered leftist, communist, or remotely pro-human rights. We need to appreciate what he saw revolution lead in *other* European nations: anarchy. To avert chaos at home, a decision was made to clamp down on all rabble-rousing freedom seekers. On August 4th, 1936, Metaxas officially and formally *put a lid on democracy by outlawing it*, as if such an action could take place in Greece, and he did it for a minute. He even went so far as to imitate an action he observed that had taken place in Nazi Germany: he launched a massive book burning in several Greek cities, primarily focusing on those considered "pro-democratic." Among those ancient Greek classics deemed objectionable and banned were included such works as *Antigone* by Sophocles and *The State* by Plato. More than 445 book titles were banned by the regime's censorship.[13] Metaxas was pleased with himself for creating stability; others would have been in cold shock by his severity.

As an outsider looking in, it would seem that the king leaving at critical mass for *any* reason would send a troubling and double message to his subjects. Knowing they were largely unable to defend themselves in these dire straits, they would have felt abandoned, disappointed, and vulnerable. The king made known his wishes from the safe distant shores of Egypt; however, Greece *did* attain some semblance of stability under Metaxas. Still, there was a heavy psychological tax to pay: dread and austerity that fell like a pall over the country. Ultimately, it would *not* be Metaxas who would deliver the death knell to little Greece. For now, he held it all together, all under the taut skein of a smooth but thinning membrane of national compliance. *This* is the Greece into which my father was born on December 3, 1935, deep in the Peloponnesus in the ancient port town of Sparta, Gythion.

If you Google-earthed "Gythion" on your smartphone, you would watch the earth revolving on its axis in your palm as you observed it honing in on and over olive-green three-fingered extensions located in southern Greece before sweeping down onto this Maniot town, which is situated inside a slightly recessed dip of a concave curve located on the upper right side of the second digit. I learned that this portion of Greece is particularly patriotic, and they had the reputation of being pro-royalist, so I would imagine the people there were extra resentful of the dictatorial actions of General Metaxas and anyone serving under him. What had worked well for Metaxas earlier in his career while he was a military leader, undoubtedly that which would have been what the king admired in and needed from him, contributed to his being selected as the stand-in leader. It took, and he stayed. Yet the very quality that proves your greatest asset can become a liability in other circumstances. However, when it is all said and done, regardless of which side of the political fence individual Greeks found themselves on or arguing over, *all* Greeks remember and admire Metaxas for *one word* he uttered with pride and fury that resonated within every Greek citizen. You shall soon learn what this was.

What no one could have foreseen was that Metaxas would remain in power for a mere five years; he died on January 29, 1941, of a throat abscess that resulted in pernicious and incurable toxemia. We will get to that time later to connect this and other cataclysmic events that lay waste in my father's childhood world. For now, keep in mind this change in the guard and the sense of uncertainty caused by regal desertion and the consequential imposition of a dictator. It *had* to have been highly stressful for the country when Metaxas came to power, and yet this would be child's play when compared to living through the madness and mayhem of *two* wars occurring on this small country's rocky soil. *No other country in the world has experienced such a maelstrom.* And there would be an unseen price to pay for the havoc wreaked on this society's psyche and system. We now can fathom how a turbulent time could have breached and broken something foundational within the corpus of my father's parents.

Junk in the Genes

It ought to come as no surprise to you that stress adversely impacts the body at the cellular level, but you may not be aware that *your body cannot distinguish between physical pain and anxiety.* It produces the same cocktail of chemical responses to alleviate what it perceives as an assault or a threat to its well-being. That our bodies can and do respond to stress serves a good purpose: it is meant to let the body (and you) know that help is (or needs to be) on the way to alleviate the current detrimental state. A perfect example of dealing with panic and peril would be when your country is at war when there is nothing individuals can do but ride out the storm as they huddle, hide, and pray they survive. Such denizens would live in a state of chronic stress: uncertainty and deprivation would be their staples as they eked out an existence for themselves in the new normal of *their* day. How might the stress of living in a country at war for nearly a *decade* impact the person at the foundational, building-block level? Could the war produce a war within the body? On top of that, what about the collateral damage of two stressed-out persons — practically strangers — in a new marriage, where the husband would feel a sense of frustration, perhaps failure for not being able to provide sufficiently for his family, and his young bride would be forced to live like an alien among in-laws who resented her *and* her sons for their imposition and dependency? It sounds like a recipe for disaster to me.

There may have been no *overt* signs of revolt or chaos in 1935. Still, while living under the country's new dictatorship and closer to home, residing within a wrought family unit, there *had* to have been anxiety and ill will steeping like ingredients brewing in a witch's broth. Such internal antagonism could have led to mutiny deep within a person's constitution. I cannot know with certainty, but I wonder and speculate. To support some gut hunches I had as to how my father could have been born with such a rare disease as Huntington's disease (HD), I "leaned not on my understanding" (Proverbs 3:5) but made investigative inquiries as to what molecular conditions might have been in place for this to have occurred. Although we *can* explain the genetics of the complex trauma that is Huntington's disease, which assaults with a vengeance specific regions of the brain, no one knows *how* the disease came to be in the first place. Furthermore, no simple cause-effect justification exists for how one child acquires it and another avoids or escapes it unscathed altogether. The *why* is on God, something that neither I nor anyone can divine this side of heaven. I do not vex myself over this stark and unvarnished truth, let alone succumb to a sense of fatalism, considering it to be some "it-is-what-it-is" reality. To concede that we *cannot* know all or at least not enough *yet* is by no means a copout or concession. *Everyone* has some tale of woe, affliction of the flesh, or heart hurt. No one is exempt.

That said, over a decade later, I still seek to understand as best I can what happened to my father at the atomic level, all the more so as he bragged about his gene pool, just in not so many words. Even the word "gene" comes from the Greek word γένος, which means "offspring, family, race, nation, kind"[14] or generation. How could his stock *not* be of consequence to him? He never saw *this* errant gift coming to invade his produced generation potentially. I am looking at it in retrospect now, but since the pain of his loss has waned, I find that there remains a longing to journey to the disease's origins, so with a steely heart and wizened eyes, I will share with you what I learned. I hope it might help *you* one day; I promise to keep to the facts we need for a rich appreciation.

A Closer Look at What HD Is Doing in and to the Brain

The first area I want to explore further is what sort of physical *effect* or impact could have arisen on or within a person's system as a result of living chronic hardship or ongoing trauma, as did my dad's parents. It turns out that living under duress has a definite impact on the mind and body. Where jargon is technical, I must quote information I obtained. According to the Yale Dept. of Psychology, "pain and stress are both adaptive in protecting the organism, [as in the case of] physical injury or starvation. However, if either of the two processes becomes *chronic*, it *can lead to long-term 'maladaptive' changes in physiology…* resulting in… *compromised well-being.*[15] Acute stress triggers "the activation of hormones that have receptors concentrated in the limbic brain including the hypothalamus, amygdala, hippocampus, and prefrontal cortex. In the limbic system, excess amounts of glucocorticoids… *have long-lasting effects on cellular function* (emphasis mine)."[16] There are these things called glucocorticoids, which are powerful anti-inflammatory compounds, and "they have the ability to *inhibit* all stages of the inflammatory response."[17] Inflammation, whether in the brain or other parts of the body, is almost always a *secondary* response to some primary disease-causing substance or event, like Huntington's disease. In other words, the brain gets in its own internecine war! This leads to the brain responding to the "faulty wiring" installed, but in reaction to this transgression, matters are made worse by the brain sending out its squadron of fighter cells. These fighter cells get tangled up in the affected areas of the brain and end up *expediting the dying off* of these areas, chunk by fragment by piece.

One type of immune (or "fighter") cell found to be present in extraordinarily high concentrations in the HD brain is called the microglia. The microglia, in turn, "release various inflammatory mediators that contribute to the long-term occurrence of inflammation in the HD brain," *resulting in damage and cell death.*[18] So, it's a double whammy: the disease causes brain inflammation, which causes the body to send out steroids to fight the inflammation, contributing to an unhealthy and excessive clustering of cells with the best intentions. *The net effect is that it all leads to premature cell death at uneven rates in different pockets of the brain,* and I can attest to you that no two Huntington's patients exhibit the same manifestations. I will show and tell you more about the harmful effects on these specific parts of my father's brain later; suffice it to say for right now that the disease-ridden brain will be further compromised under conditions of elevated environmental pressure.

Passing on Huntington's Disease: The Buck *Starts* with a Mutation

At this point, you might counter and contend that hundreds of thousands lived in such a harrowing state. What had this to do with my yet-unborn father? When you combine the long-lasting effects of stress on the body — on *either* of his parents — with the fact that *his* father was a middle-aged man *not* in his physical prime, there exists the *increased* possibility that he passed on spermatozoa with a genetic aberration or abnormality. The likelihood of such a phenomenon occurring increases more than you might know. Let's look more closely at my dad's father. According to a recent article in *Scientific American*, "By starting families in their ... forties and beyond, men could be increasing the chances that their children will develop ... diseases often linked to new mutations." This source also informed me that unlike women, whose eggs are present all their life, "sperm is continually generated by dividing precursor cells, *which acquire new mutations with each division*. Fathers passed on nearly *four times* as many new mutations as mothers." It is "the *father's age* which accounted for nearly all of the variation in the number of new mutations in a child's genome, *with the number of new mutations being passed on rising exponentially with paternal age*" (emphasis mine).[19] Not only that, but another aspect of genetics is how DNA gets passed on copies of the gene, the various versions of which are called "alleles." These alleles may occur alternatively at a given site on a pre-assigned chromosome, and there is an *anticipated* amount that gets replicated or repeated for a *normal* expansion or amount to result. The problem with persons who inherit HD is that this process of repeat expansion of the alleles goes haywire and keeps on proliferating, like a strand of spaghetti that goes rogue and gets longer and, therefore, thinner, more brittle, and likely to break off. Additionally, this process of repeat expansion "happens way more often in the production of sperm than in eggs."[20]

Do I know for a fact that bad seed caused this to happen? No, I do not. Furthermore, I want to inform you that not all mutations are harmful. Spontaneous changes *do* serve a purpose and can provide benefits like adaptation to environmental factors that are less than advantageous. To investigate what a gene mutation is and in what light I should evaluate such an occurrence, I discovered that a mutation is "a change in the genetic makeup of a living organism."[21] This resultant change can either be beneficial or detrimental to the living organism. This source told me that "the main benefit of mutation is *survival*. Most living organisms are currently alive due to successful mutations." I learned here that sickle cell anemia, lactose intolerance, and atherosclerosis are all diseases that arose in response to disadvantageous environmental circumstances that gave rise to these genetic mutations. So, was *this* what happened to my father? I did *not* find any evidence that Huntington's disease was one such that cropped up for some future benefit or need. Was it his father who unwittingly dealt the losing hand? I would never have known this, too, but then I wondered how mutations begin.

I learned that genetic aberrations, sometimes labeled "spontaneous" genetic mutations, and which *technically* are termed "de novo" (i.e., *new*), fall under two major categories:

(1) The first are <u>hereditary</u> mutations inherited from a parent and *present throughout a person's life.* These so-called "germline mutations" are present in the parent's egg or sperm cells (which are also termed "germ cells"). When an egg and a sperm cell unite, the resulting fertilized egg cell receives DNA from both parents. If *the DNA [from either parent] has a mutation, the child that grows from the fertilized egg will have the mutation in their cells.*

(2) The second is <u>acquired</u> mutations [which] occur during a person's life and are present only in *specific* cells... Environmental factors can cause these changes... or can occur if an error is made *as DNA copies itself during cell division.* Acquired mutations in those cells *other* than sperm and egg cells) *cannot* be passed on to the next generation. In other cases, the mutation occurs in the fertilized egg *shortly after the egg and sperm cells unite.* (It is often impossible to tell precisely when this mutation happened.) As the fertilized egg divides, *each resulting cell in the growing embryo will have the mutation.* Some cells that arise from the cell with the altered gene will have the mutation, while others will not. Depending on the mutation and how many cells are affected, the mutation may or may not cause health problems. Most disease-causing gene mutations are uncommon in the general population. Such spontaneous or *de novo* mutations *may explain genetic disorders in which an affected child has a mutation in every cell in the body. Still, the parents do not, and there is no family history of the disorder* (emphasis mine).[22]

In short, it is precisely at the moment of a child's conception that the inception of this disease gets put in motion. My father had this strike against him before the stroke of his birth would commence.

I am sure you still can recall from a high school biology or an introductory health course the short unit on genetics where you learned how we come to receive half of our genetic material from our father and half from our mother. Each egg and sperm, in turn, contain a *different combination* of genes. It comes down to basic math whereby the embryo receives 23 chromosomes from the mother's egg and 23 chromosomes from the father's sperm, adding up to 46 in total. The first 22 pairs are identical or nearly identical; it is the 23rd pair contains the sex chromosomes X or Y. Huntington's disease is *not* a disease that is connected to this sex chromosome and is *not* more likely to occur in one sex over the other; it is an equal opportunity affliction. When egg and sperm cells unite, these chromosomes join together and *"randomly exchange genes between each other"* before the cell divides. Each gene within a cell exists in two versions, one inherited from each parent. Often, these genes are identical, but "occasionally some paired genes occur in *slightly different versions,* called <u>alleles</u>."

There may be two to several hundred alleles of a gene, although each person can only have two genes. One allele may be dominant and "overpower" the other recessive one. Genes usually exist in a healthy form, but sometimes, the gene is imperfect or damaged. Genetic disorders arise *"when an abnormal gene is inherited, or a gene changes or mutates* (emphasis mine)."[23] So, when I told you earlier that Huntington's disease is an "autosomal dominant" one, what I meant was that if and when the child receives the one mutant Huntingtin gene from the (likely one) parent, the child *will* get the disease. To acquire the disease means alterations *will* take place in the development of the child's brain starting at ground zero, day one: conception. The manifestation of the person who has the disease will most likely not become noticeable or pronounced until middle age when the body's normal aging process commences, first with imperceptible changes, then with evident, undeniable, and disturbing alterations.

Contemporaneous with the very month I am writing, brand new information has just been released from the Paris Brain Institute that, for the first time, shows that "Huntington's disease alters nerve cell development in the cortex — a brain region largely affected in people with the condition — *before* birth, leading to changes in *overall* brain development as early as the prenatal stages (emphasis mine).[24] I continue sharing from this source, which also states that there is increasing evidence suggesting that "the disease may interfere with prenatal neurodevelopment, *resulting in a thinner cortex,* which is the outer layer of the brain that controls thought, behavior, and memory — abnormalities in the striatum, which is involved in motor function and cognition."

All these abnormalities disrupt the "division-maturation balance of progenitor cells." I had to look up what "progenitor cells" were to proceed. Progenitor cells are "biological cells more specific than stem cells in that their purpose is more differentiated; *they are supposed to divide only a limited number of times."*[25] With HD, this number has increased *far* too many times! The way this expansion has gone berserk reminds me of a clunky old photocopy machine that, when heated up, can sometimes misfeed the paper in several places. When you open up the machine to extract the mangled papers from any number of slots in its core, they can be crinkled up like a paper accordion, smudged with excess ink, or even torn. I will show you what this looks like in my father later on. An excess of these progenitor cells compromises the pool of dividing cells that give rise to nerve cells that the brain needs, and the first trimester is when you need a lot of neural cells to be generated!

The implication for the fetal brain with the Huntington's disease mutation is that "there is a shift to maturate early and, as a result, *you generate fewer neurons* at this specific time during [critical] development."[26] I apologize for the extensive quoting. As I tell my students, it's better to have too much documentation than not enough when providing critical data that could not have come from oneself. And like strands of Greek history which can quickly run together and blur indistinguishably, so much so that it is hard to keep from going down rabbit holes, it isn't easy to separate the strands of the connective bytes of relevant genetic information, but I can't *not* do the topic justice and my father respect. That said, I always think it is more important to see the bigger picture and remind ourselves that we are each unique. There is variation among human beings; we are much more alike than we are different, and we are remarkably so. The DNA of all human beings living today is 99.9% alike,[27] but, as they say, the devil is in the details.

When I join all the physical factors together, I continue to speculate how my father could have acquired the disease and from which parent. (After all, I don't *know* if it spawned from his father.) How is it that Huntington's disease spun out for the first and only time in our family's history through *my father*? The short answer is that *one* of his parents was most likely an "asymptomatic carrier," I will explain this to you in another chapter when you learn where things went awry in a portion of his gene code. Will I ever know whether he inherited the gene from his mother or father? No. Yes, I have speculated that it is more likely that it came from his elderly father living during a highly stressful time, which may have compromised *his* middle-aged cellular and, therefore, genetic system. Could the disease have come from his mother? Yes. We cannot be sure because it would have been impossible to test them genetically at the time. Plus, as neither they nor their other two sons had HD, the notion of investigating this wouldn't have been a thought. My father's parents didn't live to see or know their youngest son had it. Later on, as I wondered which of my dad's parents could have been the culprit or carrier, I scoured my memory for hints or potential clues. *His* father, my papou, had a peculiar tic, albeit ever-so-slight: he would make frequent quick and light sniffs as if he did not want his nose to drip, and he shuffled, his heals rarely leaving the floor. His mother, my yiayia, in her eighties and nineties, exhibited some faint

Parkinsonian tremors in her hands. She would repeat herself, especially particular stories, like small bundles of her life's fables. Still, neither of these scenarios would I describe as quirks or behaviors due to anything other than the expected results of an aging brain and body.

As I round this chapter's closing, I want to synthesize it together because you will meet my father in the next chapter. You have seen how Hercules, half-man and half-god, came to be born and in what capacity he is unique as a hero in Greek mythology. You have learned the particular forces in Greek history, some ancient and enduring, others vivid and time-dependent, that preceded mere months of my father's birth. In March of 1935, when Eleftherios Venizelos was in power, din, discontent, and discord were in the air, and dire consequences would result in any number of places. I have presented to you the impact of being born to his parents who, in their union, bore my father. They possessed the unique cellular aggregation that would give rise to his disease. Oh, but we are greater than the sum of the two halves from which we come. The theme of the double is universal and, therefore, connately familiar to us all. Whether we see this dichotomy manifested in man versus monster, the battle between the flesh and spirit, or body and mind, something in us recognizes we come from the primordial slime. Still, we also celebrate the fact that of all life, "God created man in His own image" (Genesis 1:27). Why else would we be so captivated by stories like *Beauty and the Beast* and *Dr. Jekyll and Mr. Hyde* or classic horror movies like *The Wolf Man* and *Frankenstein*? If you have a tender heart, you might even have shuddered when you saw the good Doctor Frankenstein unknowingly implant a criminal's brain in his creature's cranium. Surely, we could see the proverbial writing on the wall; this was *not* the case for our family or my father. I suspect that those who have bi-polar disorder understand better than many just what Alexander Pope meant when, in 1733, he described our ambivalent state in his *Essay on Man*, which I compress for you here:

> Placed on this isthmus of a middle state…,
> [Man] hangs between;
> In doubt to deem himself a God or Beast;
> Born but to die and reasoning but to err;
> Chaos of Thought and Passion, all confused;
> Created half to rise and half to fall;
> Great Lord of all things, yet a prey to all,
> Sole judge of truth, in endless error hurled;
> The glory, jest, and riddle of the world.

And yet, despite our imperfect and messy "middle state," I close this chapter by humbly giving thanks to God for life itself, my life in particular, and the parents who met and conceived me in love. How can I *not* continue to explore just how "fearfully and wonderfully" God made my dad (Psalm 139:13–14)? Yes, *especially* the "fearful" aspect that would afflict him in the decades to come. Let's now meet my pop when he made his entry into the world.

Chapter 3

Donkey's Milk and (Un)Luck of the Draw

"You created my inmost being; you knit me together in my mother's womb. I praise you because _I am fearfully and wonderfully made_; your works are wonderful. I know that full well. _My frame was not hidden from you_ when I was made in the secret place, when I was woven together in the depths of the earth."
— from Psalm 139:13–15, underscore mine

****

"Sometimes I feel like a motherless child
Sometimes I feel like a motherless child
Long way from my home…
Sometimes I feel like freedom is so near.
But we're so far from home."
— From "Sometimes I Feel Like a Motherless Child," Unknown (1870's), emphasis mine

****

"The steps of a man are established by the Lord, And He delights in his way. When he falls, he will not be hurled down because the Lord is the One who holds his hand.
— Psalm 37:23–24, emphasis mine

****

"The New Colossus"
Not like the brazen giant of Greek fame,
With conquering limbs astride from land to land;
Here at our sea-washed, sunset gates shall stand
A mighty woman with a torch, whose flame
Is the imprisoned lightning, and her name
Mother of Exiles. From her beacon-hand
Glows _world-wide welcome_; her mild eyes command
The air-bridged harbor that twin cities frame.
"_Keep, ancient lands, your storied pomp_!" cries she
With silent lips. "Give me your tired, your poor,
Your huddled masses yearning to breathe free,
The wretched refuse of your teeming shore.
Send these, the homeless, tempest-tost to me,
I lift my lamp beside the golden door!"

— by Emma Lazarus (1883), emphasis mine
****

"A true hero isn't measured by the size of his
strength, *but by the strength of his heart.*"
— Zeus in Walt Disney's *Hercules* (1997), emphasis mine

As with my previous two books, *Connecting the Dots...* and *Living Stones*, I launch many chapters with pithy quotes that put me in the frame of mind and mood for what I am getting ready to share with you. I also hope they pique your interest and that you will see their message unfold and come to life in the following pages. Counter to the chronological order of transporting you from the topics of Hercules to Greek history to Huntington's disease, three unlikely bedfellows about my father's life and the character developing therein, the quoted axioms I've chosen here are in no particular order. This chapter will be my greatest challenge because — thankfully — although I have never personally lived through any war, I am compelled to sift through specific portions of Greek history to breathe life into the testimonies my father and his cousin have told me. They will provide the framework for my father's formative years in Greece.

Let's start with the portion I've selected from Psalm 139, beginning with the part where it says we are "fearfully and wonderfully made." Though a boy with spunk and pluck, who could have ever known that within his constitution's core, the "fearful" part of a "secret place" within my dad was yet to be seen, meaning, when and in what manner his enigmatic disease would make its debut? His many "wonderful" parts would always impress and please me! Next, while my father never knew the orphaned pang of being a *motherless* child for five years, he was undoubtedly a *fatherless* one. I'm certain that when they were forced to flee the motherland, he would have already been used to the aching sense that things would no longer be right in the world. He became just another causality, a statistic, a victim of war, but also one who thirsted for freedom *and* food, and maybe, just maybe, the chance to return to his paradise restored, a home now horror-haunted.

I don't want to leave you with the impression that my father was downcast or dejected: quite the contrary! It is no lie that hardship can make you either grow bitter or become better; my dad, buoyant and optimistic by nature, would be the latter. Many years later, one evening, when I was visiting my dad, and he and I were sitting side by side eating cherry chocolate ice cream and catching the Disney version of *Hercules*, I was struck by the truth of what this cartoon Zeus would say about his son. Indeed, this was how I felt about my dad! His might was based upon the pitch and passion of his heart. Such timber led him to move many mountains during his life. You will discover how this young Greek pioneer made his way and forged a destiny in America; his can-do spirit knew no bounds!

To better appreciate what the wondrous and welcoming monument my father beheld in the near distance — the Statue of Liberty — as he approached the land that would become his new home, you should know how the inscription at its base, written in the form of a Petrarchan sonnet, got its title, "The New Colossus." As a proud Greek, I am eager to share that the *original* Colossus of Rhodes was one of the Seven Wonders of the Ancient World. It is a massive statue of a male figure built around 280 B.C. that was erected on the Greek island of Rhodes; most of it was destroyed in an earthquake in 226 B.C.[28] Ancient accounts state that the Colossus of Rhodes was created in honor of the sun god Helios to commemorate the Rhodians' successful defense of their island against a siege. It reportedly stood about 110 feet tall atop a 50-foot platform.[29] Now fast-forward and globetrot over to face our 305-foot-tall Lady Liberty. You may already know that the French sculptor who designed the Eiffel Tower and conceived the Statue of Liberty are the same, but you may not be aware that her face was made in the image of *the sculptor's mother's face*, surely longing for her viewers to sense a maternal tenderness.

By the time we get to the part in this chapter when my father came to America, you will better appreciate what those famous words within could have meant deep in his heart's core because he was one of the "huddled, homeless, and tempest-tost." And as a boy starving for father and food, he would have been glad to exchange home and heritage for what her flame glowed and held in store. His father would have been one of the first waves to have spied her because "it was in 1892 when the U.S. government opened a federal immigration station on Ellis Island, ... and between 1892 and 1954, some 12 million immigrants were processed on Ellis Island before receiving permission to enter the United States."[30] My "papou" — my grandfather — was from among these millions. The last name of the woman, whose now renowned sonnet is "The New Colossus," is engraved on a plaque at the entrance of the statue of Lady Liberty. It is Emma <u>Lazarus</u>.

It occurred to me that this poet's surname, *Lazarus*, is also apt when considering my dad's emigration story. Like the man from Bethany whom Jesus raised from the dead, my father would later describe *himself* as feeling like Lazarus "come back from the dead," his spirit resuscitated when he stepped onto this uncharted land. Little would he know that in addition to his small bindle of belongings, he transported within himself a biological burden that was yet to make itself manifest. Let's now return to our next episode of Hercules as I bring you up-to-speed through what amounts to my father's first twenty-five years, and that includes not only the sweep of history he lived through but a revelation of a specific portion of his gene code that would wreak havoc decades later. I will conclude this chapter with my father and Hercules, who, at the same time, were getting married to the love of their lives. First, let's see what baby Hercules was up to.

Hercules' Youth

If you recall, Hercules was the product of an illicit union between the incorrigibly philandering Zeus and mortal Alcema. Right off the bat, Hercules' mother, Alcmena, was prudent enough to be wary of Hera and her motives and machinations, so soon after she'd given birth to Hercules in the fields of Thebes, *she decided to abandon him there.* As the story goes on, the goddess Athena takes a stroll with Hera when she spies the babe. She takes a shining to the young tike, so Athena attempts to trick Hera into caring for this hungry and abandoned infant. She asks Hera to feed him, which she does. However, upon taking the young Hercules to suckle from herself, the hungry Hercules evidently latched on too hard. Wincing in pain, Hera flung the baby boy off, and in so doing, a spray of her milk "spilled across the sky,"[31] which allegedly is how the Milky Way was formed. He was then placed *back* home in Alcmene's nursery for the Alcema to raise her son. Six months later, Hera hatched her first murderous plot. One midnight, she sent a pair of "prodigious azure-scaled serpents [to their home] with strict orders to destroy Hercules."[32] Even at this tender age, Hercules' strength and robust sense of self were clearly evident. Unlike his twin brother, who, upon seeing the serpents, shrieked and climbed out of their bassinet, _Hercules grabbed both snakes by the necks and squeezed the life out of them._ This image is iconic.

Meanwhile, his mother, Alcmene, roused from sleep purportedly by Zeus, reflexively leaped up from bed and, with a mother's instinct, ran to check on her boys. What she and her husband saw would stop them in their tracks: Baby Hercules was giggling with glee, holding a dangling dead snake in each hand. He handed them over to his "dad," Amphitryon. Both of them bewildered, the parents checked in with their fellow Theban and the famous blind prophet, Teiresias, who confirmed that the baby was destined to do mighty deeds, that when he grew up, "he shall be the hero of all mankind."[33]

Life went on, and his dad, Amphitryon, made sure Hercules would have the finest education and the best tutors possible — something every Greek parent wanted for his child. And sure enough, Hercules received the well-rounded education of his day, including being taught wrestling, boxing, horseback riding, fencing, archery, and how to drive a chariot, play the lyre, and sing.[34] He was also taught astronomy, literature, and philosophy. As we would expect, Hercules excelled in everything that required physical strength and ability; however, he failed at music. Whether he was either not particularly fond of singing or wasn't good at it, or, as one source put it, whether he had a slothful "sluggishness of soul,"[35] his music teacher criticized him, which quickly led to an altercation between the two. Not knowing his own strength, Hercules hit his teacher over the head with his lyre and accidentally killed him! When Hercules went to trial for this murder, he successfully defended himself by claiming he had merely been taking up for himself and that his teacher had beaten him for his so-called stubbornness. In the end, he was acquitted. That said, Hercules in no way intended to kill this man, and he *was* sorry, yet this would *not* be the last time he experienced remorse over something he did.

Hercules' Early Adulthood

As any parent would today, to keep his teenage son out of further trouble, Amphitryon decided to place Hercules in a new environment among different people: he got him a job herding cattle away from home. Here, Hercules remained until he was eighteen years old, continuing to grow in stature, strength, and stamina. Conversely, his height has been described as "not above average stature"; Hercules also reportedly loved roasted meat and barley cakes.[36] The then eighteen-year-old Hercules would leave this ranch ready to make his mark on the world. Soon after doing so, he heard tell that a ferocious lion had been pillaging and killing the cattle of his dad and their fellow Theban neighbor and king, so Hercules took it upon himself to track it down and destroy it. He bludgeoned the lion with a club made from the wood of a wild olive tree and fashioned for himself a pelt from this lion's hide. Then, our hero topped it off by donning a fierce headdress made from the formidable jaws of this lion. Can you imagine it? This, too, is a celebrated image of Hercules you can easily find. During this time of the hunt, the king was so grateful for the help that he tried to devise an excuse to keep Hercules around even after the job was done; that way, he could continue to feel safe. Not only this, but the king also became determined to continue his lineage through Hercules. He invited Hercules to stay with him, and in keeping with the hospitality of his day, he offered his eldest daughter to bed with him. This king supposedly had fifty daughters, and unbeknownst to Hercules, a different daughter visited him each night until he had slept with all but one (who, some sources say, later became a virginal priestess of a cult dedicated to him). Details get sketchy and conflicting here, so let us remind ourselves that this is a myth, but the point is that although, by some accounts, he impregnated a number of these girls, "Herakles *never realized* that [the king] had more than one daughter."[37]

Our story continues elsewhere, this time in defense of Thebes, the land of his father. Having successfully eliminated the danger of the lion, Hercules made his way back home to Thebes. On the way, he ran into some Minyan heralds heading there to collect tribute from King Creon of Thebes. They had recently defeated the Thebans at war and were exacting a steep tribute from them. Unimpressed, peeved, and feeling freshly empowered from his recent exploit, Hercules took it upon himself to right the wrong and proceeded to grotesquely maim these heralds. Then, he made them return King Creon's tribute *twice* over. Naturally, war ensued. Hercules armed his fellow Thebans of every age and successfully led this group in battle; however, they succeeded due to Hercules' cunning. He ambushed the Minyans in a narrow passageway, temporarily blocked up two tunnels, and stealthily snuck into their camp by night, where he then stole their horses and bound the men to trees. What a sight!

After this, he dedicated an altar to Zeus's victory in returning to Thebes. Out of gratitude, King Creon rewarded him by offering him his eldest daughter, Megara's, hand in marriage, and the two settled down to a period of peace and prosperity. Nothing is known of Megara before her marriage to Hercules, but we can assume that Hercules was deeply devoted to her based on what happened next. Little could Hercules have known then that this happy marriage would eventually culminate in "a series of disasters in everything which related to his family life."[38] I am now ready to blend and blur my father's life and the Herculean myth together by harkening back on the interlude of my father's life leading up to his getting wed.

Pavlos' Boyhood

I have been looking forward to discovering the information I'm getting ready to share with you for as long as I can remember, and by that, I mean since I was a little girl. When I started learning Russian, I tucked away Churchill's famous quote about this country, saying she is a "riddle wrapped in a mystery inside an enigma."[39] *The same can be said of my father's youth — especially* the decade he lived in Greece. Most books contain chapters that are neatly uniform and proportionate in length chapters. You will not find the case here; I'll tell you why. I not only do not apologize for Book 1's chapters' gangly and unwieldy length, but I celebrate that what was once a blank page for me has now become the longest chapter in my book and brain. Eureka! Discoveries have been made, curiosity quenched, and celebration completed! I have been like a miner digging for hidden gold in my search and rescue mission to find and fill in the many missing gaps and puzzle pieces in my father's largely unexplored past and blanketed background. No, it is not a fully fleshed-in account, but it will more than do.

May I present *this* tray, heavily laden with pomegranates, plump grapes, wild mountain honey, walnuts, pistachios, golden raisins, and many memories? I do so with honor and humility, knowing this is a second-hand account. I have picked this precious fruit from trees once forbidden and inaccessible. So, I linger and will relish our time together here, gentle reader, as I unfold what amounts to a decade, roughly 1/7 or the first 14% of my dad's life. He lived in Greece in this period, forever leaving its mark and stain on him. Today, if I think I'm going through something incredibly challenging or chafing, I consider what my dad must have experienced as a boy, and then everything ostensibly arduous pales for me. I feel the sting of shame that comes when ease, comfort, and convenience make a man soft. As I was reading about portions of WWII and the Greek Civil War, the urgent question was: how long would this madness go on? Could wrongs ever be righted? *Much* later, he would finally return to visit and explore, but to get at the *core* of my father, we must carve and chisel through much marble to get to the man, my father, whom God had long since formed from ash and dust and clay. Let's you and I discover how history, geography, and biology converge upon my dad's genesis.

Less than a week away from a full moon shining bright, my father, baby Pavlos, was born on a plain and simple bed at home, the same as were all babes of the day; he would be his mother's last child and final son. Perhaps my father could taste tension, could sense his mother's discontent; maybe his digestive system produced excess acid, but in any event, his mother's milk had soured, and as an infant, my father had colic. One method of the day used to combat an aching belly and soothe my fitful baby was to give it *donkey's* milk. They didn't use terms like "lactose intolerant" back then. My father informed me that if that didn't work, like when babies became too loud or fussy, their parents would make tea using poppy leaves, no less. Their children were quickly soothed, and the grownups could relax. You can imagine my wide-eyed dismay! Such was the Benadryl of their day! I heard no extraordinary accounts of my father strangling snakes, but as a young boy in Greece, no doubt he would have had a few chances to smash stray scorpions hiding in a corner here or there. Whether millennia of fecund Greek history were distilled in him or he was born with an extra dose of grit, my father's robust self-confidence was already healthy and apparent as a youngster.

One of his closest cousins and playmates was Vivian; in fact, she would become like a sister to him. One of her favorite stories to tell of my father was that when they were very young children in their hometown of Gythion, my dad would proudly announce to Vivian that he knew the road — likely a dirt path — home so well that if he covered his eyes with his hands, he would get there just the same. He did just that; his cousin was supposed to point him enough in the right direction, and he could make it the rest of the way on his own. Eager to get the best of him, she was only too glad to oblige this request, but she pointed him in the direction of the nearby river, and right straight into it, he walked. As with the stories of Hercules, more than one version exists. Another time, I was told that my dad walked over a small footbridge and fell smack dab into a creek. Regardless, the point I took was that his young ego was already hale, and likely he was also somewhat gullible. This story foreshadows an aspect of my father that got played out when he was an adult. Unlike many men, my father had no sense of direction but no problem for young Pavlos! He would dismiss a wrong turn here and or a misstep there with a shrug of his shoulders, saying, "Well, *that's* okay!" There were no strikeouts for him, no possibility of *ever* looking foolish. Should he have gotten lost, my father would ask any number of innocent bystanders for directions; it was as if he were taking a survey, and somehow, he always got to his intended destination.

Myth in Man As a Boy

I can attest that, like Hercules, my father had this "perfect confidence" about him, not an offensive arrogance or snobbish hauteur but rather an inspiring self-assurance. (We will delve more into the more complex aspects of Hercules' nature later on.) No matter what life seemed to dole out in the form of some obstacle or challenge, he had no qualm or doubt that he could surmount it — and likely in a single bound. Whereas Hercules had a balanced education, working on developing mind *and* body, my dad was just another kid on the block, probably running around with older boys, all of them like a young pack of pups. This would have been his childhood during relatively peaceful times until he was roughly five years old, which would place us in 1940. As far as an early education goes, my father could not speak of his primary schooling in Greece because he had either had precious little or none. He knew his letters, but that was about it; his education was as stunted as his penmanship could attest. He would have spelled words phonetically, but that was it. At the point when he would have gotten ready to go to elementary school is precisely when his family would have had to have left the port town of Gythion to make their way to their mountain home in the village of Agios Nikolaos to hide from foreign soldiers invading their coastal town.

You will learn how far my father advanced in his chosen field, which was extraordinarily focused and bright but also a man dominated by passion. In this sense, he was similar to Hercules, not insofar as that intellect was "not strong, [but that] his emotions were *apt to get out of control.*"[40] Certainly, my father could be a fiery man, and you never doubted where you stood with him. I am sure that as a mischievous little boy, my dad's boundless energy had him bounding about like a little Billy goat. Where Hercules was taught archery and fencing and learned how to shoot a bow and arrow as a boy, my dad knew how to use a slingshot. Even as an adult, I can recall how he would turn back into that scrappy lad as he showed us his children his prowess, hitting any target we'd set out for him. Whereas Hercules learned how to shoot a bow and arrow and enjoyed wrestling and boxing, my father's generation would have no formal training in fighting; should the mood or moment arise, these village boys would pelt pebbles or stones at the target of the moment.

After all, my dad was from Mani, and for centuries, this folk had a reputation for being stern and hardy people; if they are nursing a grudge, they can stay stoic and stone-faced, nursing a grudge for years. Maniots are known for throwing rocks from high off the lookout towers they constructed for themselves deep in the Taygetos mountains. These people are also renowned for their vendettas and feuds, not to mention hightailing it back and forth to and from Crete to cool tensions or hide. My father was filled with vim, oil, and vinegar; he came by it naturally. His oldest brother, described to me as a "sensitive boy," daily walked with an older cousin to harvest salt from the broad, flat pads of stone at the rockier edges of the seashore. Just to be a bully, this cousin would throw salt in my young uncle's eyes, and I'm sure he had to keep from crying to avoid further harassment. Yet, returning home then and just a few short years later, during the thick of the war, when my father's family was living up in the village, *he* would be the "man" for his two younger brothers. During the years when their father was in America, my Uncle Kolya would be the helpmate to his mother, and decades later, as a result of this interdependency that had developed between them, complicated enmeshment arose such that it would have been unthinkable to *force* him to leave home when he became an adult. And try, though I'm sure he did, he was neither willing nor ever able to do so.

I can still remember seeing his bedroom for the first time: to me, it looked no different than it might have when he was in high school, with a single bed neatly made and a student's desk nearby, except that instead of textbooks piled atop, he had tidy stacks of paperwork from his job at the bank. He is one of the victims of this particular generation of Greek boys who became men too soon and never left home, suspending their troubled boyhood into agitated adulthood, sub-consciously ever on call to protect their mothers from the horrors of war. Only once, while sitting with my father and the both of them out on the balcony of their apartment building in Brooklyn, looking out on the horizon past the Verrazano Bridge in the near distance at sunset, did I hear and feel their unity when they sung together a plaintive song familiar to them both from those problematic days long gone by. Typically, they co-existed in a frazzled state of bitter resentment, likely to erupt in sharp shriek if any landmine were trodden upon. They lived behind silent walls of longing, like a truce they'd secretly made.

Not all was bad, and like all kids whose imaginations are active and engaged, this child's play of the day was not unique, even though the toys might be old-fashioned to us. On calmer days, the boys would play jacks or "tavli," backgammon, the national pastime of all Greek men. My dad told me that the boys in his boyhood town would often play soccer with a makeshift "ball" made up of cloth tightly bound up strips, and they would kick it about, using designated items as substitute boundaries or goalposts. Likely, the field was outside the church courtyard, where youngsters in Greek towns and villages *still* gather to play today. I can hear them now — boys yelling or arguing about whether the ball was in or out of bounds. These boys were a band of brothers who would walk arm in arm, three of four at a stretch, ready to conquer life, laughing or cursing, with dark hair tussled and faces smudged. Rather than snips and snails and puppy dog tails, *these* boys would catch cicadas or June bugs and tie strings between the thorax and head of the armored bodies so that— *voila* — they would have mini choppers that could fly about at will. These were the remote-control helicopters of my Father's Day and imagination!

Decades later, one time, our father channeled the spirit of his childhood and had us kids follow him to the field next door to our house. We watched him silently and with avid interest as he made a homemade kite from my mother's daily newspapers, some sticks, and a ball of string he produced from his pocket. He fashioned a tail from strips of rags he pulled out from the other pocket. Holding the homemade kite in one hand and the excess string and tail in the next, my father then bound across the field, surely in the same way he did decades before as a boy, going faster and faster, elated as we all watched his kite successfully get caught up by an obliging gust of wind. Up it went, far into the clouds. He called us to him so we could take turns holding that string, peering gleefully up into the sky at the flapping but mighty kite our dad had made from nothing. There was a bit of a prankster in my dad. Though he purposefully withheld traumatic stories from his youth to shield my sensitive younger sister, who loved all creatures great and small, he did slyly share with me that this pack of boys would catch and capture tiny frogs, then carefully blow air into their mouths, *past* the point of expansion to a level where they would explode. Had it existed, PETA would have been fuming, but these were tough times for spunky boys looking to make mischief.

Years later, when *we* were children, my dad once performed another magic trick out on our driveway he had learned in youth. One cool fall weekend morning, he decided to inflate some innocent, colorful balloons for us as if for some private birthday party. He produced a strange canister filled *not* with helium (He) but with hydrogen (H). What a difference that vowel made. Oh, sure, they inflated all right. After he'd filled and tied them off with string so we could hold our balloons high over our heads, he would light a rag wrapped around the end of a long stick and ignite our balloons, and *BOOM!* His homemade bombs would explode, and we were in shock and awe, so impressed with our daring dad. That same extended stick with this primitive rag would also be used with gasoline and light so he could torch any bagworm nests in the trees of our yard. Thankfully, he never did this in the fall.

Hercules had a *much* more conventional, uneventful, and well-rounded education than my father when he was a boy in Greece. When the war started and his family headed for the hills, my father would have been ready to enter elementary school, so although he spoke Greek, his formal learning to read and write would have been limited to whatever he happened to observe in the village, and that probably would have been next-to-nothing. Greeks value their education very highly, so my dad was zealous for success in our early education as if to make up for lost time in his youth. He was the best cheerleader a child could have wanted where school support is concerned. For example, when I was in elementary school, he would sit beside me for what felt like hours to help me with math.

As you've seen, life provided many opportunities for him to perform living lab experiments; plus, he held Mother Nature and the animal kingdom in awe for its myriad processes and adaptabilities. When he read aloud to me when I was a child, it filled me with the desire to do so as well because although, and perhaps because he was hardly a smooth reader in English, every syllable he uttered held promise and excitement as if he knew we were getting to the good part, and it was all good. I can't help but wonder if he read with such enthusiasm in part because his early education had been interrupted, thwarted, and suspended; therefore, he was all the more animated at the prospect of sharing this experience with his eldest, who, sitting on his knee, could hardly wait for his command in Greek, "Γυρίστε το φύλλο" — "Turn the page!"

Later, in high school, he "forbade" us from even entertaining the thought of getting a job to buy this or that item for ourselves; he said our "job" was school. Only my sister dared to disobey and got a job at Wendy's to furnish her own choice of clothing. Even in college, when an elective course I was taking took precious time from more serious subjects for my major, and my grades began to falter, my dad came to the rescue. Lamenting to him that I felt like I was drowning, my father became the squeaky wheel. He both called and wrote to the school's administration so that, probably to shut him up, I was granted permission to drop the course without penalty. I was amazed and relieved; it was just another day for my dad, who likely said, "*No problem!*" God knows what he may have told them. However, education involved more than academics, and music was another crucial part of the song of his life.

In the day and time when you provided your own entertainment, my father's mother, Dimitra, learned to play the mandolin from her older brother's first wife, whose name was *also* Dimitra. This Dimitra adored her younger sister-in-law — my grandmother — and my grandmother, in turn, happily emulated this woman and learned to play the mandolin. Sometime during the war, my grandmother's mandolin was confiscated or stolen, and decades later, when my father wasn't a well man, he would go from pawn shop to pawn shop in Brooklyn asking, pleading, or gruffly demanding to know if they had her mandolin. Where Hercules was taught to play the *lute*, when dad's family got to Brooklyn, my father took up learning the *violin*; it has the same strings as the mandolin. I, too, fell in love with the sound of the violin, and one day, coming home from first grade, marching about playing the air violin, evidently after I had heard some stringed music in music class, I was allowed to take music lessons. Much to my consternation, often when I began to practice, my father would come in my room — ostensibly to better tune my quarter- or half-sized instrument. Still, in reality, it gave him the opportunity to commence practicing *his* favorite piece, Pablo de Sarasate's gypsy piece, *Zigeunerweisen*. With eyes closed and his bow suspended on the G string, he quickly got swept up and carried away on a better wave of his past.

I'll never know if my father was like Hercules, who, if you recall, was disciplined for his *lack* of obedience to his musical teacher, Linus. Still, as the youngest of the three boys and likely a rascal, he would have been subject to having his ear curtly tugged, as are many Greek children who misbehave. This amounts to a one-second swift yank of the earlobe by the father, or as was likely the case for my dad, by his ever-attendant big brother the moment a misdeed or defiance occurred. As a youngster, I put this to the test when, once with this brother, my Uncle Kolya, *and* godfather, I dared say, "Hush up," he warned me what would happen should I ever say that again. Like Pandora drawn to her box, I did, and I earned my right to that speedy trial and punishment by the yank of my ear.

Speaking of my dad's big brother, once they moved to Brooklyn, my Uncle Kolya, not their father, would teach my father to drive. "Taught" may be a stretch because my father was never a good driver. Every street was his to drive on as he wished, laws of governance, be gone. I can still hear my mother erupting with a scream of "*Paaaaaul!*" for the countless chances he took passing some slow car over the double yellow lines or, perchance, driving up the wrong side of the street to correct a wrong turn, always with unassailable confidence. On the other hand, Hercules was taught to drive a team of horses and control his chariot by his earthly father, Amphitryon, the first trainer Hercules had in life.[41] I do not doubt that his driving was more adept. However, similar to Hercules, my father had another adult in his life to whom he would look up and who would become a remarkable mentor to him. We will return to this relationship at the point in our story when my dad was an undergraduate studying at Brooklyn College. Meanwhile, let's pull back the curtain of Greek history to when my father lived in Greece.

Life in Greece Part 1: Waves of Invasions, 1935–1941

For me to focus on what amounts to one short decade, that is, from the time when my father was born to when he left Greece when he would have been a starving lad just under eleven years old, feels like trying to take hold of a dust speck with a lasso. It is barely a blink in time, but what a turbulent epoch it was! What strife! What confusion! What savagery! There is no other country in Europe so unassuming, yet geopolitically in such a critical position that underwent a fierce fratricidal war smack dab in the middle of the Second World War! *This* is the land to which my father was born, and although I am no historian, I will peal the skin of this lemon and give you its pulp and pith and zest. Admittedly, to share his story, the more I studied and decided what and what not to include, the more it felt like I was untangling thick knots from a ship that got wrecked and mangled in a tidal wave. I do not pretend to have but a layman's understanding of these coagulated events; native Greeks will no doubt want to insert comments and corrections, but others will be stilled by wonder in all that got packed in those seemingly innocuous years, starting with his birthdate, December 4, 1935 to February 5, 1946, when my father and his two elder brothers and mother, along with hundreds of other war-weary and weak Greeks, took that frigid week-long voyage to Ellis Island, NY, where faint hopes got resuscitated and families tearfully rejoined. No, my father's story is not unique, but it is exceptional.

These formative years in Greece would shape his psyche no less than the genetic disease with which he was born would strike life *and* limb later on. No one will ever know which came first: the chicken or the egg, that is, whether the scars of growing up in the thick of two wars or my dad's genetic time bomb would impact him more greatly. To better appreciate the compound that is my father's background and biology, it is vital we set the dramatic stage into which my father was born and peer at its constituent elements. I will uncover both for you: first, a layer of Greek history during the first decade of his life, and this will be further subdivided into two halves, then a buckshot smattering of genetic background as it pertains to Huntington's disease. I will bring us up-to-speed and place my dad at the same life marker at which then stood Hercules, that is, the occasion of each man's wedding. My dad would have been twenty-five in 1960, but for now, let's time-travel together to a year or so before my father was born. Just what was going on in his corner of the world then?

The World into Which My Father Was Born: Greece in 1935

Just north of Greece, resentments were festering in Albania and Bulgaria; *both* countries were sore at Greece for signing the Balkan Pact in February 1934, putting Greece in cahoots with Turkey, Yugoslavia, and Russia.[42] The long and the short of it is that these two countries found themselves seeking retribution; to that end, they were willing to make a deal with the devil to regain lost territories and gain influence in their backyards. As you will soon see, so much of what happened in Greece in the critical years that followed, there is a knee-jerk pattern of action-reaction, but the breakneck speed, thrust, and direction at which this happened frequently brought about unpredictable and overlapping outcomes, like a cluster of interconnected events going wildly viral. You only need to remember two actors for this part of the plot of our play who will serve as the villains to Greece: Italy and Germany. There are too many players to count or name; therefore, I will keep to the major players.

I hope my Greek readers will forgive me for my truncation. The aggressive rate of expansion of these two countries reflects the voracious appetite for domination and control of their leaders, Benito Mussolini and Adolf Hitler. The leader in Greece at that time was a man named Eleftherios Venizelos. On March 1, 19<u>35</u>, in the northern Greek City of Thessaloniki, there was an assassination attempt on Prime Minister Venizelos' life and a near-successful coup d'état. Although Venizelos tried to make his voice heard while exiled in Crete, he became ineffectual and passé. In fact, not only did he *not* return to Greece, but barely a year later, he died there in March of 19<u>36</u>. Somewhere between these two Marches, the monarchy was restored one month before my father was born in November 1935. Greece overwhelmingly voted to restore itself to its constitutional monarchy classification. King George returned home and appointed a new prime minister who, as it turns out, immediately got into power disputes with him, and the king ended up quitting. This man's name is Ioannis Metaxas, but though he was Greece's most potent player until 1940, he was hardly the only one who vied for control.

What or who else would be a persistent power player in Medusa's head of Greek politics? <u>The Greek Communist Party</u>. You have my word that the only acronym of the plethora that existed to which I will refer is that of the Greek Communist Party, the KKE. Suffice it to say, this party also had military branches and offshoots that did their bidding. Why is the KKE worth mentioning? The Greek Communists were highly organized, single-minded, resolved, independent, and quite efficacious in their defense efforts; that withstanding, they *also* became problematic for those *officially* leading the country. How did the KKE gain traction? When, in their estimation, the official Greek leadership failed, waffled, or worse — did nothing to contend with more prominent players or counter other countries that were basically bullying or pushing Greece around, the Greek Communist Party swiftly and efficiently organized itself in such a way to doggedly assert itself against the Goliaths, even though it had no *sanctioned* authority. Can you feel the seeds of civil discord brewing at this early juncture *and* see how the KKE could have gained both a foothold in the Greek political scene *and* a sense of bold and brash self-confidence? The Communist Party appealed most to those idealistic, zealous, freedom-loving, and authoritarian-hating Greeks who were "riding on a *global* wave of communism's appeal."[43] Ultimately, they would have looked to the Soviet Union for direction and support, but ultimately, they got nothing. I will inform you here and now that my grandmother's brother became a member of the KKE, no doubt, as a result of being frustrated with the sycophantic local yokels who proved maddeningly inept at fighting or dispelling foreigners and fascists.

Meanwhile, Venizelos and a few other key players unexpectedly died in the spring of 1936. Now left with a power vacuum, Greece was facing an especially "grave crisis...with the dictatorships of Hitler and Mussolini threatening the peace of Europe."[44] Therefore, by process of elimination, Genera Metaxas became appointed Prime Minister in April 1936. My father would have been a four-month-old infant, and *his* father would still have been with his family living in Gythion. General Metaxas was now promoted to Prime Minister. Although *technically* he was pro-monarchy/pro-king, with forces menacing abroad *and* the KKE's organs steeping within, Metaxas took swift and decisive control of the chaotic situation. In August of 1936, he declared a national state of emergency, established martial law, and dissolved parliament indefinitely.[45] In no time at all, Metaxas had full and unlimited authority in Greece; his dictatorship would last for the next five years.

Before I proceed any further in telling you about the state of Greece while my father was in the first five years of his life when things were *relatively* calm, I should like to remind you now that it was Sigmund Freud who suggested that the first five years of a child's life, which includes the moral code of the parents, "is crucial to the formation of the adult personality."[46] And because I will never know *their* mindset, the best I can do is to probe the fundamental leaders' actions of the time to speculate how my grandparents' psychological landscape was shaped. I'll return to General Metaxas in a moment, but at this point, I find myself curious about King George's mindset. Remember that although the king was still officially in control, Metaxas had the real power. Perhaps Metaxas did his dirty work for him and then, step by step, inexorably came into his own.

Interestingly, the Peloponnese region from which my father came was considered "the traditional center of Greek royalism," Metaxas's party fared poorly here. Still, the king determined Metaxas was the best man to "impose order" on Greece.[47] What was King George thinking to have handed over his power to what amounts to the dictator that Metaxas appeared to be? It turns out he left to save his own skin; survival by any means necessary would become his life's theme. Let's remain neutral if for no other reason than to peer at the part of Greece my father is from, which, as I intimated, held nostalgia for the monarchy.

Leadership during My Father's Life in Greece: King George II (1890–1947)

Suffice it to say, King George was initially distressed about his finding it necessary to live in exile in England for twelve long years before his return in 1935; I learned that he had a love-hate relationship with the Brits.

While there, it turns out that he adopted a more Western attitude towards Greece and Greeks: although Greeks had a romantic temperament, they were essentially "savage."[48] Therefore, when Greeks voted for him to return, he came to rely upon his general-turned Prime Minister to make the difficult decisions, and Metaxas was only too willing to oblige. Furthermore, in response to the worries of the impoverished Greek people already beginning to rise in revolt, Metaxas called for a "new order" in Greece, arguing that the Great Depression proved the failure of democracy and that fascism was the solution.[49] It was also no secret that Metaxas was a Germanophile and exhibited a Germanic style and approach to his exercise of control. He was making practical efforts to squelch Communist movements in Greece. While he was back In Greece, King George was no doubt privately glad *someone* was putting a lid on these discontent groups and helping to avoid a potential mess; therefore, he continued to give Metaxas *carte blanche* and let him have his way. This would *not* include seeking aid from others.

Five years later, the Brits made King George retract his support of Metaxas when it became evident that Greece desperately needed the help of *England* to combat the Nazis. Winston Churchill courted and befriended King George, effectively persuading him to accept help from England when he found himself between a rock (the Axis powers) and a hard place (Greek resistance factions) and needed assistance. During the German invasion, when things got really rough, King George (again) left mainland Greece for Crete in 1941 but then went on to live in Egypt for years. Finally, when the coast was clear, and he could return to Greece in 1946, he did so; here, King George would remain until he died in 1947. He delivered his most memorable quote about all his moves: "The most important tool for a king of Greece is a suitcase."[50] Of course, he wanted to return to Greece but was prevented time and again, initially by various Greeks who resented his support of what amounted to their *own* dictator. He was a stubborn and rather paranoid man to many, where British overtures toward Greece were concerned. Had he returned to his fraught and frothy homeland earlier, he would have been or become a lame or dead duck. Even Churchill appeared to have turned on him and forced him to abdicate for a regent appointed in 1945.

By the end of March 1946, not even one month after my father's family emigrated to America, the monarchists had won the election. This event led Churchill to return that following September, as the king was clearly in over his head and unable to deal with the magnitude and severity of the problems. Greece was facing economic collapse and was still fraught with political fractures and instability. Less than six months later, in the Royal Family's summer palace in a suburb of Athens, this insecure and embittered man died on April Fool's Day 1947, technically from arteriosclerosis, but more likely from lost pride and a broken heart. This would have been one year after my father and his family left for America. Let's come back to square and focus on the man who was large and in charge during the *first* five years of my father's life.

Ioannis Metaxas (1871 – 1941)

Who was this General Metaxas? Although he was very much a dictator and one who harbored pro-German sentiments, Metaxas would best be remembered as the man who stood up to the brash Benito Mussolini. This complex, decisive, and controversial leader was the perfect transitional figure because he balanced a royalist stance domestically with a pro-Greek nationalist agenda in the global arena. Ideally, I hope to carve out with surgical skill a tiny corner of the world upon which my father's would-be shattered life was built. It was during a time when the world's *and* his birth nation's histories cataclysmically collided as if Greece was a marble that got stuck between two flipping paddles in a mad pinball machine. My dad simply knew it as his boyhood.

Let's take a closer look at Metaxas since he was in charge during the first half of my dad's years in Greece. On March 5, 1936, King George II appointed Metaxas the Minister of Defense, a post in which he would remain until he died in 1941. The king was grateful (and indebted) to Metaxas for his cunning, his military prowess, and his swift and accurate reading of the pulse of Greeks at the time. Metaxas spoke bluntly and openly about the possibility of a civil war, and most politicians and the king feared getting caught on the losing side. At the same time, alliances were quickly made and undone.[51] For the time being, George did remain in Greece, but he was out of the limelight *and* out of the heat. As I said, he let the more forceful and capable man do the difficult work of leading this fragmented country.

Metaxas' first act was to declare a state of emergency in Greece, and on this day, he dubbed Greece "an anti-communist state, an anti-parliamentary state, a totalitarian state."[52] The political significance of this appointment was monumental since, in *spirit*, Metaxas was a dedicated royalist; however, in *fact*, and to his core, he was a military man who possessed a forceful, authoritarian style of leadership. There would be no voice of dissent or pledge to cry *"Freedom!"* heard or seen on *his* watch. Indeed, his was a non-parliamentary regime in Greece. Was Metaxas effectively suppressing the labor and communist party from gaining a foothold? Yes. Was there a price? Indubitably. I have already told you about his reputation for being autocratic, albeit for the good of Greece as he saw it. However, the situation was more complicated because he was considered a "Germanophile."[53] I can't tell if it is because he was attracted to the rank-and-file order and efficiency of Germany's already well-oiled military machine or if it was their culture's reputation for demonstrating the capability to execute a single-minded purpose with a focused strategy without any messy sentiments or costly acts of compassion to keep them from achieving their goals. Greeks tend to quarrel among themselves too much to achieve a unified and higher ambition readily.

Although Metaxas *did* have a vision for a "Third Hellenic Civilization,"[54] his objective was nowhere near the scale that Mussolini or Hitler had for their countries, which was worldwide domination. Furthermore, Metaxas had no broad base, let alone any adequate popular support, but at the end of ends, it was apparent that Metaxas was concerned for the welfare of Greece and Greeks. He would never buckle under the demands of the likes of Italy, yet at the same time, he wouldn't have wanted to have raised any ire from ruthless Germany. Maybe Metaxas intuitively and subconsciously knew the Nazis Party under the Führer, the despot Adolf Hitler, was going to be able to reach its aspirations. Perhaps he didn't want Greece to get subsumed or caught in the wake of its destruction. Likely, he, too, wanted to create a "modern and efficient state"[55] of Greece.

Repressive measures aside, which is easy to dismiss from the safe sidelines of decades and thousands of miles away, Metaxas completed many public work projects and took steps to alleviate Greece from the impact of the worldwide Depression. Ultimately, Greece's demise came about from getting caught between Scylla and Charybdis, the infamous mythical sea monsters described by Homer's *Odyssey*, only now it was Italy and Germany. Mussolini's expansionist plans for his "New Rome" made the double trouble wielded by this dynamic duo all the worse: it boiled down to Italy's marching through Albania to get to Greece. The very notion of Italian hegemony would have been ludicrous to any Greek!

It would help if you understood that Greeks and Italians have similar temperaments and Mediterranean lifestyles, perhaps because they occupy similar spots on the planet forever. In my travels, I have heard the Greek-Italian cultural connection as "one face, one race," even temperamentally similar enough to dub these small southern Mediterranean countries "kissing cousins." While Greece's glory and cultural-philosophical contributions predated the Italians, Rome's reputation for being the superior military machine is renowned. Today, they argue over who makes the best olive oil. Even though the Italians' sense of fashion, style, and art is heads and shoulders above that of the Greeks, Italians, like the rest of the world, are drawn to a core of freedom, a sense of balance, and the quest for wisdom which resides in the breast of every Greek.

Suffice it to say a handful of other neighboring countries would adversely impact Greece at this time, but I will simplify matters for expediency's sake and mention that the ever-ready and helpful British were critical to Greece's viability. Under the rulership of Metaxas, Germany was preoccupied with designs further north, so you might say that Greece wasn't directly on Hitler's radar or on the front burner as far as plans for his *immediate* expansionist goals went. This fact was solidified in August of 1939 when representatives from Nazi Germany and the Soviet Union met and signed the Nazi-Soviet Non-Aggression Pact; Hitler could plow ahead with countries in closer proximity to Germany. Meanwhile, little Italy under mighty Mussolini got the wink or nod or sign of okay from Germany to proceed with plans to rip through Albania and invade Greece, and this is when the mess really began. Having already annexed Albania in the fall of 1940, Mussolini made up some fabricated excuse to position Italian troops on the Albanian-Greek border, something to the effect that Greece was tiptoeing where it ought not. Albania obviously didn't mind, and we can infer that Hitler looking the other way would indicate his tacit approval for Mussolini's designs in Greece. In fact, Italian troops were already crossing the border into northern Greece!

What made Greece an attractive area to try to interfere with or possess? It certainly wasn't an abundance of natural resources it contained in its rocky soil. Oh, no. It was location, location, location: the *thousands* of miles of shoreline and direct access to the Mediterranean, not to mention *dozens* of steppingstones or landing pads of islands upon which to hop or position oneself to face bulky Turkey. Mussolini would accost Greece from her north and west; contrapuntally, later on, England would seek to deliver aid and ammunition from the south. Germany would eventually have its way wherever and however it desired. Anxious Greeks stirred the pot from within by shaking their fists and wagging their tongues at these would-be conquerors. No matter what people may say about Metaxas being a dictator, in the end, he was more pro-Greece than pro-self insofar as he was trying to assert his will in the international arena. He had declared Greece's neutrality in September of 1939. Therefore, on October 26th, 1940, when looking on with envy at the conquests Hitler was already steadily making, Mr. Mussolini got greedy and grubby for an accomplishment of his own. He literally woke Metaxas at 3:00 in the morning to inform him that *he had three hours* to accept the "terms" he was presenting to Greece. These weren't terms so much as an ultimatum that announced, "Ready or not, here we come! Like it or lump it! Take it or leave it!" But this was no game of hide-and-seek: Italy was going to invade Greece whether or not Greece would roll over and take it or not.

Mighty Metaxas, furious at the unmitigated gall of Italy, of all countries, to make such demands on Greece and him (and at this hour), responded with one word: "*Oxi!*" This was an emphatic "*No!*" Winston Churchill said that for the Greeks, this was "their finest hour."[56] This day would be the dawning of the Greco-Italian War, lasting until late April 1941. Meanwhile, mere months before Greece proved soundly victorious over the Italians, General Metaxas unexpectedly and out of the blue died from complications due to an abscess in his pharynx. The timing could not have been worse, and the country's fate was left to a cacophony of bickering voices coming from weaker men, not that anyone could have prevented the wave of Axis momentum that took on such horrific force. You need to know that the decade of the 1940s is considered "the most devastating and deadly in Greek history."[57] Until they escaped and left on the second of February of 1946, my father and his family would experience the direst pangs of this epoch. How apt that they set sail in this month, whose name stems from the Latin word, *Februarius*, meaning "to purify"[58]; it became my family's transition time, bringing them to a new land and halcyon life.

Triple Whammy and the Big "No!"

During my childhood, I'll not forget my mother warning us children in hushed tones, "Never ask your father about his childhood," so shrouded in mystery and mayhem that we dared not bring our dad back to murky or vivid nightmares merely to satisfy our childish curiosity. Eventually, after my parents' divorce, my dad would unseal this inner vault and tell me stories from this chapter. It was almost as if he went into a trance; it was like watching him open up his fresh box of horrors, yet undeniably sprinkled with moments of unparalleled sweetness. I was yet largely unfamiliar with how the historical pieces fit together, let alone transpired, so I'm providing a framework for us to house the mishmash of my dad's memories and stories, which I'd heard but were as yet disconnected shards. Much will be missing, and many facts persist that defy fathoming, but I hope to have captured a whisper of the spirit of these times my dad lived through. I remain ever-mindful not to get subsumed by the tangle of personalities and multitudinous interconnected branches of Greek political factions within parties. Another desire of mine is to investigate the impact of how war created post-traumatic stress disorder deep inside my father's young frame and fragile psyche long before the term "Huntington's disease," or its acronym **HD** came about in our awareness. I will provide personal anecdotes to give flesh and blood to cold and chilling facts.

Let me draw a couple of maps from 1941 in broad brushstrokes, which I scoured over while reading this history. I take delight in maps; they help us see the bigger picture, which is invaluable. The first map below[59] shows wave upon wave of thick red arrows, indicating the source, direction, and degree of invasion, starting north of Yugoslavia and Bulgaria, zig-zagging inexorably and determinedly southward, as if Greece were a toilet bowl towards which all forces were aimed to flush. Eight stubby arrows siphoned down to four, and then these became concentrated in two areas of initial penetration in Greece, then re-fanned out to three arrows reaching across central Greece, not failing to neglect finally penetrating the Peloponnesus with two final parting gifts of elongated spears of condensed attacks terminating in Kalamata, a city located one "finger" over from my father's. Only three faintly-dotted lines of help coming northward from Crete indicated British lines sending filaments of succor to mainland Greece and the Monemvasia in the east-most "finger" of the Peloponnesus. The second map[60] to the right of the first also arrested my attention. It is labeled "The Balkans 1941: Invasion of Yugoslavia and Greece, April 1941." Though vast and detailed, my focus here became riveted on what transpired in the Peloponnesus. I looked at this land, the three-fingered "hand" of my father, and saw four red veins of infiltration across the top, with the first arrow distinctly aimed towards the Messenian left "finger." This was achieved first by brushing alongside the capital of the Peloponnesus, Patras, then dropping down to the westernmost side of Messenia, exiting out through its tip. A second launching point began by entering through the Corinthian Canal at Corinth, then unfurling out in three directions. The first stubby vein isn't too far to reach to accommodate Nafplio. The second one scurried straight over and down to the major Messenian port city of Kalamata, situated just west of the Mani finger. And then I saw the third arrow that maligned the Mani by heading straight through and exiting a tad further south of my dad's port town of Gythion, on the east coast of Mani.

There is no way that Axis forces wouldn't have stopped in Gythion if but to raid and rest before plunging further south and east to a smaller and more practical point of exit in this middle "finger" of Mani. I do not know the name of this port of exit, but it looks to be less than an hour's drive away from Gythion. Perhaps it was the older port of Kotronas; maybe it was Kokkala; I don't know, so I'll call the whole thing off. Why would I detail this march of madness? Because I can so easily and fitfully see the terrifying trifecta of this three-way invasion, like the three-headed dog Cerberus, that got instigated with the Italians, then continued with the follow-through of the Goliathan Germans, and then Bulgaria would get in on the action up north and east. I know no European country during WWII with a time slot known as "The Triple Occupation."[61] No wonder my dad, as a lad, couldn't tell if the raiding soldiers were Italian or German! It was *both*!

And while Germany officially retained control of Athens, Thessaloniki, Crete, and the Greek border alongside Turkey, "the Italians occupied the rest of the country."[62] Backed up by Germany this time, the Italians got a second chance to maraud and humiliate Greece, and the Germans, not *entirely* trusting the Italians to be successful in their campaign, would have scoured and sniffed out areas that might have needed reinforcement to ensure Axis success. So, while Italy lost to Greece in their *initial* invasion, they were decidedly glad to take what they could get and to be "permitted" to work alongside bigger-and-badder Germany by "getting" to have their way further south, and this would include the area where my dad was from. Not even two years later, in 1943, Greeks would undergo shock waves of the Massacre of Kalavyrta in the northern part of the Peloponnesus (halfway between Patras and Corinth), where Germans retaliated for the Greek slaughter of their own sixty soldiers with over five hundred Greek civilians.[63] This part of Greece would have felt *wholly* ravaged and ready to drop had it not been for their guerrilla fighters fighting back tooth and nail and keeping embers of hope alive. My dad and his family would have been in hiding up in the village by then; surely, they would have heard of what became the bloodiest Nazi massacre in Greece — *and* in the Peloponnesus at that. I now return to the time right after Metaxas' death in January of 1941 when my dad would have been just five.

It would be an understatement to say that no one could have anticipated the level of resistance and gutsy push-back the Greeks brought the over 100,000 Italian troops that poured into Greece. As I have mentioned, Greeks squabble vociferously with fellow Greeks but unite against a common enemy like nobody's business. Against all odds, they did it against the Persians and would do it again against these Italians. Perhaps recalling this historical lesson, even Germany opposed Mussolini's unilateral design and foolish move. From the inception of the Italian invasion in northern Greece in October of 1940 until Hitler's follow-up blitzkrieg of April 1941, Greeks not only repelled the Italians, but they also forced them to retreat into Albania. Greek soldiers were so fired up that they valiantly evoked the battle cry of "Freedom or Death!" the motto of their homeland adopted back in 1821 when the Greeks won their independence from the Ottoman Empire. Of course, this success proved costly and exhausting, and even though it was worth it in the minute, there would be no rest for the weary in the next hour. They didn't stand a chance, and the real trouble hadn't begun.

War II and the Civil War in Greece: An Overview

Those six *months*, which brought about a burst of pride and glory and gain, would be followed by a bust of six *years* of Greece being pummeled by outsiders, and that's not including self-inflicted wounds springing from discord and disagreement from within. Storms within storms were brewing beforehand, so the war within the war overlaps and would spin out its own knotted and disastrous combustion. The *worst* tangled mess that is the Greek Civil War did not happen until *after* WWII, but it overlaid with and got amped up because of it, like some VIN diagram gone haywire. WWII is said to have begun on Sept. 1, 1939, and ended on Sept. 2, 1945.[64] The Greek Civil War is reported to have lasted from 1941 and ended in 1949, and within this period, it can be further broken down into four phases.[65] My father was present and accounted for in three out of four stages. Because it would be so easy to get consumed and subsumed by interlocking events and their associated details and personages, I will divide and conquer this complicated time in history for you by providing a thumbnail sketch of these two wars, the one worldwide, the other hardly civil. So as not to get entangled or bogged down, each will have its own devoted paragraph, and I will funnel information pertinent to either Greece or my father. Finally, and most essentially, I will exit our historical mini-series by peering into my father's experience as best as possible.

After Mussolini's failure to conquer Greece in his quest to become the conqueror of the Balkan Peninsula, Hitler, no doubt irritated, found himself having to clean up this mess. Initially, Hitler wasn't focused on the southern part of Europe at all. However, he soon found himself strategizing that Greece could be a stepping stone to Turkey, which was but a stone's throw to Russia, and *that* was a tantalizingly strategic prospect in his quest for world domination. Therefore, on April 6, 1941, Hitler launched what was known as Operation Marita.[66] German soldiers crossed right on past and through the previously inviolable dotted line known as the Metaxas Line, which was drawn between Greece and Bulgaria. The natural and most practical point of entry would be through Macedonia and the northern portion of Greece, and what better way than through its second-largest city, Thessaloniki, then charge southward through to Thermopylae (where 300 Spartans held off the Persians in 480 BC), and finally marching straight for Athens, but that wasn't all, let alone the end. The Germans continued through the Corinthian Canal into the Peloponnesus. They advanced to other key ports, including Patras to the west, Kalamata and Monemvasia to the south, and Nafplio to the east. The Germans also invaded Crete, and although the Cretan fought like savages, famously shooting down German soldiers as they were parachuting down like rats from the sky, ultimately, they proved unsuccessful. From Crete, the Germans could zig-zag back up through the Peloponnesus or hop eastward to other Greek islands, which might prove strategically advantageous to them should the need arise.

Greece in the Thick of WW II: 1941

You need to know that time and again, more than any other country, it was the British that came to Greece's aid. Please also keep in mind how closely King George was aligned with England. After Metaxas died in Athens on January 29, 1941, unsurprisingly, King George exited stage right and remained watching from the sidelines in Egypt. Of course, after Metaxas died, he installed *another* royalist as prime minister to take charge of Greece. The ancient Greek motto, *"Come and get it!"* this new prime minister famously resurrected with the promise, "We will fight!" Neither he nor the already-spent Greeks could have fathomed an "avalanche" of German divisions— with *ten times* the strength of the Greeks" — would have considered invading their country. With calm, cool, collected, and cruel efficiency, they just kept on coming in, merciless "wave after wave" upon the "lamentably inadequate" Greek forces.[67] To add more barbarity to the blow at Greece's esteem, twelve days after Germany invaded Greece, this new prime minister who had just replaced Metaxas committed suicide.[68] I'm not kidding. So, while many Greeks either hated or loved Metaxas for his overbearing but stabilizing ways, that period in Greece was child's play compared to the chaotic and terrifying turbulence that would ensue from the power vacuum that was left.

I would imagine that *another* unfortunate bi-product would be anti-monarchist resentment for its failure to provide tangible and effective leadership, and this, too, would not serve Greece as a whole well during the very time that the British were trying to come to the defense of Greece which at least they recognized for its strategic value. After all, Greece would be the final frontier whereby Germany could sew up its sphere of domination in the south. Greece was the ninth country to fall to Germany in the early 1940s.[69] Although Italy was given dibs to the southern portion of Greece, do not think that Germany wasn't present and accounted for as well. Later on, I learned from my father that the Germans were more than displeased with the Italian's overall sloppiness and slipshod inefficiency, so much so that they went the extra mile and forced over 50,000 Greek Jews in Thessaloniki onto trains and deported them to concentration and labor camps; it is mind-numbing to comprehend that only around 1,200 Jews remain there today.[70] Having visited the Jewish quarter in nearby Beria in 2015, I would say that this figure is a stretch at that.

While I'm at this sidebar, it is incumbent upon me to tell you that though you are already well aware of Hitler's campaign to eradicate the Jewish people, there were many other "undesirables" and nationalities he wanted to eliminate to fulfill his aspirations in the field of eugenics. But that's not all. In his desire to create an "Aryan master race," on **July 14, 1933**, the German government promulgated the "**Law for the Prevention of Progeny with Hereditary Diseases.**"[71] This law mandated the forced **sterilization** of specific individuals with physical and mental disabilities or mental illnesses. Individuals subject to the law were those men and women who "suffered" from any of the nine conditions. These included: "hereditary **feeblemindedness**, schizophrenia, manic-depressive (or bi-polar) disorder, hereditary epilepsy, **Huntington's chorea** [my underscore], genetic blindness, deafness, severe hereditary physical deformity, and chronic alcoholism."[72] Oh, Lord, whom did they *not* deem as base? The law also allowed public health officials to apply this law to those "asocial elements" who were seen to reject German social values. I would be remiss if I did not mention this horrifying fact here, knowing that had my father's disease been apparent at the time and had he been living in that part of Europe, he might have been murdered. But I digress.

Later that April of 1941, on the heels of the failure of the Italian campaign and shortly after Germany invaded Greece, tens of thousands of British were sent to aid Greece under Greek command. Nonetheless, it was still nearly impossible for those British-backed Greeks to maintain their focus on cutting off supplies to the Germans. Not only did Germany prove masterful at ferreting out exposed pockets and unprotected flanks, but their "blitzkrieg" method of attack proved indomitable and unassailable, so overwhelming was it and were they. Of course, Greece did enjoy a few minor albeit glorious moments of brave and impressive actions, including blowing up strategic bridges and railway lines. Another more symbolic act of defiance occurred one month after German troops had raised a flag bearing the swastika over the Acropolis; two daring Greek teenage college students dared to sneak up and tear it down.[73] Ultimately though, the advancing Nazi forces demonstrated "overwhelming tactical and technical superiority against the Anglo-Greek forces."[74]

Even though most military action occurred in northern Greece, German troops marched straight down to its capital, Athens, and didn't stop there. They even made themselves a makeshift bridge from which to cross and gain control over the Corinthian Canal, the gateway into the southern section of Greece, the Peloponnesus, the portion of Greece where my dad was from. At the time, Corinth was being used as a strategic launching point for the British Navy to send help to Crete and other islands. Not only was Greece invaded and dominated by Germany, but it was at this point that Hitler next put into effect a deadly three-way chokehold that would strangle Greece.[75] This strategy would be more commonly or innocuously known as the Occupation of Greece, and the plan was that Bulgaria got the northern swath; Germany dominated Athens, Thessaloniki, and Crete; and the Italians got in on the action and were permitted to hector the rest of Greece. The purpose of Hellenic domination was not merely to add another notch to Hitler's belt: Germany also controlled Greece's natural resources and plundered her economy, which included "confiscating crops, stealing foodstuff to feed soldiers, and extracting coal and minerals for energy."[76] Even Mussolini reportedly said that *"the Germans have taken from the Greeks even their shoelaces..."*[77]

In just three short months, by June 1941, Greece was a defeated nation.

Russians like to take credit for being the country where the turning point of WWII occurred, that is, where <u>Operation Barbarossa</u> got botched by Hitler's failure to appreciate what a harsh Russian winter and her vast and snowy territory could do to his Axis forces. A friend of Adolf Hitler reported Hitler having once said, "If the Italians hadn't attacked Greece and needed our help, the war would have taken a different course. We could have anticipated the Russian cold *by weeks* and conquered Leningrad and Moscow..."[78] Other historians argue that if Greece had surrendered without any resistance, which in so doing, consequently brought about a forced delay and shift of Axis resources, it would have enabled Hitler to implement his Operation Barbarossa in the *spring* [79] rather than the reality of invading Russia not until *June* 22, 1941. Some historians use this argument to assert that the Greek resistance proved the pivotal turning point in World War II. Later, in hindsight, Hitler said that of all the nations Germany fought, *"the Greeks were the bravest and most gallant."*[80] Inspired by the Greek resistance during the Italian and German invasions, Churchill also remarked, "Hence we will not say that Greeks fight like heroes, but that *heroes fight like Greeks."*[81] Surely, all can see that this period in Greece was nothing short of awe-inspiring and heartbreaking.

<u>WWII Part 2: A Puppet Government Installed and Axis Powers Exit Greece, 1941–1945</u>

From 1941 to 1944, an Axis collaborationist puppet government would be installed in Greece, and subsequently, Greek resistance groups were popping up all over the place. Some worked with the British, but it was the Greek communist factions who proved the most effective in launching successful guerrilla attacks against occupying powers. Therefore, during the remainder of WWII from 1941–1944, the time when my father was living out the tender years of five through nine, is precisely the period when Greece was squarely under German domination, when Italian forces were *also* still present and active, when British and those Greek forces cooperating with the British were feverishly trying to counter the German occupation, and at the same time, the military branch of the Communist party and *its* army were also striking out with deadly force against *both* the Germans and — truth be told — *anyone* who was occupying Greece or countering them. What madness! What fury! What desperate times! Like mad dogs biting at their own flea-bitten and mangy tail, these Greek Communists were so mistrustful they proved to be violent towards fellow Greeks whom they even suspected of working (i.e., "collaborating") with <u>non</u>-Greeks of *either* side! And because the Communists were so organized and well disciplined, even though the Greek countryside was mountainous, they conducted an effective and savage guerrilla campaign.

Meanwhile, Italian troops were spent and collapsed in the summer of 1943. Perhaps consequently, less than a year later, by the summer of 1944, it became apparent that Germany too would be soon withdrawing from Greece[82]; *officially*, German forces began leaving Greece in September 1944.[83] Various Greek resistance forces harassed the retreating Germans on their way out, and concurrently, those Greeks who, out of self-preservation (or "cowardice," if you'd asked a member of the KKE), collaborated with the Germans "in the *Peloponnesus*, Macedonia, and Thessaly, were slaughtered"[84] (emphasis mine). Contemporaneously, the Russian Army was marching steadily and decidedly through Eastern Europe, advancing to Germany to strike the final death blows. By December, with Germany effectively crushed and undone, the political state of Greece was left in shambles; it would remain to be seen who would be in charge of this tragic mess. As the Germans withdrew from Greece, anti-communist factions merged and combined with the KKE to take final stabs at their now-parting common enemy. By the end of that year, it would be the better-coordinated Greek Communist Army that seized control of much of Greece (but *not* Crete), yet such an action would not go unchallenged. Now, the infighting would combust.

Infighting, Deliverance by Percentage, and Dénouement

With Germany and Italy out of the picture, Greece was left barely hanging on, their sense of peace and unity hanging by a thread. Plus, Greece's self-inflicted cuts were still bleeding. Recollections of the many murdered were still fresh and sharp, the economy was in shambles, and the political scene was still in flux and volatile. Open fighting between the Greek Communist forces and anti-communists broke out at the beginning of December 1945. This would be two months *before* my father and his family left on *their* Good Ship Lollypop. Prime Minister Churchill visited Athens on Christmas day of 1945 to make peace with the Greek Communists, but that turned out to be a bust. I now want to make you aware of a sneaky secret arrangement made at the highest level between the two most commanding men in the world at that time (as Hitler had committed suicide in April of 1945). This power play ended up providing CPR to a beleaguered Greece, which, with no one in charge and many jockeying for leverage and control, had become like a maniac hacking away at his nose *and* spiting his face. At stake were democracy, freedom, and the lives and fortunes of thousands upon thousands of innocent Greeks.

That preceding October, something called the "the Percentages Agreement" was made; it was an informal pact made on a simple slip of paper in a clandestine meeting between Joseph Stalin and Churchill about *post*-war plans for a few small and, by and large, impotent countries: Greece would be divvied up such that the *British* would retain *ninety* percent in control of Greece to the Soviet Union's *ten* percent.[85] Romania would be in the opposite proportion, and Yugoslavia would be split down the middle, 50/50. It was like two giants were playing a secret game of jacks, and the fates of men were being tossed around like they were incidentals or mere child's play. Meanwhile, the scrappy and ever-zealous Greek Communists, alive and well, willing and able, fought fiercely to fill the power vacuum in Greece. The following will be the Reader's Digest version, which will complete our account for this decade. Only afterward will I come back and have us walk side-by-side with my dad.

After Churchill was replaced in July 1945, British forces continued to hold steady in Athens but refused to get involved *elsewhere*. Instead, the Greek government's nascent army took on the unenviable job of crushing the communists. By this time, the Greek Communists were practically rabid from a mindset now stuck in purge-and-attack mode. Along with the eradication of all "fascist sympathizers," they even became intent on dismantling the Greek Orthodox Church. What had started as a noble effort to expel the Nazis morphed into a group of thugs who committed violence against *anyone* who wasn't with *them*. Here is the ugliest part of what amounted to Greeks turning on Greeks. Although consistently outnumbered, the communists were "veterans of guerrilla warfare and fought well."[86] There was no *one* leader in Greece for *anyone* to trust fully, and every action from among the many who fought for control was either heavy-handed or oppressive. Delicate and respectful diplomacy — there was none.

In my reading, I witnessed many men fighting from every angle while an exhausted populace continued to get pummeled, caught in their crossfire. The internecine struggle that began in December of 1944 advanced in full force from 1946 and continued to its termination in August of 1949.[87] It was like a boxing match between brothers duking it out that went *twenty* rounds, and as horrified as you were, you couldn't turn your head away, so you, too, ended up fleeing the scene of the crime. As would so many Greeks, my father and his family left their home and native rocky soil in the winter of 1946; it was the season of death. Some twelve months later, in early 1947, Britain formally withdrew from Greece, but the American military tipped the tide in favor of the official Greek government after 1948. Thankfully, new leadership emerged in Greece, and some men proved noble and capable of steering Greece onto a path of peace and healing.

The Greek Civil War and the Greek Communists

By this time, the tables had *long* turned from needing help from the Communists to counter the Nazis; now, the Communists and the Red Scare of Soviet domination had become a threat in their own right! Therefore, President Harry Truman provided the new Greek government aircraft and training to combat this *new* wave of *native* contenders.[88] As I have indicated, the savagery of the Greek Communists seemed to know no bounds. Fortified by American help, Greek government forces methodically and successfully pushed the rebels deeper into the mountains. The Greek Civil War climaxed in August 1949 when the final frontiers of the communist strongholds were destroyed. The fighting quickly faded afterward as even Stalin himself ordered the Greek communists to declare a cease-fire.[89] From 1946 to 1949, it is estimated that Greek Government forces suffered about 48,000 casualties; furthermore, some 158,000 Greeks may have died altogether as a result of the Greek Civil War, which is still considered to be *"the twentieth century's most brutal civil war"*[90] (emphasis mine).

As fate would have it, just one month *after* my father and his family sailed away, Greece would have an election in March 1946 that would be the first step towards realizing the Truman Doctrine of 1947. This formally marked the point at which when the United States would get involved in Greece's affairs, again stemming from the aim to counter communism's aggression and cancerous spread there, and that included any lingering Soviet influence associated therewith. To round the corner of this decade and give you a monetary idea of how devastated Greece was, I mention the Marshall Plan, also inaugurated this year. Its overarching purpose was to provide long-term economic and humanitarian aid to sixteen non-communist Western and Southern European countries, Greece being sixth in line.[91] Because of its plundered and underdeveloped economy and then still-active civil war, Greece was a region of unique and particular concern. It was deemed that aid and a $700 million package would be doled out systematically over a few years until it was determined that Greece had become sufficiently stabilized; this would not be a reality until 1952.[92]

Greece As the Backdrop for My Father's Upbringing

The birthing pains that drive me to relate to my *father's* experience in the war, from the time they had to leave their port town to the moment they had to hide in their remote mountainous village, are now entirely upon us. Before I back up and push, I will ask you again to please bear in mind that, unlike any other country in Europe, little Greece had to contend with *both* powerhouse Axis bullies who would elbow her into a corner of their domination. This would have her ricocheted right into a mishmash hodgepodge of incompatible homegrown gangs that seemed to propagate by the year, each of which was nobly trying to come to *Greece's* rescue *and* to gain its *own* vainglory. Apart from Greece's traditional allies in France and *especially* Britain, at the tail-end of WWII, the United States came to the rescue and dealt with the behemoths of Germany, Italy, and the Soviet Union, albeit in different capacities.

Rankling resentments among Greeks now arose between those who had escaped abroad in 1941 — and my grandfather would have been among these — and those who endured the Occupation, which would include those who resisted the occupiers *and* those who collaborated with them, those still pro-king and those *actually* in charge. Running amuck thick among them all were the fiery Greek Communists, trying to assert their will and ways.[93] This was a recipe for disaster.

Why exactly did my dad's *father*, my papou, leave when he did? Sensing impending danger and considering all his options, my papou took a calculated risk and became one of those who ducked out and left the country shortly after Metaxas died with the intent purpose of finding safety and succor on distant shores. After all, his first voyage, which had landed him in America on June 12, 1910, proved rewarding: he had already picked sweet fruit from his labor in the restaurant business; therefore, it would be a natural consideration for him to return and save more for *his* young family. Eventually, they could join him there in peace and prosperity. At least, that was the plan. How could my grandfather have known that the world and Greece's hardly civil wars would amp up with such ferocity that he could not see his wife and sons for almost five years, as standard travel would have been suspended? He could not.

A Time to Starve: The Hunger Games

By now, you may be wondering if you inadvertently purchased an annal of Greek history. To fill in the gaps and crevices of my ignorance regarding this dark period my father experienced, I plunged into half a dozen books and more than fifty articles to explore the history that made such a profound impact on my dad from his living through these five *years* of wars. I would disrespect my father and be remiss in my reporting to you if I did not flesh out the period that *should* have been the most innocent portion of his life. Before recounting my dad's account and stories, I have one more historical episode to cover. After Metaxas' death, when my grandfather had already left to make good and save up, it would take but mere months before Germany had officially and wholly taken control of Greece. You have seen how this quickly led to Germany ransacking the Greek economy, ravaging its cities, and looting villages for both food and commodities.

Meanwhile, to prevent supplies from falling into Axis hands, the British implemented a naval blockade; this was understandable. Yet the unintended consequence and bi-product was a *massive* food shortage in Greece. Greece had a double chokehold on her from friend and foe, antagonism and aggression from every direction and within; the nadir of these two wars would last for nearly two *years* in Greece. The Germans turned deaf ears, and the Italians shrugged their shoulders to Greek cries for help. The nutritional situation, in particular, became so desperate in the summer of 1941 that Greece was in the throws of a full-blown famine by the upcoming fall.[94] The food shortage was particularly dire, especially during the first winter of Greece's occupation (1941–42), coupled with hyperinflation. British historian Mark Mazower said, "This was the worst famine the Greeks had experienced [since] ancient times."[95] The famine soon spread to regions like the islands, cities, and villages outside of Athens. Two hundred and thirty miles south of Athens, where my father lived, they also felt acute pangs and effects of this starving time. I remain in mind-numbing shock as I offer you these stats and descriptions:

> "As many as 50,000 people perished during January and February 1942 [alone], and all together, by the end of the Occupation, approximately 300,000 people had died as a consequence of famine and malnutrition. Hard hit were infants and children...[96] "Children wandered pale and skeleton-like along the pavement shouting 'I am hungry' so that residents…would be moved to give them something if they had anything."[97]

In the meantime, although reluctant to lift the blockade, the British agreed to a compromise, and grain shipments were allowed to enter through Turkey. The International Red Cross got involved and eventually brought wheat, and various other international war relief associations organized resources that made their way into Greece. By the end of 1942, there arrived a steady wheat supply to the country's biggest ports, and the mortality rate did fall; however, the prices of almost every commodity skyrocketed, and the food situation "remained grim until the end of the occupation (1944)."[98] For Greeks, the word "occupation" is still synonymous with famine and hunger due to the harsh situation the Greek population faced during these years. In fact, stockpiling unnecessary amounts of food and an "irrational fear upon seeing an empty pantry" is still colloquially called "occupation syndrome" by Greek people since this behavior was prevalent during the postwar years.[99] You will see this theme of want throughout my father's life; I have barely begun comprehending it. So, where exactly was my dad throughout all of this? We will return to the world from the perspective of my young father now, starting with when he would be forced to leave his birth town and hide in the remote and mountainous village of Agios Nikolaos.

My Father's Account of WWII and the Greek Civil War: Family Stories of Hiding in the Hills to His Hegira

My dad's earliest accounts of what life was like during the war, which he eventually and bit by bit shared with me, start in 1941; he would have been six years old. I have already recounted some of his recollections during innocent days *before* war interrupted life. I place us now at the start of the Occupation, but that would have been before they headed for the hills. The reality of war set in like a ton of lead when soldiers entered *their* section of Gythion. As a young boy, unless he had listened to their accents or language — which he would not have at age six — my dad could not have discerned whether the soldiers were German or Italian, as *both* were present. Later, my father confirmed and admitted that during the raids, he didn't know "if it was the Italians or Germans" that were ransacking their town. I learned it could have been *either*. This would have transpired *after* the initial defeat of the Italians up north and when Germany came to clean up the mess and take control, which would then blur and blend into a host of invasions in Greece by the Axis Powers. Germany and Italy permeated and penetrated the Greek countryside and made their way southward, wreaking havoc and leaving a wake of terror. Instead of learning his A B, C's, and the three "R's," an undoubtedly confused and frightened little boy would have to stay home from school, but this was certainly no school break or holiday! Going to school would hardly have been the last thing on his mind. This would have been the time right *before* they made the semi-permanent move that would have them hiding in the nearby mountainous village of Agios Nikolaus for some *years*. And when it was time to go, time was of the essence; precious little could be brought along.

I wonder how my grandmother would have felt facing the choice of risking staying in her own home and possibly being murdered or packing up her boys and heading to her husband's village, where she would have to live with her unloving in-laws without her husband for God knows how long. Neither option was palatable; only one was viable, so she was left with a no-contest choice: it was time to go and hide or to stay and maybe die. Therefore, I wonder what my dad would have thought when he saw his mother burying valuables in their small backyard. Perhaps he caught sight of her furtively digging holes to hide their silver, a few household items, and maybe even jewelry. I wonder what she would have said to her young sons the morning it was decided they would have to leave. What would it have been like to suppress her fear and be sure not to convey a tone of worry while feeling the ache and inevitability of moving without her husband? How long would she have to live with these troubles and the uncertainty, not to mention her in-laws, in the days and perhaps months to follow? How could she have known it would be five *years* she and her boys would feel stuck *yet* grateful, in safety *and* starvation?

With her husband abroad and therefore, unavailable and inaccessible, she would follow the lead and directive of her older brother, her guide and idol. I can't help but think that she must have known that he was becoming increasingly involved with an underground covert organization. He was among those who comprised a group of local Greek men who simply sought to restore order; after all, no one else seemed to care what was happening in *this* neck of the woods in Greece. Her brother — my great uncle — was a member of a guerrilla group of Communists who took matters into their own hands to at least keep *their* families safe from murderous marauders and invaders. After all, these men knew the lay of the land, who could be trusted, and what actions they could risk to ensure the safety of their loved ones. Feeling alone and scared, my young grandmother would naturally cling to *and* put more responsibility on her eldest son. Conversely, she barely might have noticed her youngest, my father, who probably would have affixed himself to his next older brother, the middle son.

In times of war, all bets are off as far as practicing accepted ethical codes and moral standards go, and later in life, my dad still possessed a neutral stance towards taking shortcuts, bending the rules, and cutting corners to save money. His actions still spoke of survival by "any means possible"; opportunism was born early in him. I suspect that as a desperate lad, he likely pilfered foodstuff. I do not know this for a fact, but I can see it in my mind's eye. Things quickly erode and get sketchy where my dad's jagged recollection of the series of events goes; there are gaps and lurches for the lack of facts, evidence, and transitions. It reminds me of the various renditions one finds in the mythology of Hercules, where one source says this and another that. What rendition is accurate? What variation is false? Regardless, what I utter here is *not* fiction. My dad once told me that in his hometown of Gythion, *there was a pit where they would throw corpses* away to keep them from rotting in the streets. He said that *dogs could be spotted darting among the heaps of dead, scurrying and scavenging for limbs or digits to carry off and eat elsewhere.* He told me of *the stench of rotting flesh he could never forget and the smell of smoke in the near distance.* His cousin, Vivian, whom I've already introduced, corroborated these horrific revelations.

As I shared what my father had relayed to me to her, she would quietly nod in assent, pick up the threat of this conversation, and add a few more harrowing strands for me. The tipping point in their *having* to leave came when Vivian's mother, who was married to my grandmother's oldest brother, dared to show loyalty to her beloved husband and bold defiance to the enemy. One morning, it turned out that one of the children in the family had inadvertently let out the family's male rabbit, either wanting to play with it or perhaps to do something mildly mischievous. The family had only had two male and female rabbits, and as times were already getting really tough, *both* were needed to provide for future sustenance. Little Vivian's mother went out in search of the missing rabbit. As she was out and about looking for it, Greek *counter*-resistance soldiers (i.e., those *against* the communists and paid by other foreign entities to do their "dirty work") saw her and, perhaps vaguely recognizing her, made some crass remark about her husband, who, if you recall, was part of the local resistance *and* a communist. Knowing that they were talking about her husband, she said to them in bold defiance, *"If you say something about my husband, I kill you!"* She was shot on the spot and killed instantly. Next, they cut off her fingers and slit her pierced ears to steal her jewelry. In shock and horror, someone in the village witnessed this and immediately ran to look for her young daughter, Vivian. That person found her "crying and crying" because she had been searching for but not finding her mother. When they went back to find her mother, they found only her body, and "she was missing her fingers and ears." I do not know if little Vivian saw her murdered mother or not; her story stopped just shy of that moment. I can only pray she didn't. After that, for nearly two years she would barely speak.

With her mother murdered, Vivian and my dad (as well as my dad's next older brother) would become as close as brother and sister, a bond they kept all their days. My grandmother had lost not only her sister-in-law but a dear friend. Her niece, little Vivian, barely six at the time, was named after *her* grandmother as was custom, but decades later, Vivian would name *her* daughter after my grandmother because although her father would get remarried and have three more children, my grandmother became like a mother to Vivian, and they would remain close throughout life. This relationship became all the more precious to my grandmother because, in Vivian, she would find the love and loyalty of a daughter, a love so different from that of a son. At one point, much later, I recall my grandmother shaking her head, her eyebrows curved up at a 45-degree angle from chronic worry, and lamenting to me with exasperation, bitterness, and heartache, "Sons! *No good*! Better one daughter than a meeeelion sons! You like ee daughter to me!" This odd declaration was the distillation of decades of disappointment. Her relationships with her three sons would be complicated, tarnished, and ultimately unfulfilling for *any* of their hungry hearts. Meanwhile, the time had come to leave, so they might have lived, but we are not yet at that point in our journey.

Because my grandparents, my father, and Vivian are all dead, I no longer have access to any primary sources from which to inquire; therefore, I cannot tell you by what means my grandmother and her three sons made the approximately twenty-five-kilometer journey from Gythion to Agios Nikolaos. In my mind's eye, they piled up like the Beverly Hillbillies or the Joad family in *The Grapes of Wrath*. They likely got a ride in someone's car; maybe they walked with others in silent but determined tightly knit groups; perhaps they rode on donkeys. There is no way that road would have been paved in the 1940s, so now, double the time it would have taken for my family to trek there. If you used Google Maps to take you from <u>Gythion</u> to <u>Kokkina Louria</u> (which means "red bands" or "red straps"), the village from which my *grandmother* comes and which is *on the way to* my grandfather's village beyond and higher up, you would learn that this distance is 18 km (11 miles). If you want to go to the pinnacle of this road, you will end up at <u>Panangia Yiatrissa</u>, which is at the pinnacle of this mountain. From here, the shimmering waves of the broad sea are in the far distance below; the wind and sun caress your face. Here, the monastery named "Our Lady of Healing," a reference to the healing powers Greeks believe the Virgin Mary possesses, is situated. Arriving here brings us up to a distance of 38 km (23.6 miles), so I will now guesstimate that the distance to Agios Nikolaos, which is situated *between* these two points, would be 25 km or 15.53 miles. During those days of hiding, I'm sure their prayers were on fire and as potent as the aroma of wild oregano in the air. They would have been grateful for the ancient homestead God provided. Although I cannot tell you by what means they got to Agios Nikolaos, let alone how long it took to get there, I do know beyond a shadow of a doubt that they were driven by fear and hunger and hope. My father never lost the latter.

Decades later, I have been to all the places mentioned above, perhaps half a dozen times. I light a candle in honor and remembrance for them now. Today, I can easily drive up to and come upon the sleepy small square of **Agios Nikolaos**, the area no larger than a full-sized basketball court softened into a circle. You would find a few trees that would provide shade, a store with a front porch from which you could buy orange juice or beer, or a small bowl of peanuts as you sit in those diminutive, colorfully painted, straight-back wooden chairs ubiquitous in Greece. The houses surround it, radiating up and out of this center, and the lone diminutive church is also within the circle of square one. You could continue to the next village if you chose not to stop here in this square. Each village you come upon is like a bead on a band of an ancient bracelet that takes you to the jewel at its peak, Panagia Yiatrissa. As you peer around the bend along the outer rim of Agios Nikolaos, what might seem like a broad shelf that terminates in a cliff appears. Here, you would spy a tiny graveyard that overlooks a small valley even further below, and you might wonder how *any* holes could be dug in this rocky soil. At the same time, you try to read about the lives of those whose epitaphs are engraved in these mighty slices of standing tombstones. This is the one spot on the planet where I see my surname etched on marble slabs, standing in the bright sun. My father would *not* be buried here, but as a boy, surely, he went there to explore or to play hide and seek, so desirous was he for fun during those dark and dire days.

Another cousin of his, the village priest (or "Pappouli" as he is affectionately dubbed) who lives there today, walked me to the house which my father lived, which *his* father had built, and which his father's father staked claim to, as I have told you. This spry man wearing a monastic blue robe and donning his simple black *kalimavkion*[100] (conical head covering), with a posture still straight as an arrow, had a beard like Santa's and twinkling eyes as blue as an azure sky at high noon. We stand eye-to-eye, dead level with one another, as I would with my father in his later years. This was pleasing to me. Pappouli led me familiarly around by the arm, smiling and proud as punch to show and tell me (in Greek) all these places that provided shelter for my dad. His mind and heart were on happy fire.

I seek to briefly mention Freud's theories about early childhood development, which speak the truth about these critical formative years. I'm sure you all are familiar with his assertion that "personality develops during early childhood"[101] and that early experiences "shape our personalities as well as our behavior as adults." Freud asserted that we mature through a series of stages during childhood and that if we do not have adequate nurturing and parenting during the first decade of life, we can get "stuck" in that stage for want of what wasn't provided. As adults, we subconsciously develop defense mechanisms to compensate for that deficiency or stunted, thwarted, or shattered part of our psyches.

This all seems like common sense to me, but when I read the more clinical terminology, I realized I was onto something that could help us sympathize with my father in his adulthood. The dread and anxiety my dad *had* to have felt, the paternal abandonment he *must* have perceived, and the recollections of raw hunger he endured would do a number on him and his adult psyche. The term "post-traumatic stress disorder" did not come into use until the 1970s, and it was used as the diagnosis for psychologically afflicted soldiers returning from the Vietnam War.[102] My father had no such label, let alone self-awareness, so I now attempt to give form to this nightmarish fog that he would much later push aside. We will return to this topic when we re-evaluate his core personality to assess how Huntington's disease warped and intensified certain aspects of his personality. Even in adulthood, my dad had an uncanny sixth sense about him, as if he possessed a wild animal's instinct or an alertness for whiffing out "danger, danger," be it those who doubted or disobeyed him, disrespected, or discounted him. He knew when secrets were being kept. Later, he tended to hoard certain items for all those "just-in-case" moments of hypothetical impending disaster. His "you never know" mantra impacted what he saved and purchased. Needs always trumped wants, and many wants were unnecessary luxury items.

For now, know that the five-year span while my father lived in this village will offer few concrete facts and barely a glimpse into his days there. My imagination has spun a mental reel of my father's daily life. I saw its dirt floor; I imagined the icon corner over there. In this recess, prayers were whispered, candles and incense were lit, and select saints were called upon and commissioned for extra help. After all, surely it couldn't hurt! Maybe the boys scuffled or sat at a table where the men would speak of the latest snatches of gossip or news of the war they'd heard. I cannot know what they must have felt, but that they huddled here for almost five *years* gave me pause and an inkling of the gravitas and emotional scarring that *two* wars wreaking havoc would produce. However, there must have been closeness, intimacy, worry, and depravity. Living on his *father's* land and the house that his *grandfather* would come to possess, my dad, his mother, and his brothers probably would have felt *relatively* safe and sound. Still, at the same time, perhaps they felt like they were imposing upon the half a dozen already dwelling in that tiny home. Nothing mattered more than bare-bones survival.

The School of Hard Knocks

My dad would have moved from his birth home to the little house in the mountains within months of his starting *the first grade*. Only now can I better appreciate that when he attempted to write in Greek as an adult, his penmanship was still like that of a kindergartner: he pressed so firmly into the paper that any words or formulas could have been confused for ancient Greek etched in marble slabs. By the time he was in college, his penmanship would not only be legible, but it would be as straight as an arrow and small as if he were trying to squeeze in as many organic compounds as possible. Now leap forward to his final five years: you would be in shock to see his longhand; though still heavy, it had become grotesquely large and loopy, thanks to his disease "*kicking in,*" as he used to say. He never got the hang of spelling or punctuation in *either* language. Perhaps he was read to; most likely, he was not. His schooling and education would not resume (begin?) until he went to the States at eleven. And there, he would have had to catch up *and* learn a new language. There were no helpful ESL classes at whatever public school he attended in Brooklyn. Any "learning" that would have taken place in the village would probably have been along the lines of memorization of a Greek nursery rhyme or prayers he would have been expected to recite, perhaps even done routinely, like a daily vitamin, some stock and store, and salve for his soul. These prayers would never leave him.

Seeing how playful and animated my father could get with *us* as kids, as he was such a free spirit, I would be willing to bet that the time he spent in Agios Nikolaos created a suspended state of boyhood in him, one that would want to come out and play when he felt safe and sound as a dad. He had not got his fill, and he could have cared less that he looked foolish to others. He was *our* king of the hill and the only grown-up willing to play hide-and-seek or "peeking Tom" around the float on our lake with the same abandon as we did. Some speak of having children bringing out a "second childhood" in them; for my dad, it was a chance at a new first. He told me that up in that village, the young boys there would run around and chase each other, seeking optimal chances to launch rocks at the weaker "tribe," as if this were some predecessor of *Call of Duty* or cowboys and Indians (perhaps for them, Greeks-vs-Turks) all rolled into one, "just 'cause." In mischievous glee and misguided rage, my dad's older brother would occasionally throw rocks at his mother. I was also told that when this uncle was a youngster, the older men in the village gave him Greek moonshine— *raki* — also "just for kicks." These men would likely have circled around a small table or two at the square, playing *tavli* (i.e., backgammon) and drinking raki, and discussing whatever shards of news they might have picked up on their transistor radios or from a lone passerby. What menial tasks might my father, as a boy, have done during these dire days? Nearby, just about a thousand feet from the village and off the main mountainous road is a small olive orchard. Decades later, my father would point it out to my brother, and fourteen years later, my brother retraced their steps and shared it with my sister and me in 2011. I'll take you there now.

In the Garden and the Starving Hour

My brother, sister, Bonnie, and I walked along a diminutive dirt path off the main road just beyond Agios Nikolaos. A chorus of cicadas surrounded us. Our hands, of their own accord, reached out to touch the tops of the tall, parched grasses, and our eyes were drawn to thick clusters of the most amazing small, intense, ochre-yellow flowers. Only today have I looked over pictures of when we three traipsed as we explored and discovered through research that these flowering golden perennials were wild fennel. An online source revealed that travelers and sailors used it to transport fire, and in an ageless time before this, according to Greek mythology, Prometheus, who stole fire from heaven for man, hid the flame inside these fennel stalks.[103] We gravitated towards the center of this field, where we spotted an old outbuilding with terracotta-tiled roofs, the standard type used throughout homes in Greece and southern Europe. This structure of the outbuilding was about the size of a one-roomed house, except that its walls were built atop centuries-old stone protected by a thick layer of ugly cement. Time added the finishing touches of dried grasses adorning the craggy rock, like carpet. The roof had corrugated tin patching where terracotta tiles were missing or broken.

As my brother recalled memories of his trip there with our dad in 1997, I couldn't help but notice that my brother looked relatively small, standing next to one of those overgrown prickly pear cactuses that are so common in Greece. They can grow to be fifteen feet tall[104] and group together in what looks like giant expansive compounds. Adjoined to this building was a makeshift outdoor oven that was imperfectly frosted in a slathering of cement, no doubt poured over the original oven used when my father was there. It even had thoughtful indentions for olive oil, pots of Greek oregano, or other necessities. A plastic chair sat beneath it as if waiting for its person to return and rest from a day's hard work trimming olive tree branches or perhaps to check on a loaf of rustic bread baking within. In the near distance, you can spy half a dozen barrels used as beehives; I do not doubt that my dad and the family there appreciated any drops of this ambrosia offered to them during that time of scarcity. In fact, of all the European countries, Greece consumes more honey than any[105], a habit from their millennia-old simple lifestyle and salubrious diet.

As an older man living alone, my dad maintained the Mediterranean diet without ever calling it such; it came naturally to him! And he was always pleased as punch to announce that his kids had *"smarts"* and *"good health habits,"* as if *this* were a badge of honor worth bragging about. I suppose it is: you are honoring the physical temple *you've* been given. All that notwithstanding, the Mediterranean lifestyle my dad lived as a boy was combined with austerity or imposed asceticism he never forgot. Once, my father told me that one of his "duties" had been to tend whatever handful of sheep they had, so while we were there taking it all in, my mind transformed this tiny field or farm into the one where my father, as a boy, might have led their sheep or fed the goats, be they one, two, or a few. I can just see them grazing on whatever tufts of desiccated greenery they could find here and there. He was no shepherd the likes of David. Still, I would be willing to bet drachmas to donuts that he, too, in his own inchoate way, would have echoed prayers as did David, who cried out, "O Lord my God, in You I have taken refuge; Save me from all those who pursue me, and rescue me" (Psalm 7:1). Up in that small house nearby where his father had been missing, I imagine that my father and his two brothers would have slept on sheepskin, probably the softest material their skin would touch. Perhaps it soothed their young selves lying three in a row.

Nearly half a century later, after my parents got divorced and while a man living on his own, my father would snuggle in bed underneath a flokati rug with no desire or need for sheets made from Egyptian cotton or silk to separate him from said "blanket"; it was still his covering of choice. Every now and again, my father would give me a few crumbs of details from his stint of starvation. I think he blocked and buried a *lot*. Once they got so desperate for food, they even tried using ground acorns as a makeshift replacement for wheat to be able to make bread. It was so awful that *"even the dogs wouldn't eat it."* My dad told me that *"they would wipe themselves leaves,"* and without a doubt, they would make do in some designated spot off in the near distance. The distressing sense of persistent hunger never left my dad, and as kids, we used to joke that "our family never had leftovers in the fridge like *other* families did." As soon as we children would be excused from our dinner table, my dad would quietly wolf down whatever was left on our plates as if he were some human vacuum cleaner or vulture or "bottomless pit," as my mom often described him. Not only that, but he also never drank while he ate, and he later told us that this was because he didn't want to *"fill up on liquids"* or use valuable space in his stomach for mere fluids. As she watched her husband polish off the rest of the food without seeming to gain an ounce, my mother never ceased to be dismayed. However, *none* of us ever heard the sound of his belly churning and rumbling from starvation, never heard him likely quietly moan in his sleep, dreaming of food *not* to be found, and never listened to the whiz of planes roaring overhead, instilling a palpable fear like a bomb detonating in one's soul.

My dad never complained, lamented, reflected, or induced guilt in us, his children, for having the *privilege* of luxury and unspoiled innocence. Life was for the living, and he had just been surviving. Later on, when we kids were in high school and if our family occasionally went out to eat, a rare occurrence, he would gruffly instruct us *not* to "fill up on crackers and bread" that "*the food was coming,*" as if we ought to keep a clear path and pouch for the good stuff. However, much later, in his final years, bread is precisely what my father would head for first when eating out! His hand darted out for the bread brought to the table, and if it were still warm or extra crusty or garlic-y, he'd immediately ask, "*More, please, and do you have any olive oil?*" He was drawn to the elemental, and often, he would take home almost an entire meal as if *it* were dessert or, maybe, having already stuffed himself with their staff of life, his doggy bag would contain a meal for foraging later.

Why do I draw out facts from fragments of life in the mountainous village of Agios Nikolaus, using my imagination to flesh out my dad's life days? The village of Agios Nikolaos translates into English as "Saint Nicholas," and it became their gifted place of refuge for five *years*, starting in **1941** to when they fled Greece in the midwinter months of **1946**. To help you better reference this point in history in a more electrifying manner, I'll compare my dad's dreadful ordeal to Anne Frank's living nightmare, who, along with seven other members of her family, would hide in an attic from 1942 to 1945. Mere months after she was murdered, fate brought a narrow window of escape that opened up for my father and his family, and they grabbed it for all they were worth. Let me bring to your mind events that were transpiring in Greece during the *first* stage of its civil war, which overlapped by several months and actually got going *before* Nazi Germany's official invasion of April 1941 and its subsequent occupation of Greece, which, as I've said, ended in October 1944, the month Germans would withdraw.

Final Days in the Village and the Choice to Leave

War may have been coming to a close for most of Europe, but it was far from over in Greece! The Greek Communists quickly attempted to fill this vacuum of the Germans exiting and commenced fighting Greek royalist guerrillas fortified by British troops. The shaky coalition government that was formed disintegrated a few weeks later, and a bitter civil war broke out in Athens on December 3, 1944.[106] I will venture an educated guess and deduce that during the stint between the latter phases of the Greek Civil War when another coalition government was in place, <u>my grandmother would have obtained the official paperwork to leave Greece and join her husband in America</u>. Copies of this document, which I ordered and now hold in my hands, designate as the date of completing their Immigration Visas to be <u>January 22, 1946,</u> for both my father and his two brothers and January 28 for my grandmother.

Thus, smack dab in the middle of *this* particular phase of the Greek Civil War, which began in early December 1945, from the time when the Greek communists had (temporarily) accepted defeat and disbanded their forces, to two months later in February 1946, just one month before a general election was held in Greece in March 1946 allowing the royalists to be back on top,[107] is precisely when my then ten-year-old father and his family fled to America. They were hardly alone. In the history of twentieth-century migration to the United States, Greeks began to arrive in their most significant numbers after 1945, fleeing the economic devastation caused by World War II and the Greek Civil War. Indeed, "from 1945 until 1982, approximately 211,000 Greeks emigrated to the United States alone."[108] Another source I found identified the Greek Civil War in terms of its proximity to the closing of WWI by delineating its two-stage phase: December 1944–January 1945 and 1946–49, during which Greek communists <u>un</u>successfully tried to gain control of Greece.[109]

Economic and political reasons continued to motivate Greeks to leave in search of safety because of the continuation of the crippling consequences during the *second* phase of the civil war during 1946-1949. Most of these emigrants at that time *"came from rural areas,"* [emphasis mine] and they would supply both the national and international labor markets.[110] <u>My dad would have been from among this cast of people</u>. To put this particular Greek exodus in a broader perspective, "more than one million Greeks migrated in the wave which mainly fell between 1950 and 1974. Most emigrated to Western Europe, the U.S., Canada, and Australia."[111] In short, my father was one drop in the tidal wave of war-weary Greeks running away from home.

Sweet Land of Liberty

I do not know precisely when or how my family left the village in Agios Nicholas to make their way up and through to exit the Peloponnesus, then traverse the Corinthian Canal so that they might reach Athens, where they would have completed their emigration paperwork, but I *can* easily imagine them huddling with hundreds of other Greeks, standing at the designated ship dock in the massive port of Piraeus, and holding a worn leather suitcase containing a few worldly possessions in one hand and the hand of their loved ones traveling with them in the other. I'm sure they looked shell-shocked yet alert, silent but restless. By and large, I would think that they would have felt numb, but hope was somehow hovering right with them there, too, as they "fixed their eyes not on what is seen, but on what is unseen" (2 Cor. 4:18).

Meanwhile, they prepared to board an other-worldly, titanic luxury liner. And what of the ship that would transport them thither to the Port of New York at Ellis Island? The Gripsholm Swedish-American Line started its transatlantic cruises in 1927,[112] but it was during World War II that some of the Gripsholm ocean liners were used as repatriation ships; they made over thirty voyages to exchange prisoners of war, diplomats, women, and children between the warring nations,[113] including Italy, Germany, and Japan. For this reason, one line of these cruise ships, the M.S. Gripsholm, earned the nickname "Mercy Ship."[114] <u>My father, his mother, and two brothers boarded its *sister* Swedish cruise ship, the **S.S**. Gripsholm</u>, which, I assume, was one of the liners used to transport beleaguered Greeks (and others from allied nations) to safer distant shores. I suspect that while they got themselves settled on this ship, my family members would have been crossings themselves and saying prayers audible only to God: "*Κύριε, ἐλέησον*" or "Kyrie, eleison," which means "*Lord, have mercy*." Their prayers were answered; looking back, even today, I can see that "because of the Lord's faithful love, [they] did not perish, for *His mercies never end*" (from Lamentations 3:22 HCSB, emphasis mine).

I learned that in 1952, one of the SS ocean liners made the voyage in just three and a half days, so perhaps on that winter's day, the second of February 1946, it might have taken closer to an entire week. Though seafaring vessels were in high demand during WWII, the U.S. government could charter this fleet of ships painted white and lit up with bright lights at night to broadcast their protected status. Enemy governments agreed to give the vessel safe passage.[115] My father must have stood agog facing the massive diesel-powered cruise ship, which was modeled after one of Sweden's most famous castles,[116] and walking among its luxurious interiors must have seemed to my young father that he was standing in some temple illuminated by God (Rev. 21:22–23).

You may think the boys would have bound about like young goats, exploring this grand and lavish ship, testing their freedom, and feeling the exhilaration from the liberating sense of no danger lurking about. Such was not the case. It was only much later, when I was in my twenties, that my father told me that "*he looked like a poster child for starvation*." He had that tell-tale sign of a bloated belly. Therefore, I am forced to reconsider my wishful thinking that he was unaware of his condition because others like him were in the same boat. He would have been too weak to play. His self-description of *"looking like a scarecrow"* got me wondering why, and then I looked into how the body conserves itself in the manner it does with such evident cost. Over prolonged time, with radically insufficient caloric and nutritional intake, arms and legs become emaciated, and the skull's skin covering gets so eerily taut that it makes the person look like a skeleton or some haunted ghoul. I shuddered to imagine my father in this condition and then probed into why starvation and a bloated abdomen go hand in hand. Malnourishment expressed in this shocking manner is due to insufficient protein intake; we all know this.

Even if my dad survived on whatever they had scrounged and scraped and skewered, it was clear there wasn't enough meat, and a lack of protein "disrupts the normal functioning of the lymphatic system."[117] One of *its* specific functions concerns how the flow of internal fluids, including water, is monitored. The long and agonizing story is cut short; there's not enough pressure to push the water through capillaries back into the bloodstream, so fluids accumulate in the abdomen. This pooled liquid in the gut "impels it to bloat."[118] My dad just felt like he was starving to death, so when he and his brothers came to discover that there were *three* sumptuous meals served *daily*, they must have made their way to the dining halls like bewildered little zombies coming back to life and then — to behold *ice cream* offered with no limitations! It must have felt like manna falling from heaven for these famished lads. Indeed, my dad said that *"they made themselves sick from eating so much ice cream."* These boys were hardly purging themselves on purpose to repeat this sweet affair as myths report of the ancient Romans, they who would gorge then intentionally vomit, all but to make room to continue their gluttony. These boys were ravenous as wolves, but their compromised systems were too weak to ingest such an overload of fat and sugar. Still, I'm sure they didn't mind how sweet it was! Finally, landing in a safe harbor would have been like a miracle, too.

I wonder what it might have been like for my father and his brothers to look in the near horizon and see the Statue of Liberty, like some oddly familiar, giant Greek goddess or maybe even a mammoth sculpted version of the Theotokos ("God-bearer," the title of Mary). In her left hand, she held a torch that would shine a light on the pathway to their father; he was waiting for them near her base. Oh, they must have been giddy with anticipation! Often, they had to have felt like *fatherless* children, so to peer at this titanic woman who promised peace and plenty would have stirred their own "yearning to be free," and for the first time in such a long time, their hopes and prayers would find deliverance. How they landed and where they were admitted was a process that was efficient, albeit slowly accomplished.

Between 1946 and 1954, Passenger Lists of ships with a destination of New York were compiled. Immigrants landing at Ellis Island went through processing, whereby they were admitted by recording their entry as organized by Date, Steamship Line, Classification of Passengers, and the voyage route.[119] I possess a digitized copy of the archived page entitled "LIST OR MANIFEST OF ALIEN PASSENGERS FOR THE UNITED STATES" who were sailing from Piraeus, Greece, on the S.S. Gripsholm on **February 2, 1946. My father's name is located on List 34, number 16**, right beneath his mother's and brothers'. For identification purposes, fifteen columns must be completed. The first six on this list comprise one's tax status, name, age, sex, marital status, and calling/occupation. Under column 7, it gives the abbreviation "do," which, although I could not find out what this stood for, I assume it meant "dependent of." Next comes a revealing category entitled "Read" and the one next to it, "Read what language." As a teacher, I found it haunting that only by my grandmother's name was "Greek" written; this space was *left blank* for all three sons, who had received *no* education to speak of for half a decade. Following this, the last sub-classification under this number eight was "write," again, for my father and his brothers, a telling blank remained in the box.

Only the oldest son, four years older than my father and two years senior to his next brother, had the shell of more normal days indicated by his being classified as a "student" rather than merely "*do.*" Categories 9 through 13 read as follows: "Nationality (Country of which citizen or subject)," "Race or people," "Country," "City or town, State, Province or District," and finally "Immigration Visa, Passport Visa, or Reentry Permit number." How these were completed would be as one would anticipate, except for the *final* one. Here, in all caps, written next to my Uncle Kolya's name, is typed: "HOLDS US PASSPORT #823 ISS. AT U.S. EMB. ATHENS JAN. 22, 1946." For my *next* uncle, there is a ditto that reads, "IN BROTHER KOLYA'S US PASSPORT #823 AS ABOVE." However, by my father's name for the five categories 9–13, you will find "do" *dittoed* six times. (Column 11, "Place of birth," is subdivided). Never having been to the States, I don't know how my oldest uncle would have been issued a US passport other than perhaps because his dad had been issued one. Recall, if you will, that their mother was issued what I assume was an Immigration Visa precisely six days *later* on "January 28, 1946." Column 14 is for "Government officials only" as it concerns "verifications of landings, etc.," and the final column identifies the Country and City or Town, Province or District. I hovered here and stared a moment because for all the rest of the Greek passengers on the U.S. Department of Justice's Immigration and Naturalization Service List 34, you would see "Greece, Athens" for this last column 15. Not so for my grandmother and her three sons; you would notice that the "City or town, State, Province or District" my family indicated was "Laconia." A word about this word: According to Merriam-Webster,

> "laconic" comes to us through Latin from the Greek *Lakonikos,* which is derived from *Lakon,* meaning "native of Laconia." It has been with us since the 16th century and has sometimes been used with the basic meaning "of or relating to Laconia or its inhabitants." In current use, *laconic* means "terse" or "concise," thus recalling the Spartan tendency to use the fewest words possible.

Before we leave Greece for good, allow me to tarry here for a moment to tell you about the portion of Greece from which my father springs. Technically speaking, <u>Laconia</u> is a regional unit in the southeast portion of the Peloponnesus comprising five municipalities.[120] You might be impressed to learn that the capital of this prefecture is Sparta, and forty minutes due south is its ancient and modern port, Gythion, where my father was born. Gythion is situated in the <u>Mani</u> Peninsula (i.e., "finger"). Because it is technically on the *inner* portion between the two right-most peninsulas, Greeks further delineate it as being in the Mesa ("Inner") Mani. I describe Mani for you here only because I firmly believe that a decade of living in this terrain *also* shaped my father's psyche and outlook as much as his being from Laconia would imbue within his *modus operandi* with its laconic stance. "The Mani," as it is called and which is about 30 km (roughly 19 miles) in length, is

> "a mountainous region that is mostly treeless and almost completely barren, though the hardy olive thrives there and land is cultivated wherever there is enough soil to shape a terrace. Small villages are often situated on seemingly inaccessible mountain ledges."[121]

I tell you this here and now because this harsh terrain that helped keep him from harm's way also created an unassailable aspect to his personality that enabled him to push himself both to survive and to surmount unique challenges later in his life, and this would also include a contortion of his brain and frame decades later in life. We are not there yet. It is high time to have him land and take his first steps on new soil, that is, the city streets of NYC. We are a few moments away from the long-overdue reunion with their father. My dad and his family would have been among the crowd of these Greek "huddled masses," those "homeless" passengers who landed at Pier No. 97 at the foot of West 57th Street.[122] He, too, would have undergone "a required examination by the immigration officials," and he would have been issued a stamped landing card upon completion.[123] Finally, with their luggage brought to them by one of the ship's stewards, my father and his two brothers and mother would step into the brisk winter air, slowly making their way among the swaying masses of people eagerly and silently scanning for the sight of their loved ones.

The Reunion

The following account is one of our family's most treasured heirlooms as it pertains to my dad's biography, and to be honest, after having waded through the research necessary so I could locate and put together the many missing puzzle pieces from my dad's youth, I appreciate it all the more. This is no apocrypha. My dad never had "a way with words," as he put it; therefore, he was all the more amazed when I could complete his sentences with swift accuracy and prescience as if I were magically drawing a rabbit out of a hat, and he would shake his head in awe. Here is the story of their reunion. My Uncle Kolya, the eldest son, who was fourteen then, would have held his brothers' hands to keep the three of them together as they made their way through the dense crowd. I imagine my overtired yet determined grandmother was tucked in close and right behind him and her two younger sons, perhaps holding her suitcase. Born in 1913, she was precisely nineteen years younger than her husband (b. 1894) and nineteen years older than her eldest son (b. 1932), and this midpoint position that made her the fulcrum between the two weighted more heavily in favor of her son; the gravitational pull towards him was undeniable and powerful. My Uncle Kolya would be like so many eldest (or only) sons of this particular and peculiar generation of Greek men who would often find it impossible to sever ties with their mothers.

Suddenly, like a lighthouse keeper who spies his native land on the horizon, my Uncle Kolya's frame stiffened in spontaneous and restless excitement. He quickened his pace, and his two younger brothers knew by the sudden squeeze of his hand that their brother had just spotted their father. Had it been up to him to ferret his pop out, my father might not have been so sure, as it had been so long since he had laid eyes on him. Within a few moments and feet of reaching their *patera*, my quiet and dapper grandfather, dressed in a protective overcoat that covered his three-piece wool suit and donning his neat fedora, which he habitually wore, got down on his knees with arms outstretched to take in his sons with all of him. At that sign, all three boys ran for their father, and they fell onto him, hugging him and holding onto one other tight to ensure this was no dream. I see my father clinging to his father like a baby monkey to its mother, breathing him in and not wanting to let go for fear it might be another one of his nightmares where he would wake up and find his father still gone. Uncle Gerasim would have been laughing and crying simultaneously, and Uncle Kolya, tears streaming down his face, would have held onto his father and let himself cry like a boy for having had to have been as strong as a man during those hard years. My grandfather would have kissed his boys as he held them close, one tangled love knot of father and sons. And then, he told his sons to *reach into his pocket* as he said he had bought a treat for them. He would have kept his shock in check and grief to himself as he beheld *and* held his boys' wasted frames. A man of few words, he would have wanted to give them, at the very least, a little something as a token of welcome to America. The boys pulled out a Hershey's chocolate bar, one for each of them, and for just a second, they gazed at it as if it were a bar of solid gold before they hungrily tore open the wrapper and bit into its chocolatey goodness. My father told us numerous times that *he had never tasted anything so sweet in all his life.*

It was after my parents' divorce that this sacred little story came out, and every year after that, for his birthday, one or more of us would mail my father the biggest Hershey's chocolate bar we would find. To this day, the tradition continues, and the memory remains. Meanwhile, as my grandfather would have been cooing soothing words of affirmation to his hungry sons, his eyes would have reached out to drink in his wife, still to him his young bride. After five years of absence and separation, this thirty-three-year-old mother of three who finally faced her then fifty-two-year-old husband might have felt like she was greeting a stranger, a ghost, or some old man for all she had borne without her mate those years of yearning. No doubt, she would have experienced many mixed and conflicting feelings at that moment, but in the greatest measure, a wave of *immense* relief would have washed over her. He would then have stood up to embrace his precious wife, rocking back and forth, his hand gently cupping the back of her scarfed head, promising never to *let her go.* So much making up for lost time, tenderness, patience, and assurances of a tangible nature would be needed to bridge the gap between the past and this unfamiliar present. In the meantime, it was high time my grandfather took his family to their new home at 1589 Bedford Avenue, Brooklyn, N.Y., all the more so since it was freezing out that frigid gray day in February, and his wife and sons would soon be feeling the cold in their bones despite their warm reunion.

And so, life began again anew in this unfamiliar land of the plenty and with a people so varied. What you and I would consider a typical snapshot of any portion of the populace in the United States, what with, as Whitman would express, "the varied carols I hear," our panorama of ethnic, racial, and nationalities and vibrant array of religious and linguistic expressions a blur and blend of dulcet tones, my young grandmother found a perplexing and unsettling cacophony. Nothing was pure or right or good anymore, and although she was eternally grateful to have her boys out of harm's way, new and more insidious threats she believed she was facing: those that could tear her family apart through the seduction of the senses and appeal to self over family, secular over sacred, another nation supplanting her heart's home. As I have been told, the section of Brooklyn they lived in at the time was predominantly Jewish. The Italians lived not too far from them on Flatbush Avenue, and much later, my dad would love to take us to eat Nathan's hotdogs on Coney Island.

Perhaps because Greece is a country where 98% — and this seems to me a conservative figure — are Greek Orthodox,[124] the very definition of which, in Greek, ὀρθοδοξία, means "*true* worship,"[125] my grandmother felt like an alien living in enemy territory. In this place, she was surrounded by heretics, strangers, bumpkins, and heathens. After surviving five years in a village tucked in the Taygetos Mountains, she felt vulnerable and exposed again, even though bellies were full and she could sleep at night. Plus, now she too would need to find work to help her husband provide for their family, all the more so because the Greek immigrants' drive to *save, save, save* money was a near obsession. The inner mantra of "*You never know...*" drove *both* my grandparents to work to have the resources to buy the only thing that would anchor in them a sense of security and solidity: *land, land, and more land.* And eventually, that's what my grandfather would do. Always planning ahead, I am told that, even after long hours at work or in the wee hours of the morning on his days off, my grandfather would walk around different parts of Brooklyn to search and find what property might be available for him to purchase and build onto.

Roughly a decade later, he would do the same in and around Athens, Greece. The total of his pursuits in Brooklyn would result in his building a three-story apartment building on 9*** 3rd Ave., where *our* family would visit them from the early 1970s on, and in Greece, three places, one of which was a swanky apartment in a more aristocratic and older section of Athens;

another closer to the center of this capital that itself was comprised of two apartments, and a small summer home, three narrow streets down from the pebbly beach that he built in an area not even incorporated just outside of Oropos, itself 38 km. (23.6 miles) north of Athens. Why do I mention these places to you? Some fifty-five years later, after my grandmother and Uncle Kolya had passed, my father came to acquire these Greek properties (by buying out his remaining brother's portion). In turn, not even three years after this, when my father was deemed incompetent, I would decide what to do with these properties. We are not there yet, so I want us to rush back to when my father would have newly resumed (or started) his education in the States. He would have been in the fifth grade, illiterate in Greek and English, and hardly fluent in this land of the free and home of the brave. There was no ESL class, resource teacher, or guidance counselor to shadow or show him the ropes. Even in adulthood, my mother reported that my dad had particular difficulty with double consonants — "Did 'rabbit' have one or two 'b's'?" — and he was always fascinated by idioms, also something which he never could quite master, but that's just peanuts, just "spilled milk under the bridge," as he might say. Whenever he tried, my mother would shake her head or giggle; we kids looked at him as if he were our Martian. In short, he had a bumpy start in this new safe haven.

The Interlude

Somewhere within the first two years of my grandmother and her sons reuniting with my grandfather when their new life was beginning to solidify into normalcy and routine, something didn't take, couldn't gel, and my grandmother remained discontent as she bristled at the discordant and "barbaric" languages she heard all about her. Besides her own nuclear family, she saw precious little familiar, and she felt overwhelmed by what seemed to her new and even more insidious threats. She was again on guard with redoubled concern for her sons' moral welfare and cultural integrity. So much temptation! Such little present of lasting value! That said, I can't help but contemplate that my father *must've* felt hope and possibility inflate his lungs. Like one of the characters from the 2003 movie *Lost in Translation*, I would be willing to bet that my grandmother would lament to her husband after he got home from working long hours in the restaurant, probably a diner, "I feel so alone, *especially* when other people surround me."[126] Not only that, but she had not even gotten to say goodbye to her mother; she missed her something fierce. I have reason to believe my grandmother had since become pregnant, and she did not wish for her child to be born in this foreign land where everybody and everything was "all mixed up." What was my grandfather to do? The only thing worse than missing his wife and sons for five years was finally having her here, and it turned out that *she didn't want to be here.* My father told me that my grandfather "sold all the furniture in their house" to acquire enough money to send his wife and sons *back* to Greece.

To this day, I remain in awe of his generosity and wisdom that his wife would have to see for herself that a return to Greece could only be temporary, and he was right. My father never told me what he felt about this move. Still, curiously, when I was in high school, I came upon a manilla folder in his filing cabinet in the back closet of his office that had written with a sharpie in his heavy stroke, "TWINS," and inside was a single sheet of notebook paper that said that when they returned to Greece, his mother had had twins, and twin *girls* at that and that they had died at birth. Admittedly, I had no business looking at this file, but I did; furthermore, I never confessed my nosiness to verify the truth of this tragedy with my dad. Decades later, I was still unable to corroborate this with his cousin, Vivian, so this may be another unverified account of some secret, similar to some alternate version from a subplot in the myth of Hercules. However, if we do take it to be true, it would give rise to explaining why my grandmother was so insistent on returning to her native soil, which, although no longer burdened with *two* wars, was still amid the froth and fury of its civil war. She wished for her child to be born in her birth country, and she longed to see *her* mamma. She did not return to her home, sweet, home alone: she also uprooted and took her boys with them, and their brood of four went back to Greece. This would have been in 1948 when her three sons were 17, 16, and 15; the Greek Civil War would have been within a year of fizzling out and grinding to a halt, but a lot can happen in a year.

I don't know when these twin girls— if indeed, there was a pregnancy — were born, but Dad also *wrote* (but never spoke) that they died at birth. Vivian confirmed that my grandmother *did* get to see her mother one last time. As fate would have it, she was actually with her mother when she died. The night before she passed away, her mother, that is, my *great-*grandmother, had a premonition that she was going to die. She instructed my grandmother *to look after her niece*, Vivian, who, if you recall, lost *her* mother to murder. I do not doubt that my grandmother would have been glad to honor her mother's request, all the more so as she would have no daughters of her own. But still! What an unforeseen calamity to deal with upon returning home! Although Vivian remained in Greece with her father, his new wife, and their children, she and my grandmother would remain close throughout life.

Many years later, my grandmother would tell me in private in her broken, clickety-clack English, "Sons?!? No good!! I take one daughter for a meeeeelion sons!" I should translate for you here and supply what was implied but missing in such a declaration: sons are the ones who leave you and break your heart; only a daughter will be the one to come back and care for you when you are old and alone. Technically, that didn't exactly turn out to be the case because my Uncle Kolya, so connected to, or better to say, enmeshed with his mother for his long being her little helper in those dire and desperate days, never could, as my father put it, "cut the umbilical cord," and live on his own. Such would create a beast of a man fraught with resentment, neediness, bitterness, and entitlement that scarred his soul. I felt sorry for this man who was my uncle *and* godfather, and I somehow thought I understood him in a way I could never put into words. And so, with her mother dead and the pregnancy producing a miscarriage, what else could possibly go wrong? Evidently, my grandmother did not do the math before they left because when my Uncle Kolya turned eighteen in December of 1948, she received an official notification that he was eligible for the Greek Army and that it was time for him to enlist. The Civil War was *still* going on, and he was needed. Oh, the agony of it all! She had not anticipated this! There was nowhere to run, nowhere to hide, and she *could* not suffer any more loss —*especially* not her eldest son. Consequently, in agony and defeat, she gathered her three sons and sailed back to the land of the living and to her husband, who was waiting for her, tired, too, but again with open arms.

Second-Class Citizens

Part of returning to the business of surviving and *thriving* in America also involved the often-overlooked transition of what it means to assimilate. How could they retain their identity, lifestyle, and heritage in a land that was, by and large, *Anglo*-based? How would they maintain a shred, semblance, or modicum of the values that had served and imbued them with a sense of *who they were* for longer than could be possibly remembered? *Could* they even? What unanticipated difficulties or unique challenges would they have to face and overcome? Each member of my father's family navigated this paradigm differently, and the net result for my father was that he would sever himself from his family and their sphere of influence and set himself on a different course, orbiting around a *new* gravitational pull of what amounted to assimilation. I am the product of his defection, but we are not at that part, and I do not want to give the impression that his Greek core ever detached from the retina of his persona. In fact, quite the opposite, and much later, it would be the pitch that held him together as he was falling apart. Upon returning to the States, this time for good as far as claiming America as her primary residence, my grandmother got a job as a seamstress in a tailoring factory and worked "very hard."

Years later, she told me she would take the bus to her job every day but never learned to drive. With her husband working long hours in the diner and her boys back in school, out in this bright and brave new world, she soon experienced a subtle but discernable phenomenon that she could not have foreseen and for which her husband had not prepared her: discrimination. According to Vivian, my grandmother "liked to make herself up and look pretty," and she bought her boys and all of them "good Italian shoes" — only "the best" for hers! Much later, when I met my grandmother as a five-year-old, I fled in fright at the sight of her tangled and twisted phalanges. I was witnessing the result of decades of abuse, cramming those D-width Greek feet into high-heeled, pointy-toed shoes that were to bring her closer to civilization and acceptance. Outside the diner, my grandfather, like some Greek Frank Sinatra, habitually dressed in a three-piece suit and remained in it even at home, so used was to "dressing for success," *long* before such was ever a clever phrase or maxim.

Vivian's husband, Alex, shed light on what life was like for the swarthy southern Europeans who had newly emigrated to America. He said, "Greeks and Italians that came to America and did second-class work." He explained their mindset: "Obviously, by how my grandmother dressed herself and her boys, *she never wanted them to be considered second-class citizens.*" Therefore, for my yiayia [grandmother], who, along with my papou [grandfather], made sacrifices so that their family could succeed, for my father to have "married for *love*" and not only that, unbeknownst to them, but to one who was a <u>non</u>-Greek, would have been a spurning and insult to all that they had worked for. Rejection was tantamount to betrayal, and this act of treason would not soon be overlooked, forgotten, or forgiven. Indeed, the *only* item my father inherited from *his* father was a single wool suit, now a relic from days gone by. I am told that my grandmother spent a *lot* on her middle son's education, including her preparing a bonus, extra-credit tray of a Greek dessert that was her hometown's specialty, *diples*, but she did *not* do this for my father. As you soon shall learn, this was likely due to my dad's great fondness and practical adoption of Professor "Papa" Chagaros, my dad's chemistry professor at Brooklyn College, a gregarious Greek genius, a man who himself had married a non-Greek, a woman from England. And this was one more ball that got things rolling toward leaving *this* land of Greeks, putting my father on his life's odyssey.

It would take him *half a century* to return to his native port town of Gythio; Odysseus took only twenty to return to Ithaca. Thomas Wolfe would famously pen, "You can't go home again," my father would indicate its truth for him by prolonged droughts of absenting himself from Brooklyn. Maybe he didn't want to be a boy in a bubble. Perhaps it is more accurate to say that he no longer had a home to go to. His mother's inductions of guilt, the overbearing nagging, her lamentations, the woe, her suspicions, and the dire warnings were too much for my hopeful and ever-optimistic father to spend any appreciable time around. This world of hers was clouded thick as if with incense, and my dad felt squelched, stymied, and suffocated. He yearned to breathe, to escape *this* ship stuck in time inside a bottle. As it turned out, it would take not too long for this spirited boy and youngest son to be guided by his impulses and version of the American dream. I will share how my father forged a future for himself on this foreign, albeit fertile soil.

I doubt that too many Greeks of my father's generation can say they sailed the seas *twice* to make it to America even once. Still, this second time took, so my dad, who shared a room with his older brother Gerasim, buckled down and did what any young immigrant does to forge a way in life that is not yet clear: study, study, and study. My dad later complained that one of the reasons he hated cigarettes so much was that his brother Gerasim smoked in their bedroom while he was doing his homework. I can see their single beds separated by a desk, maybe two, school books piled high, and a few clothes thrown over their chairs. The boys were responsible for seeing that they had done the household chores and at least started their schoolwork before their mother got home. I am told that Kolya began dinner so that by the time his mother returned from the factory, she could finish up and have them eat together. Because restaurant work requires long and often late-night hours, I do not know if they ate with their father every night, but I have seen with my own eyes his quiet presence bringing peace and a sense of security to his family. You may think I could describe any family in any state or country, but this is not entirely true.

From the time my grandmother and her sons returned to the States to *stay*, which I would approximate to be near 1949, it would take two more years of them living as ξένοι, "xeni," or "foreigners" in America before my father became "naturalized." No wonder my grandmother remained xenophobic: she never really felt like she belonged, nor did she ever accept this country as hers. It was on permanent loan. What does becoming a "naturalized" citizen entail? Would one be artificial or not fake without such a certificate, like some counterfeit watch? One had to draw a line in the sand and take a plunge and pledge; it became both desirable *and* necessary for my family, who would only go back to Greece for R and R.

According to the online source, "The Difference between Naturalization and Citizenship,"

> Naturalization is "the process wherein a person born from *another* country acquires citizenship and nationality of another. Naturalization is given to people who are immigrants *to* the US . . . who entered the US on student or working visas. In applying, [my dad completed Form N-560]; these people must have permanent residency in the US *for five years*. They must also pay the filing fee, *pass the citizenship test*, and have no legal impediments"[127] (emphasis mine).

I possess and now hold my dad's original certificate of citizenship in my hand. I can imagine that for my then fifteen-year-old father, this coveted document may as well have "been stamped with the gold seal and framed in a gold frame...[It] *matched the dream that was hung up in [his] head.*"[128]

Even though the four of them returned to Greece for about half a year, they did not have to start their count back to square one after that interlude. The date from when they first arrived, Feb. 2nd of 1946, to October 34 of 1951, the date on my father's Certificate of Citizenship, No. 11-26427, is *five years and seven months.* By the late 1950s, my industrious grandfather had saved enough to purchase property and build a three-story apartment building with his hard-earned money. And though my grandparents would return to their native soil nearly annually and reside there for an entire season, America *did* become their home. They would die and be buried on American soil in a cemetery very much like Brooklyn itself, where crossing a path would place you among a different ethnicity or nationality, be it a host of Greek souls over here, Koreans there, or Italians just beyond. Here, too, space was at a premium, and these dead souls would live like apartment dwellers, only instead of dwelling stories high, caskets were stacked deep. My grandfather went first on May 11, 1982, so his casket is at the bottommost of our family's inverted pyramid; then twenty years later, on Christmas Eve, 2003, his widowed wife joined him and was placed atop his (with how much soil in between, I know not). Barely a year and a half year later, on June 14, 2004, my ghost-of-an-uncle and shell-of-a-man, forever unable to live with or without his mother, joined them and would be the final, tick-tack-toe, three-in-a-row, topmost and final member of our family to seal fates and fortunes here. I can say to you that less than five years after my Uncle Kolya was buried, my father passed away, and I would be the one to choose a burial spot for *him*, but more on this later. We are still in the land of the living with so much opportunity yet to be explored!

One of my favorite subunits to teach in modern American literature is that of the American dream. There is no better or more cherished example than *The Great Gatsby*. We should heed Fitzgerald's admonition not to cheat or take short-cuts to achieve success and, even more essentially, not to be one of the "careless" ones who disregard, use, or leave one for dead those of a lower economic bracket, perceived status, or class, or violates those of a different class. To guarantee success here, my father would do everything "right" according to the formula: he would catapult himself to success through education, and he worked *very* hard at his studies, a circumstance which *also* necessitated overcoming a language barrier. No other member of his or our family would earn a doctorate. Not only that but eventually, he would go the extra mile and do post-doctoral work in his chosen field of organic chemistry at M.I.T. no less, that is, until his own burgeoning family compelled him to seek more lucrative work than what academia provided.

Meanwhile, during his undergraduate days, his mother still attempted to keep her boys sheltered and isolated, fearing that their Greek identity might smudge or run or become diluted or corrupted by associating or fraternizing with non-Greeks. I'm not sure if this was due to her chauvinism and nationalistic pride; perhaps her xenophobia heightened by her experiences in the war, or maybe it was because of her keen intuition that whispered to her there were other defections aside from political ones. It would be she who felt the sting of discrimination herself, and then, due to some proactive self-protection, perhaps she rejected *first* to lessen the *anticipated* sting of feeling shunned. That shift in mindset is another bi-product or casualty of war, a mind game that preserves and pollutes. I suspect her suspicious mind came about from a combination of the above. All I have to do is read the description of my father's Naturalization document, which describes him as a 5' 5", 120-pound fifteen-year-old brown-haired and brown-eyed single male whose complexion is "dark" to know that this clarifier of hue or indication of pigmentation shade was not mere happenstance. His description also reveals the long-term effects of malnutrition on his spare teenage frame. Being "dark" bears the mark or negative connotation of being wrong or evil as opposed to the "light," which connotes pure or good. Further, being "dark" in America, where the color of one's skin has been systematically used as a means of discrimination for *centuries,* would add an official marker that this person was *not* one of the dominant culture's background, that is, of Anglo heritage.

Life for a non-W.A.S.P. would have unique challenges in dealing with stigma by stain. While I do not pretend to *begin* to compare his experience to that of African Americans by *any* stretch of the imagination, I would argue that having a swarthy complexion *did* have a bearing on his self-concept and on the paths that he chose for himself. In delving into this fascinating and wholly overlooked topic, I came upon a paper called "THE SOCIAL PSYCHOLOGY OF IMMIGRATION: THE GREEK-AMERICAN EXPERIENCE,"[129] which for me was like striking gold, like talking to a medium for the insight it provided me into the mindset of my father, he who would not speak of scars that were invisible but undeniable. Perhaps that is what I am doing now. It was also like perchancing upon poison because amongst the seemingly innocuous normative expectations and rich opportunities we celebrate offered here in America, I advertently stumbled upon some not-so-subtle forms of bigotry. I then began to connect the dots as to how the very nation in which my father was thriving would also contribute to his severing ties with a chaotic, war-torn country from which he and the rest of his family fled, a land that he had once called home. There are apparent costs to the benefits of becoming a part of America's wealthy "melting pot," including those that would tacitly encourage putting one's heritage in the back seat, except in the expressions that would have been light, celebratory, but nonessential. To "melt" implies a burning away of something; for my father, that would eventually mean cutting the cord to his Hellenistic roots. However, strands remained and would never dissemble themselves from him.

Therefore, I am not implying his "Greekness" left him; that would have been as unthinkable as performing a blood transfusion to a different type. He would remain G-positive! However, my dad would forever straddle these two lands as if he had been our very own Colossus, except that he had one foot planted firmly in America while the other still hovered precariously over Greece; such an awkward balancing act that was! To camouflage their Mediterranean hue and history, some Greeks attempt to go through life incognito, even going so far as severing syllables from their gangly and polysyllabic surnames that are "all Greek" and weird to a more sanitized version that might pass as having sprung from a less-complicated Anglo-American culture. A branch of my family living in New Jersey did just that, lopping off half the syllables of our surname, and it goes by one, now possessing only two. My father did nothing of the kind, but his desertion was more complete. I suppose had she known, his mother might have diagnosed it as a type of "Stockholm Syndrome," whereby the captive takes on the sympathies of his captor; however, this term had not yet been conceived. Maybe she would consider her son weak, having fallen prey to the seductive powers of ease and comfort under the bright American "sun comes out tomorrow [and] clears away the cobwebs and the sorrow."[130] That "tomorrow" would be *today*, and its promise and potential gripped my father. My take is that with a heart open and hopes high, my dad flew straight into the arms of an American girl with whom he fell in love, she who had no war wounds or heavy emotional baggage. *She* did not expect him to bear some grave cross. She was a small-town, Midwest American woman — his very own village girl! Falling for her must have felt like another D-Day liberation for him, but we are not quite ready to make their introduction.

As a boy, I doubt that my father would have been aware of the particular immigration law of 1924, "whereby *Greek* immigrants were restricted to the *lowest* immigration quota than any other European group"[131](emphasis mine). Why would this be? For what reason? I read this article, which shed light on that which, in hindsight, I can see made a profound impact on my dad's self-concept, value construct, and decision-making apparatus. Discrimination produced the collateral damage of resentment that would worm its way out years later, suppressed but never squelched. I will share but two points from this article because they expose a subtle disgust that my dad would feel in varying degrees at different times. How odd to escape war but to land in a land of power, potential, and protection that *also* bears prejudice instead of peace. The first point concerns itself with the pressure to conform to the social norms, which, on its basis, would discriminate against Greeks. Since this type of antipathy was *not* racial but *national*, its impact would *not* have been noticeable to mainstream Americans but was discernable to Greeks. I would argue that my father fell into the category of Greeks who swallowed the "if-you-can't-beat-'em,-join-em" outlook. Feelings of adequacy would come more readily if one blended and took full advantage of all opportunities.

My father catapulted himself to material success by furthering his education, but doing so in his way led to an abandonment his parents never saw coming: he basically ran away from home. Leaving the fold felt like exhilarating freedom to my father, as if *he* were his family's Icarus flying towards the splendid sun. In the substrata of my father's subconscious, the decision to liberate himself from his war-torn past, as well as the current and never-ending harangues from his termagant mother, was made easier because he had long since learned to tune out her nagging, like a layer of superglue she poured to preserve their unity and way of life. Instead, he would surrender a part of himself to this foster land for his greater gain and good as if *he* were his sacrificial lamb; he would not be thwarted! Indeed, he became one of those Greeks who

> "sacrificed *the substance* of Greek culture to keep only a Greek cultural facade, such as church attendance, folk dances, Greek food, ethnic parades, and the like. [He made] no attempt to analyze in-depth the meaning of Greek culture or to explain its symbols, study its history, literature, or art. Such in-depth cultural plunge *may have been psychologically too difficult to bear...*" (emphasis mine)[132]

Please bear in mind that my dad's associations with Greece were knotted up in sharp recollections of war and ravelings of the nitty-gritty of his heritage, so it was just easier and simpler to make a clean break and run for it. He tried to separate the wheat from the chaff and lost some of his essential grain, but at least he knew he was of the wheat even while growing up among the tares. For my dad, Greece remained a land of pride *and* nightmares — all the more so as he had been forced to return when things were still amuck. Other than speculating that because the reality of war had become normalized and blurred with his family life in Greece, I can't tell you why he didn't remain in the Greek community in the States as so many do. My father certainly had no premeditated plan to escape or move away. Recall, if you will, the catalytic converter in my dad's life: the man who became a father figure to my father. Long before my dad ever met my mom, like a baby duckling, he followed the lead of his favorite professor, a Greek man, who showed my father kindness, understanding, affection, and a new direction. Only then, when my dad was at graduate school in Indiana, some 800 miles away from the centripetal forces at home in Brooklyn, did he meet and fall in love with my mother, and "the holocaust was complete."[133]

My parents both said that we, their children, were the best thing that came from their doomed marriage. Looking back, I attribute my dad's decision to marry my mom in significant part to a simple pain-avoidance, pleasure-seeking impulse. Blended in with his drive and energy, I also believe he was divinely endowed with a healthy dose of hope- the kind that springs eternal. Everything about my father's *modus operandi* confirmed and asserted —as if his soul could speak — "As for me, I will always have hope" (Psalm 71:14 NIV). Such a positive outlook cannot be merely attributed to his being naïve or the youngest, carefree child. Nearly a decade spent suckling worry and endurance is enough to take the wind out of your sails. I believe the likes and scope of which my dad possessed were divinely endowed. His brother, two years older than he would have to place an ocean between his mother and him to enjoy his freedom and independence fully, but unlike my father, he married a Greek girl and became one of those Greeks who delved deep into his rich history while living in Tehran, Iran; Alexandria, Virginia; and finally, in Heidelberg, Germany. Like Greeks in the tavernas, my uncle would play fierce games of backgammon with his best friend for hours on end. This, too, would become an adored pastime for my father and me, his eldest daughter, for many years to come. My father eventually settled down in the hills of a small town in East Tennessee, but his pleasure always centered around food, so he became our family's beacon of Greek dishes and dances.

I now return to the second point from that article I told you about, one on which the vast majority of Greek-Americans heavily came to rely to feed their faith; it is the same source as long-forgotten relatives who lived during the dominion of the Ottoman Turks would use: <u>Greeks have always turned to the Orthodox Church for respite, revival, and restoration</u>. Not too long before my parents wed, my mom had come to reject not only the church but the trinity, whittling three down to one and eschewing the divine in the process. Therefore, my more modern mother naturally would have been repulsed by the medieval institution of the Greek Orthodox Church, what with its thick incense, eerie, other-worldly Byzantine chants, ancient, long-bearded priests, and misery-rich Byzantine icons. For my dad, this was home, but not for long. Absence became his path of least resistance. Only when our family made its annual two-hour trek to the nearest Orthodox Easter service did I realize that this amounted to a veritable pilgrimage for my father. As he sang along and responded *en masse* with his fellow Greek parishioners to the priest and fluidly crossed himself, finishing up the sign by closing the door and gently touching his heart at the end, somehow not of his own will, yet with all his spirit, did I realize I was getting a glimpse at a portion of my father that was *his nascent core self,* and I was hungry for more.

Only after my parents divorced and the dust had settled did I realize the sacrifice my father had made all of those years to keep the peace and appease his wife. It took no time for his spirit to resurrect and return to the church after their split, and Christ was still there waiting for him! Ironically, the First Amendment, which guarantees every American to worship as they would see fit, enabled Greeks to fly unnoticed beneath the radar and maintain a portion of their "Greekness" intact and still in concentration. Precious little melted down or burned away; impurities were left pure! And although my father was never a devotee of the church to the degree his mother was, she who for decades to come would cry that her (two) sons of desertion "never even gave to the church," his faith was indeed and indelibly stamped on his soul; he, too, belonged to Christ.

Just how and why did the Orthodox Church in America become more sacrosanct, "more Catholic than the Pope," than it ever might have been in Greece? In the States, the Greek Church became the center of gravity for Greeks because of what it provided, that which was sorely missing. In the following excerpt, I share with emphasis salient portions that make clear what the Greek Orthodox Church provided Greek Americans. It gave them

> "*a sense of belonging,* which Greek society did for the Greeks living in Greece... Many Greek immigrants channeled their love for their cultural heritage toward their Greek churches, which they felt they had to give up in an Anglo-dominated society. This is why we have today the seemingly unexplainable, if not contradictory, phenomenon of completely anglicized third and fourth-generation Greeks zealously supporting the Greek Orthodox Church: *their Church touches them as deeply or as completely as does one's place of birth or country of origin.*"[134]

I ask you to pardon me for this lengthy quote, but for me, it captures a spark never extinguished in my dad's core, as if he had held a candle within him; his faith and form remained aglow after all those years. My mother asserted that his faith was only skin-deep, that his "motions" made in the church were "performance-based" done through rote memory recalled. I beg to differ. I saw a man whom God "strengthened with power through His Spirit in his heart through faith." My dad comprehended — knew the love of Christ, one which surpasses knowledge, and *he was filled to all the fullness* of God" (adapted from Ephesians 3:16–19, emphasis mine). As we pass through the threshold that takes my father to his adulthood, I know that I cannot fill in the blanks of what constitutes daily life while he was in high school or college. Such detail *du jour* isn't my focus. Instead, I'll now move to tell you about how my dad was given the green light, or as he would say in later years with his warbly voice, "permission" to take flight and make a nest with a cardinal from Indiana. However, unlike our mythical hero Hercules, whose wife Princess Megara was given to him in marriage by King Creon, my dad would claim the woman he desired with the passion and fury of a titan.

It's Only Chemical, Logical

By the time my father entered Brooklyn College, his father was approaching sixty years old. His reserve, age, and quiet passivity around the house, as compared to his on-edge and often anxious wife, would make it less likely for my father to seek advice and direction, let alone comfort from his own "pateras" or father; he was hardly a "pop" or "dad" to him. Being the youngest son and kid brother who was kept close to his mother's apron strings and far from "stranger danger" long before such a label was coined, my guess is that *my father was not taken too seriously among his family.* The youngest may be adored, but their voice and vision may be taken less earnestly than those of the older siblings, that is, until something inside them stops and says, "Enough!" Family dynamics shift and fade and reconfigure, but some roles get frozen in time, and I think my dad had had enough of being the "μπούφος" ("boufoss"), that is, the dunce among his brothers. My mother learned that it had always been my dad's role that stretched on into adulthood — one for which he had a knack anyway — to make his mother laugh.

A boy on the cusp of manhood might understandably seek someone *other* than family to validate him as worthy of respect and assure him his dreams held merit and his goals were attainable. My dad decided he was more than the class clown or the family jester; he'd show them! He was "more than a conqueror" (Romans 8:37 NIV). At the time, he took that eight-minute walk from his house on Bedford Avenue to Brooklyn College, heading straight for the now-familiar lecture hall or perhaps a laboratory nearby, where he would discover the realm of chemistry. He had become enthralled by its characters, codes, and complexities. This invisible world of such exquisite order and dynamism was introduced to him by a professor who became no less influential on his life than the subject that had captivated his mind. Both took him by storm! Brilliant, gregarious, affectionate, and kind, this mustachioed man became a father figure to my dad. We all have a small and select handful of people who have profoundly impacted our lives, and Professor Basil Chagaros was my dad's guardian angel and mentor. From him, my dad learned that the sky was the limit and we are only limited by the scope of our visions, and my dad was a dreamer. Who would have foreseen that my young father, with his bright and creative mind, sought order and possibility within the periodic table of elements? Who would have imagined that the Russian chemist and inventor of the periodic table, Dimitri Mendeleev, and Linus Pauling, winner of two Nobel prizes in chemistry[135], would become my dad's superheroes?

Decades later, when I first moved into my dorm room as a college freshman, my dad was delighted to give me a colorful poster to adorn these institutional walls: it vividly depicted the periodic table of elements. *"Was I not thrilled?"* was the look he gave me. Only recently did I learn that in addition to Pauling's more popularized work, whereby he made a connection between taking large doses of vitamin C and lowering one's chances of getting the common cold[136], in the circles of chemists, he is considered *the* most outstanding chemist of the twentieth century and the founder of molecular biology.[137] Why do I mention this to you? Unbeknownst to my father, Pauling's discoveries "made it possible for geneticists to crack the DNA code of all organisms and *develop techniques to help prevent the inheritance of genetic disorders*" (emphasis mine).[138] What that my father's disease, which yet lay unexpressed in his youthful frame, could have been one of those that was prevented. All I knew was that my father was a "vitamin fiend," as he would label himself.

You should know that for Greeks living in the States, as far as labor goes, if one didn't settle in the groove of the conventional Greek line of work in the diner or restaurant, then one ought to at least go for the gusto and become a doctor or lawyer! But a *chemist*? What was he *thinking*?!? As a young man, my father's dad started working as a chef in the U.S. Navy during WWI. My dad's parents' expectation for him was that, like his father before him, he would *also* go into the restaurant business. And why *else* is this a tendency? I learned that "the Greek story is just a takeover of mostly Italians getting *out* of the restaurant industry and moving on to less demanding work."[139] As with the wave of Italians that preceded the Greeks in coming to America, the easiest jobs would be in the service industry and, more importantly, where one didn't have to know the language. English is a Germanic and polyglot language and would be challenging to learn. My dad never mastered English, nor did he pay much attention to the fact that he hadn't attained beyond a bare-basics proficiency in his native tongue's grammar. My father's verbal blunders, mispronunciations, and mixed-up idioms were a source of endless entertainment for my mother and us kids growing up.

By the time the *1960s* came around, most immigrants who had arrived in the first third of the twentieth century had already become Americanized. Moreover, at that time, Greek people in the U.S. were relatively newer and fewer in number than the Italians and were *"not* as Americanized."[140] As a result, they were *also* not pressured to become as normalized or mainstreamed as the Italians had been. They complied in part to avert the not-so-subtle and unpleasant effects of discrimination for being dubbed "dark." Therefore, as you can see, it would have been natural for my father to follow in these footsteps, *but my father was a rebel...* with a cause! Leaving his familiar fold felt like unshackling iron links of love that connected the individual to his community. At the time, he just knew he felt stifled and wanted out. Later, when he explained his career choice to us kids, he would say he was *"cooking with chemicals,"* an odd-sounding justification I'm sure he wished could have satisfied his parents. His two older brothers also bucked this system and chose different paths, but they never left the Greek fold. One might argue that becoming an American for my dad involved accepting my mom's core values and priorities by proxy. This new citizen hailed his right to pursue "life, liberty, and happiness." However, taking on the new did not mean getting rid of the old; beyond sense and form, surviving within my father was a sublimation of the ancient Greek ideals of "virtue (or excellence), glory, *and duty.*"[141]

My dad would have entered Brooklyn College in 1953 and been slated for graduation in 1957. I would like to say one final word about "Papa Chagaros," this beloved professor who hurrahed my father when none in his family gave him anything but grief for his unorthodox choice of major. Part Almost every summer when my father was an undergraduate student, Professor Chagaros took his motley crew of young Greek undergraduates with him to Chicago, where I'm told that he conducted lab experiments at such a spectacular scale that he needed all the help he could get. And who better qualified than a posse of willing, able, and educated Greek students who would gladly do the grunt work for food or a leg-up in their career in the form of a coveted connection or recommendation? My dad told us that at times, he had his arm up to his elbow deep, stirring vats of experimental solutions that only much later did he realize contained carcinogens of high concentration. That same softly hairy forearm of his I knew and loved as a girl that would plunge into a pitcher of orange or grape juice to break up the clods of frozen concentrate was the same stirrer that had waded through sludge and slime of God-knows-what. Indeed, doing such just might have been how he ingested poisons that permeated and affected his system at the cellular level, but we are not there yet. My father never criticized his professor for taking such risks with his students when conducting his experiments.

My buoyant dad went through life impervious or oblivious to any negativity, criticism, scorn, or doubt concerning something he was passionate about. And he was a man with a plan —multiple! In fact, naysayers only spurred him to succeed and surpass their meager expectations. He'd show them! This "Teflon" mentality never left him; only later, *sadly, it also applied to his fantastical thinking and wishes more than it did realizable goals and plans.* When it was apparent he was not sound, he would express unfiltered and half-baked thoughts that would have best been left unsaid for their preposterous nature. Yet, somehow, they possessed a pinch of plausibility or a kernel of truth. To our expressions of doubt or chagrin, Dad would counter, *"IIIIIII don't think so,"* like he was some Greek Superman and fortune teller rolled in one. I'll bet Hercules thought no less of himself. In better days, his complete confidence would take him to unchartered waters to claim a woman who was a foreigner to himself. After he graduated from Brooklyn College, the commencement ceremony for which, decades later, he told me that he was still disappointed that his parents did *not* attend, he entered graduate school at Purdue University to complete his master's degree in organic chemistry. Let's return to my dad's post-secondary education and voyage to Atlantis; after all, in settling in on a chemistry major, my dad struck out on his yellow brick road, a path that would lead him *not* to Kansas but to Lafayette, Indiana.

Flight Take 2 and a New Chemical Compound

Most children have heard how their parents first got together and who was the one who dared disturb the universe.[142] I learned this lore from my mother because I had often asked her to tell me *their* "Beauty and the Beast" story; I loved it so much. Not dissimilar to my father, but for polar opposite reasons, my mother, who was also attending Purdue at the time but as an underclassman, reeled with giddy delight to partake of the broad world waxing wide in her backyard. There, she was introduced to members of the international community, and I believe she relished her taste of *this* new world. Those from South and Central America, Palestine, and Greece were among the flavors and hues exhilarating and alluring to a young woman with a deep need for more than shades of pale in life. Had she attended another school, her major would have been art, but home economics was all she got at Purdue. Still, there *had* to be more to life than her hometown's version of an antiseptic, squeaky-clean, prescribed, and circumscribed lifestyle, allowing for no variation. Her passion for aesthetics, art, and design and a complementary focus on light, warmth, and texture brought aesthetic bearing to life when she met people from exotic lands. *Life* became her art, and she became intoxicated with new and alluring music, tantalizing cuisines, and these unfamiliar and beautiful people. The airtight seal came off, and she felt alive! For a bright and curious young woman with an artistic temperament and a shy nature, she was drawn like a moth to the light; those with a zest for athletics or more of the same need not apply.

Now an octogenarian, my mother still looks back on these as some of the best days of her life. Why, at the time, she even dated a young Greek boy, a man named Teddy Stethakos, a gentle soul and one whose mother had been sweet to my mom, affectionate even. How could my mother have guessed that when she met my father — or rather, when *this* Greek man, who, as if struck by Zeus's bolt of lightning, fell in love with her on the spot — would come with odd baggage that she wouldn't know *what* to do with, let alone fathom how it got there. After all, *her* experiences with befriending these deliciously different foreign men had been like one long, fun, and fantastic Greek Fest. How could she have foreseen that life with my dad would *not* be like endless days of baklava and gyros and romantic strolls around the Parthenon? In fact, he never took her to see the grandeur of Greece, as it was yet the land of emotional landmines for him.

Evidently, *there was this dance. . .* Don't so many love stories begin like this? My mother was standing off to herself, just watching this exhibition of living exotics, when whom should she see in the near distance staring at her as he made his way over to her, but a dark-headed Greek man (*not* god) in tortoise-shelled glasses and wearing highwater khakis held up to his waist by a thin belt. Handsome? My mother's sister said my dad looked like Tony Curtis, but my mother saw a man with a demeanor more similar to that of the young comedian Jerry Lewis. My dad was not the cool one; he was no suave and debonaire Dean Martin. He was a young Greek geek, and he was smitten. Perhaps she was drawn to his herculean energy, already spilling over like some billy goat; she knew he would go places. He asked her to dance, and she nodded. Their elements collided, and my dad became a noble gas to her ethereal regions. All I knew was that their song was "Misty," and I do not doubt in my mind that as my dad held his future wife in his arms, she was doing her fifty's swing to his Greek circle dance for two, and somewhere deep inside him where he had no words, he felt the lyrics give voice to his heart. As hands touched, bodies glided, and his eyes communicated the words he willed of my mother: "*Look at me. I'm as helpless as a kitten up a tree, and I feel like I'm clingin' to a cloud. I can't understand — I get misty just holding your hand...*"[143]

My mother never knew what my dad had told this Teddy Stathakis, whom she had been pleasantly seeing, but Mr. Ted no longer came-a-courtin'. My father pursued my mother like a bloodhound, following the scent of success and a woman he'd claimed as his own. My father's singular-minded pursuit of her, along with a romantic possessiveness, spoke volumes — and without words — that *no others need apply*. I am reminded of the finality with which Emily Dickinson's soul chose her beloved: "I've known her — from an ample nation — Choose One —Then — close the Valves of her attention — Like Stone."[144] Later, my mother confided that my dad had never been in love before and that *she was his first.* I know no more of their courtship, only of the astonishing speed with which my father switched gears and hats from romance to realism when they said their "I dos."

On a bright and cheery <u>Christmas day in Jacksonville, Florida, in 1960, my parents were married</u> by a Unitarian minister in the house of my mother's aunt, who had encouraged "otherness" in my mom. My father had since received the stamp of approval from her aunt's husband, a professor of psychology, who attested my dad was "brilliant." I can't imagine that the service could have begun to quench my father's expectation of what this holy sacrament would look like. Compared to the ornate and highly symbolic ceremony of the rite of holy matrimony in the Greek Church, where after petitions have been made, prayers offered, and candles lit, the couple receives a literal crowning, this would have felt like going through the drive through at McDonald's for a happy meal! The priest takes two wedding crowns, or "stefana," blesses the bride and groom, then places the crowns upon their heads.[145] Nothing of the kind *here!* Even for a simple man like my dad, there was not enough majesty due to this sacred sacrament, this once-in-a-lifetime moment! The *Greek* version of the best man is the one who performs the interchanging of the crowns three times; he bears witness to the sealing of this union. The Holy Trinity of Father, Son, and Holy Spirit were present and accounted for! My dad had *no* best man, let alone *any* of his friends or family present. Why? He did not brave the elements and inform his family of his sacrilegious union, which was *hardly* a wedding! He would receive no crown or ribbon to symbolize their unity with Christ. He would have no priest who, on behalf of Christ, blesses and joins them in holy matrimony.

Instead, there was a Unitarian minister in a simple suit officiating, not to mention a random young boy who made many a photobomb here and there. God may have been watching, but Jesus seemed not in attendance. Not only that, my mom no longer viewed the Son of Man as the Son of God, let alone her Savior; she was too smart for her good. Instead, she would have been *thrilled* to marry this foreigner of hers in such a homey yet unconventional setting; contrastingly, my dad had to have been left puzzled. Was this even legit.? He probably wondered how, with no crowns bestowed by Christ, they would ever truly be king and queen of *their* home. There were no Greeks present "to speak now" in admonition, let alone "forever hold their peace" about what God had joined that Christmas Day. Twenty-two years later, my discontent and lonely mother would put it asunder, and their less-than-perfect union would cleave in twain. My dad kept any doubts or denunciatory thoughts he might have had to himself, smiled broadly at his very own American bride, and they said their "I do's." This was the same year *Never of a Sunday* came out, and America seemed obsessed with all things Greek. As it turned out, my mother would never forget her Christmas wedding date because my dad could never remember their anniversary.

Another revealing aspect of their matrimony was that none of my father's family attended the wedding. As I briefly mentioned, he *never even told them*. He knew that this was no way to start a legitimate marriage in their eyes. For them, uniting with her was tantamount to sleeping with the enemy; it meant leaving the fold and abandoning his tribe. Such betrayal for all they'd done and been through! He could feel their fury from a thousand miles away. Why wake these sleeping giants? It was *enough* to contend that his wife could *never* understand the underpinning love-hate feelings he held for his church, the pressure *and* peace he concurrently felt from the icon of God staring down at him from the mosaiced ceiling in its basilica. So, now to deal with the ire of his tragic parents, who would rain on his parade *and* plans and dreams? No, thank you, not today.

Afterward, my dad had asked my mom in passing if they could *also* get wed in the Greek Church in Chicago; she must have looked at him like he was a loon. It was not brought up again until we children were born and baptized because his parents told him (no doubt, in harsh tones) that they *should* have had a *proper* wedding to validate or sanctify their union (according to the Greek standards of the day) and thereby *legitimize* any future children of theirs. Even though official Greek statutes on this matter would eventually become relaxed, privately, my grandmother referred to us as "illegitimate" because of my parents' egregious oversight. It's like the first wedding didn't count because it was not taken seriously — as a holy sacrament. It's a shame I came to learn this only later because I thought my grandmother and uncle referred to us by the synonym for "illegitimate" because we were not full-blooded Greeks.

Meanwhile, my mother must have wondered where this energetic and enigmatic man who had pursued her with such passion and romance had gone. From wooed to wed, my father expected my mother to don her new role as Wife swiftly and all that this entailed; plus, he was still in the throes of graduate school. My mother did not receive a copy of the Greek playbook on What a Marriage Looks Like; otherwise, she might not have bought this farm. Instead, disappointment and regret became her companions. Star-crossed lovers and strangers in the day, my parents got off to a rocky start, but on *that* sweet day, they smoothly sailed away on their lifecraft, headed for many successes and an impending disaster, and I'm not referring to their divorce.

The Genetics of Huntington's Disease

Although my father's Huntington's disease had *decades* yet to go before it made its disturbing debut, the seeds were already sown, so now, it's time we take a look at what was happening to him on the genetic front. It seems oddly apropos that in choosing the field of organic chemistry, a discipline that whittled down the alphabet to *four* letters — Hydrogen, Oxygen, Nitrogen, and Carbon —my father would inherit a disease that further stripped it to *three* letters where it concerned *his* genetics. Ultimately, genetics interfered with a portion of *his* organic chemistry. I've seen his many college notebooks neatly filled with brilliant little helixes, with their lengthy, hangman-like extensions where he'd completed complex equations as if he were a beekeeper with his own productive and orderly hives. Life was so much messier than this world! As it turns out, his disease would trump his ace and carve the alphabet to a mere *three* letters in a genetic code that, when played out, would afflict him in the years to come. Who could have guessed that his Huntington's disease involved the DNA segment known as a "CAG trinucleotide repeat," [146] whose count has gone far awry? Let's delve into this mire to make sense of what would make my father eventually lose his.

Huntington's Chorea: A Deadly Dance

In the previous chapter, I speculated how Huntington's disease could have been inherited in the first place. Not only that, but I couldn't help being struck by the irony that the name of this disease also happened to be the name of my mother's hometown. What are the odds? What kind of sick joke was this? I speculated to my mind's content because I would never get the opportunity to do genetic testing on *his* parents; plus, I won't get to know why the fallout from the Fall got expressed in *this* particular manner in my *dad*. The bottom line is that one of his parents was the "asymptomatic carrier." If I were a betting person, I would speculate that his father triggered its reality into being, which, by extension and expansion, got activated in my dad. There would have been a higher probability for the spontaneous and random mutation to have occurred within his father. However, I could be wrong; perhaps the genetic marker lay dormant and waiting within his mother's ovum.

Whereas the last chapter was speculative, in *this* chapter, my focus could not be more focused, precise, and concrete. I need to go into the history of how the disease came to be discovered and named, and I must not expound upon the fascinating research into identifying the marker or gene for Huntington's disease within the DNA molecule. That said, I will give you a trio of dates to provide you with the context of the disease's discovery to pave the road for when *our* family received its shocking confirmation about my dad having chorea. You will make this discovery in two chapters to come, but for now, I will set the stage as we investigate the locus of a genetic crime scene; we will be like private detectives, you and I.

In 1872, in his paper called "On Chorea," a physician by the name of Dr. George Huntington isolated the protein, dubbing it the *huntingtin* protein, that was the guilty culprit for sparking this shocking disease's induction; he would then give the first clinical description of the disease that would bear his name.[147] By the 1960s, in Dr. Huntington's honor, it became known as "Huntington's chorea" and then "Huntington's disease." In 1983, when my parents were divorcing, Dr. Milton Wexler quietly found a DNA marker for the HD gene.[148] He isolated this marker close to the unknown gene affected and "pinpointed it down to the tip of the short arm of chromosome 4."[149]Then, just one decade later, in 1993, the HD *gene* was found, like some lost Dead Sea scroll discovered, and when its "text" was read, the particular mutation that resulted in the disease was identified. (We discussed mutations in the previous chapter.) These breakthroughs helped launch the Human Genome Project, which started in 1993 when genetic testing became possible. Thirteen years later, my father would take such a test not once but twice to *"double-triple check,"* as he wanted to say, to deduce what might be the cause of his obvious but unidentified disorder.

The Huntington *gene* contains the instructions for producing a *protein* that contains the DNA, and because it was discovered after the gene, it is called the <u>Huntingtin protein</u>. The mystifying script housed within the gene that causes Huntington's disease is in our *DNA*. Knowing to get tested and then "read" for this code, which might conclude with a diagnosis of HD, would only be possible if you saw the eerie effects manifested in your middle-aged loved one; their abnormal movements and peculiar behavior might then prompt you to have him to check, to take what is called a "predictive test."[150] We would have my dad take this test in the winter of 2006, with results known in January of 2007. Suspicions of a disease I had not even heard of came back *confirmed*, but I am getting ahead of myself. Let's get back to the A, B, and C building blocks that we would find on none other than the *fourth* of our twenty-three pairs of chromosomes. A particular trio of amino acids on the number 4 chromosome numerically connects our triune of myth and man and math, merging the birthdays of both Hercules and Pavlos on the fourth of the month to the x-marks-the-spot chromosome #4 with its aberration. From when we first began noticing the slight and random tic here and there or wondering about a random or bizarre outburst over something seemingly inane to when we would seek outside help with our Unsolved Mystery, it would take a few *years*.

Some viewed my dad's confounding behavior and peculiar movements as that of the normal aging process in *him*. Some secretly speculated it was Parkinson's. Still, we weren't taken aback; my dad always moved about in his *own* way anyway. Who cares what others think? Still, the undeniable reality was growing on us all —except for the very one afflicted — that something was off and not quite right. How could we *not* gasp or grin at his lurchy, herky-jerky movements? They were comical in the way that physical comedy can make you laugh. Day by month by year, he was becoming something of a village oaf to us, albeit he was *ours*. You can't put a date on the disease's manifest inception because, technically, the disease began at conception. Also, *each person's rate and display of its visible expression differ*. I would hazard to guess that for my father, HD made its first visible spark when he was in his late forties, and it would take roughly a decade for this flame to grow into a brush fire.

Eventually, I would become his fireman, but let's return to our "in the beginning." As it turned out, this macabre dance of divine nature — as if St. Vitas had been resurrected here and now — got kicked out in our dad from the genetic slot machine. Spinning out its odd, foreboding code that might *seem* like a stroke of bad luck, mere chance, or an unfortunate occurrence to us mere mortals, but this is *not* the case. From the moment we are born, we all are on the path leading to death; it's just a matter of *how*, not when, and none of us gets to choose or know how or when we die. Yes, progress has been and will continue to be made in preventing or circumventing this or that means of disease. To that end, I want to inform you that every penny of royalties I earn here will go towards research to reduce or correct the effects of this disease. In the meantime, as we forge ahead and examine both my dad and this disease, I recall hearing that God watches out for children and fools; therefore, in the case of my father, I am grateful that "the LORD supports all *who fall* and raises all *who are bowed down*" (Psalm 145:14). I'm sure He already has.

Just as I was picky in deciding whom to introduce you to in terms of the various leaders and sub-groups involved in the Greek Civil War, now, I will select some of the microscopic mire that was transpiring within my father on the cellular level. I hope to share the instigating mitigating causes that led to the collateral damage and fallout in my dad's frame and mind. I will hold your hand as we take baby steps out onto the invisible playing field where the action was taking place, where a tiny but giant revolt led to a very different type of civil war: a cog in the wheel, a genetic abnormality, and malfunction. An imperfect life doesn't abort God's mission, so we will read how my dad's plot got twisted with a single mis-stroke on his fourth chromosome; it did not change who my father was that God intended him to be.

My presentation will not be as exhaustive as what you'd find in a textbook; that would hardly be desirable. Instead, I will focus on my dad's genetic drama's critical scenes and keynote actors. Some terms you will already know or recall; others will be novel or technical. This journey we are getting g ready to embark upon will be inward and on an infinitesimally small scale. I would like you to consider it as if we are stepping into the Dutch graphic artist M.C. Escher's geometrical masterpiece, *House of Stairs* (1951). You can get lost in its three-dimensional optical illusion that makes you feel like you could be any mannequin-like faceless person sojourning on a staircase with no beginning or end, like a double-slinky with steps installed. You are going inexorably downward on a seemingly endless escalator that spirals down and inward to the very center of an unseen universe where life unfolds and then blossoms before your eyes. Only in my father's case would there be an aberration, a glitch, a bump in the road, a knot inside his noggin that got sewn in his fabric.

I am sure you can easily recall that cells are the building blocks of life and that the nucleus is the center of the cell. Without a doubt, you also understand that after the miracle of life takes place when God's foreordained particular sperm and exact ovum unite. These two become one, complete with celebratory fireworks, and there comes the frantic business of subsequent cell division so that the embryo's development and growth can occur, all with stunning beauty, incalculable precision, minute detail, and rich complexity. No one but God could orchestrate the physical masterpiece, which is you; after all, we are made in His image (Gen. 1:26). But just as "the whole creation groans and suffers" (Romans 8:22) from man's willful disobedience that resulted in his subsequent banishment, *we who believe in Christ Jesus* will know no *spiritual* death. It is on God's watch as to when we *physically* expire. We anticipate and look forward to a restoration, a breathtaking *perfection* of what's yet in store for us, and we've only seen His Son, but I'm getting ahead of myself. Let's return to the mired metamorphosis shortly after my dad's conception.

The A, B, Cs of Genetics

Our plunge to the cellular level will feel like we are on an otherworldly *Journey to the Center of the Earth*; let's expand the scope of our pinpointed focus. Inside each of the zillions of cells we have is the nucleus, the Ground Zero, which contains the directions for each cell. At conception, one-half of the zipper strand of all the genetic information you will ever have comes from one parent; it joins and zips up with the same strand belonging to the other parent, and though your future is up to you, your genetic fate is sealed. Then comes God's math: cell division commences at your nascent core as this embryo concurrently, miraculously expands via multiplication and differentiation into all the designated parts and pieces and various functions thereof within your body's complete construction. Prepackaged within the cell's nucleus are twenty-three pairs of chromosomes. Except for the sex-determining pair of chromosomes, the rest of the twenty-two pairs of chromosomes look pretty much the same. Think of a pair of chromosomes as two squiggly strands of confetti that are pinched together in the middle; in actuality, they are more like foam noodle structures that are the packaged form containing your DNA, and this stands for deoxyribonucleic acid. It turns out that, in its essence, biology is chemistry! Perhaps they resemble the delicate dance of a couple of seahorses doing their tango. And here we arrive at the moment of hushed awe and respect because DNA is *the* code, the master architect's blueprint, God's rulebook for constructing your entire corporeal self!

The complete set of your DNA is called your *genome*, and it's all organized the same way, even though the *content* is as unique as each snowflake. The complete DNA instruction codex, or genome, for a human "contains about 3 billion bases and about 20,000 genes on our 23 pairs of chromosomes."[151] No wonder geneticist Dr. Francis Collins, who guided the Human Genome Project (1993–2008) in mapping and sequencing the billions of DNA letters that make up the human genetic instruction book, called the arrangement of these letters *"the language of God."*[152] I love visualizing the DNA within these chromones, with their double helix containing tens of thousands of genes, like some double spiral staircase with thousands of twinkly lights carefully strung around them, as if they were millions of fireflies all aglow packed with energy and information, except for efficiency's sake, here they are compacted into super tightly-looped, back-and-forth coils, in a concentration similar to the unbelievable number of rubber bands that get packed inside a golf ball; however, here it's the *genes* that are contained along *each* of the double-stranded DNA molecules. Now we are getting to the nitty-gritty of your matter: your genes hold the DNA, which contains "the information needed to build the cells of a living organism *and* pass traits to offspring. Such traits include number of limbs, blood type, eye color, and <u>risk for certain diseases</u> (emphasis mine)."[153] Such "risk" implies the potentiality for mutations like the **huntingtin gene** to arise, leading to the impending reality of Huntington's Disease.

Oh, how apropos that the word "gene" comes from the Ancient Greek word γενεά, which means "generation, descent."[154] Just as any alphabet is comprised of a certain number of letters, our DNA has four chemical subunits of DNA, but the "words" of the DNA are always only three "letters" long. These words are called "codons,"* and when adequately formed, they create "sentences," which are proteins. What happens with a person with HD is that they have a "run-on sentence" of the would-be normal Huntingtin protein. Back to living chemistry 101: these building blocks of information in your DNA, which all lead up to the formation of you, are, as a grouping, called *nucleotides,* which, along with other elemental ingredients, march together in specific lines and form to form an actual *strand.* The nucleotide is the building block of the DNA and holds the genetic material responsible for passing characteristics from generation to generation.[155]

As I touched upon before, there are only four "letters" of nucleotides, and like children's wooden toy box letters, I now present to you the nucleotides of (1) adenine (**A**), (2) thymine (**T**), (3) guanine (**G**), and (4) cytosine (**C**). We are concerned with three of the four letters. The precise order or particular sequence of these bases determines what biological instructions are contained in a strand of DNA, and they do *not* mix-and-match pair up—these letters "like" combine in specific set and predictable ways. Chromosome #4 has the trinity of CAG, comprised only of these three letters in that order. However, I will cover how often it gets expressed in just a minute.

Please remember that while the **nucleotide "blocks"** are the constituent ingredients of the nucleic acids in the ***DNA strand,*** the **amino acid** is the building block of ***proteins***[156]; the amino acid is the most basic unit of the protein. Like many other proteins, the huntingtin protein contains the amino acid *glutamine.* In people with HD, however, *there is an excess number of glutamines in a particular protein segment.* These extra glutamines come from having too many copies of the corresponding codon (see above*) with the letters C-A-G in their chemical code of DNA. In short, HD results from having *too many copies of C-A-G* in the DNA that codes for huntingtin protein. That is why HD is often referred to as a **"trinucleotide repeat disorder.**[157] As the number of repeated triplet CAG (cytosine, adenine, guanine) increases, the patient's onset age *decreases.*[158] This inverse proportion makes for bad math and a bungled outcome. Furthermore, because the unstable trinucleotide repeat can *lengthen* when passed from parent to child, the age of onset can *decrease* from one generation to the next. People who have excessive repeats *always* incur Huntington's disease. It has since been suggested that the mutation tends to increase with every generation it gets passed onto, and this rogue huntingtin protein gains further traction, expressing itself even more vividly and grotesquely.[159]

Genetics Gone Haywire: A Gluttony of Glutamine

I now turn to the genetic landscape of my *father,* whose initials are PGA; this backstory concerns itself with the nucleotide CAG. Each DNA sequence *also* contains directions for completing a host of specific tasks in making you: creations within creations! The culprit that would forever alter my dad's life and longevity would be a misfit form of the particular protein named the huntingtin protein. And no, that is not a typo: Huntington's disease is caused by a *mutation* in the huntingtin gene, also called the HTT gene; among geneticists, it is more frequently referred to as the IT-15 gene.[160] I laugh nearly maniacally at the vast understatement of "IT," standing for "interesting transcript."[161] I should say so! Like a quarterback with a secret playbook, the genes *within* the DNA possess the game plan instructions, one of which is to *make proteins,* sometimes called "the building blocks of life." But what happens when an errant play is called? Where, how, and in what manner does the garbled message get expressed?

As I probe into that which is *not* the usual occurrence and examine the effects of an abnormality, indeed, a super specific oddball spinout on a critical yet unseen level, I state for the divine record that *God makes no monsters or mistakes,* just mighty men who are frail, each in their way. And so, before we proceed, I quickly recap the fundamentals to refresh them for myself: chromosomes are those long spindles that contain our genes, and the gene is a wee segment of the double-helixed DNA strand within that chromosome. Also present and accounted for are specially- and specifically created *proteins* the gene encodes.[162] If genes encode proteins, and proteins dictate cell purpose or function, then the free flow of information within these cells involves transcription and translation. That's enough jargon for here. How data gets is not as vital to our story as in the delicate, finely tuned mechanism of intra-cellular communication. A mistake will be made if any part of the think-tank is marred. Then we arrive at our now familiar case in my father's flesh. The outcome of all these intermarried processes and molecular activity is mainly rote and predictable, yet *how* we get there is concurrently complex and sublimely unique. Now and again, we get some surprises. So now let's go to the crime scene where the accident occurred.

To study the cause of this rare disease, we must pause on the fourth stairstep of the staircase of twenty-four pairs of chromosomes and get introduced to chromosome number 4. **Chromosome 4** is the largest of the twenty-three pairs of human chromosomes; "it contains around 1100 genes."[163] You get one copy of chromosome 4 from each parent, forming a pair. Chromosome 4 spans about "191 million DNA building blocks (base pairs) and represents more than 6 percent of the total DNA in cells."[164] Gene mutations on chromosome 4 have been linked to genetic disorders and, "in particular, those that include neurological and neurodegenerative disorders like Parkinson's *and Huntington's diseases.*"[165] A chromosome mutation is an unpredictable change that occurs in a chromosome.

Although there are many possible reasons for malfunctions, and such errors relative to the entire human population are astonishingly rare, the changes that result in HD are explicitly brought about at the point of conception *when the nucleus begins its cell division,* and, as you recall, the child gets one set of chromosomes from each parent. **In my dad's case, the structure on *one* of his #4 chromosomes was compromised during cell division when, ironically, it is time to multiply (that is, to *copy*) the aggregate of genes on them**. There are several ways the chromosome structure can change, and one of them is called duplication, when "extra copies of [the IT15, a.k.a. huntingtin] genes are generated on the chromosome."[166] Not only that, but the proteins around which the DNA strands are tightly coiled can *also* get adversely impacted in a fluke duplication process, and one of these results in the huntingtin protein. The region of the HTT gene contains a particular DNA segment known as a <u>CAG trinucleotide repeat</u>. Next, I'll expand upon our knowledge of this familiar trio.[167]

Let's plumb the depths of what's going on with these viable building blocks in the Huntington gene. As you recall, this gene contains a repeated span of the three nucleotides, C-A-G, that give further directions to encode for the amino acid *glutamine*, the "G" of the CAG sequence. What brawn this particular amino acid has! Of the three acids, *it* is the guilty culprit, the villain in this convoluted accident, because when an excess number of glutamines, in particular, has arisen, *it can cause a buildup, spillage, or a sloshing over of itself with detrimental effects in so far as the manifest expression goes.* There is another crucial molecule we must get introduced to here, if but for a moment, and that is the RNA, which stands for Ribonucleic acid; this molecule is essential in various biological roles such as coding, decoding, regulation, and expression of genes.[168] All of this amounts to a communication that becomes a matter of life and death. You'll see.

Suffice it to say, the genetic code is the set of rules used by living organisms to *"translate" information* encoded within genetic material — you know, our DNA, which is "like an archive of *blueprints* for proteins"[169] — into proteins. This translation is accomplished by the ribosome, which links amino acids in an order specified by the so-called "messenger" RNA (<u>mRNA</u>) to carry amino acids and to "read" the mRNA three nucleotides at a time.[170] During the critical stage of protein production called "translation," the cell's protein factories process a copy of the DNA — the so-called messenger RNA. However, **in patients with Huntington's disease, the messenger RNA contains an unusually high number of consecutive CAG sequences**, and you now know that the CAG includes a building plan for the amino acid glutamine. In my mind, I see this process as a pre-configured assignment of interpreting highly classified information, which, in turn, will ultimately determine an aspect of *what we become*; this is not to be confused with *who we are*. It seems to me that some microscopic clandestine think tank is assigning each of its members a specific and compartmentalized role in reading, translating, and conveying God-given instructions from the top down. We only see the result.

Therefore, any errors in the DNA would result in defective proteins, and then the détente accords are off; communication breaks down, and an aberrant message is sent. The huntingtin protein is essential for the organism's survival. If the protein is defective, brain cells may die.[171] We all have the huntingtin protein, but the damaged one becomes the resultant *mutant* Huntingtin protein. An unexpected and irregular increase in the size of the CAG segment leads to the production of an abnormally long version of the huntingtin protein. **The elongated protein comprises smaller, toxic fragments that bind together and accumulate in the neurons, disrupting the normal functions of these cells. The dysfunction and eventual death of neurons in some regions of the brain underlie the signs and cause the symptoms of Huntington's disease.[172]**

Less than five years after my dad died, scientists identified a structure of molecules regulating this huntingtin protein's production. In 2013, one geneticist, Dr. Sybille Krauss, indicated that "we were able to show that this complex binds to the messenger RNA and controls the synthesis of defective Huntingtin." When the scientists reduced the concentration of this complex of molecules in the cell, the manufacture of the defective protein was turned down, as if it had become unplugged. Dr. Krauss continued, "If we could find a way of influencing this complex, for example, with pharmaceuticals, it is quite possible that we could directly affect the production of defective Huntingtin. As it is, an increase in the size of the CAG segment leads to the production of an *abnormally long version of the huntingtin protein.* What that this kind of treatment would *not just treat the symptoms but also the causes* of Huntington's disease."[173] Oh, what that this could be!! However, we are not there yet, and that is not the focus of our story; I just felt compelled to share with you *what might become a reality*, but for now, we must stick to what *was* and *is*, so I return to our messy tale here of what happens with there's too much glutamine in the cocktail. In my mind, I see our DNA Slinky with glutamine juice splattered onto the fourth step, which has become sticky; our soles will get stuck. As I am no geneticist, at this point in our sketch, I must quote what I cannot verbalize for you otherwise. I find the following description particularly lively, as if physics, chemistry, and biology were engaged in a brutal battle deep within my dad's brain:

> Because glutamine is a polar or "charged" molecule, <u>the overabundance of glutamine causes links to form within and between proteins</u>. Htt molecules [the HTT *gene,* which provides instructions for making the huntingtin *protein*] <u>"stick"</u> to one another, forming strands held together by hydrogen bonds. <u>Rather than folding into functional proteins, they develop into tangled, rigid groupings known as protein aggregates</u>. These fibrous protein aggregates accumulate and *<u>interfere with nerve cell function</u> <u>by entrapping key cell regulatory factors</u>*.[174]

It is due to the erratically expanded CAG, mainly that finicky G therein, that this toxic mess is created. <u>The CAG segment is *typically* repeated 10 to 35 times</u> within the gene. In people with Huntington's disease, the CAG segment is repeated <u>36 to more than 120 times</u>.[175] Among individuals with between **40 and 50 repeats — and this accounts for "an estimated 90% of people affected by HD worldwide,"** which included my dad — statistically speaking, "CAG repeat length has been shown to account for approximately 44% of the variation seen in the age of onset."[176] Other (environmental) factors also contribute to the age of onset of HD in these individuals. Genetic testing identified that my dad's CAG counts — the *pair* of them which are located on that #4 chromosome— were 23 and **41**. As I mentioned earlier, we don't know from which parent *he* inherited his 41, let alone the count of the silent carrier's one. The count of the *normal* CAG trinucleotide will always be overshadowed and dominated by the nefarious one whose count went into calamitous overdrive. A picture says a thousand words, so I'll show you what this looks like by displaying an average count in contrast to the defective one over twice its length. To bring it closer to home, I'll put in **bold** when we pass from Dad's 23 to 41 repeats:

CAGCAGCAGCAGCAGCAGCAGCAGCAGCAGCAGCAGCAGCAG
CAGCAGCAGCAGCAGCAGCAGCAG**CAGCAGCAGCAG**
CAGCAGCAGCAGCAGCAGCAGCAGCAGCAGCAG
CAGCAGCAG

Let's now dive deeper; there are critical numbers within numbers. To recap, individuals with an abnormally large number of CAG repeats in the HD gene produce a mutated version of the huntingtin protein, which contains too many glutamines. The HD gene (IT15 gene), which encodes huntingtin, is located on the human chromosome 4 and consists of 67 <u>exons</u>.[177] An exon is any part of a gene that will encode a part of the *final* molecule essential in various biological roles such as coding, decoding, regulation, <u>and expression of genes</u>.[178] Think of these exons as sub-units or sub-sections on the protein where chunks of information are stored. In protein-coding genes, exons can include sequences that code for amino acids — including our now familiar glutamine — and untranslated sequences. The disease-causing mutation is a CAG repeat expansion within exon 1 of the HD gene (HD exon1). The CAG repeat is then translated into a type of stretch. **The disease will manifest when this stretch "exceeds the critical length of 37 glutamines (pathological threshold),"** whereas 8–35 glutamine residues in huntingtin are tolerated by neuronal cells."[179] It's black and white, yes or no. I repeat to emphasize that *everyone* has the huntingtin (HTT) gene, but only those with a *mutated* form of the gene will develop the disease. When it's all said and done, this amounts to a minuscule percentage of people, which may explain why you may never have heard of this disease before. I know it as the disease that *would* have killed my dad, that is, had not *another* disease taken him more swiftly and less painfully had HD had its way. Regardless, it shook my world and robbed me of my dad "before his time," as they say.

We will observe the slow train wreck caused by the damaged DNA that has its final fallout in our brain and bearings. Since we know *where* the error occurred on the Huntington gene, let's look at what this excess count of the CAG stretches looks like and learn how its imperfection mars the map or directions. This huntingtin protein is "very large" and "seems to have many functions, *especially as the brain is developing before birth*,"[180] yet all this is not fully understood. Although the huntingtin protein's exact function is unknown, the mutated protein is thought to be responsible for the widespread neurodegeneration in HD.[181] The DNA "likes to stick to itself, forming a structure like a hairpin,"[182] with the Cs and Gs of the CAG fusing. I visualize this portion of the DNA as spaghetti that will stick together while boiling (with no added oil) and come out in ropey clods. When a mutant gene gives faulty instructions during cell division, there is a tendency for this replication process to get stuck and then for *more* copies of the CAG to insert themselves than is usual. As a result, the translated protein huntingtin contains disease-causing expansions of glutamines that "make it prone to *misfold* and *aggregate*."[183] I imagine this like a stack of misfolded clothes, already in an already too-tall stack, ready to topple over from the effects of its height *and* not being folded perfectly. This misfolding protein strangles and murders nerve cells in the brain, and there are specific parts of the brain. I will tell you about the particular and peculiarly impacted areas in the next chapter. This alien form of the Huntington gene very gradually accumulates in aggregate chunks and specific parts of the brain; these chunks are actually "sticky lumps of proteins within the cells that cause the death of the cell"[184] over the life of the person as if some rogue message got encrypted in a plane's flight's management system that turns it into a kamikaze plane on a suicidal mission at the time it is in full flight. The plane wobbles in the airways of the affected person's brain.

I find it fascinating that these clumps of piled-up CAG expansions are "trashing" their local environment so that even structures that could clean up this mess are neutralized! These aggregates demonstrate their toxic functions, which ultimately lead to neurodegeneration, and this is nothing short of the death of cells and, in particular, *the decay of some regions of the brain*.[185] Amazingly, safety features built into the cell might usually correct or regulate the impact of such protein misfolding, including breaking down and clearing out these misfolded protein clumps, like taking out its own garbage, but this gets impeded. Why? Instead of getting chopped up and recycled, the shards of these proteins enter the cell's *nucleus*. Because the sequence of the amino acids on these proteins is off-kilter, they pile up and remain there, creating a putrid environment in the nucleus, which has "very detrimental effects on the cell."[186] These clods of rogue huntingtin proteins even "kidnap" other particular proteins[187]and prevent them from doing *their* job, one of which is to help the neural cell (in the brain) survive. In genetic-speak, the defense of the cell is referred to in simple terms as "the chaperone system."[188] And if the load of these messy stacks of huntingtin proteins *exceeds* the capacity of the cell's chaperone system, the job of which *would* have been to clear the "traffic jam" of aggregated proteins accumulating in the specific parts of the brain, does not get done, and neurons get strangulated. These clumps of defective protein heap up and scar the neurons, which cannot survive and reproduce."[189]

In short, with a diminished or damaged chaperone system, no "clearance machinery could signal to the cell that emergency measures are needed to avoid apoptosis," that is, cell death. How can I not mention that the word "apoptosis" stems from the Ancient Greek word, ἀπόπτωσις, meaning "falling off," as leaves do in autumn?[190] I suppose falling leaves are an apt image because these neurons also break down and fall off over time. This gradual decomposition-like process of these mutant proteins may help explain the relatively late onset of HD compared to other diseases.

Normal degeneration of the aging brain takes time to happen because the rate of replacement of cells slows as we get older, so with the *addition* of these particular damaged and dying neural cells not getting replaced or swept away, like a log jam deep in the cranium, the picture of what HD looks like in real time develops like a Polaroid snapshot before your eyes somewhere midway in the person's chronological spectrum. Since we don't know how many years are apportioned to us, it's impossible to give an exact age or precise moment that you will witness this *Invasion of the Body Snatcher* in your person with HD play out in real time; all you will know is that it's fact and neither film nor fiction. The slow strangulation of the brain that snuffs out life before its seeming time is most likely why my dad died at 72, a "spring chicken" — an analogy he used to show how young he thought he was. He would not live to be an upper octogenarian like his parents. Of course, environmental factors impact the rate of progression, but our focus in this chapter has been on nature, not nurture, and time plays a part.

It takes *years* for this detonated time bomb to explode; you probably won't notice the fallout and effects in your person with HD. Why? That's because its discernable launch typically (though not exclusively) doesn't occur until somewhere in middle age when the normal aging process accelerates cellular degeneration all over the body. So, little by little, an odd gesture here, an unusual outburst there, or an unfamiliar lack of awareness are all the clues you get. These quirks are easy to write off or dismiss for quite a while — until they get more vivid and shocking, and then you can't shut your eyes any longer. When I recall my dad's odd mannerisms or his tendency to repeat certain behaviors or phrases or movements, it seemed like his brain was stuttering or getting stuck as if his thought was a record on which a layer of dust particles clustered together, which causes the needle to get stuck in a groove, and with the same maddening sense, you hear that syllable hiccup over and over and over again in the song, with the crackles in the groove overlayed audibly as well, until it moves on because of a random incident in life that jolts it along. It ruins the song that you love. While no one suspects anything, throughout one's life, "this mutant huntingtin protein which is silently forming clumps in brain cells" [will eventually] cause them to become damaged and die."[191] When protein misfolds and amasses inside nerve cells, *the nerve cells die off*. This grand central station of commotion occurs in the brain within a few specific regions. How can you tell? The damaged brain can no longer give a clear command, and this glitch is expressed through "lost muscle coordination, a decline in cognitive abilities, and behavioral abnormalities become apparent."[192] This decline is like watching your parent turn into Frankenstein's monster in slow motion; you may mock, weep, or become exasperated as you watch the one you love become a caricature of their former self. The next chapter will rivet our attention on the particular portions of the brain that become impaired. Let's now turn the page to our last subtopic and look at the likelihood of HD getting passed on and to whom.

Probability and Statistics

What are the odds that a person would inherit this aberrant gene? Thankfully, precious few do, something to the tune of "between 1 and 3.9 percent of the general population"[193] have the mutant HD form. The chances of a child inheriting the gene mutation from the carrier parent are exactly 50/50 because you get one chromosome from each parent to make up your own uniquely combined pair. If you acquire the one with the HTT gene from the afflicted parent, you <u>will</u> have HD because the gene for Huntington's disease is a *dominant*, not recessive, trait.[194] Autosomal dominance is the term used to refer to "a pattern of inheritance characteristic of some genetic diseases."[195] "Autosomal" means that the gene in question is located on one of the numbered or <u>non</u>-sex chromosomes; in this case, as you know, it is on the fourth one. "Dominant" means that a single copy of the disease-associated mutation is enough; that is all it takes to induct the disease. (Contrast this to a recessive disorder, where *two* copies of the mutation are needed to cause an expression.) How is this so? You get one chromosome 4 from your mom and one from your dad, and because this is a *dominant* gene, if the affected one combines with the normal one, the aberrant chromosome trumps, and the person loses. It's the same odds with each child the couple produces. It does *not* skip generations. If you do not inherit the gene, the disease stops in its tracks, and you can sigh in relief for dodging a bullet. It's simply a stark black-and-white, yes-or-no, duck-or-goose outcome for the person at risk if one of their parents has HD or is in that invisible gray area with more than 26 CAG repeats but less than 40. [Please refer to the table below.]

Since the likelihood of *both* parents having this expanded gene *or* spontaneously occurring from either parent is so low, we can render this scenario negligible for its high improbability and, therefore, irrelevant to our study. It is *not* related to sex, so there is not a greater likelihood for either sex to inherit it. That said, even though there is no greater chance for either sex to inherit it, there *is* a higher probability for the expansion to be longer in males than in females.[196] Unfortunately, if and when this gene does get passed on, there is a tendency called "anticipation" such that the copying takes off where it started. The CAG count usually gets higher with successive generations where it is inherited. One such classification is "juvenile HD," which occurs when the disease develops before the person is 20.[197] Here, the CAG count for it usually starts at 55 but can be as high as 100 or more[198]. Its effects begin early, devastatingly hard, and fast, and medication to mollify its debilitating effects is typically called for. You may think all of this is t.m.i., too much information. Still, I share with you what *I* had to grapple with as I silently and anxiously devoured article after article, secretly wondering about my siblings' and my odds at this casino table of unluck.

Number of CAG repeats	Outcome
< 26	Normal range; individual will not develop HD
27-35	Individual will not develop HD but the next generation is at risk
35-39	Some, but not all, individuals in this range will develop HD; next generation is also at risk
> 40	Individual will develop HD

[199]

Conclusion

All of that notwithstanding, you should know that HD is not the only disease where DNA information is improperly copied, communicated in damaged form, and possibly passed on. Interestingly, more than a dozen diseases are caused by this expansion of the three-letter polyglutamine diseases. In *all* cases, these elongated proteins tend to accumulate in "indigestible clumps that cause the cells to die,"[200] but it is a slow death. As rare as it is, Huntington's disease (HD) is "the most common inherited neurodegenerative disease, and uncontrolled excessive motor movements and cognitive and emotional deficits characterize it."[201] I will show you how this made its entrée in my father later.

As we round the corner of this chapter to follow our story's plot in the next, I am struck by the breadth and depth of what we have covered, all the better understand that which we can never fully know or fathom; there are so many mysteries unto themselves within each of us. It is quite one thing to review the myth of the demigod Hercules, who led a charmed life in youth, and it is quite another to make this myth come to life in a man like my father, who possessed strains of greatness marred by matter unseen. You have witnessed the scope and scale of two wars my father lived through, where geography and chronology intersected in his life's graph as if we could chart destiny on an X and Y axis. What but the sense of impotent rage one would surely feel if he learned he'd been dealt such a hand? When one of Robert Frost's daughters died as an infant, in anguish and defiance, he asked God *why this could have happened*. His answer was, "What but design of darkness to appall? – **If** design govern in a thing so small." Here, Frost seems to imply that not only was there *no* reason for why she died, but that there is no order at all, like no *one in charge*, as if God is either uncaring or not so powerful. Respectfully, I couldn't disagree more. God can *neither* be omnipotent but not omnibenevolent nor omnibenevolent but not omniscient because that would abnegate His positive qualities in their supremacy. Though logic is lacking, there *is* sense in my dad's tainted gene pool. The buck goes back to and starts with us.

If you viewed my dad's brain like it were a Rorschach test with some of his inkblots smudged or blemished, **we do not get to judge the value of a man's life by the outcome of a genetic test, a degree earned, or one's self-acclaimed pedigree; instead, it is by the love he breathed in and out of his heart's life.** Just as the third daughter on *Fiddler on the Roof* married someone outside the faith and my dad married someone of a different nationality and culture, I saw with my own spiritual eyes the "Spirit in the inner man" deep within my passionate father. The Holy Spirit dwelling in his very mortal flesh would comprehend "what is the breadth and length and height and depth [of] the love of Christ which surpasses knowledge" (from Ephesians 3:14–19). All wounds, all imperfections, all transgressions, all crimes, and every hurt and scar "as far as the east is from the west, *hath He removed from us* (Psalm 103:12 KJV). And though this is a lesson in faith and perspective that has us looking far into the unseen distance of a future restoration, let us come back a little closer to my dad's life in the next chapter, where we shall meet back up with Hercules in his early marriage. Hercules' unintended catastrophe relates to my father's crumbling marriage and an unseen disease marching silently on toward its entrance.

My father soon after they'd emigrated to the States
when he was in elementary school.

My father playing the clown among his now well-dressed family.
He would have been a freshman in high school.

This picture was taken for my father's Naturalization
document when he was a teenager.

My father trying to look cool, standing in between
his next older brother and father.

W.+l P..l Anabakos — June 1958

My father and his adopted "father" and favorite professor
(of chemistry). Here my dad is 23 years old.

Chapter 4

Grit, Grace, and the Path of Greater Resistance: 1960 – 1984

"Ρολόι κομπολόι"

Ένα ρολόι μου ΄χες χαρίσει
που το κοιτούσα όταν αργούσες
που το κοιτούσα όταν αργούσες
και το ρωτούσα αν μ' αγαπούσες

Θα το δώσω το ρολόι
και θα πάρω κομπολόι
να μετράω τους καημούς
και τους αναστεναγμούς

Τώρα δεν είσαι στην αγκαλιά μου
και την καρδιά μου η ζήλεια τρώει
τι να το κάνω τέτοιο ρολόι
κάθε του χτύπος και μοιρολόι
   — <u>Άννα Μπακιρτζή</u>

"Watch Worry Beads"

You had given me a watch
which I looked at when you were late
which I looked at when you were late
and which I asked if you loved me.

I will give in the watch
and I will take worry beads
to count the sorrows
and the sighs.

Now you aren't in my arms
and jealousy eats at my heart
what should I do with this watch
each of its beats a lament.
   — Lyrics by Anna Bakirtzi (1967)

"Good character is not formed in a week or a month.
It is created little by little, day by day. Protracted and
patient effort is needed to develop good character."
– Heraclitus (540-480 BCE)

"Worse than a true evil is it to bear the burden
of faults that are not truly yours."
by Euripides (~485– 406 BCE)

As challenging as the previous chapter was to marshal in, it is time to crack open another bittersweet chapter in my father's life. We are now here, but *this* chapter goads me differently. In chapter 3, I wove together historical events, including some staggering particulars in my dad's youth. Then I fused it with the genetics of HD so that you would better appreciate my father's core mindset and values. In *this* chapter, you will become better acquainted with who my *dad* became; our focus here is to have you appreciate the man *before* the disease bungled his brain. Unlike the last chapter, where I included dates and historical events to articulate when this began, that ended, or how some genetic process was transpiring, there is nothing neat and tidy about trying to differentiate my dad's innate personality from his disease-riddled one. Like some hungry vulture, HD pecked away at the shell of his identity and nature. It snatched parts and pieces of him, laying waste to his personality, but at a tortuous amble; however, the heist was not complete.

You already know that my dad was a man of science and one with a great passion for life. HD would erase him down to his "Greek nub," as I was want to describe him in the last years of his life. We are not there yet. Where his "normal" life ended and the disease's conquest began proves to be like two jagged and erratic overlaying parabolas on his life's graph. The HD version of himself would grow increasingly apparent to all but himself, yet called out by none. Life circumstances announced its arrival. While my dad was in the fullness of his manhood in his thirties, his HD was present but not accounted for. It had not yet begun to whittle away parts of his wits; bit by bit, this started in his forties. We had no "ready, set, go" or the crack of a shotgun to know beyond a shadow of a doubt that "it" was to make its debut. Instead, among *this* chapter's quarter of a century, HD would make its fleeting and sporadic cameo appearances in the form of, say, the slip of an expected moral code or some usual but hyped-up emotional response. We just thought our dad was having one of his weird moments. We told ourselves that, other than he wasn't like other American dads, he was still alright; there was nothing wrong with him. This was also true; we just didn't realize we would get a bonus feature. As I said, none of us knew what "it" was. Later, when he was pushing fifty, the terminating point for *this* chapter's focus, we would catch in the corner of our eye the faintest flicker of an erratic movement in his comportment. Mildly amused, we would chalk it off to some untamable Greek moment where freedom trumped order, even if in his body. If we weren't embarrassed or amused, sometimes we were a little envious of his ability (or lack of concern) to say and do whatever many wished they *could* have.

As I began this chapter, I admit I had difficulty picking a cut-off date, year, or occasion that declared he "had" it. My focus and aim now will be to mete out the meat and potatoes of who my dad was before his early symptoms occurred. Once you become familiar with my dad's ways and means — and maybe even come to love him — and after that, learn all about what that time bomb would do to his brain, then you will be prepared to join me in the rest of his bumpy rollercoaster ride during the last score or so of his life. I will now march us up to the significant, life-altering event of my parents' divorce, the line in the sand for *this* chapter's finale. At this life junction, we will switch bait from tragedy to trauma, from indiscernible to the undeniably apparent in both mind and manner in the next. You already know that he was *born* with the disease, but HD is not like cancer or some devastating car wreck where you can point to a clear before and after. No, it stalks and sneaks and steals your beloved while leaving precious shards of them in its wake.

I look forward to giving you glimpses of his intrinsic ways and means *rather* than scribing some blow-by-blow chronology. First, I'll share relevant memories from the score of years when I lived at home under my parents' roof; then, I'll highlight aspects of his personality so you can grasp who my dad was before the raid began. For the final third of this chapter, I will present a mini-primer of the particular parts of the brain that get altered due to the genetic aberration you learned about in the last chapter. Cause and effect, action and reaction, behavior and consequence, it's still my dad, truth or dare, catch him if you can. I will show you and tell you about my dad's before so you can better sympathize with him when the after begins.

This Chapter's Epigraphs

If you have read either of my two previous books, you are familiar with my proffering a few quotes to launch the chapter and prepare our minds and hearts for what is to follow. I use them to set the stage: iconic moments and favorite family fables that will reveal my dad's primal self. The first quote is an excerpt from my dad's favorite Greek song; it brought him ecstatic joy, and he listened to it often with his eyes closed. Without knowing the words to give shape to the feeling I had, even at five, I could tell there were other places my dad had been to and loved and missed. I just knew I wanted to be there with him because of the sense of yearning he showed! The etymological roots of the word "κομπολόϊ" (komboloi) evolved from "κομποσκοίνι," the Greek word for "prayer rope."[202] My dad did not possess one, but I'm sure in his mind's eye, he fondled one. Unlike the rosary beads you find quietly caressed by those speaking to God in many Catholic-dominated cultures, prayer is not the primary purpose of those who handle the komboloi in modern Greece. Perhaps the act is something for fidgety hands to do; I suspect it means something different to each man. Usually, the length of worry beads is "approximately two palm widths" and has a short tassel at the end. This string of small, unbreakable beads carried by many Greek men walking about is commonplace. They hold, finger, and flick this band of beads with machismo, pomp, and circumstance as they stride and stroll. To me, the form of the hand's movement is similar to that of Greek priests who hold and firmly swing out the incense-emanating censor as they walk up and down the aisles, except here, it is a tiny, quick upward flick; if its sound were notated on a sheet of music, we would add the term *staccato*. It's a soft clack that becomes as familiar as men playing with pocket change. The click also reminds me of backgammon pieces being moved to their destined spot on the board or the aggressive throw of the die hitting the wood as men play *tavli*, backgammon, outside Greek coffee shops.

In my research, I discovered that these Greek beads can be fingered and counted quietly, for, as the lyrics speak in this song, "in every knot, I say a prayer." We had worry beads displayed in our home like some vestige or modern relic of Greek culture in a museum, but I never saw my father pick them up or quickly flip them. Still, "Watch Worry Beads" lyrics spoke to my dad. His parents gave him an Omega watch, which he loved, and I'm sure he glanced at it frequently when my parents were dating. My mom was habitually late, and I'll wager his heart secretly wondered if she would ever come to love him. If, at its root, jealousy comes from a fear of lacking, my father's insecurity manifested itself in the form of the green-eyed monster. At times, his jealousy could overtake him. It's little wonder that this deadly sin would impinge upon him: he had already lost more than he could bear or bring to mind, his native, craggy soil. Therefore, I would imagine my dad flicking those komboloi beads. He was ever the optimist but also a man praying that love would never leave him. Let's move on to Greek philosophy.

I next chose a quote by Heraclitus because it reminds me of my father's life motto, "patience and persistence," which in Greek is "υπομονή και επιμονή"; these two Greek words are near homonyms. Greek philosophy is chock-full of sage advice on developing good character, and its more oriental orientation highlights that nothing of substance or true success comes quickly; instead, protracted and patient effort is what is called for to develop sound character. Though my dad's energy could be as intense as if one were standing next to a bonfire, his *modus operandi* was to set his sights *far* ahead and march the steady, long-haul trek to enable him to accomplish incredible feats in life, be it gaining his doctoral degree, or later, running a marathon or two or five with a broken heart. I next chose a quote from the Greek playwright Euripides, who gave voice to Hercules in dramatic verse from the original myth.

Though no martyr, I could call my dad a victim of twisted fate for reasons you already know that stem from historical and hereditary reasons; *these* constitute the "burden of faults *not truly his*." He would *also* be blessed *and* cursed with selective and willful ignorance, making him naively blind to problems right under his nose. His natural tendency and life habit was to look farther down the pike and see the potential rather than the actual. However, he was no mere dreamer. Part of being the eternal optimist translated into my dad's swift dismissal of ingesting anything that he deemed harmful or interfering, which, as a youngster, he had no choice but to bear, either while he lived in war-torn Greece or under his mother's thumb. Later, he refused to take *any* responsibility for the demise of his marriage. Instead, a brusk bewilderment and rage were his mental garments; such a mindset came from a boundless optimism where the possibility of failure *did not register*. I'll start by sharing relevant memories from the score of years when I lived at home under my parents' roof; afterward, I'll select highlights of his life and personality so you can discern who my dad was to his core before HD presented itself. When I mete out this chapter's portion of Hercules' life, let me now cut to the chase and give the spoiler alert that while we *do* come to the pivotal and devastating turning point for *Hercules,* which, as you may already know, in a fit of madness, he murdered his wife and children, thankfully, *there is no such parallel of manslaughter with my dad.* That said, my dad would experience trauma, which modern psychiatrists tell us is second only to death in terms of its crushing impact, and that ugly event is divorce. He'd already suffered through war, but he would never have seen marital fracture coming. It broke him.

My father was as devastated and in as much despair as was when our demigod Hercules unknowingly committed *his* crime of passion. During a hallucinatory state, he imagined himself killing perceived enemies. Since no such parallel exists, I will offer you the personality features of Hercules' which my father also possessed in his mental landscape. This is how I will tether their stories together. This is no bare-bones biography, and my father's tales will not be confined to linear progression; instead, we shall explore his thematic expressions in common with Hercules. In the latter portion of this chapter, you will peer and probe at the specific parts of the brain that became altered due to the genetic aberration you learned about in the previous chapter. The particular segments of the brain most impacted by HD cause certain behaviors to get either inflamed or dampened as the disease gets cranked up. You'll witness this in the next chapter. Let's return to where we left off with Hercules; he had just married Megara when we last met him.

Hercules' Madness and Manslaughter

As is the case in any investigative reporting, I not only found the original myth offering us a glimpse into the life of Hercules, but I came upon two play versions as well, one by Euripides, called *Hercules* (written c. 420-415 BCE), the other by Seneca called *The Madness of Hercules,* (written between 49-65 CE).[203] The myth is the briefest and offers a pale exploration into Hercules' core values; however, its chronology and storyline are the most true, so I will use it as the sequencing framework for my account. That said, although the playwright Euripides flips the order and has Hercules performing one of his labors *before* the multiple manslaughter, I find his delving into Hercules' mindset worth sharing because my dad also possessed a stoicism that bears sharing. According to the *mythological* account, with Hercules fresh back from his relatively recent exploits and successes in Thebes, his *early* years in marriage to Megara had to have been happy ones. She bore him three sons, and Hercules was devoted to Megara and his family. Bliss and contentment would prove to be a sure sign that change was on the way. Still fuming over her husband's infidelity, which produced this brave demigod, Hera continued her rant. She never ceased being bent and determined to exact her revenge upon Hercules to get back at her husband.

The crimes of the father would surely visit the son. After all, she is the goddess of marriage, and Zeus's son would be a constant reminder of her husband's infidelity. Ultimately, Hera bewitched Hercules into believing that Megara and his sons were his enemies. In his deluded state, fearing for his and his family's lives, one starless night, he went into protection mode and savagely murdered his wife and their three sons.[204] According to the original *mythological* account, Hera manipulated Hercules to send the Fury of madness upon him. Not being in his right mind, he mistook his children for those of Eurystheus, his cousin and King of Mycenae, and in a fit of blind rage, he first attacked his brother's son, but somehow, he managed to escape. Then, in his deranged state, Hercules mistook his loved ones for enemies, shot down with bows and arrows his children, wife, and nephews, and then "flung their bodies in a fire."[205] He massacred them all![206] When he came to, he found himself in his "blood-stained hall with the dead bodies of his wife and sons around him."[207]

It was his stepfather, Amphitryon, who informed Hercules that it was he who had killed his own dearest but that it was not his fault because he had been out of his mind. Unlike our contemporary society, which would have furnished him with a defense attorney who would have encouraged him to take a plea of innocence because of insanity and do time for involuntary manslaughter, Hercules would not hear of taking what he considered the coward's way out by accepting such an excuse. He alone was culpable! Instead, wildly grief-stricken and not knowing *what* to do to make up for this heinous act, initially, he "shut himself up in a dark chamber for some days."[208] What came to him next was to rush out and kill himself to atone for this crime of passion.

Had it not been for his best friend, Theseus, who clasped Hercules by his still-bloodstained hands and offered him encouragement and a different perspective, he might have succumbed to plans for self-slaughter. Even if he hadn't followed through, Hercules was sure that he would live a life of shame and ridicule after that. Instead, Theseus told him, "Men of great soul can bear the blows of heaven and not flinch. Even so, suffer and be strong."[209] Thankfully, Hercules was dissuaded from committing suicide. Still, unlike Theseus, who did *not* believe his friend was guilty of murder he did not *knowingly* commit, Hercules remained convinced that he should do time for the crime in *some* capacity. After all, he *still* felt like a vile pollution and loathed himself. He had killed his family! There was no blaming the gods for this. Oh, no! To blame Hera wasn't even a thought! Therefore, he continued with Theseus from Athens, where he'd initially left home and then moved to Delphi.

You may recall that Delphi was an important ancient Greek religious sanctuary sacred to the god Apollo and home to the famous oracle of Apollo, who gave cryptic predictions and guidance to inquiring individuals. The oracle — the Pythia or priestess — would answer questions from visitors wishing to be guided in their future actions.[210] Having arrived in Delphi, Hercules understandably sought to consult the oracle so she might instruct him how to atone for this egregious sin. The oracle told him that the punishment would fit the crime and that, considering what he did, "only a terrible penance would do that."[211] She indicated that Hercules would have to visit King Eurystheus and serve him to repent for what he did.

As the story goes on, he submits to the oracle and willingly goes to his cousin, King Eurystheus, to do whatever he demands to be made righteous again. How could he refuse? In turn, King Eurystheus would decree that Hercules would have to complete twelve arduous and nearly impossible labors to atone for what he did to his wife and children.[212] According to the chronology of the *myth*, the next portion of Hercules' story is the one that launches him into *the* most famous of all escapades of the demigods: his "labors." Dear reader, I need to give you a heads-up that these "labors" will take place in Volume 2 of this book to tell my dad's story. At that point, I will have us switch protagonists, and we will move from focusing on my dad, our "Hercules" in *this* portion of the book, to me, his daughter and would-be caretaker. I will be doing the *herculean* tasks in the second half. My dad's life will continue from noun to adjective, crime to punishment, and destiny to deliverance. However, there is nothing "normal" about a man "accidentally" killing his wife and children, let alone inheriting Huntington's disease. In the meantime, let's jump back to what the *playwright*, Euripides, rolled out in dramatic rendition: who

Hercules was. Through this prism, I will expound upon who my father was before his disease came to the forestage.

Since Hercules is the figment birthed in some Greek imagination and is not an actual person, we can read myth and dramatic accounts of this larger-than-life figure, but no biography exists. Other than miraculous tales and quasi-historic accounts, we have no other account to vivify his personality traits. My dad was flesh and blood, gut, heart, and soul. Just as Hercules was an anomaly in his family and community for being half god and half man, you will see how my dad aligns with Hercules because he was odd-man-out in our family. And although he became an American citizen, his spirit was ever and always Greek. My dad often acted as if he was a demi-god.

Pride always doth cometh before the fall, but acceptance and acknowledgment of our role do not. Hercules *accepted responsibility* for a tragedy contrived by an *outside* force (i.e., Hera), which *he* brought to fruition, albeit not in his right mind. My dad's marital "death" came about in part because he rejected any part he may have played in bringing about its demise. It was not Hera but his heredity that wrought my dad's brain into a state of an unsound mind, but, like Hercules, he was not made of the same stuff as the rest of the mortals in his family. Hercules had no more say in his parents' illicit union than my dad did in combatting the disease he unknowingly inherited. And while Hercules knew who his father was, my dad had no notion from whom he had inherited a ticking time bomb that would detonate in the gray of his middle age. Neither my dad nor *any* of us would learn if he inherited the defect from his father (or mother) or whether it came about spontaneously, like some improvised move in a Greek dance. Also, in inverse relation to Hercules, it would not be my dad who murdered his wife, but in leaving my father, it was my mother who nearly "killed" my dad's spirit. Know *I cast no stones*. I have not walked in either's footsteps. Was there a fate or force exacting its revenge upon my dad and his sins, or perhaps the sins of his father? No. Again, I return to the stark reality of our fallen flesh and broken world, which only finds its future restoration through our Savior and ultimately in the new heaven. Let's come back to earth and tell our story.

As you now know, Euripides' popular *dramatic* account of this myth flips the sequence of a few events and even has Megara escaping Hercules' murderous clutches. The appeal of a heroic hybrid of man and God is undeniable. However, let's look past the multiple versions of Hercules and focus on the primary sources of the myth. The original Greek narratives of Heracles are "frequently treated with a *religious* importance _beyond_ that of the other mythic heroes."[213] In his play of Hercules, Euripides honored this religious hue and incorporated "a prayer vocalizing the unlimited power of the gods and man's _inability to change his sorrowful situation_."[214] Maybe Hercules needed worry beads of his own.

The degree to which Hercules was manipulated by a goddess such that he lost his sanity required an equal and counter-balancing dependence on *other* divine forces to recalibrate his moral equilibrium and rectify his wrong. Hercules' comportment of strength, fortitude, valor, and determination for which he is so well-known, is fundamentally based on an abnegation of self and chiseled self-discipline which subordinate personal wishes or desires to achieve the greater goal, which, in Hercules' case, was a vindication of his wrong-doing and expiation of sin. After all, no one but he took those lives. This is what makes him a "spiritually complex persona."[215] No, my father was never guilty of the murder of his wife, let alone of infanticide, but he was an outgoing and willful man with a ferocious temper. He also possessed an incredible reserve within that enabled him to achieve success and endure hardships that might leave others pale or panting. Let's take a look at this inner strength.

The Choice of Hercules: The Path of Suffering

How are *Hercules'* moral fiber and life's pitch reflected in my *dad's* personality and values? It is an attitude, posture, and bearing toward life that both men adopted and radiated. When Hercules was a young man, not knowing what course of action or direction to take, he sequestered himself to contemplate the matter further. He found himself facing a fork in the road as to which path to take, and he confronted two goddesses at the start of each road. The alluring and comely one named Kakia (or "Vice") offered him a life of ease, delight, and comfort. The other goddess, also beautiful but humble and modestly attired, was called Aretê (or "Virtue"), and she forecasted an arduous path for him with significant losses and sufferings, that is, "one that would require hard work where he would encounter many hardships."[216] Hercules chose the latter, accepting that *good does not come from ease*. Such is a seemingly innocuous but life-altering decision we all must make, whether in the magnitude of some harrowing moment or a pivotal choice confronting us on how best to conduct ourselves.[217]

This critical decision is what Socrates famously called "The Choice of Hercules,"[218] the story is recounted by the historian Xenophon in his collection of Socratic dialogues called *Memorabilia*.[219] Xenophon was a student of Socrates. In it, we find the compelling argument that appealed to Hercules: "Nothing that is really good and admirable is granted by the gods to men without some effort and application."[220] Hercules concluded that the gods set the price at a high premium for genuine, meaningful, and lasting satisfaction. Truthfully, such a high-stakes commitment is required for gain and glory or in the pursuit of excellence. Does not Jesus promote the same when He uttered a parallel paradox to His twelve, "If anyone wants to be first, he shall be *last...*" (Mark 9:35). Of course, Jesus was a real man, the Son of the living God, and our Savior. Hercules is a myth; he comes from the mind of a man God created. And as the Apostle Paul would remark in his re-evaluating temporal hardship when contrasted to the gain of glory and Christ, "I consider everything a loss,...garbage" (Phil. 3:8 NIV). No, I am not melding myth with messiah. May it never be! However, I *am* suggesting that Hercules imbues the value that suffering for the good carves a finer character and promotes others over self. My dad also leaned in this direction, except that "others" for him began and ended with his family.

In a way, we can find the same expression in the path of Hercules in the passion of Christ Himself. The origin of "passion" traces its roots to the Latin word *"passio,"* which means "suffering, enduring,"; the notion behind it is an acceptance or taking on "that which must be endured."[221] Why else would Jesus famously require of all of His followers, both then and now: "If anyone wants to come after Me, he must deny himself, take up his cross, and follow Me... For what good will it do a person if he gains the whole world, but forfeits his soul" (from Mt. 16:24 and 26)? He led by an example nonpareil: contemplating excruciating death on a cross for all mankind's sake, Jesus submitted to His father with "soul deeply grieved..., saying, "...yet not as I will, but as You will" (from Mt. 26:38–39). Again, let no one think I am suggesting Hercules is like our Lord and Savior; banish the thought! However, we *can* find merit in an ethic they both lived by: a self-denial not for its own sake but for the greater good. It denotes a pledge to do what is right based on devotion to God and "adding self-control, perseverance, and love" (from 2 Pet. 1: 6–7 NIV).

My Father Blazes His Own Path

And like his namesake, the Apostle Paul, my father, Pavlos, in his own way, would spend his life trying his best to "fight the good fight of faith" (1 Tim. 6:12), which necessitated *putting himself last* —not that it came easily. Though the Greek Stoics' heyday was in the third century BC, fizzling out around Christ's time, the Romans revisited the stance. In 180, Roman Emperor Marcus Aurelius famously said, "The impediment to action advances action. *What stands in the way becomes the way.*"[222] The Stoics took Hercules' choice as a metaphor promoting the ideal that the means to achieving the good life. They said it was better to face hardships, rise above them, and excel than to "embrace easy-living and idleness, and allow your soul to shrink [where] personal deterioration or stagnation results."[223] I think that neither Hercules nor my dad sought self-actualization. Still, somewhere in the blood, sweat, and tears of their core, they accepted that it takes grit and pushing oneself to achieve success, and both of them were willing and able to do so, each in their own way and for their purposes.

Bringing the path of virtue up to speed and date, I can see that such a mentality aligns and rides in tandem with the immigrants' notion of how the American dream operates. To gain the coveted destiny of "life, liberty, and the pursuit of happiness," many immigrants have followed the recipe for achieving success, which calls for working hard, sacrificing, getting an education, not to mention a little luck and pluck and many prayers. You need not be a god or one who comes from a particular background, hue, or family to more than make it.

Although my dad did not have the tragic impetus or moral imperative to rectify wrongs, as did Hercules, he *did* accept the tenet that he would persevere through adversity and expend himself with all vim and vigor to accomplish his goals. My dad was also a clever and practical man, and he garnered help and curried favor when, where, and how he could; Hercules was no different. Both Hercules and my dad were willing "to face obstacles and overcome them, uncomplaining, by following the rougher path in life — *the hero's path*."[224] That said, neither claimed such a title. There is one significant difference between our hero and my dad: whereas most people naturally *prefer* to have support — be it the proverbial dangling carrot or pat on the back — someone, something, or some positive thought, initially, my father fed off the *opposite*. How so? He made good use of his figurative "stick" — his parents' grumblings, which expressed doubt, disbelief, disappointment, and the like.

My dad adopted the "I'll-show-them" mentality and distilled the toxin of low expectations, negative feedback, and life-sucking pessimism into a mental fuel that spurred him on to success *and* vindication. This was not asceticism for its own sake but a self-generated fortitude, and *despite* their skepticism, he would reach his goals. Like Hercules, my dad didn't need auditory invectives to apply pressure to squeeze out some action for and from himself. Perhaps it is because he already felt like a winner: he had survived two wars in less than a decade; therefore, what more could life do to keep a good man down, especially here in this land of plenty? Maybe the fact that he was the "boufoss," the fool of his family and ever the kid brother, made him feel free because no one took him seriously. After he left the state to pursue his academic aims further, perhaps incredulousness turned into walls of silence. And can you imagine when they finally met his American bride? There *had* to have been wailing and gnashing of teeth! That was the last straw!

He would shield and insulate himself from their firing squad of reproach and recrimination by living several states away. A byproduct of getting ahead (and leaving them behind) was that, like Hercules, he flexed his mental muscles and proved his doubters wrong. He was his super-hero! It also didn't hurt his odds that he left home and joined forces with a woman doing the same. He felt liberated again by releasing himself from his family's confining or prescriptive expectations! Even though my dad's head may have been in the clouds, like Hercules, he always kept one foot on the ground. Later, as Hera would hound Hercules, my dad had HD nipping at his heels.

The story of Hercules does not concern itself with the mundane details of daily life, nor is this account of my father a strict biography. Although I carry the chapters along natural, chronological lines, my overarching aim is to underscore the ways and means with which he came into this world, his innate personality and outlook, which both life and he would shape. These inherent qualities predate when and how his disease would distort his frame and warp his mind. I will identify and highlight the quintessential attributes of my dad's disposition and nature by using specific themes in Hercules' life as my guideposts. You will see my dad come to life. Like Hercules, my dad had one strike against him that began before he was born; however, unlike our demigod, my dad's being born with a disease was not caused by some jealous goddess but by the original pair's disobedience to God. The subsequent punishment due to us all got played out in my dad's "defective" genes, and a disease was birthed in him, which ended in his (likely) early demise. It's as if he came with faulty wiring. That Christ took on and up sin to reverse the course of human history; my dad celebrated every Easter without fail.

Unlike Hercules, I do *not* believe my father had an epiphany or the moral compunction that Hercules demonstrated, but then again, my dad never committed manslaughter, let alone struck anyone. Instead, he "killed" any dreams or plans his parents may have had for him — *not* by beating them but by *joining* this wild, wild west. They preferred observing America from the safety of their plastic-covered armchairs in their living room, watching John Wayne westerns. What my dad shares with our mythical hero is that enviable self-confidence, zest, stamina, and drive that would have him leap buildings in a single bound. The lyrics to the song "Mighty Hercules," sung at the start of the animated cartoon, which came out the year I was born (in '63), could easily have been referring to my dad. Though far from perfect, my dad — *my* hero — would also spend his life "fighting for the right, fighting with his might with the strength of ten ordinary men. [He had] virtue in his heart and fire in every part."[225] Like Hercules, my dad was driven to accomplish greatness in his universe; they both tasted bitter defeat due to their failings close to home. Though a curious man where the natural world was concerned, when it came to intra-personal relations and interpreting the complexities and contradictions of the human heart, my dad was a blind man who couldn't read brail. He was our ostrich. Time and again, he buried his head in the sand and pretended nothing wrong had happened until the moment or problem passed. The wrong remained ignored, but sediment was still underfoot.

If he did become heated in an emotionally charged argument, my dad's temper flared like a skunk's spray radiates. He got louder and more furious as the conflict ran its course. You will see that, like Hercules, my dad could be explosive. Afterward, he swiftly went silent and deadly, like a man stewing in vinegar, as was the case when Hercules went into self-imposed isolation. We, his family members, got put "time out" — his wall of silent fury — until dad came to and normalcy resumed. Though headstrong and willful, my dad usually avoided confrontations like the plague, especially if the situation called for taking a stand for some right that was not *his*. Rather than rock the boat, his go-to was to gossip or malign his "enemy" behind their back, like some old village woman.

Let's resume and quickly finish up the loose ends where I left off with my dad in the *last* chapter; in so doing, we'll ready ourselves for *this* chapter's parallels and departures between Hercules and my dad. What that I could have been a fly on the wall when my father finally informed his parents that he had married an *American* girl. Did they drop the phone? Did they go cold and send a loud and clear message through audible silence, conveying their doubt, disbelief, and unmistakable disapproval? Did they cry, scream, and shout in froth and fury? Yes, probably all of this and more. With him would end their Greek-only family bloodline and heritage. What could be worse? My dad's heart cried, "Love trumps all!" This was *his* girl. That I know what happens next is due to my mom's reporting, *not* my father's. Mom told me that a close friend of his parents was sent down from Brooklyn to Atlanta "like some spy" or emissary to visit the happy newlyweds. This man's assignment was to check on my dad while checking out the new wife. I'm sure the report that was sent back was less than glowing. My mom said that although they knew she was of the "Heinz-57" variety, they wanted to ferret out if she had any German in her heritage. That would have been a deal-breaker, something more than they could bear; my mom was hurt and bewildered. Wasn't *he* the foreigner?

Sensing their anxiety and wanting to reassure them that, in part, she *did* marry their son for his ethnicity and to more fully introduce herself, she wrote them a long, carefully composed, and I'm sure, imploring letter. *Surely*, they would see the light! There was no phone call to reassure her that it had been well-received. Not too long after that, she found a letter addressed to her lying in their mailbox. Inside and at the bottom of the envelope was *her* letter to them, "ripped up into a thousand pieces." She was crushed. Again. How did my dad respond? Likely, he did nothing. My dad studied for his final exams during their Christmastide honeymoon, even while his bride and he lay side by side on a warm beach. He was oblivious to his bride's sighs and quiet dismay at his lack of attention. Instead, he simply blocked out or ignored others' discomfort or disappointment if it interfered with his higher aims or tasks at hand. That which had served him well to bear pressure and deprivation as a youth would severely stunt his capacity for empathy as an adult. No one bore this more than my mom; to the world, he was ambitious, happy, and headed for success.

Before I proceed further with my dad's life, it is time to shift the flow and direction and refer to specific themes as defined by Euripides in his dramatic version of Hercules. They will serve as my guideposts for what I choose to tell you about my father. Even though my grander scheme is to honor my father, first, I've got to show you who he *was* before you learn what he *became*. I will not get bogged down in marital woes or family bliss. So, what themes will frame who my father was for you? How do they relate to Hercules? These Euripidean themes include "ambiguity, dichotomy, hope, identity, moral responsibility, opposites, and theology."[226] I will sequence them in a manner and measure that *I* find helpful as if they were folders into which I will place critical documents, files, and selected content of my father's life. I will combine the themes of "dichotomy" and "opposites"; that only makes sense, but we won't get into theology in how Euripides presents it until much later, during my dad's time of dying. That said, sporadically throughout this chapter, you will notice that I refer to New Testament principles that touch upon my dad's life and cardinal values. I'll continue to connect myth and Scripture where applicable. As I recall my dad's life, I'll distill his character, personality, priorities, and temperament to their purest (though not perfect) state *before* they became tinctured and tarnished by HD. From then on, my focus in this chapter will be on my dad's real life, not Hercules' imagined one. Let's dive into the theme of "ambiguity" and see how it played out in my dad.

1. <u>The Theme of Ambiguity: Science</u>

When you hear the word "ambiguous," you might attribute this qualifier to one who is wishy-washy or indecisive; let me assure you that this is *not* the case with my father. At a tertiary glance, two areas that might seem irreconcilable but coexist seamlessly within my dad include his being both a man of <u>science</u> and <u>faith</u>. Not only this, but he subscribed to going as far as one could in <u>education</u>, yet at the same time, I would consider him an *<u>anti</u>*-<u>intellectual</u>. Let me explain. You already know that my father majored in chemistry. Although he may have been swayed towards studying this subject under the caring influence of a Greek professor who took him under his wing, it was not unnatural. Indeed, he viewed the world through the lens and mindset of a scientist, that is, one who finds himself questioning, probing, seeking, and problem-solving to satisfy his curiosity and wonder about the ways of the world, particularly those at the organic, invisible level. He was fascinated with how matter operated and was drawn to figure out how elements interacted in different contexts. He investigated the back story to discover how everything we see comes to interact. He would take glee and say, *"Water is H_2O to us chemists!"*

Once, when he helped me with my advanced placement chemistry in high school, I'll never forget that I got the distinct sense that the elements were his best friends; he understood their attributes and tendencies like we knew the personalities of our friends. He let me in on a secret, taking delight in announcing that *"the goal of every element is to become a noble gas, and they will lose or gain anything to do so!"* Truth be told, he was versed in this cryptic language of organic chemistry better than he was in the English language; furthermore, he could recall their numerical order better than he could recall our birthdays. For my dad, from the outside looking in, chemistry made order in spheres that could be chaotic, confusing, or contradictory. Perhaps by proxy or substitution, I believe it also helped make sense of the nonsensical world of his youth. Unsurprisingly, he was drawn to organic chemistry because my dad was passionate about life and possessed the mental acuity to probe her furthest mysteries.

I hold my dad's black leather, hardbound, gold-lettered dissertation submitted to the faculty of Clemson University for the degree of Doctor of Philosophy in the chemistry department from 1965. Its musty smell emanates when I open it up to peruse a few pages, and it makes me smile. Long ago, my mother told me she had typed his dissertation in the acknowledgments; however, it is dedicated to "the memory of N.B.C.," his beloved professor. The title of his thesis is "Studies in Resin Acid Chemistry." As I leaf through its sixty-four pages, I encounter terms twice the length of my four-syllabled surname, charts of foreign chemical structures that look like the hexagonal tiling in a honeycomb-like scaffold, and some of the "tiles" have circles drawn within them, and others, either trapezoids or what look like little houses connected. If his dissertation title sounds vaguely familiar to you, it is probably because my dad was working with the resin acids and essential oils that come from certain types of coniferous trees. He aimed to purify, prepare, and "convert [the resin into] potentially physiological active derivatives through various synthesizing methods." His charts include such gripping labels as the "Grob Reaction," the "Rupe Rearrangement," and "Ring A Contraction of 1-Ketonorordehydroabietane," among others, not to mention a preparation of this and a derivation of that.

You can imagine my surprise that one of the stabilizing acids he used throughout his research was supplied by "the Hercules Powder Company." His research had him experimenting with ketones, steroids, and various acids and interpreting data obtained from chromatography. The only words I recognized were ammonia, benzene, aldehyde, hydrogens, and alcohol; I couldn't tell you what a "bulky, angular methyl group" was. I think you get the idea, but his brain didn't break just for the world of science. He was constantly "problem-solving," as he would put it. That said, the issue at home dealt with mechanics or plumbing; all bets were off. Sifting through these pages has me better appreciate his pride in announcing that as a chemist, he was "cooking with chemicals." It turns out he *was* a chip off the old block! Like father, like son! It's just that this was *his* "recipe book," even if I still can't tell you what he made. In short, his extrapolating and brainstorming produced the best results in the crucible of *chemistry*, and there's no doubt he knew this was his gift.

When my father left academia for his first job in the industry, at an engineering and project management corporation called Bechtel in Columbus, Ohio, he would moonlight there and began to do experiments on his pet project, which involved a plant in Greece he had first heard as an old wives' tale called the bitter pickle plant. I have seen it growing wild over scrubby places in the Greek countryside, and its fruit looks like a pinky's-length gnarly, knobby little cucumber. Decades later, I learned from relatives that my dad asked them to send him packages containing this dug-up plant from Greece. Even now, looking back, these relatives still shake their heads and chuckle over his eccentric request. Aside from the fact that the bitter pickle plant can be eaten, I recently read in an article that it has properties that can help fight diabetes, lower cholesterol, cleanse the liver, and boost the immune system.[227] This plant, alternately called "bitter melon," contains a high concentration of antioxidants which "functions as a powerful defense mechanism against illness, and [it] also helps <u>fight free-radical damage that can cause various types of cancer</u>. In 2010, a study published in the Pharmaceutical Research Journal stated that bitter melon *has* <u>anti-carcinogen and anti-tumor properties</u>" [emphasis mine].[228]

There it is in black and white! Without understanding the science, let alone his methodology for distilling the compound from its concentrated juice to harness its cancer-fighting properties, I have complete confidence that my father possessed the expertise, vision, and drive to unlock and harness its potential. He would have started this project in the early to mid-1960s because we lived in Columbus from 1966–1969. Cancer is the second leading cause of death in the United States,[229] so to have been able to put into production such a pharmaceutical would have been *monumental*. What happened? Based on what my mother told me, I inferred that my dad was moonlighting his research and doing experiments *at work*, using *his employer's* equipment and resources.

Eventually, he "got caught," as she put it. No, they were not interested in his research and were quick to point out that there was a conflict of interest to be working on this pet project on their dime; such was unethical. I deduced that he was expected to resign, so we moved to a city in upper east Tennessee where a fellow chemist friend of his worked and helped him find employment. Eventually, he got a job as a chemist at Eton Kodak. His purpose was to take projects conceived of and done on a small-scale, experimental level in Eton's parent plant in Rochester, New York, and expand them for production-scale capacity while anticipating and circumventing potential mishaps or avoiding problems that might pop up. This required his vast knowledge of the raw materials' properties being used and his expertise in successfully performing various reactions transformed on production scales.

My dad's analytical mind was not turned on or off, depending on whether he was at home or work. If for Shakespeare, all the world's a stage, for my dad, all the world was a lab, and he was ready for experimentation at every turn, be it in the kitchen, his backroom (i.e., an office and lab combo), or out in nature. For example, in the last house he lived in, he converted his conventional heat pump to a thermo-electric one by pumping up water from a natural spring on his property so that its perpetual water flow would become an energy source that generated power to run his heat pump. It costs pennies to the dollar for *"Mother Nature's free power."* He did not need to hire someone to figure this out or install it. When I was in my thirties and would visit him, I was as likely as not to be greeted by him wearing a stopwatch like a necklace around his neck. He was *that* concerned and familiar with the operations of his efficient system; if it kicked on too early or late, that might be an indication that he needed to clear natural debris or mucky detritus from its entry at the head of the spring water, which impeded the flow of water from freely entering the pipe and heading for his heat pump system.

As I have mentioned, he was constantly *"problem-solving,"* as he put it. As I grew older, I became more appreciative of his wonderment or curiosity about how the properties of things interacted or functioned, right down to the infinitesimally smallest level. It was a natural for him. That said, he relied on his cunning and instinct when it came to penetrating the mystery of the nature of women and the complexities and contradictions of the human heart. His mind often led him astray here, but he would neither see nor say such. He also became absorbed by the workings of animals and Nature, but I'll say more about this elsewhere. For now, suffice it to say the world was both his oyster and his lab.

Faith

For those of a more conventional mindset, it might be natural to say that the flip side of the man of science would be the man of faith; that both coexist would be a clear sign of our broader theme of ambiguity, which I am addressing here. Though I will now consider my father's faith, please know that reason and faith coexisted harmoniously within him; there was no dichotomy or contradiction here. His faith had *plenty* of room for entertaining abstractions and esoteric matters, including science. Speculation and hypothesizing came as naturally to my dad as it does with the priest whose faith is robust enough to engage in conversations about God and theological doctrine, human nature, and puzzling circumstances in the world. Anyway, my father's faith was like that of a child, and I believe God blanketed him in protection.

Faith transcends and defies our desire to give form to it with explanation or justification, and my dad was ever at a loss for words when it came to expressing the nuances of his heart's language. He could not explain to my mom *why* he was a believer — he just *was*. For better or worse, but much to his relief and delight, I often finished his sentences, especially if we touched upon intangible regions like the farthest limits of human experience, including death. *"You have suuuuch a way with words,"* he would confide in relief to me. At times, this amounted to my becoming his medium, and when he would struggle to put his feelings into words, I could become his emotional whisperer or soul's translator. It didn't help that he wasn't a native speaker of English. No wonder he often couldn't generate the precise word in English to match his mindset, and he had a searching look as if he was momentarily blindfolded and attempting to pin the tail on the donkey. Spending a lifetime trying to furnish just the right word was like playing "Marco Polo," I got really good at getting warm. He was no unsolved mystery to *me*. His nods of approval, smiles of relief, and shaking his head with eyes saying, "Eureka, she found it!" all confirm that I understood him.

I tell you that to tell you this: unlike my father, although I was not raised in the manner and measure that *he* was in the Orthodox Church, where there are *no words required* for the parishioner to initiate, only those to be chimed back in unison with others in a mass rote response following the priest's first utterance, I *can* assure you that beyond a shadow of a doubt, my dad was a believer in and follower of Christ. He absorbed the church service with his whole being, and Christ was the center of his soul's attention, albeit flanked and buttressed by Byzantine icons, church elders from the past, and the local priest, all of whom were ready to provide backup. You may say that one's physical presence in church does not reveal or indicate whether one has decided to accept Jesus Christ as one's personal savior. You are right, but that is certainly not the only way *God* evaluates the state of our soul. *Who are we to judge, let alone know, the relationship a person has with Christ just because his justification or coming-to-faith testimony doesn't resemble ours?* The proof is in the pudding, in the fruit we bear for Him in our life. It seems to me that when my dad fell in love with my mom, he dropped out of favor with his family *and* the Greek community, which, as you know, includes the Orthodox Church. It made life less complicated for him to take the path of least resistance, so he took an extended sabbatical from the *Church*. Still, Christ never left nor forsook my dad (Heb. 13:5). I could tell by the look in my dad's eyes that he never abandoned his faith or his Savior. When my parents split, one of the very first things my dad did was to come back to the church. I know Jesus was glad, and it was very good for my dad.

If you have read either of my other two books, you are already aware that I spend concerted time and focus discussing the difference between the Eastern Orthodox and Protestant — especially evangelical — approaches to Christ; that is *not* my purpose here. My point is that my father's being a man of faith does not contradict his being a man of science. I think it's spectacular to witness both housed in one person! Oh, what that my father could have expressed how the two were reconciled and coexistent within him because so many folks think it cannot be. Some contend that the further we explore and explain the world around us, this disables and divorces us from faith in the Father, Son, and Spirit. I observed in my father an unassailable belief that creator and creation are as inseparable as our existence is from His reality. Without Him, simply nothing could be.

Before my parents got married, my mother practically interrogated him about his core religious beliefs, and, according to her recollection, "he ran out of the room." Her fiancée did this *not* because he was troubled or vexed over the icon of *"the eye of God staring down at him"* but because he faced her firing squad of disapproval of these ancient theatrics. It's true; he did share with her a disdain over hypocrisies observable in any number of disappointing ways among both priests *and* pastors; the institution of His Bride got in cloudy collusion with the world. As a young man, my dad adopted a view like Nikos Kazantzakis, who was threatened with excommunication for his criticism of the Church in his controversial writings. This Cretan writer's famous epitaph reads, *"I hope for nothing, I fear nothing, I am free,"*[230] and it echoes my father's heart's sentiment.

Despite his steering clear of the church, I return to focus on my father's faith, which never left him. At the time, there was no Greek Church within two hours of where our family lived. Despite whatever unresolved differences my mom and he had about deciding which church they might attend, he put his foot down and insisted that his children be baptized in the Greek Church. He sought God's stamp of approval for his babes even if his marriage had not been legitimized in the Greek Church. One sacrament done was better than none! Without fail, come high water, he attended the midnight Pascha Greek Easter service, which was nearly always roughly two weeks off from the rest of the world's date. He distinguished the different dates *not* by referring to the Gregorian and Julian calendar but by simply differentiating between "Greek Easter and American Easter." It seemed to me that Greeks were deadly serious about their mournful-looking Christ; meanwhile, we looked for pastel Easter eggs and gobbled up chocolate bunnies and jellybeans in our brand-new Easter outfits.

Once, when standing next to my father in the midnight Pascha service, I quietly glanced up and caught a glimpse of the man familiar to me, yet one whom I also did not recognize. With no words uttered to capture what I saw, I witnessed his becoming one with the body of Christ in the Orthodox Church. As they say, he was "in the spirit," and I sensed he was thirsty for *His* Spirit. Invariably, he would then reflexively reach over and take hold of my hand to share the life of this moment. Still, our family would usually leave when it was time to go outside the church *en masse* after lighting the candles within to commemorate the moment of the Resurrection. Later, when I was in college and had lost a lot of weight one particular semester, I'll never forget my father leaning over and whispering to me that I should go up to the altar and have communion *"because I was ready."* I figured that he meant that my recent and relative abstinence from the things of this world was a means to a purification of sorts.

As I stated, my dad made like a homing pigeon after my parents' divorce and began attending the recently built local Greek Orthodox Parish. Fortunately for my father, as it was contemporaneous with his divorce, the first Greek Orthodox community in the tri-cities dates back to the early 1980s. In the mid-90s, a permanent home for it was founded in Bluff City, taking the name Christ the Savior.[231] It was the size of a small banquet hall with a makeshift narthex and came complete with a portable iconostasis. It became his home base, and he no longer had to drive two hours or wait on the priest's monthly visit to some lone Greek house in our hometown. In fact, from the home he bought to this parish was less than a twenty-mile, door-to-door drive.

Only much later, when *I* came to faith and began reading the Bible, did I perchance upon Proverbs 22:6, which foretells the truism that if we "train up a child in the way he should go, even when he grows older, he will not abandon it." Of course, I immediately thought about my dad. During the last decade of his life, he would bow his head in prayer before eating — his hand reaching out under the table searching for mine, or he would cross himself whenever he thought of a dearly departed family member. I could see the miracle of faith resuscitate into a resurrection of a very human kind. I will come back to this topic again before we finish his tale. For now, I'll move on to explore one more area within the theme of ambiguity in my dad's life, and that is the see-saw of heralding education on the one hand and anti-intellectualism on the other, which amounted to elevating the simple to the sublime.

Education

By now, you can appreciate just how important education was for my father and other immigrants like him: it was the key to success, but for a man like my father, soaking up the setting of academia produced a life of its own, and it brought him great joy and satisfaction. I have all three of his diplomas facing me, starting with the one from Brooklyn College (1958), his MS from Purdue University (1961), and his PhD from Clemson University (1965). Back in the village, he would have done life with relatives and close friends known to the family. In college, the tightly knit band of brothers who made up the chemistry department created a covalent bond based on their common intellectual pursuit. It mattered not if they were from India, South Carolina, Boston, or Greece. This would have been such a stimulating and satisfying time for my father because he also had that spirit of scientific inquiry *and* pride of ethnicity fused in his frame. I recently found some black-and-white photos of my parents at a party for those in his department in Cambridge. There was a fantastic swirl of varied shades of people from different ethnicities and backgrounds, but whose common denominator was their passion for chemistry. My mom wryly quipped that a party with many men with PhDs in chemistry was "not your typical party." Undoubtedly, she implied that their sense of humor was droll, quirky, or even corny compared to their high intellect. Nonetheless, I hold one picture a little longer that someone had taken of my parents dancing together, and I saw *their* magic.

To work in the lab with other like-minded men, hearing the sound of a fluid being poured into an Erlenmeyer flask here, the purr of a Bunsen burner being turned on there, glancing over at a colleague bent over and scribbling down observations and notes in this corner, or watching one of the professors crushing some compound with mortar and pestle in his station would have been like home, sweet, home to my dad. Not long after my parents were married and my dad had completed requisite extra courses at Georgia Tech in Atlanta, and now with a child on the way, my parents packed all their worldly possessions in my dad's black VW Beetle and drove to Anderson, South Carolina where my father would earn his doctorate. I, their eldest child, was born in 1963, and by the time my next sister was born in Boston in June of 1965, my father was doing post-doctoral work at M.I.T. He was at the top of his game. He felt on top of the world and unstoppable: a little Greek boy who knew no English had, by age twenty-nine, obtained the highest degree in education possible, married a woman of *his* choosing, and was now employed at M.I.T. and in the great city of Boston, no less. Here, he would contribute to his sphere of knowledge and make a home with his young family in a duplex near Cambridge. What could be better? Let's get back to my dad's education.

I was so proud that my dad did post-doctoral work there at M.I.T. my siblings and I erroneously thought this was a bona fide degree that eclipsed or superseded his Ph.D. Having attained this summit degree and feeling like he had "made it," you should know that <u>my father evaluated everyone he met through the lens of their "getting an education."</u> To be blunt, if they had no education or, worse, showed no desire to pursue their education, they were on the bottom rung of my dad's caste system. Whenever he met someone or saw their surname in print, his brain would go to work and first figure out their ethnicity. Naturally, he would initially home in on persons like himself of a non-WASP heritage; next, he would inquire about their job or vocation. It's not so much that he hob-knobbed with only those with doctorates — that was hardly the case! But he did gravitate toward those actively pursuing or had accomplished a post-secondary education. He would be a cheerleader of the former and a cohort of the latter! Improvement always begins with *renewing the mind* (Rom. 12:2)! Most folks go on auto-classification mode when they learn the side of town and neighborhood you live in, see the brand of clothing you wear and the car you drive, or hear your speech. My father's criteria for judging a person's merit always began with their educational endeavors and accomplishments; the cherry on top was if that person cared for and celebrated his heritage. He introduced people the same way a Native American would name a person after some animal or element in nature that he resembled or something he had conquered. So instead of telling us this or that person was Sitting Bull, Black Hawk, or Cheyenne, he would smile and say, "This is Taj from Calcutta who got his doctorate at the University of Chicago," or this is "Steve Belusky, whose father immigrated from Poland. He is a physicist working at Oak Ridge." Playing a musical instrument also resonated with my dad; he had a passion for the full spectrum of musical expression, both refined and raw; the former finds its place with us here now.

Since my father had always loved music and had played the violin in high school, he attended the symphony too, not because he was a snob or wanted to hobnob with the cultured, but because he craved this music and appreciated the richness, order, and depth that classical music offers and fills you as few other types of music can. He didn't get pop music; it was like junk food for the spirit. It was customary for our family to go to the symphony; we didn't know it as "highbrow." When I was in high school, my father took me to Carnegie Hall to hear the violinist Isaac Stern perform, and as I glanced over at him, he was all ears, giddy with anticipatory delight; so was I. We took his mother, too, so that she could get out of the house. She, on the other hand, would browse the program and whisper to me the origins of the names of this or that player; I could tell she was particularly scanning for Jewish or Russian names because that would have confirmed her in the filing system who went where or did what in this mixed bag of a nation in which she resided and died, but never would call home. Contrapuntally, my father's zeal for all people, places, and things revolving around higher education sustained his primal spirit that knew no bounds. It was like we had our very own barbarian, and his love of the elemental proved a double-edged sword in its own right. Let me explain.

Anti-intellectualism

I'm not sure how my father managed "to retain the spirit of infancy even into the era of manhood," as Ralph Waldo Emerson said, but he did. Usually, one would consider the opposite of education ignorance, but for my dad, it meant an attraction to the simple things a person often passes by or takes for granted as they grow up. Not so for my dad. He never read Thoreau, but he would have approved of his decree to "Simplify, simplify!" My father had a passion, energy, and spirit that one typically finds in children, who are naturally in awe of and do not lose their sense of wonder over the essential elements in nature, be it a rock, a leaf, or a flower they discover and then gleefully bring to their parent. It's like every day was the first day of creation for my dad, and he was exuberant about sharing it with us. His inner joy and zest for life had us (and, for sure, me) following him like he was our Pied Piper or Pan the goat man, our very own shepherd. Some of my earliest memories of him revolve around our making discoveries together, as if we were the original explorers of the continent's primordial slime and feasted on mud pies.

In Cambridge, when I was two, he and I made our first snowman, and with snow up past his knees, he lifted me so I could insert the carrot for its nose. Two years later, at age four, in Columbus, Ohio, he and I graduated to rolling mounds of snow into massive white logs, transforming them into frozen tiers as a base for our snow fortress, never mind an igloo! He didn't ask or expect me to be anything I wasn't, including neat and tidy, prim and proper, or full of sugar and spice. He and I were too busy mining for life's gold. When I was five, we performed our own curious circus act: he would lay on his back with his feet outstretched and locked together, with his hands grasping his knees closed. Next, he would take hold of my hands as I stepped onto the soles of his feet, maintaining my balance as he raised me. Finally, I let go of his hands and slowly stood straight up. This is how we made our father-daughter pyramid.

For this village boy turned modern man, being a father was the very best a man could ever be. Not only did the family come first for our cave father, but he might be suspicious of others as a potential enemy. He could whiff out a fake or fraud like a bloodhound could a fox, and just as if he was some brute bouncer, you could tell by the furrow of his brow and the tilt of his head if he detected false words or lies. He was on-call to squelch the fake news of our day, which might beguile any of his family to the land of phony. Any display of pretense, false humility, or condescension based on one's wealth, societal status, or economic class alone brought out the competitive beast in him to show he could outwit, outsmart, or outperform those whose worth was found on a pedigree *not* attained by blood, sweat, and tears or at least, pulling oneself up of by the bootstraps of one's own efforts and education.

In grade school, I was embarrassed that although we lived in an affluent neighborhood, I didn't understand why my parents had no intentions of joining the country club like all our neighbors did. It made no sense to me. What was the point of living here? There were to be no tennis or golf lessons for us, no shopping for clothes with high-end logos, and no boasting based on love of football, state college, or the southern region in which we lived. My dad was not only odd-man-out in this respect, but he would show a complete lack of regard for that which the prevailing culture deemed cool, proper, or even "normal" because, for him, merit was based on survival, smarts, and sweat. His democracy ran deeper than party lines; he had a reputation at work for "treating the President of the company the same as the janitor," something I've always been proud of. What that he could have garnered the respect he craved. While I would not consider my dad a hypocrite, he did hold double standards and held himself to no bounds, rules, or credo made by any person other than himself. As a result, I believe we all were somewhat entitled and viewed ourselves as better than those for whom convention was king. But in the privacy of our home, our dad was often the fool.

One undesirable byproduct of living with a man who knew privation meant that although he sure did clean up nice, like some adolescent boy, he gravitated toward the path of least resistance where his appearance was concerned. At home, he wore a handful of tried-and-true articles of clothing, one of which was a pair of tie-dyed tan and white jeans. And if it were summer, my mom would have to remind him to wear an undershirt to dinner. He wore a pair of Golf sneakers that looked more like sandals over time. He also donned a one-piece, super-stained pair of "dungaree" coveralls, as he used to call jeans. This was his appointed uniform for mixing up chemicals or gardening. When our family went on vacations, he took that as his cue to take a break from shaving, which, for some men, might bring a casually unkempt or sexy look, but in the case of my dad, it made him look homeless.

Being a literal Spartan had its figurative application where his spending habits were concerned: spend as little as possible. Once, while visiting his parents, we stayed at the Waldorf Astoria Hotel in NY. To save money, he had us kids drag our sleeping bags through the lobby so as not to have to order a trundle bed or — heaven forbid — another room. We looked like gypsies getting ready to set up camp. The ten-hour annual trek to our (maternal) grandparents' lake cottage meant we would have to spend the night in a hotel, so back in the days before "Kids Stay Free," my dad would have us duck down in our station wagon so we would evade the view of the management who otherwise would be sure to count six in our vehicle. We knew the drill: the quick downward motion of his hand behind the front seat would command us to *"Get down! Get down!"* That said, though we all would stare at my dad in confused amazement, he might try to make the trip straight through in one day, preferably with only "pitstops" to fill up on gas (and not to relieve our bladders). It wasn't a thought that we would bring *"goodies to munch on"* along the way, so our Plymouth Fury often smelled of hard-boiled eggs and ripe bananas. My mom proved victorious in Corbin, KY, because we got to stop and eat at the original Kentucky Fried Chicken. We felt like royalty eating out on the lawn in picnic fashion! As the terrain got flatter and we counted cornfield after cornfield, the closer we got, the faster he went. Double lines were no deterrent to my dad, who treated them as a double green light for taking a chance to pass. I can still hear my mom shrieking, *"Pauuuuuuuul!"* as we faced head-on vehicle after vehicle or even a wide combine before whipping back into our lane at the last second.

After he drove like a bat out of hell, we finally arrived, and while we kids sprung out, liberated from our steel cage, my dad walked like the living dead. He headed for the sunniest spot in the yard, and like some happy hound, he would lay down on the warm grass and use it as a flat stone (or his shoe) for a makeshift pillow. He would close his eyes and bask in the heat of the sunshine hitting his face and body, snapping the first two digits of his toes and twitching his mustache in reflexive delight as he relaxed from the drive up. All things elemental came first for him, so my dad, our very own caveman, was also one who preferred meat cooked over fire. I believe he would have set up his kitchen around the grill if he could have. Still, as it was, when it was time to prepare the meal for us, you were likely as not to find him attending to a whole salmon on his trusty grill or a makeshift "Cuban grill," as he called it, which was a whole dug in the ground where he would set up a primitive barbecue. If a rotisserie were unavailable, it would be his favorite way of cooking lamb.

A final example of this flip side to his being an educated man is an odd one. He went by his own unconventional and unexpected code, one that he applied only to himself, and that was to avoid reading or taking in knowledge that would impede, curtail, or undermine his original thoughts and innate creativity. He was considered by many to be a genius in his field of chemistry. Like Sampson knowing that cutting his hair meant losing his strength, my dad didn't want to ingest what others in his field had done so that his mind wouldn't be influenced, shaded, or hampered by others' methodologies and fixed ideas. Although my mother did subscribe him to a thin journal called *Science News*, which didn't have too many pages and succinctly delivered the latest news from the various fields of science, his impulse was not to scrutinize too closely what other chemists had done because he didn't want to consider or be swayed by any particular methodology as a foregone conclusion or sole approach.

It's no wonder that when it came to reading, I knew of only three books he ever read: *Gone with the Wind*, which for him was probably like an introduction to American culture; *Oblomov*, a nineteenth-century Russian novel about a member of the landed gentry who enjoyed the simple pleasures of life but slept his life away; and *The Godfather*, which my dad had on his bedstand like some others might keep a Bible. Speaking of the Bible, someone once gave my dad a Bible after he retired and invited him to their Sunday School class. He went there enthused and full of interest and questions for the others in this "school"; faith was not an issue for him. The sum effect was that his attendance in Sunday School was brief; they didn't know what to do with this pioneer, this Greek Paul Bunyan, who sought to satisfy his inquiring mind but meant no disrespect to God. He greatly admired the Cretan author Nikos Kazantzakis, not because he loved or had read any of his many works other than like *Zorba the Greek*. That one spoke to him. My dad — our Zorba — appreciated the rebel in the author.

A mind open to possibility cannot be predicated or dependent upon man's customary laws, conventions, or logic. Whenever my dad would play chess or cribbage with his father-in-law, all bets were off, and he would astonish him by making unexpected moves that defied rationale. Only later would my grandfather shake his head in amazement that some unorthodox move of my dad's led to victory. When my dad and I played backgammon, he showed me no mercy; he was as ruthless as a conquistador for how well he knew the rules of this game where luck meets skill. As if he were Adam on assignment to name the animals around him, he preferred exploring the natural world around him. If we visited any town with an aquarium or zoo nearby, my father would take us, and we'd likely be the last to leave. I could go on about my dad's penchant for the primitive and primal, including the other end of the musical spectrum he adored, village music, be it from the Greek islands or the hollers and hills of east Tennessee. I'll switch gears and shift to the following central theme in Hercules' life, which also reverberates in my father: moral responsibility.

2. <u>The Theme of Moral Responsibility</u>

In both the mythical account and Euripides' play version, there is a particular focus on Heracles' moral character. By this, I mean that since

Hercules believed in the gods' supremacy, which was based on the premise that they could do no wrong, he would not plea bargain and argue that as a mortal, he oughtn't to be culpable for the egregious sin he had committed, all the more since it was accidental and without his awareness. He refused to point a wagging finger or place blame on the gods' machinations or Hera's manipulations. No, if the gods did exist, they must also be perfect; therefore, he would shoulder responsibility for his actions, including the burden of punishment for wrongdoings. He decreed his own guilty verdict and sought a punishment to fit the crime. Hercules should be heralded for no reason other than his resolve to take responsibility. Our age rarely bears witness to this type of voluntary atonement.

In the case of my father, though eventually driven mad in the classical sense by having the tough luck of bad genes, he never committed familicide. That said, his peacock pride often would have him contend that, correct or not, he was in the right. The difference between Hercules and my dad lay squarely where each man placed the blame for their marital "death." Hercules killed his wife and considered himself blameworthy; circumstantial evidence and Hera mattered not to him; the buck stopped with himself. On the other hand, my dad did not hold himself accountable for the failings in his marriage and assuaged himself by announcing he had committed none of the "biggies": he had not committed adultery, gambled, or squandered dollars; he abused neither alcohol nor his wife." He had a good job; no one could accuse him of being a bum! Weren't these the reasons that made a marriage tank? He could fathom no other reason that a vow could be broken. Therefore, when his wife left him, with eyes puffy from sleepless nights and wild grief, bewilderment, or righteous indignation, he would ask me, his eldest, *"What's so wrong with me?"*

Unlike Hercules, who chose to take up his cross for his transgressions — his somnambulant-induced manslaughters — my father would be more like Adam and blame his Eve for their marital fall from grace. She ate the apple; his hands were clean. Meanwhile, leading up to the decline of their marriage, the rest of us watched him cover his eyes, ears, and mouth and ignore the writing on her wall that she was falling out of love with him. However, this is neither the time nor the place to account for their break. I now lift my dad to highlight the trio of roles that were as indivisible from him as skin is to sinew. Umbrellaed beneath the theme of moral responsibility, I'll have us examine four key expressions that encompass who my dad was. I'll start with his role as *patera,* father. From this, I will fan out a host of areas where my dad demonstrated Hercules's sense of responsibility; they came naturally to him, and the first is that of provider. The second role I'll delve into is my dad's being a natural teacher; this sprang from his being a life-long learner. Finally, my dad demonstrated his innate respect for life by being "a <u>health nut</u>," as he would describe himself. I consider this also to be his respect for and show personal accountability for the gift of life itself. To the last drop, he enjoyed what we now call an "active lifestyle." Let me now tell you what fatherhood brought to my dad.

Fatherhood

I don't want to give you the impression that my dad was perfect. He was not. I'll touch upon his flaws in the next section, which deals with our third theme of dichotomy and opposites. My focus here and now is to share who my father was at his core: a man proud to be a father. If he did nothing else in life, he sired and reared children, his progeny, and his name would carry on meant more to him than anything else. Incidentally, the word "core," in Latin, means "heart,"[232] and my dad's heart contained certain fixed and immutable features that never left him, even when his frame faltered and his mind declined. Within my dad's mental heading of fatherhood, you'll find three broad areas: his readiness to play with his kids, his desire for family togetherness, and a drive to be in control and prepared for survival.

My earliest memories of my father are ones filled with joy and fun. Maybe because he missed out on much in his childhood, as an adult, he liked to do things as a *collective*, so he would play *with* us, not just watch us. It could be argued that he was reliving his childhood, but I think his spirit was just as eager and, on the move, ready to explore the possible as it was his first go-round. Such a mindset is more in keeping with a child's innocence and eager hopes than the adult who has become wizened, prudent, and cautious. In this sense, my dad remained a kid, and we were drawn to a bigger version of ourselves for our ringleader. He was re-living nothing; this was a first for him, too! And we had no war on our turf. Therefore, adventures with my dad frequently held a possibility of danger, yet I was never scared. I suppose it's no wonder my mother often drolly commented that she felt she was raising *five* children. When our family got its first canoe, my dad was thrilled! He could hardly wait to take me for a ride in a nearby river; I may have been ten. My mother dropped us off, and we carried the canoe to a broad, shallow, and gentle portion of this river; it flowed as slow as a sluggish stream. In we went, and before you knew it, we met a fork in the river. My dad intended for us to cross over to take the left fork, which was calmer. To do so, we had to cross the increasingly agitated waters that were quickly building up speed as the river increased in depth. We reached those stiller waters. Instead, the canoe got turned around, so we went down the river *backward* at a breakneck pace. In an instant, we turned back around and found ourselves mere yards away from heading straight towards a tree! Its lowest broad branch stretched out and was parallel to the water as if making it ready to block us.

To avoid what seemed like an imminent crash (or decapitation), I thrust my oar out, and upon contact with that branch, we immediately flipped the canoe. I still remember being submerged and looking up from underwater, watching in helpless wonder the orange interior of the canoe flash by overhead. When my head bobbed up and I gulped in a draft of air, I scanned my swirling surroundings, but my dad was nowhere to be seen. I screamed for him, and like some echo, some familial walkie-talkie, he yelled back at me from the middle of the churning river, so we knew each was at least alive and close by. I spied another tree with a branch extending over the river fifty feet ahead, so I readied myself to grab it and take hold for dear life. With the river still coursing swiftly, I latched on to that branch in the blink of an eye as the current swiftly thrust the rest of my body under and past the branch now squarely under my chin. I now saw my feet straight out in front of me. The force of the water flow was doing all it could to relinquish my vice grip on that branch.

In the next flash, I spied my father miraculously inching his way out to me on that same branch, then positioning himself behind me, and then he edged us both safely to the shore. (Somehow, unseen by me, he had managed to swim over to my side of the river.) Completely soaked, we scampered up the bank like wet dogs and made our way to town to the closest filling station to call Mom to retrieve us. It turns out that there she was, filling up our station wagon. When she caught sight of us, I didn't know what would happen first: she ran to me, but it looked like she wanted to murder him. For me, my dad was my hero; for my mom, he'd racked up another zero. The canoe was long gone, but later that day, my parents did spy it on the back of another man's pickup truck. They knew it was ours because my father had neglected to register our canoe and affix the requisite decal on its side. After all, what was the worst that could happen?

While many might have thought that my dad was reliving his childhood with and through us, we, on the other hand, couldn't have imagined what might have prevented him from having a so-called "normal" and carefree childhood. Early on and unbeknownst to my dad, our mom instructed us to avoid a who-knows-what reaction in him by saying, "Do not ask your father" about his early childhood memories. We felt this would have been equivalent to opening Pandora's box and peering into an abyss of his perilous past. Why bring on pain on purpose? Therefore, we were purposefully kept in the dark about the disturbing days of war, pillage, and hiding to keep us all feeling light. We didn't need to know such things anymore, other than the lack of good that might show itself from dredging up those dark days. Still, it remained one of our unsolved mysteries, and my dad remained mum. Still, this time, we were unwitting fellow survivors with him of *his* choosing. I'll recall a few other examples of my dad's gravitational pull to be with his *own* and do things *together*, come what may.

It was from my father that I learned to swim. It wasn't his lesson so much as my desire to jump into his open arms. His broad smile, open face, and eager eyes beckoned me as much as his enthusiastic shouts joyfully bid me to join him. How could I resist? Jumping into his arms felt more like taking flight. Immediately, he would put me on his back, and I held onto his furry shoulders as I looked over his balding buoy of a bobbing head, and off we went in the direction of the middle of the lake or sunset, whichever came first. If you watched the pair of us, you would see my dad performing the breaststroke; I felt like I was riding a dolphin. Later in the first winters we spent after we had moved to Tennessee, my dad would occasionally volunteer to take us kids sledding on the long slope of the golf course behind our house, where, if you got a good running start, you'd end up sailing straight into a frozen creek at its base. We piled up with him in our red sled and took to the most treacherous hills near our house. As children, we were sometimes more scared than thrilled to see what "hill" he would have selected for us to sled down. Likely, it involved the steep embankment where we would sail airborne for a few seconds, with the promise of landing squarely on our coccyx or in the frigid creek — on purpose. We didn't know whether to laugh or cry; likely, we were doing both. Sledding with Dad became all the more memorable because we were his co-conspirators for agreeing *"not to tell your mother"* about our misadventures. He was fearless but not reckless, a lover of life, and an unsentimental realist. His zeal for Nature and openness to endless possibilities continues. Once, he brought home a hawk as well as a black snake that had been caught nearby where he worked; they were his show-and-tell for us!

My dad knew no fear, and he would be as likely as not to grab and hoist barehanded a mammoth snapping turtle onto the back of his truck and then *"relocate it,"* so it wouldn't get hit. He had luck and pluck. At my grandparents' lake cottage, he climbed a ladder to its topmost rung, then shimmied to a pole he'd set between two parallel giant trees, hanging onto the pole with all fours like a monkey hanging upside down so he could hang a swing for us kids. Once he jumped out of my grandparents' pontoon onto the shoreline to chase and scoop up with his bare hands an ancient mamma catfish, moving like a squirmy submarine in amongst the lilies and muck, with her thick blackberry ooze of wriggling fry following closely behind her. When my youngest sister announced she wanted animals, her wish was my father's command. She had a veritable Noah's Ark of stuffed *and* real animals in her bedroom and the backyard. No request was too weird or impossible for him. In addition to bubble-eyed goldfish and black mollies, she had heaven knows how many parakeets, a hutch with rabbits, banty roosters in the backyard, and even an oddball Guinea hen. We had a family puppy that was like a sibling to us. However, there was a definite distinction between man and beast, and when Dad saw too many felines replete with fleas slinking about the house, the pragmatist and chemist in him put two and two together, and I was secretly commissioned as his cat catcher, so he could euthanize the surplus population around our house.

He possessed the kind of inner freedom that made you sense that *anything was possible*, but he was also sensitive about what his children were exposed to. He was especially alert to *"outside influences"* even if they invaded our world through electronic means. Let me explain. Soon after my brother was born, we got our first RCA colored TV, and so mesmerized by it were we that my dad stormed in one morning and told us that he *"was going to throw the TV out the window,"* that we all were spoiled and needed to go play outside. We scampered out quickly because we could definitely imagine Dad throwing the TV set off the roof as if he were Godzilla. Two final examples of our being involved and thrilled by the light danger my dad flirted with included a game we dubbed "Peeking Tom," which he played with his three daughters around the float just past our grandparents' dock. It was like playing hide-and-seek: we girls silently hid behind one of the floating metal drums, and then we would wait for the "monster" to appear out of the depths. Suddenly, our dad would come up from the bottom of the lake, like the Creature from the Black Lagoon, and surprise us. The remaining strands of his long combover hair would lay across his face like seaweed, and he would say in a mock Chinese accent, *"Peking Tom!"* We squealed with frightful delight and tried to get away to the other side of the float, but my dad would whip the float around so vigorously that it felt like we were in a cyclone. Looking back, any of those barrels could have easily knocked us in the head, but it wasn't a thought then.

Not all adventures involved danger, and my father was always ready to explore any nearby and new frontier of upper-East Tennessee. However, since my mom did not trust that he possessed a modicum of better judgment, let alone common sense, she declined every offer to hike. Ever the foreigner, my dad felt like one of the original settlers, and he was eager to join the ranks of Lewis and Clark, so he joined a local hiking group. One of the most memorable hikes he took me on with this group was to Mount LaConte, and later, visits home from college included his taking me on whitewater rafting expeditions in West Virginia. He loved the area we lived in so much that he would offer to chauffeur me on zig-zaggy, back country roads just so I could photograph anything of charm and beauty that caught my eye; he recognized my gift for spotting beauty. Anyway, this was an opportunity for my dad to spend one-on-one time with his eldest daughter. Where we went mattered not; it was always about the journey for him. By then, my parents were divorced, so I'll return to the time before our family was fractured and refocus on more foundational days with my dad.

My father never insisted or dictated that we *had* to do things together. Unlike Chris Griswold, my dad made no proclamation or an edict for his family to partake of his vision. Life was at its best for him when we could all be together; I believe it made him feel as safe and secure as it did for him being tucked away under one roof in the village during those harrowing times. What that *his* father could have been there and never left his sons! We were unaware of such stirrings in him. Anyhow, in upper East Tennessee with a Greek dad and Hoosier mom, a scientist, and an artist, we were odd men out, strangers in a strange land. I'd never met any family like ours. We resided in a neighborhood nestled among an eighteen-hole golf course; our house was closer to its country club than the entrance. It felt as if my parents out-snubbed these socialites, whom they saw as ones whose culture extended no further than the fairways of their backyards. We had the odd last name and not a relative within five hundred miles. In fact, each of us kids would seek out adults who would become surrogate relatives and anchors for us.

If my dad considered us an anomaly, he didn't let on; he conducted himself with pride as if we were the original settlers due to our just desserts. We were made of the sterner stuff from which our neighbors came generations ago. They had no recollection of a heritage that went further than their grandparents' memories but not of a home on distant shores. "*Heinz fifty-seven!*" my dad would label the folk around us, which didn't include their dogs. That said, by and large, the people from East Tennessee can and do trace their roots to Scotch-Irish origins, and discovering their love of mountains and music brought endless delight to my dad. One of his favorite things to do was to take us to the Carter Fold, a musical performance and concert venue near Hiltons, Virginia, which was "dedicated to the preservation and performance of old-time country and bluegrass music." There, we'd listen to the village music of *this* locale.

Bluegrass music satisfied my dad's soul, for with its fast and furious fiddle sawing, tinny banjos sounded similar to bouzoukis, thumping stand-up bass pumping life into all, and mandolins fiercely and gently strummed. Many from the audience of all ages were eager to buck dance and could hardly wait to come up front; for my dad, continents were connected. He felt at home in the hills all over again.

Togetherness for my dad also meant we ate together, and this was as serious an affair as if we took communion daily. Invariably, his sternness produced an overwhelming desire for my second sister and me to laugh. I can't tell you how many times I chortled my milk after glancing at some hilarious face she made over which we'd giggle in wicked delight—his stern glance at us and momentary pause from chewing only made it worse. My dad was never one to watch too much TV unless there was a documentary, especially if it was about nature travel or classical music. Like our very own Walter Cronkite, he'd yell for us to come to watch TV right then as if he had a special news-breaking announcement of national importance.

Even when I was an adult, living two hours away from him, he would call me on the phone as if I was no farther than the next room to tell me that Itzhak Perlman was playing on PBS, Emeril Agassi was cooking Mediterranean or National Geographic had a special on the Great Coral Reef Barrier. In my earlier childhood, he would sit riveted to Mutual of Omaha's Wild Kingdom like most men do watching football. Earlier still, when he would take notes for his studies while watching the evening world news, I sat beside him scribbling nonsense or underlining sentences from my latest *Ranger Rick*. It wasn't until after the divorce, when I visited Dad at his house, that I learned how primal his need for togetherness was. Sometimes, he'd inch his foot over and clasp mine with his bare toes as if they were eager to play footsie; he had done this since I was four! And always, if we'd have to drive somewhere together, be it to the grocery store or later, to a doctor's appointment, often with Greek music cranked up in my car, it would be just a matter of time before I felt his hand pop over in a quick grope to hold hands with mine. It wasn't a thought but his heart's reflex to do so. Maybe it was a way to make sure no trauma like he'd experienced as a youngster would ever take us away from him, so he was always ready to hold on tight to us. His love was palpable and messy and real.

This preference for togetherness took on a foreign hue even to us, his American family: my dad blurred the lines of ownership to mean "what's mine is yours and yours mine." Whereas it seems that most Americans prefer to have clear boundary lines delineating the property and possession of what belongs to whom, even within one's own family, this was not the case for my dad. His herd mentality meant that he saw no crime in using my mom's toothbrush, and they typically shared a glass at dinner, even though my father rarely drank when he ate. When we'd take our annual summer trek to my grandparents' lake house, he would never ask for his own drink; instead, he would ask to take *"just a sip"* of mine, and I'd know that he could practically inhale a third of it in one gulp. The same held true for his grabbing his favorite road snack, Peanut M&M's, so I just put them out on the shallow shelf to the left of the glovebox within his hand's reach. When I bought my first bike, which I'd saved up to buy with my own money, it was not I but my dad who was the first to jump on it and give it a spin to the end of the circle and back while I stood by mouth agape in dismay. I'll now shift gears and relate evidence of the ferocity with which my dad became a provider.

Provider

I don't think my dad's being a provider was learned or adopted so much as innate. He didn't "protect and defend" because this was the man's expected or designated duty to his wife and family. Still, because we were "bone of [his] bones and flesh of [his] flesh" (Gen. 2:23). He also innately knew affection and affirmation were as essential to our spirits as air to our lungs. It was that elemental, and his provision fed belly and soul. Without a word spoken, and should the need arise, we knew in our gut he would kill, die, or steal for us. My father's notion of what it meant to provide stemmed from his core commitment to providing two of the three basic human needs: food and shelter; mom saw to the third. Except for the crack in his code that occurred while navigating the murky waters of divorce, he never wavered or faltered in his giving.

During that period, he was beside himself and not himself then; plus, unbeknownst to us, his disease was beginning to make its debut. Since I've already shared with you the deprivations he experienced as a boy during the war in Greece, it should also make sense that he would never let his children experience hunger the way he did. No, not on his watch! And while I did not consider my father a remarkably generous man where material things were concerned (as, by and large, they were not essential to him), we never wanted for food, and good food at that. It would be illogical for him to have us fill our Mother Hubbard cupboards with *"junk food,"* which he categorically called all processed food before there was a term for it. Unlike many men who don't like to go to the grocery, my father would be on-call like some paramedic or ER doctor if we ran out of milk or some provision my mom told him we needed. No matter what, my dad was always ready with a checkbook to buy groceries, and this extended well into our adult years.

Even when I was nearly thirty, most of his visits to me would include a trip to the market where he would offer to pay for at least part, if not all, of my groceries, just like a king would provide for his subjects. The same was true for gas in our cars when we visited him. I also don't think I've ever seen a man more appreciative of the food or meals served him. My mom cooked well-balanced meals of endless variety every night, and each one was for my dad, like his first meal and the Last Supper, and he showed his approval and delight by the size of his bites and the sounds of pleasure which issued forth from someplace deep within. Everything about him told us all to "behold, and it was very good" (Gen. 1:31). As an adult, when I prepared a Greek frittata-like omelet for him for breakfast or made one of my Greek salads with homemade dressing (which time and again, he said I needed to bottle and sell) or during the days when my brother as a young adult would fix dinner for just the two of them, it was like the first meal of creation. He would look up in gratitude, pleased as punch, and say, "*Soooooo tasty!*" There were staples for my dad that were ever at hand, and we were never without them. I can still see the large Jiff jar that he used to keep his wild oregano from Greece in; the use of that herb ensured any meat would have a hint or whiff of Greece in it. Cheese was his go-to meat and potatoes, and we always had commercial-sized wheels of County-Line extra sharp cheddar cheese in the fridge the way you might find briny barrels of feta in a Greek marketplace.

On the rare occasion that our family would go out to eat, my dad ordered us "*not to fill up on bread*" and that we should "*save room for food.*" However, later in life, I saw that my father *could* eat "by bread alone" (Matthew 4:4), well, that and a little, no, a *lot* of olive oil. When mom was getting supper ready, it was not unusual for my dad to come to our bedrooms and, like some personal maître d', offer us cut carrots and celery "*as an appetizer*" while we were doing our homework. Also, during the earlier years, when my parents together or dad alone would prepare Greek dishes for parties they might host or attend, I saw that my dad was as at home in the kitchen as any woman. When he'd make us homemade "*Greek French fries,*" as he'd call them, or a tray of his father's homemade rice pudding, or we kids would get the less-than-perfect samplings of spanakopitakia or some honeyed delight if my parents were entertaining others, I experienced a little taste of heaven on earth. I was grateful for those delectable tidbits.

Later on, in my early college years in the early 1980s, when my parents were still together, and the whole family would come and visit me, it became a tradition for my father to take us out to Red Lobster. We felt like royalty before the sumptuous spread of seafood that covered every inch of the table. Whenever he would visit me on his own, knowing how much I adored it, he would greet me at my dorm room door with a large, chilled container of Neptune salad as if he were Poseidon himself hand-delivering it to me. Whatever foodstuff we wanted was on hand at his house, or if something was missing, no matter the hour, we'd head to the grocery — or "shody do," as I pronounced "grocery store" as a toddler and which he'd still use as our secret code for us to head on our mission; it was never a trudge or chore. It was a blessing!

The yang to the yin of my dad's being a provider of food was *shelter*, and for a Greek, such wealth was measured in *land*. I've shared that my mom cared for the clothing; my father focused on food and land. I think my dad would have been content to be covered in lambswool, looking like a cretin hobo; maybe that's why he saved all the hides of the lambs he slaughtered all those many Greek Easters. Perhaps he wanted to weave his flokati rug. When my parents divorced, and he was clearing out a side closet of some of his stuff in the carport, he pulled out stiff hide after hide; they were stacked one atop the other like wooly cards. Those were in the days of our family's lamentations.

I return to my dad's gravitational pull towards longing for land. They say a man's home is his castle, but my dad was more moved by owning the land beneath his feet. My mom made his castle our home, and she furnished our nest with an eclectic blend of antique and modern Danish furniture and decorations from all over the world. Nothing matched, yet it all fit and made sense; African statue carvings, Peruvian tapestries, Greek dolls, and oil paintings of mountainous Tennessee landscapes made by local artists adorned our shelves or walls. Tucked in amongst this and that furniture, many a houseplant thrived. We drank from amber-colored plates and local stoneware. My dad would have been content to drink from a jelly jar. Likely because my dad did not see much wood used in homes while he lived in Greece, he adored that our house had wooden paneled walls; what my mom hung on them was immaterial to him.

After their divorce, to make his humble apartment feel more like the home he left, he rented every painting the local library had to offer and hung them hither and yon on his living room walls with no regard for rhyme, reason, or taste. However, his bedroom walls were entirely bare except for a single portrait of a young maiden with a thoughtful expression, and it didn't escape anyone's notice that she resembled our mom. My mother told me that my father felt like he had arrived when they bought their first home in Columbus, Ohio. It was a palatial English

Tudor mansion, and my Uncle Kolya carried a snapshot of it to show his friends in the same way grandmothers eagerly shared pictures of their grandchildren. It was too much for my parents to afford, so they ended up selling it. The house that became the home we were raised in was one my mom picked out; my father assented and claimed stake to it like he was one of the original settlers.

We lived there from 1969 to 1984, the era of my youth and the golden years when our family was intact, and my dad felt whole. One of my parents' biggest battles took place soon after my brother was born, and my mother saw we needed to shift rooms to add a bedroom. To do so, she decided it would be advantageous to add another room for common space — a family room! Her plan was practical: we would use three of the four existing brick walls surrounding the patio, then add a fourth wall, roof, floor, and, *voilà*, a new room! She could already see it in that architect's mind's eye of hers; my dad just saw money down the drain. He pouted, screamed, and stamped his foot: if any money was to be spent, it ought to be used to buy the empty lot next door. My father's desire to own more land was connected to possessing plenty of basic staples to sustain his homestead. However, where my dad imagined future gains and greater security by acquiring more land, we just saw a boring, empty field with more grass to mow.

My mom won that battle, and though, at first, my dad refused to step foot in "the new room," as it was forever called, he came around. In fact, it became everyone's favorite room. Perhaps in foresight as to what might draw my father into that room, my mom installed a Franklin stove, and after that, at the first call for frost in the fall, my dad turned part lumberjack in what became his near obsession with furnishing wood for that stove. Whenever my dad built a fire, he loaded that stove to maximum capacity such that our evening fires looked like a small inferno. Had his wee bonfire thrown out a spark, I suppose it could have burned our house down. My father never worried about such matters; his face was suffused with a glow of satisfaction. Then again, maybe it was the heat from his furnace. With the new Franklin stove in the new room came the need for firewood, and my dad foraged until I believed he found every stick of available free firewood within the surrounding counties. By this time, he had a pickup truck, something he was sure made him look like one of the locals. Load upon load of wood did he bring in and stack in front of the brick planters adjacent to our front door? Our home began to look like Fort Knox. If we saw a logging truck barreling past us, my boyfriend at the time would joke with me and say, "There goes your dad!" After the divorce, when my dad bought the house he would live in for the remainder of his life (except the last two years), its main selling feature was that its interior walls were covered by several types of local wood, including wormy chestnut. The house's exterior was plank cedar, and when he re-roofed it, he chose thick shaker planks. It boasted to have not one but *two* fireplaces! Sold!

He soon bought and inserted a Buck Stove in its downstairs fireplace and fed it wood as he would us food; it kept the downstairs toasty warm. Truth be told, when I inhale deeply in my *heart's* memory, I can easily recall the scent of my father: he smelled like pine resin. He undoubtedly ingested it as a lad in Greece and as a man from his hearth. In later years, after his eldest brother passed away, I saw his single-mindedness for possessing land resurge, and in a near frenzy, he bought out his second brother's share to own all three familial properties in Greece. In this respect, we might better compare him to Antaeus, a mythical giant who is said to have gained strength by being connected to the earth. My dad may have called Greece *"a pile of rocks,"* but he gladly grabbed several stones when the opportunity availed itself.

The final frontier of my dad's ingrained moral responsibility as "provider" connecting him to Hercules revolved around his being alert for inclement weather. It, too, became a near compulsion of his, and he showed an ever-readiness to come to our rescue where driving or transport was needed, come rain or shine. I have already described his near obsession with having enough wood; perhaps living in fear and uncertainty during the war years got transmuted into his need to gather sticks and forage for food when he detected ominous forces of Nature looming over us. His radar-like vigilance stemmed from the childhood trauma of having to be ready at the drop of a hat to drop everything and head for and hide in the hills. Only now, it wasn't foreigners that threatened invasion or mayhem, but actual storms looming on the horizon — or his children leaving for the wild blue yonder. It all produced the same feeling in my dad.

Though never a boy scout, my father's motto was "Be prepared." He always knew when and how much snow was predicted and notified us kids on the telephone as if the National Weather Service had employed him to alert us his children. If I happened to be standing next to him and he could tell I was cold, without a thought, he quickly peeled off whatever overgarment he was wearing. I never had to ask for a coat or blanket; he swaddled me in his blue parka or would bury me in a pile of blankets if I gave the word. And if I didn't call him to tell him I'd arrived safely home from driving through sketchy weather, his peace would lie in the balance. My dad was willing to sacrifice time and resources to be wherever and whenever he was needed or called. I think he possessed a paternal protectiveness that might have been expressed in more chivalrous ways in bygone days. He never treated us as damsels in distress, but his loyalty and allegiance to his children were bound in his blood. Hercules may have had a steed or chariot; my dad had his trusty van. Later, he would come to our aid in a pickup or any of his VWs, be it the *"racy Rabbit"* or "junkie Jetta," as he was want to say.

How he reacted to a hypothetical or perceived loss of an adult stretches back to how he felt as a boy when it was the German or Italian troops raiding their village. We didn't get how virulent this pang remained in him; he wasn't even conscious of it himself. The "scarcity principle"[233] creates a mindset founded on the reality or perception that *one's access to available resources is limited*; therefore, one does whatever one must to hold onto things for self-preservation's sake. Later in life, my dad hoarded certain random items like Wal-Mart plastic shopping bags, and where his parents covered their furniture in plastic, my dad used towels or carpet samples my mom brought home from work, whether in his car or high-traffic areas in his house. He double-wrapped items in his fridge, so you might not know what was inside the mummified casing. Later, he even told me he had hidden items in the attic of one of the properties he owned, but I never found it. In short, life for my dad became a game of survival of the scrappiest, and he could be a fox for himself and a wolf for his family. His van was provisioned with all the just-in-case tools one might need, and when I bought myself my first car, he proudly presented me with a brand-new ratchet set in one hand and a pair of jumper cables in the other.

His "gifts" sprung from his urge to provide us with the practical *necessities* of life, never our coveted *wants*. From college to young adulthood, he was our master packer, private U-Haul backer, and personal life-tracker. I'm sure he would have gone from sea to shining sea had we asked him. Like Hercules, he lifted many times his weight our belongings and would sweat and strain and stagger until all was where it was intended or requested to be. Once, he tied my then-dead car to his back bumper with a thick rope to haul it back home as soon and as cheaply as possible. No problem! We had our funereal caravan, and I was steering the coffin car. His notion of taking care of us at that time also included making sure we had transportation, but here, he faltered, and once he gave me a car that practically had no breaks; another time, it was a diesel rabbit with an anemic alternator. I felt like Fred Flintstone jumping my car off by letting it run down a hill so that I could kickstart it. Really, though, I can't complain. In one of my most desperate times, he paid off the balance on the first car I bought; this amounted to several thousand dollars. Just as Hercules went to aid those in need, my dad was also on call to strong-arm any element that threatened our homes.

Also connected to my dad's love of wood was his readiness to subdue trees or limbs. Seeing as how my house is in the hole of a donut, which is all woods, my dad was on it to cut down spindly pines or leaning trees, but by the time he offered his services, his HD had progressed enough such that it wasn't safe for him to handle his trusty chainsaw. He owned two, and both were professional-grade, top-of-the-line, so when he pulled the starter, the kick-back was so strong, it nearly lifted him off his feet. He didn't seem to notice and would wield his trusty sword to hack down any tree that threatened to topple over or snap, and he was game for any lopping off any other limb I might want down. Once, he fell a tree, and it fell right on and knocked out the power line to my house, but that was a mere accident — *no biggie* —no one had been hurt! He cut a check to fix it that day as I stared at his apparent lack of concern.

To protect our home from small four- or six-legged invaders, and since he was a chemist, Dad skulked along the perimeter of our houses, carefully pouring his homemade lethal concoction to rid us of vermin and termites. Decades later, I found his aluminum jug with "DDT" written crudely with a sharpie on the front. Another time, he commissioned my brother's help and affixed an oversized copper wire to my fuse box so that my house would never feel the effects should lightning strike my home. He also bought me my first snow shovel in case I got stuck at the top of the hill. His housewarming gifts included a grill and a kitchen table he had made for me in a woodcarving class. They were emblems of food and hearth my Hercules always hoped I'd have. Anyway, what could be tastier than meat cooked over fire? I can see him pushing his beloved grill from his garage onto a cardboard that covers his gravel driveway to cook whole salmon for us.

To that end, the most impressive feature he added to his home happened when he converted his conventional heating system to a thermo-electrical heat pump, whereby he channeled a steady flow of water gurgling in from a natural spring up to his house. This natural flow of water provided a perpetual source of practically free energy! Taking advantage of President Jimmy Carter's offering of a tax incentive in the late '70s to implement alternative energy sources, long before our current era where, for some, it has become in vogue to "live off the grid," my dad found a cheap way to heat and cool his house — *"for pennies"* he would gleefully announce. No doubt, this satisfied his inner imperative always to be prepared because you never knew when the chips would be down, the bottom might fall out, or you might find yourself in dire straits. And yet, he remained the titan of optimists! As prepared as he was, what my dad never saw coming and could not have imagined having to face was a Goliath of disease more deadly than war and invisible to the naked eye. It lay like a time bomb ticking inaudibly inside him. That time is not yet nigh, so we now turn to the second manifestation of my dad's expression of moral responsibility. This one came about without effort or training because he was a natural teacher.

Teacher

I don't know how much teaching Hercules did, but we can read that he was a stalwart leader when he was a younger man. Teaching is also leading and need not be confined to a classroom. My dad had a curious mind but longed to share his discoveries and newly acquired information with us. His enthusiasm was infectious, and before you knew it, you were swept up and captivated by his Discovery Channel spirit. The delight he took in Nature was arresting. I have a sweet recollection of us lying side-by-side on our living room floor in Boston; we were both mesmerized as we gazed at the fish in his tanks. I would have been three or four. At the time, he had two tanks, one freshwater, the other salt water, one stacked atop the other. The soft glow of the light, the iridescent flashes of wafer-thin, angular angel fish darting among tufts of water plants, and the gentle flow of bubbles from the aerating pump humming behind would calm our busy natures. He and I are of a similar temperament. Off to the side was a singular fishbowl with seahorses in it, and I can still remember him getting down on his haunches to face me and explain that it was *"the daddy seahorse which takes care of its young."* I knew he meant the same to me. My father may not have had a pouch or birthed us, but he cared for his young as they grew.[234]

Seven years later, my dad decided to try breeding Betta Fighting Fish, and he set up the requisite environment by dividing the tank in two by placing a perfectly cut piece of glass to separate the two sides. Again, for him, the hallmark characteristic of these fish was that it was *"the daddy fish that makes the nest for his babies."* The female is kept nearby and in sight but temporarily unavailable to spur the male into making his frothy nest of air and saliva; he becomes motivated to produce his nest of wonder in hopes of captivating her with his skill set.

When the foamy nest was complete, my dad would carefully scoop up the female and drop her on his side. Then we all waited with bated breath to see if she was sufficiently impressed to check out his nest; meanwhile, he hovered, waiting for her underneath its surface. Like a sports announcer, my dad whispered, *"If she's receptive, they will mate."* The male collects the fertilized eggs in his mouth and transports and deposits them in the nest."[235] The female is scooped up again and sent back to her side. In the meantime, the male stays nearby and makes sure no eggs fall out of his nest to fall prey to predators; if one should drop, he quickly scoops it up with his mouth and redeposit it. These babies, or "fry," hatch in three days,[236] and they're pretty much good to go. Again, the lesson was loud and clear to me about how proud my dad was to be a father and that he took an active and vital role in the home. My dad also taught us never to put two males together in one tank because they were so possessive and territorial that they would fight to the death. My dad was also highly territorial; he didn't even like other male relatives in the house, or so it seemed to me. They interfered with his flow and farrow. Likewise, even in his dreams, mighty Hercules fought to the death when he perceived others encroaching upon his domain.

Whatever struck us kids with wonder, my dad was all in, and he let us explore this or that to our heart's content. The world was our oyster, and he was our deep-sea diver, ever at hand to educate us about the wonders of the world. Another early childhood memory occurred when I was about five, and we visited a farm. Seeing a clutch of chickens, I got curious about what a rooster's coxcomb and wattle felt like, and I shared this with my dad. He thought nothing of chasing one, capturing it with his bare hands and then holding it securely so I could touch the wattle. Defying danger (and, likely, rules), he did the same thing at the zoo: gently but firmly, he took hold of a curious baby elephant's trunk, which it had stretched out, groping through the bars in hopes of pinching an offered handful of peanuts. Dad did this in a flash so I could feel its soft, smooth, and moist interior. As much as he loved to lay in the sunshine, he was also like a baby sea turtle, inexorably drawn to the sea as much as they. It is elemental and elementary. Much later, after my parents' divorce was finalized and seeing my dad gasping for sense and life, my brother, sister, and I knew the best medicine in the world would be to take our pop to the ocean, likely where he came from. We drove non-stop, and when we arrived late that night, my weary dad did not go to the hotel room. Instead, he walked directly to the beach and lay on the sand, letting the moonlight bathe his face and the saltwater lick his toes. We had no doctor's order, and we didn't need him to teach us what to do; we just knew what fit the bill and would hit the spot. Hercules' children never got to see the day or time when they would care for their father; we only got a sneak preview then.

I'll resume his role as a teacher by recounting a few more examples given in no particular order other than how they naturally occurred to me. He was eager to share his discoveries with us, answer our questions, or solve problems we had, be it explaining through analogy or, more likely, demonstrating. Once, proud as punch, I tried to turn the tables on my dad and show him what the latest marvel, my newly acquired Magic Slate, could do. My show-and-tell involved presenting what I had written with its conjuring stylus to him. Then, with an upward snap of the plastic sheet, I made what the inkless stick had penned disappear. Wasn't he impressed? Smiling, my dad did the same; only *he* squiggled a line on the pad with his *finger* and not the stylus provided! That was his trick on top of their magic!

Even earlier, as a toddler riding my horse, he added to my bouncing pleasure by creating the clip-clop sound effects of the horse. Much to the amazement of the other adults present, I mimicked the exact sharp clacking sound he made with his tongue at two years old, and off we went to the imaginary races. When I was eight, he gave me the coolest present around: a set of transparent pink glass clackers, and they made the same impressive sound as when he popped his belt. (They probably could have doubled as a weapon.) Like some unintentional but successful lesson in physics, he showed me how to make those clackers go on seeming automatic, whereby through a rhythmic up-and-down motion of my wrist while holding onto the string they were attached to, they would ricochet back and forth on the highest and lowest contact points, like a double pendulum modulating in fast motion. It made the modulated clack of a sharp gun report cracking. Speaking of physics, my parents had a billiard table in their bedroom, which provided endless opportunities for me to learn more about action-reaction, the relationship of angles, the dynamics of power, and the value of a light touch. During the lone year, I tried out for and became one of the fast-pitch softball pitchers, and Dad was my catcher *and* my fan in the backyard where we'd practiced.

When it was apparent in elementary school that I was having trouble with math, my dad swiftly brought a chalkboard easel into my room to tutor me. He made practice makes perfect fun because he got excited over every step, leading to success. Later, when it turned out he could not help me penetrate the mystery of the unknown variable x in Algebra 1, he commissioned the help of his best friend from college, who also happened to be an engineer. There was no badge of shame for my not doing well; *it was just another equation to solve and extra practice* that always proved to be just the ticket for him. Helping me with my advanced placement chemistry was a *treat* for him, and I always felt that he was telling me about the properties of his relatives and how thorough and intimate his knowledge was. And where some children's parents seek to instill a sense of responsibility by insisting that they work to pay for their car insurance, my dad, under no uncertain terms, said that *"school was our job."* Even when I got to be in college and was struggling to find more time to devote to studying, my dad wrote to the dean of my college, pleading that I be permitted to withdraw from a 1-hour course that I did not need but which was consuming no less than six hours of my week. He was ever that squeaky wheel that got the (olive) oil.

The best good teachers are a hands-on lot, and my father was just that. My father was the one who first let me drive. His beige Chevy pickup truck became my first steed; I was all but twelve when he took me out to practice on back roads, and it was our secret. When it came to learning how to drive our stick-shift VW Rabbit, my dad would take me to the country club parking lot on early weekend mornings and contort his body in the passenger's seat so that he was nearly upside down, his head facing my feet. In this contorted position, he would place his left hand on my left foot, hovering over the clutch; his right hand cupped my right foot on the accelerator. Carefully, he maneuvered both my feet to that midpoint so they could feel the sweet spot the split-second before locomotion. I would glance down at that eager smile, looking back up at me as he said, *"See? It doesn't take much gas at all!"* In contrast, when I'd ask my mom to ride with me, she was as likely as not to bring and read the Sunday paper; if I wracked the car with violent spasms from a gear seized up and improperly engaged, she would calmly look over at me to signal that it was time we swap places so she could get us out of the lurch on the hill where I'd stalled out.

I cannot overstress the importance of education for my Hercules. The best teachers don't only tell; they show, and my dad's way of showing us how important education was to say to us — and me in particular as his oldest — that *"we should go as far as we could go"* that he *"would pay for all the schooling we ever needed."* There was never any talk of cost where education went; it was our sacred cow, and the idea implied that we couldn't afford *not* to go! I heard this so often that I knew I was attending college while in grade school and looked forward to it. No one could have anticipated what financial havoc divorce wreaked. Still, my parents' separating or *"quitting at peak production,"* as my dad phrased it, made it such that by sheer timing, I completed my undergraduate degree *before* the divorce decree compelled him to pay for our undergraduate education. Therefore, when I entered graduate school, I was on my own. I put that degree's debt on the Guaranteed Student Loan tab and paid on that near twenty-grand note for thirteen years. I was rankled and felt betrayed by his promise, which had gone unfulfilled, but I did not handle my disappointment well or maturely for a long time. Only when I broached my Hercules *not* as an entitled brat, brooding in indignation and demanding to know why he had reneged on his prior promise and insisting that he pay off my loan, but *as a contrite and humbled daughter* who, after all those years, confessed and confided that *she still needed her daddy's help*, did he come through. Drinking in my respect and humility, he cut a check without hesitation and hugged me like he'd been waiting for this moment. We embraced. That forgiveness was as sweet as honey. By then, he had recovered and recouped the economic losses incurred during the divorce. The life lesson my dad taught me when he paid my balance remaining to Sallie Mae, the friendly name for my ugly GSL, was that he *was* a man good to his word.

The final example I'll give to demonstrate his passion for my learning through his teaching was when he taught me how to make *soupa avgalemano*; I was not even ten. Initially, my parents prepared this classic Greek chicken soup dish together, but seeing as I was always eagerly watching nearby, he passed the torch to me. I made myself available for the critical part of his pouring the piping hot broth into the lemon-egg mixture, which I would slowly stir — "Sigah, sigah!", which in Greek means "easy-does-it," ensuring its smooth blend without the broth curdling and inadvertently becoming egg-drop soup. It became "our thing," and to this day, I need no recipe other than recollection. As I turn the page here and move from teacher to "*health nut*," as he would call himself, I will give flesh to my final example of Hercules' being a moral man. This encompassed my dad's lifestyle because it shows his values. Values worth their salt are the ones we adhere to because they compel us to be righteous and responsible. He stayed active for as long as he was able. As fate and fortune would have it, caring for his physical frame would have no bearing on what was in store for his mind. I have already shared with you how fundamental and sweeping my dad's roles as father, provider, and teacher; now I'll share with you his zest for taking life by the horns and seeing to it that it would be good to the last drop. Such was our Hercules' tainted destiny.

"Health Nut"

I have a large black-and-white photograph of my papou, my father's father, in my office. He is standing beside a flower cart bursting with bouquets, sheepishly smiling and holding onto one of the gorgeous sprays. This cart with the flowers is nearly as tall as he donned in his dapper suit and fedora hat. You would see by the twinkle in his eye that it was as if he was acknowledging to the person taking the picture that these flowers dwarf him, but he is pleased as punch to be working in retirement. He looks forward to selling his floral wares to passersby in Central Park. Many in America go about their career or job like it is a toil from which they will one day be released, as if liberation were the ultimate goal of retirement. Like his father before him, my dad would one day no longer be employed where he had spent most of his years working as a chemist, but everything about him said there is no such thing as retirement.

Not feeling tired, spent, or done, he kept on living and shifting his focus, energy, and passion elsewhere with new aims in a fresh way. It is as if life was meant to be spent in perpetual and purposeful motion; to cease would disrespect our maker who endowed us with life, and we've only one to live. And by perpetual motion, I hardly mean idly spinning our wheels or trotting endlessly on a treadmill. To utter "hallowed be Thy name" in your heart's prayer implies that we revere God by taking the bull by the horns and living the life He gave us; ultimately, it's on Him when it stops. We honor God when we give our all for Him. I believe that Hercules' heroism sprang from the fact that he kept renewing himself by taking on challenge after challenge. He didn't lie down and die with the death of his family, even though he was momentarily stunned and felt down and out. The secret to longevity and "the good life" is to live your life; you don't squander or cease until you can't. Ever. Keep your heart pumping out, love, and breathe in the same.

Staying active in diet, faith, and passions kept my dad chugging on the straight and narrow; simplicity delivered sanctity to his soul. My dad was a lifelong vitamin-taker, from the earliest days when he'd dispense those pea-shaped, oxblood multivitamin capsules to us kids. When Flintstones chewables came out, my youngest sister and brother gladly gobbled those up. We had easy access to tangy discs of vitamin C the way some children are given Communion wafers. The common cold passed my dad by; he rarely got sick, but if he did come down with the flu, it would hit him like a ton of bricks, yet it would pass through his system just as quickly as if his high metabolism burned it through its velocity. As he got older, he took even more vitamins, including Vitamin E and Soy Lecithin, and he would tell us their chemical properties and how they aided us on the cellular level. He communicated these facts using the same tone a priest might when commending particular virtues. Later, when he was in the full throes of HD, and I would accompany him to any number of his doctor visits, and when asked what medication he took, he beamed and proudly piped up, *"None! Just vitamins!"*

So many fads and trends pander to our health and diet concerns. Still, my father remained an orthodox adherent to the Mediterranean lifestyle way before it became in vogue and labeled the optimal diet long before the likes of Euell Gibbons, Dr. Oz, or Dr. Atkins gave their stamp of approval. Although a man who never got his fill of food, my dad instinctively knew that there was a spiritual dimension to health that involved a holy and wholly comprehensive approach to what we ingest. There is no magic bullet to losing weight or gaining a prosperous life by swearing off this or a New Year's pledge to that. Yes, he also drank wine but was an occasional drinker at best. Sometimes, he'd enjoy a beer, but a little red wine was good for the system and spirits! Of course, he also adored retsina, that acrid and ancient Greek wine infused with a special pine resin; it matched his inner pitch. Greeks have been drinking wine for as long as their little country has existed.

That he once made wine probably made him feel like a god-drinking ambrosia. When I was in high school, my dad got it in his mind that he was going to make wine, and make wine, he did! One day, he came home from the grocery with his car full of boxes spilling over with cartons of overripe grapes. That wasn't enough, so he returned for languishing strawberries and other berries. Although he stopped short of stamping on the fruit with his heels, like some village woman (or Lucille Ball in the famous grape-stomping episode), he pounded the fruit with his stiff fists through a giant funnel. The sludge dripped thickly into a 16-gallon carboy, no doubt one he'd pinched from work. After that, he added sugar to initiate the fermentation process, that is when the yeast consumes the sugar.[237] Then he capped the small opening at the top with a rubber stopper with a hole, through which clear rubber tubing was snuggly inserted. This tube reached the bottom of the tank, where soon, there would be the dregs of the fruit's pulp; he stuck the other end of the tube, which came out of the carboy and into a large jar full of water.

After months of hearing that incessant light gurgling sound in our kitchen's background, indicating that carbon dioxide gaseous molecules were escaping, the bubbling would finally stop. Our lab technician and vintner excitedly announced that it was done! Well, not quite. Now he could bottle the wine, which was both a comical and messy affair because the only person he could commission to help him was my then-eight-year-old brother. Our kitchen looked like a crime scene, but the result was that my dad kept our house in stock with that batch of wine for the next five years. I don't want to give the impression my dad was a big drinker; he was not. In fact, he liked to brag that he was a teetotaler, which, although untrue, indicates that wine was a staple in his home but not a necessity at his table. What you would find him drinking long before it became common knowledge in the States that there were associated health benefits was green tea.

Greeks have been drinking wild mountain tea for centuries; I'll bet Hercules had his favorite blend made from lemon verbena or chamomile leaves. With every sip, my middle-aged dad would taut the tea's ability to "remove the free radicals," which over time damaged our systems, making us more vulnerable to acquiring cancer.[238] However, there was not enough tea in all of China to keep my dad from one day getting cancer. Tea was a liquid antioxidant for him, but his usual go-to was simply water with ice — *"if you've got any"* — which he drank like many a dog, practically inhaling it in long, grateful gulps.

I don't think my dad ever heard the expression, "Go big or go home," but everything he undertook exemplified his force of herculean habit to give life his all. Until Hercules had his fit and blotted out all he held dear, he did not burden himself with self-reflection; likewise, my dad's powers of analysis and observation were reserved for the outside world. My dad was not reflective, so I'll catch you up on what brought meaning to his life outside his family and job. For Hercules, before he performed his penance, doing life meant doing battle and protecting his. My dad was always on guard for us, but three additional areas he pursued with passion included music, his business, and jogging; I'll start with the last since it ties in best with his health habits.

Even though I remember my dad doing jumping jacks and pushups after work while he waited for my mom to finish dinner, it was during the dark days that led up to their divorce that he began jogging around the neighborhood. No one told my dad to take up jogging as an outlet for releasing or rerouting his frustrations when his marriage was unraveling before his eyes. It was as though he was running for his life, and we knew if he did not vent his pent-up rage and frustration this way, he might explode. This launched a decade-long habit he continued after the divorce, and he joined a band of like-minded co-workers with whom he would run relays or local races. Incidentally, I use "race" loosely because my dad was as slow and steady as a turtle, and you could spot him a mile off. Self-dubbed a *"sweat monster,"* he would wear a sweatband, sometimes of his own making, with an ordinary kitchen sponge rubber-banded around his head. After dinner, sometimes we might not see him until after it had gotten dark. This was in my late high school days for me.

For all his optimism, my dad avoided conflict, all the more so if, in his bowels, he detected a losing prospect whereby talking might make matters real and, therefore, worse. Maybe he couldn't express himself as he intended; like Hercules, his mercurial nature and swift temper could blind him. He never saw that his rage contributed to their rift. Hercules and my father fought against that force of birth and nature that had damaged them. In a way, they were hounded by their heredity, which left them feeling illegitimate, my dad with his mysteriously acquired disease, and Hercules with his enigmatic parentage.

During the couple of years it took for the divorce to get finalized, my dad ran three marathons; I'm sure he sensed they matched the grit required to endure the break he never wanted to see or accept. Two races he ran by himself: the New York Marathon and the "granddaddy of all," the Boston Marathon. No amount of therapy could have done what running did for him. I accompanied him on his third as his "water girl" at the Grandfather Mountain Marathon.[239] My job was to keep him fortified with water poured into Dixie cups from our green Coleman camping water jug and snack-size Snicker bars. As he passed around some treacherous bend, Dad would spy me, and his pace would quicken perceptibly. When he reached me, he would inhale the water and devour the bars whole! He would grin at me, grateful I'd thought to peel off the wrappers. Later, when I was in college, and I had put on the "freshman fifteen," my dad didn't lecture or scold me; he just invited me to run with him, and his health habit got jump-started in me.

Man was not meant to live alone, so although our home and family were his first circle, my dad planted himself in the world around him to explore entrepreneurial possibilities; he also resurrected his musical activities by joining the civic orchestra. Later on, as you will see, he returned to the fold of his faith. My dad was never one to come home and "call it a day"; he converted a non-descript windowless "back room" that adjoined the laundry room into his office, which also doubled as a small makeshift lab. This was his way of squeezing every drop of life's good to the last drops out; he was naturally the kind of person to make lemonade. Sitting at his desk, he would pour over "recipes," as he would call his original formulas to concoct coolants. He was bound and determined to start his own side business and strike it rich with his solvents, hopefully to be sold on a large scale to trucking companies. My dad turned out to be a better lab tech than a slick salesman, but he kept his business afloat. We knew little about what Dad was doing with this business, but we saw him busy. He even rented a small warehouse for production purposes. As he got older, when the world no longer dealt in cold calls, door-to-door solicitations, or presenting one's ideas in person as if one were a living business card, my brother filled the gap and transitioned into taking over the business. My mother came up with the logo for the business he would incorporate, P. Chemicals Incorporated, or PKI, and it exists today under the supervision of my brother. Yes, my dad wanted to create a legacy and become wealthy.

I believe his guiding light for how to get rich (but not so quickly) was Monopoly, his favorite game next to Backgammon; his piece was the battleship. I don't know about Hercules, but my dad's method of conquering was to take his enemy by surprise, quietly buying up all the inexpensive purple properties and then, without making any fanfare, plopping down as many hotels as he could. Maybe he felt at home on Mediterranean Avenue or liked the sound of Baltic Avenue. He would eagerly purchase the railroads as if he were their conductor. He never paraded his cash, let alone carried any; he kept his cards close. Such was the same with his business dealings, even though we were aware he was persistently trying to expand his outreach; acquiring realty would have been a natural for him. Near the end of my parents' marriage, he bought a cluster of small, sketchy apartments in town. It was apparent that unsavory dealings went on there. My dad also took up residence there while waiting in limbo, not knowing whether or not Mom would take him back. He had to give up before he gave out, so next, he moved out of these apartments and bought a two-story cedar house, mainly because, furnished with its own kitchen and separate entrance, it pleased his son, my brother, who was still in high school. The house had acreage, so my dad got his homestead while my brother got his private pad. More life awaited my dad on the other side of his workday, and there was still more after retirement, but we are not there yet. We are ready to shift gears and dive into the third theme of Hercules' life.

The Theme of Dichotomy and Opposites: The Wrath of Paul

As you know, in this chapter, I am using the Athenian tragedy by Euripides to frame and blend commonalities my father shared with Hercules, especially their personalities and values. Unlike Euripides, I am not going to contort the chronology and put the cart before the horse by chronicling his labors before those horrifying homicides set up by Hera. Like the contemporary Greek philosophers of his day, Euripides shifted the focus from Hercules' amazing feats to the gods' illogical and cruel intentions that would make it possible to manipulate his mind and wreak havoc using Hercules against himself. My father may have been filled with rage over his marriage being torn asunder, but I have no homicide report.

Unlike Hercules, my father did not contemplate suicide because he never thought he'd done anything wrong, and he was too busy trying to hatch a plan to worm his way back into our mother's heart or good graces. Euripides' purpose as an author is both to make Hercules the victim of the machinations of the gods as well as to elevate him by having Hercules, *of his accord*, climb to morally higher ground by taking on a punishment that was not due to him. As a result, the gods get demoted to manipulative at best or absent at worst. This theological bend bears no weight here; my father never questioned fate or felt victimized by the gods or God. He blamed his wife as if she were Eve, yet he longed for her as if she were earning back his beloved Rachel. Perhaps you think I, as his eldest daughter, idolize and idealize my father or put him on a pedestal. No, it's high time to go the full mile. I will offer you a counterpoint, but this is no jeremiad. I aim to present you with a fair and impartial view of my dad. Like Hercules, my dad — our hero — was just another imperfect man, some might even say a narcissist. I wear no rose-colored glasses; his flaws are crystal-clear to me.

In the dramatic version of Hercules, we learn about dichotomies evident in the events and themes[240] beyond Hercules' hero, which provide challenges or counter-point views and actions in opposition to Hercules. In my dad's case, the turmoil I expose will be an inside job, even if the answer is beyond his reach or reason. So often, we can be our own worst enemy; my father was no exception. Rather than judge or revile my dad, I ask you to embrace the whole of him. We won't write off his transgressions or excuse them away like some defense attorney or astute analyst might. Nor will we blame God, the Garden, or Greece for the fact that my dad could be a brute barbarian. I can suggest that his being out-of-sync psychologically and culturally would have enflamed his hot-headed temper, at times, making my father seem a cretin or beast unrecognizable to us. Although the ancient Greeks touted the importance of maintaining harmony and balance,[241] everything about my dad seemed to point to the opposite: he was a man of passions and extremes housed in one frame, never to be reconciled. We will embrace the good, the bad, and the ugly as you witness the "dichotomous halves which show the reality of opposite destructive and constructive forces" warring within my father, our hero.

You have now had a taste of the best of my dad; now I will bear his most perturbing if for no other reason, to provide a balanced perspective as well as a guidepost for you to consider later on when you'll see how his behavior declines as his disease progresses. Alexander Pope stated everyone has their faults: "To err is human." My dad was no god, and he had a temper like Hercules. As with the dramatic version of Hercules, whereby "certain characters stand on opposite ends of one another, creating a rift between them,"[242] this would be the case with my mom and dad, so I'll touch upon the source of their severance.

For those unfamiliar with Greek ways, let me also explain that although the ancient Greeks may have been erudite philosophers, many modern Greeks, like my dad, wield their might through dramatic displays of displeasure. The dichotomy in our adaptation of Hercules is that my parents could not have been more opposite ends of the spectrum in how they expressed their anger and handled conflict resolution. Simply put, they did not. It boiled down to divergent values and pride. They say opposites attract, which was true in my parents' case, not only in personality and passion but in how they argued; this proved detrimental to their union. If my mom felt threatened or attacked, she turned into a box turtle, retreating far inside her shell. Conversely, my dad would be like a mad jack-in-the-box and pop up and pursue with purpose, momentarily putting himself back in his box only to loudly erupt again when her walls of silence didn't come down. She was a stoic to his being one of the furies, and vengeance became his. My dad blamed my mom when things didn't go his way, and he used volume over vocabulary when he lost his cool. On the other hand, my mom could decimate him with carefully selected words and quickly exit stage right.

Your soul's worth imploded with her quip that could cut like a knife, but your eardrums and sensitivities burst with my dad's sonic boom. Somehow, after an indeterminable and interminable period of silence had passed, during which all negotiations were broken off, life took the upper hand, and problems were swept aside for the need to tend to the immediate needs at hand. Later, my mom would say over and over again that she was the "buffer" between our dad and us and that she had married "Dr. Jekyll and Mr. Hyde" for how quickly he could go from gregarious, buoyant and happy to sulking, skulking, or explosive. The precipitating spark might not ever be known. If my dad did go silent and sulk and slink about, it was usually because my mom's parents were visiting; otherwise, quiet pouting was so out of character for him. If his agitation was brewing, there was no denying it, much like you can sense an electrical storm looming on the near horizon; sparks of static were sure to follow.

Typically, it was anybody's guess as to why he went off the deep end, so we tried to read for clues like my dad's mother might have read into the future by peering at the patterns of Greek coffee grounds when plunked on a saucer. My dad's brail was not always easy to read. My mom became an emotional barometer of my dad and anticipated and responded to the shifting winds, trying to keep us from feeling the effects of his volatile emotional storms. Usually, we did not know the rhyme or reason for his changing tides. He, too, did not; perhaps he could not connect the dots and pinpoint why he had lost his temper, all the more so if the cause of the eruption was related to a more profound trigger. And so if he became blinded with rage, he wouldn't pin the tail on the donkey; he would point the blame on my mom. The degree to which he got angry was often not commensurate with the "crime," not to us, his more civilized family. There was no tidy "conflict resolution," just a unilateral insistence on his part and subsonic depression registering in her until, piece by piece, she quit their "three-legged race," as she put it. My mom put her foot down and walked away; my dad fell. *My dad broke down with the same anguish as Hercules in our myth version, except this was no dream, and he accepted no guilt.* I blame neither and still love them both immeasurably. Let's chalk it off to their occupying two different solar systems in the same galaxy, and neither could fathom the planet each came from. They were like two astronauts raising four little aliens in their own private Idaho; they collided but, try as they might and did, never fully yoked; in the end, my dad's vow stuck, and my mom's dissolved.

Our Hercules here was deceived by the woman he had scorned. My mother would not remember it like this, and my dad kept blinders on until death did them part. What was it that made my dad tick? How did this relationship go so far south? What would have gone awry if my dad and Hercules had taken moral responsibility so seriously? You will need examples to give flesh to fact, flaws to faults, which will humanize our hero; then, we'll complete his prototype. With additional examples and background, you'll come to see who he was before his disease would afflict his brain and pervert his ways and means. Without judgment, let's take a gander at his trespasses.

Of the Ten Commandments, my father regularly broke the Seventh and Eighth Commandments when it served his needs. Lying to save a buck never seemed like outright theft to him; he rationalized his peccadillos by justifying that we ought not to let ourselves be fleeced by others. For example, if our family had to spend the night in a hotel, my dad would gesture with quick downward-motion pushes of his hand. We in the back seat knew the drill: it was time to duck down in the car so those at the front desk would not see that we had six persons in our vehicle. (That was before the days when "Kids Stay Free!") If there was an age limit or cut-off point, we knew to keep quiet when our dad reported an age by its half-life. No matter how tall the tale, he never missed a beat or raised an eyebrow. Going through the grocery store's produce section with him meant time for free snacks and manna from heaven; no bunch of grapes or peanuts in their hulls were safe from his fingertips. Much to our embarrassment, often, he would argue over the price of some item at the cash register like he was haggling at an outdoor bazaar in the old country. When salad bars came out, my dad would mound his plate or burger with "*veggies,*" which he dubbed all produce, as high as a bale of hay. He would never have paid for a trip to the salad bar and forget about "just one plate, sir." My dad also brought home flasks, beakers, stirrers, and other containers he'd pinched from his workplace in the same way others might take office supplies or the box of Kleenex (or a towel) from the Holiday Inn, which he also did. My mom was miffed; my dad could have cared less.

My parents loved to do bargain shopping at antique stores, but that wasn't the only source of treasures to be found. My dad also had no problem entering into buildings soon to be demolished, all the more so if my mom pointed out that this or that item "needed" to be "saved," like resplendent stain-glass windows from a condemned church in Atlanta. She would solicit his help for that rescue project, and he was all in for their scavenger hunt of things headed for destruction anyway. Years later, when my dad was buying apartments, he asked his eldest brother to borrow ten grand for the downpayment, but he never paid him back. My uncle's fury was so great he could barely stand to be in my dad's presence. My dad glibly shrugged his shoulders and didn't think twice about reneging on this loan. He justified that he'd "borrowed" it for all keep's sake. After all, his brother didn't "need" this money back because he'd inherited everything from their father. This was my dad's idea of poetic justice; my uncle called him a thief. And, thank goodness, my mom did all the bills and our taxes; when my dad was *"going solo,"* as he dubbed himself post-divorce, I saw him write off an inoperable car he had donated at triple its value as a write-off on his taxes.

I have heard that an unguarded strength can quickly become a double weakness, which was the case for my father. He could turn off or tune out pessimistic clamors or voices of doubt — this started when he was young, and without "distractions," it became possible for him to propel himself to success. However, this rebuffing or shrugging off of opinions that ran counter to his *also* produced a callous disregard for others' views, which might have been helpful to him. He simply did not concern himself with what people thought of him, and he had no problem letting them see that he didn't. Appearances mean so much to many; to my dad, it was fluff.

As kids, we would roll our eyes at him if he seemed goofy or played the fool, but we would stare a hole through him if he were rude to a server. Sometimes, we felt as if we had our very own Quasimodo[243]. Like the hunchback of Notre Dame, our dad became the object of our ridicule, not to mention a victim of others' gossip. Though he did not care about the world's view of him — that is, unless we had somehow made him look "bad" as a dad to it — he was like a bloodhound and could whiff out distance and disdain from his brood, but that's as far as it went. Like a stubborn mule, he kicked and brayed but did not root out and try to mend broken fences or lost alliances. Duly note that our Hercules here was a better father than a husband, but my dad's yo-yo volatility always caught us off-guard. We never knew how his winds blew, what ruffled his feathers, or what dropped or raised his sails.

He was a mystery to us in many ways, but I loved him beyond

measure. "They" say that the line existing between love and hate lies on a razor's edge; I say truer words were never spoken. In fact, I read that the brain cannot differentiate between the intensity it feels between these two extreme emotions. The "insular" is a brain region that determines the intensity of an emotion and whether the emotion is positive or negative. Hate and love are involved in the neural processing of what is referred to as "the arousal effect of emotion." [244] Those particular emotions with a "high arousal effect" can quickly turn from positive (love) to negative (hate)."[245] What was boggling to me as a child were the hair-trigger switches within my dad that flipped him from an average man going about his regular affairs at work, house, or yard into a madman around my mom, a fool in public, or a tyrant in our home. We couldn't anticipate which man we'd meet when, so we proceeded with caution and treaded lightly around his eggshells. We had no idea where his landmines lay or what vexing thing my mom might have done to aggravate him and incur his wrath. There was no thought of therapy for dealing with past ghosts from his Greek Van Diemen's Land. Then again, he might have just been hungry, or "ravenous," as he liked to say, because his blood sugar might have bottomed out; we had no word like "hangry" then. As an aside, HD wasn't on anyone's radar, let alone in our vocabulary.

Another significant value difference that created a gap between my parents was that my mom saw our community as an extension of her home and sought to better our immediate world to benefit us as well. My dad subscribed to the adage that "charity begins at home." While this phrase is not biblical, the Apostle Paul does tell us that "if anyone does not provide for his own, and especially for those of his household, he has denied the faith and is worse than an unbeliever" (1 Tim 5:8, emphasis mine). My dad was as adamant about this point as if he had coined it himself. This was his eleventh commandment, but it also brought out his worst. My dad fully expected everyone to abide by Christ's credo, which he also adopted as his own motto: "The one who is not with Me is against Me, and the one who does not gather with Me scatters" (Matthew 12:30). It was as if he were his little-g god in our cosmos. However, my mom was not one of his followers; eventually, she flew their coop. And this was no time for the faint of heart in our family. Dazed and confused, my dad attributed our defending mom to our being "brainwashed" and "poisoned" by her. He interpreted his world using battle terminology to express their internecine war. Despite furtively spying inside his own home to catch wind of duplicity, deception, or betrayal in ways or words, he couldn't see the writing on the wall for believing he could wield his way through sheer force of will. During the final two years, when their marriage and our household were in a ceasefire, all of us but Dad could tell their ship was sinking. Since none of us came to *his* camp, he equivocated us all with Mom and kept repeating that *she* was the *"traitor."*

As the eldest daughter, I knew my mom's side and mind inside out, so though by temperament, I am more like my father. At the time, my mindset had me empathize with my mother. While *he* hadn't been paying attention, we kids couldn't help but notice that her heart had grown cold towards him, and no effort of his could resuscitate her affection for him. From the time I graduated high school through my undergraduate years, my dad tried every which way he could to get my mother to see the greater good, to try to bring her *"back to her senses,"* to give him another chance, but her heart no longer saw him as husband or hero. United they stood; divided, he fell. He expected me to be a medium, a translator, or divine agent to find some unturned stone or missed angle through which he could worm his way back into her good graces or affection or anything —throw the dog a bone, for Pete's sake! Hercules never had to grovel, but he did do penance. So unaccepting was he of the outcome that even after the divorce was finalized, he never told his parents. I made this discovery quite by chance when, on my first trip to the Soviet Union in 1984, his mother and oldest brother met me at JFK airport for a quick visit at a restaurant before I had to board the plane. After dispensing with the pleasantries, in no time at all, they ferreted out the truth about my folks. They interrogated me as if they were the Greek Gestapo or Secret Police; then, I was cursing my dad as much as I was lamenting for him.

If I were to choose two other weaknesses in my dad that panned out in excessive displays of rage, they would be <u>possessiveness and jealousy</u>. These two emotions were often expressed capriciously in the form of the "because-I-said-so" attitude of his intended to rebuff any retort looming on the horizon. His pursuit of personal power frequently led him adrift and astray. My dad's possessiveness originated from a fear of loss based on past privations. Starting with my mom and moving out in bold concentric circles radiating from them as one, we were his; freedom to be who we made to be aside, we belonged to him, property of PGA. And while he made fun of his oldest brother for never *"cutting the umbilical cord"* attached their mother to go out and live on his own, I am sure my dad would have been entirely content if our family could have had a homestead or a family compound, with none of us traveling further than our job or the market, so connected at the hip and heart was he to us.

If he felt tremors of any distance mounting between us, it created a King Kong within him, and you would indeed find him swinging out his hairy arms to scoop us in close to him. At times, we were bewildered by this ferocity. Therefore, it was no wonder when my mom sought out ways to help our local community, including supporting our city get public busing, aiding with voter registration, and even attending meetings of the local chapter of the Audubon Society, he was not a happy camper. From the shadows and the sidelines, my dad booed, balked, and belittled her. That charity should extend beyond our home made zero sense to him. Should she leave the house in the evenings, and he had to babysit us, we kids knew he would likely blow a gasket, and so we were glad to go to bed early, if but to giggle in the safety of our rooms and escape his gargoyle-like wrath. Her absence in the evenings was not a regular occurrence, but his reaction was a given.

My mother's social life and extended family of choice were found at church. That may sound righteous, but in the "Me generation" of the 1970s, a decade that promoted self-actualization and individual awareness, my lonely and silently biding mom took hold of pop psychology like a fish to water and downed pop psych classics like *I'm Ok − You're Ok*, *Games People Play*, *Please Understand Me: Character and Temperament Types* and *The Road Less Traveled* as if her life depended upon it. They validated and affirmed her bright, new hopes for self-actualization as much as they troubled and mystified our old-world Hercules husband, who didn't see she could need anything but food and family. She found validation in secular humanistic values that exalted self and man rather than God and Son; she did not seek His Word but instead, her way.

My dad went along for the ride because going to the Unitarian Church at least meant they were attending some house of worship; anyway, there were other scientists and PhDs like himself in attendance. Plus, he became their token Greek, giving him numerous opportunities to shine and share his heritage, if but to grill lamb and dance his heart out. I'm told that once at a party, my father head and led a string of thirty people out and around a house as he leaped and gyrated and twirled like a Greek whirling dervish, holding onto his trusty handkerchief that tethered him to the rest, all of them swirling and laughing under a blanket of moonlight. My parents were also involved with a circle of friends who took turns hosting international dishes and another circuit who were involved in the local symphony in some ways. These were the good ol' days, but this patchwork quilt of our family's making also had some serious stains.

When my dad got a thing fixed in his mind to do with and for his family, there was little stopping him. The best and worst example of this, which our whole family remembers, took place when he took our family hostage during one Christmas vacation. We were visiting my mom's folks out in Arizona. One of my dad's buddies at work told him about the one-of-a-kind, can't-miss site in America called the Grand Canyon. On one of these days, Mom excitedly told us that we would see Indian Cliff Dwellers; they were caverns or caves carved into caramel-hued, stark mountains. With my dad behind the wheel of our "plain Jane" van and his family in tow, we would have had no way of guessing that another plan had hatched in his brain, and it didn't take long for him to announce where we were going: the Grand Canyon, of course! These Indian caves didn't stand a chance! The drive seemed to take hours, and he wouldn't stop for love nor money.

Popping peanut M&Ms or chewing coffee beans for sustenance and energy sounded more like he was crunching on gravel. His gaze was fixed on the Grand Canyon in the GPS of his imagination, and we could tell by the alarmed expression on my mom's usually impassive face that we all knew we were in for a ride and one driven by a maniac. It would not be wise to rile him since he drove fast with blinders on. My poor sister was whimpering and about to float or turn yellow, and we had only two 8-track tapes to drown out the silence. Aretha Franklin wasn't getting it that day. *Finally*, we pulled up in the national park's parking lot, yet my dad caught a fever somewhere along the way and crawled in the back of the van. He was sweating profusely and was sick as a dog. All he could do was shudder and huddle under the thick green sleeping bag. Ironically, as fate would have it, he missed the site altogether! I barely remember what I saw there myself, but I sure do remember what I felt.

The year I turned thirteen, our world changed forever. Weary of war and my dad's tendency to be tyrannical, my mom changed the rules and her script. Tired of our Hercules ranting and raving over every penny spent, my mom got a job as an interior designer, and while my dad was glad for the extra income and an outlet for her artistic expression, she spent her money on things that made no sense to him, like family vacations to places of educational or cultural value rather than free stays at her parents' lake cottage to drop off the kids and leave without offering to pay a penny. As the years passed, she felt ignored and taken for granted, and he felt disrespected and disregarded. Their cycle was vicious; the gulf widened. To break their stalemate, my mom started going to therapy, but when my mom asked him if they could go to therapy together, my dad bellowed, "*You're* the one who's lost it!" and clutched all the tighter to what (or whom) was escaping his grasp. As Hercules would be dazed in a dream, my dad remained clueless and did not intuit or divine or realize that his refusal to get help became the last straw for her.

His possessiveness had soured into jealousy and clabbered into suspicions vocalized. My dad would furtively sneak up and lay low to eavesdrop on conversations to weed out information he would not attain by normal communication channels. His trust was low because he feared desertion. He turned from sullen to violent when suspicions were aroused, but I am getting ahead of myself. I can tell you that he turned back into a village boy when he believed his territory was being invaded, and he pelted a rock through the back windshield of the VW van belonging to someone he believed to be a wolf among his sheep. On the night of my high school graduation in May of 1981, my mom announced she no longer loved him, but this wasn't the end. For three interminably long years, we all lived in a permanent state of limbo, not knowing whether or not our mom would stay married to him; she did not relish the thought of instigating the collateral damage of what could happen to her children, never mind breaking apart our family.

In 1983, she made the painful decision and final curtain call to leave him, but then she asked *him* to move out of the house. Two kids were out of the home, and the two that remained ended up apart, each living with the parent of their same sex. My father was shell-shocked and would become like a homeless beggar, willing to accept any breadcrumbs of hope she might throw his way, but not before he first lost his marbles and his temper. One evening, while three out of four of us children were not at home, he tried to physically force my mom out of the house since *she* was the one who wanted to be free of him. Hercules' brutality against his wife occurred while he was in a hallucinatory state; my dad was wired and on fire. My mom stayed put and clung to the cool base of the toilet in their master bath, and my dad, failing to pry her loose, threatened her by raising his fists to force her out. That's as far as it went, but he only hammered another nail in his coffin. For the moment, another stalemate was reached.

What happened next remains a blur of unknown. While I was away at college, I came to learn that by some miracle — no doubt brought on because my mother had given Dad a sliver of hope that his leaving the house would give her "the space" she needed to reconsider her decision and maybe "give him one more chance," he agreed to leave our home and house. He held onto that slender thread for *years*, but no effort on his part would bring about the "*reunification*" he so desperately sought. In that dire time, Dad became an alien; he had chosen self-exile rather than chance losing her altogether, but he did so anyway. No number of flowers placed on her windshield or tearful pleas he requested of me to commission on his behalf to her could move my mom's heart, which had by then cooled to cold. He hadn't been paying attention along the way, or maybe he had, but he refused to enter this labyrinth of complex feelings. Our Hercules had no *ah-ha* moment of epiphany in recognizing his part in their demise. At the onset of that two-year interim of her indecision, nearly suddenly, my dad lost the few remaining strands of hair atop his now wholly bald head. Seemingly overnight, the dusting of grey at his sideburns turned to a total shock of near white, like a halo of mourning framing his dome.

For the first time and only time in his life, he lost his appetite and grew gaunt. That summer, George Jones's "He Stopped Loving Her Today" came out, and I couldn't hear it without crying, drinking, or both. Their divorce was finalized on January 6, 1984. My mom brought reams of notebooks teeming with proofs, justifications, and evidence; my dad came empty-handed with a shell-shocked heart and boggled brain. My mom asked for nothing for herself but freedom and funds from him to pay for their children's college; my dad's defeat and banishment were complete. Don't think that the desire to get back together with her died any more than Hercules got over his wife's (and children's) death. Oh, no. His strategizing and *"troubleshooting"* would continue for several more years after that. The green-eyed monster was the next and final "opposite" force I mentioned, which countered the great and good in his nature. Here, I turn from his unfortunate exchanges with his wife to us, his children, and me.

I need to quash any notions that I would hold my father in contempt by airing his dirty laundry for any other purpose than providing a baseline so we can discern and differentiate between the average, flawed individual and the sick man who dominated later on when my dad's Huntington's disease had *"kicked in,"* as he would phrase it. Part of the reason that this section on "Dichotomy and Opposites" exists is to counterbalance what some might contend is unjust favoritism or unmerited favor, so I balance this presentation of my Hercules by exposing his underbelly; we each and all have one. However, my dad justified losing his temper, often with a frothy, speechless, righteous indignation. Like many, he possessed little interest in or inclination towards reflection, let alone correction; unlike Hercules, he felt no inner pang to atone, but eventually, he would come to beg.

When my father considered society's standard for what constitutes grounds for divorce, he was firm and sure *he* had done no wrong; why, he was without blemish and in no need of change! *Au contraire, mon frere!* For the record and from God's truth, "there is none righteous, no, not one" (Romans 3:10 NKJV). Before we cringe or roll our eyes over some overbearing behavior of my dad's, even then, God was "demonstrating His love toward us [and him], in that while we were still sinners, Christ died for us." Although my father was a believer, he was not one to wear his faith on his sleeve, and he did not share his faith with his children. I had no idea that while I may have been disappointed in the outcome of their marriage, *I should not have been judging either of my parents.* He just wanted to get back into her good graces; if he prayed for restoration, it would have remained unspoken. I myself had not yet taken the leap of faith. I was ignorant of the destiny of a person who had heard of Christ and remained neutral like Switzerland or hostile like North Korea.

Dad may have taken the easy way out and defaulted to my mom's default position of rejecting organized religion — primarily Protestant Churches in the South — but I contend that his faith lay dormant yet very much alive. I saw it resuscitate and blossom after their union dissolved. I think God was still demonstrating His love for my dad even though he put his faith on hold to keep the peace in his marriage. By and large, we, his children, were innocent and ignorant heathen. One fine day, I did come to believe, but my father had already been dead four years and didn't see that I had been "justified by His blood...saved from the wrath of God through...the death of His Son (from Rom. 5: 8–10). Of a certain, my pop is smiling at me now because I now share a future with him even though back then, we never spoke of such vital but esoteric matters. He didn't want to make any waves with Mom, and we didn't want to raise my dad's ire; we all knew he was capable of madness that could render him savage or sullen. The wrath of our Father in Heaven wasn't even a thought then, so I thank God for His mercy and infinite patience with us! We were all high on the high horse of pride.

I genuinely believe that in the three or so years leading up to their split, my dad's fits of rage were misappropriated bouts of emotional leakage that indicated somewhere deep in his core, he knew things weren't good between them, so by venting (or yelling), he let off steam which kept their break at bay. After he combusted and my mom relented and conformed, he felt a wave of relief, even though nothing had changed; we kids were stone-cold mystified. We never knew when the other shoe was going to drop. In those days, I used to think that my dad's short-tempered nature was as innate as his olive complexion, but I do not believe this to be the case. How we express our anger is a *learned* behavior, and my parents attended such different schools of thought; his mom screamed like a siren, and his brothers brayed like donkeys when ticked or peeved.

His father, a quiet man who kept his suffering to himself, was the odd man out in that family; my dad mimicked his mom. I am grateful that my perception of my father in the late seventies and early eighties was not the be-all, end-all "that's the way it is."[246] Anyway, I now know that "God sees not as man sees, for man looks at the outward appearance, *but the Lord looks at the heart"* (1 Samuel 16:7, emphasis mine), and my dad had the heart of seven men. I return to a short list of his transgressions and flaws that combusted into outbursts when his HD became pronounced. HD did *not* instigate *new* features; it just distorted and amplified flaws or idiosyncrasies *already present.* Each of us kids has our own opinion and recollections of who our father was and would become, but this is the eldest daughter's tale, so you get her memories of this Hercules.

Within our thematic section of dichotomy and opposites, no example of my dad's duality is more pronounced than where education and heritage overlap into a fuzzy area of gray and longing for me. You already know how important education and heritage are to my father, so wouldn't you naturally think that he would have been desirous for his children to learn to speak Greek? Regardless of the few words and phrases here and there he uttered to me as a toddler, the answer and outcome are the opposite of what you would expect. What I didn't consider then was that not only did he not have home court advantage of being a native son, but I could tell he took the most practical route by putting to route all that made life more challenging or more complicated; he'd already been through more than enough. Why drudge up what had been destroyed or bring to life old skeletons? He was doing his best to get along and succeed in this version of the American life he'd chosen. Therefore, he could afford to sacrifice language for progress or peace. Only when I heard him talk on the telephone to his parents, always extra loud and animated, did my other dad come to life, and, oh, I missed what I had never had. I have the faintest memory of going to Greek school for a short time with my mother; I couldn't have been more than four, and it was not for long. Maybe my mother was trying to jump-start learning Greek in her eldest, which her husband had not; likely, my dad was pleased, yet he was largely uninvolved. The Greek he spoke to me was relegated to our nighttime ritual, whereby he would tell me in Greek to "turn the page" of the children's book he would animatedly read to me and then "good night." Except for Greek food types, that was pretty much it.

Fast-forward to my messy days in junior high when I was making straight A's, but behind the scenes, I was also getting mixed up in sketchy activities. What pulled me back to my senses and sensibilities was a healthy pride that pricked my heart to explore and celebrate my Greek heritage. Step one involved asking my dad to teach me Greek; I was a freshman in high school. I still remember announcing that I had something vital to ask him. So, one school night, I asked him to come and say good night to me, at which point I listed all the obvious reasons why teaching me Greek was a good idea, not that I thought it needed stating. You would have thought he would have given me a welcome-home hug for asking him to teach me to speak Greek. Not seeing any light turn on in his eyes, I began begging. "Dad, *pleeeeease* teach me to speak Greek!" Instead of holding me as I started to cry, he got gruff and rebuffed me. I was floored; he hemmed and hawed and seemed awkward and distant. That was that: case closed for then, but his faltering didn't stop me, and a few months later that year, I asked my dad if, at the very least, he and I could drive together to Brooklyn at Thanksgiving. I wanted to visit my yiayia and papou! I got a swift and enthusiastic reply to that request: "Ναι!"— "*Yes!*" — and he and I started what would become our annual pilgrimage there, a mecca trip for just the two of us, and it satisfied our souls and created a special bond between us.

I got closer to my grandmother and felt a temperamental connection to her that I could not put into words. She felt it, too. I'll never forget her saying, "*I love you like ee daughter, not like ee granddaughter!*" One evening after dinner on their balcony, my grandfather and I sat side by side, silently gazing out at the Verrazano Bridge on the horizon, the sky settling into indigo but with the city's many lights still twinkling like fireflies. I confided in my father's father that I wanted to learn Greek. He smiled warmly, put his paw of a hand over mine, and then got up slowly to get something from inside. He shuffled back and handed me an ancient Greek Primer, softly telling me, "*You must practice every day!*" I nodded and promised him I would. I still have that book today, and I know more Greek than I did then; even in my father's last years, our conversations were peppered with Greek. For the next five years until my freshman year in college, my dad and I made our annual trek to visit his folks, and it was good. Afterward, he and my brother took up the tradition.

Later that spring of my freshman year in college, my papou died, and though I didn't make the funeral, my father asked me to fly with him to his forty-day memorial service or "Mnimosino"[247] in Greek. Little did I know then that I would hold the same service for my father, including preparing the edible mound of koliva[248] for him; in fact, it looked like a powdered grave. Koliva is a delicious mixture of wheat, walnuts, cinnamon, raisins, honey, and more, dusted with powdered sugar. It is meant to be shared with fellow parishioners who loved him. This particular Greek tradition and recipe predate Christianity, and they can be traced to its use in festivals as far back as the eleventh century BC! In 362, the patriarch of Constantinople began requiring its consumption during the Great Lent.[249] This is not the last time I'll refer to koliva; I, too, would make a batch in honor of my father.

Since that time, having become "connected with celebrating the memory of saints," koliva has been prepared and consumed after the memorial service by Orthodox believers. The inception of this idea can be traced to John 12:24: "Unless a grain of wheat falls into the earth and dies, it remains alone; but if it dies, it bears much fruit." I don't know how much fruit my father bore, but he ate his fill of koliva at his dad's Mnimosino. On our flight home, suspended between heaven and earth, sky and cloud, my dad wept for his father and apologized to me for not teaching me Greek. And could we please try from here on out? Naturally, I was still all in! Surely, the dichotomy in my identity grew a little fainter here, but I still have one more example of my receiving the opposite of what you'd expect from him.

Three years prior, when I was sixteen, I had the opportunity to travel to Europe with a group from high school, and one of the six countries we visited was Greece. I was euphoric as I saw people that looked like me and were happy for me. Once, on our way from Thessaloniki to Athens, our bus stopped along a dirt road, and in the near distance, I saw an older man riding a donkey who, upon approaching us, spoke directly to me from among all the students there. I felt like I was gazing at my grandfather, who was transported through time and space. Mesmerized in wonder, I gazed at the aqua-marine sea — the actual water and not some picture in a book. How could I *not* jump in this water? So I did! Down I went, and feeling something soft tickle the sole of my foot, I dove deeper and brought up a segment of sponge from the depths in triumph.

Ancient sights I had only read about came to life. I felt euphoric and resurged, connected to my dad just being in the primus locus that birthed him. My assigned homestay in Greece was on Salamina Island, a mere fifteen-minute ferry ride from Athens. Upon learning I was Greek and still had relations living there, my host family took me back to Athens on day one to meet my relatives. My dad gave me a crudely written, penciled address of theirs, "just in case." When our mad taxi driver arrived at their apartment, I rang the doorbell, but the door was already ajar. Curious eyes peered at us and me, and then my host brother and sister informed them that this stranger was their flesh and blood. Immediately, the door swung open wide, and, starting with his cousin, one by one, those inside embraced me with many tears and light kisses on my cheek: I was their only living link — and evident chip off the old block — to my long-gone father. So many "Poh-pohs" or "Oh, mys" I heard, and I was introduced to my father's aunt, whose name translates to "Angel"; it fits.

It was as if no time had passed since my dad had left, and, with my host "brother" as a translator, we all sat together eating koulourakia cookies, and I caught them up as best I could. Meanwhile, behind the scenes, the coordinator of our school's tour in Greece was working out the details with my teacher, such as whether I could stay in Greece after our official tour had ended. He said it would be his "honor and pleasure" to make this possible for me. Giddy at this prospect, I eagerly made that expensive trans-Atlantic phone to tell my dad the great news and ask for his official permission. Out of the blue, my dad bellowed, "No!" that could not stay longer than the group and extend the trip to Greece. I went cold and numb. Who was this, and why was he so angry? I begged and pleaded, but all I heard was a crushing finality in his voice of refusal. It was like Zeus had just screamed at me from Mt. Olympus; I felt humiliated, bewildered, and forlorn. It would be fifteen years later, but my next trip to Greece would be with my father. It would be our only trip, but with that trip, this particular dichotomy melted into the sun-kissed sea. Nowhere do education and heritage intersect more for me than in my choice of major in college, and I also had to contend with my dad's wrath here.

The year after my papou died and the year before my parents' divorce was finalized was the year I switched my major from pre-med to Russian, and I'll never forget that phone call home to him to inform my dad. I was euphoric: I had that settled feeling for the first time when something clicked and fit right into place. I was sure my dad would be pleased! Instead, I heard an eerie silence over the cold receiver. Then the storm hit, and I was sure my dormmates could hear my dad through the phone. *"You did whaaaaat?!? You'll neeeeeever get a job!!! What were you thinking?!?"* Now, if I had been like his brother Kolya or his mother, I might have dramatically dropped the receiver and skulked off, but I froze as if in shock, and I felt hot tears well up in my eyes. My hands went cold and clammy, and my heart was pounding through my chest. I don't recall my exact response except that I would become a professor.

Keep in mind that I declared my major as Russian just one month after Premier Brezhnev died, and the Cold War was in full tilt. You heard phrases like "better dead than red" if you were one of the few, the proud, marine-like family of us Russian majors. Once I visited or attended school in the Soviet Union, my fate and fortune were sealed. I did both. Multiple times. True to my dad's wild and wooly mood swings, he informed me the next time I saw him that he'd *"been doing some thinking."* His expression indicated that the verdict was now in my favor. Why, I could get a job with the government like the CIA, and *"the benefits would be tremendous."* He was all about the benefits!

And though this is the section where I focus on his darker musings, I must mention here that there's no doubt he appreciated my love of Russian culture. Whenever I would discuss this or that class I was taking, he would always start by asking me *"how Mother Russia was,"* like she was our newly adopted relative. Even our last trip to Brooklyn included his driving me through and personally curating Brighton Beach and Sheepshead Bay, both of which boasted having the largest Russian-American communities in New York City.[250] Whatever Russian Orthodox Cathedral was nearby, we would scout it out so I could take a picture of it and peek inside.

Nonetheless, in those early days when I was still seeking to complete or fulfill that part which yearned within my hungry, half-Greek self, my dad would sit at his kitchen table after we'd had dinner, perhaps setting up the backgammon board. He might announce wistfully, *"You grow old too fast and wise too late."* I took this to mean that he might have wished for a do-over of our upbringing. I'll never know. If I argued passionately in favor of something I'd seen practiced in the Soviet Union that I thought should be done in the States, like having the right to free education and universal health care, my dad did not counter me. He would say something vague and mystical, like, *"Sometimes you have to travel around the world to end up next door."* Maybe he was lamenting over gains and losses in his pyrrhic victory of survival in the States. Perhaps he chose his battles more wisely and let me have my say while he prayed that I might learn that home is where the heart is, and he was with us here in *this* place.

Do any of the "flaws" I have fleshed out seem unforgivable? Horrible? Harrowing? My dad did not think of himself as holier-than-thou or perfect by any stretch of the imagination. Still, when he compared himself to philanderers, drunkards, gamblers, *"worthless bums,"* or criminals, my dad counted himself a saint. My mom was more like Hamlet in carefully weighing every thought, move, and deed. In the seventies, we might have called it "analysis paralysis." It took her three years to decide that she would not remain with my dad. Because of his mercurial nature, I think she realized that neither suicide nor homicide was off the table for him; for him, divorce was a death knell. He may have known the order of the periodic table of elements; however, he could not recall the dates of our birthdays, let alone their anniversary. That was one of many cards in her Rolodex of infractions she had accumulated over twenty-three years of marriage. Unfortunately, her love *did* keep a record of wrongs (1 Cor. 13:5 NIV). As Hamlet said, "There is nothing good or bad, but *thinking makes it so,*" and my mother tallied enough marks until she reached the straw that broke *her* back.

Conversely, my dad did not keep score; no crimes were committed! He saw the world in black and white, my mother in technicolor gray. He did not blame fate or his parents or his upbringing for whatever it was that displeased my mom so, but unlike Shakespeare's Cassius, who was brooding and introspective, my dad never reflected or concluded, "The fault is not in our stars/But in ourselves," and that unfailing egoism proved to be his Achilles tendon. This is an excellent place to transition to the final focal point Hercules and my dad shared, our last themes from the drama of Hercules, which I'll combine with identity and hope.

The Themes of Identity and Hope

It should come as no surprise that Hercules' "identity crisis" — indeed, if we were to acknowledge that he had one — revolved around the fact that he was half god and half mortal. In his theatrical rendition, Euripides manipulates the order of the myth's events such that the labors come first and then the familial murder. However, I will stick with the myth's original sequence. I also find no need to describe the part of my dad's identity about his "Greek nature," as he would label it himself; this would be to state the obvious. Instead, I'll focus on what seemed like a self-applied shellack, a veneer of what my dad *thought* made him fit in with the regular Joe in upper east Tennessee. It was one of the first things we kids would make fun of behind his back. We didn't do this in a mean-spirited way; it's just that his becoming a chameleon to up the chances of being accepted in his adopted country — and in this neck of the woods seemed a dubious and doomed prospect.

Upper East Tennessee is populated by people as clannish and small-minded as those from the hills he came from across the ocean. He was Greek to their Scotch blood, but both were full of wild goats, craggy cliffs, and miles of coastline. The neighborhood in which we lived was an oasis for the affluent. Wealth and worth came from many sources; some were from "old money," and others were transplanted professionals who valued a more high-brow culture; we were the latter. Sort of. The first giveaway to our being odd-men-out was our odd four-syllable last name, which, if people ventured to pronounce, they invariable landed on the wrong syllable. My dad would sometimes try to adopt the modulation and tone he had heard in these nasally, tin-voiced natives who elongated their vowels to the point that they made two syllables out of one and cut off or truncated poly-syllabic words to a mutant dwarfed version. My dad never could get the hang of the pronunciation, but he gave it the ol' college try. Undoubtedly, these folks got an odd kick out of him attempting. However, we kids cringed or rolled our eyes; my mom just looked away. Our favorite memory of our personable dad trying to fit in or socialize was when he would try to initiate light conversation at, say, a filling station, where he was likely to get out and stretch, clean the windshield with vim and vigor, and perhaps spout off to the next guy over, "*Heeeeey there, good buuuuuudy!"* His convoluted mish-mash of American idioms or mispronunciations brought no end of delight to my mother, both then and now. There are too many to count! Betty Crocker became *"Betty Cracker"*; he bundled two idioms and came up with *"there's no use crying over spilled milk under the bridge,"* and in his final days, he would blast doctors who didn't do his bidding and hiss to me, *"But they took the Hypocritic Oath!"* He was a goofball nerd trying to be "cool"; feigned aloofness utterly eluded him, and any attempt at such had us kids smirking or cackling. He didn't mind, notice, or concern himself with our reaction to our thinking he was being a fake or fool. In the seventies, we used to say, "Give me five!" as the sign to hand-slap over an agreement or shared moment of joy. Instead, my dad would say, *"Give me three!"* and get tickled with himself. In exasperation, we would come back and say, "Oh, brother!" he would smirk and reply, *"Oh, sister!"*

We came to expect the unexpected in our dad; we just never attributed it to his being forever foreign. My father's Greekness was especially obvious to us whenever his parents called us on the phone, and he spoke Greek to them loudly. He would shout into the receiver, not because he was upset, but because it was as if greater volume was called to compensate for their distance. In those moments, we got a glimpse into our father, who had a past and identity that, for us, was like a black hole, a galaxy unto him entirely unknown to us. He was my favorite living artifact, and I wondered what it was like for him to live so far from his native, rocky soil. Two other features of East Tennessee endeared this land to my father and made him call this part of the planet his home: the mountains and the music. Upper East Tennessee is the most mountainous part of this state; one could go on a different hike every weekend of the year and not run out of new treks. Only when I traveled to the Peloponnesus for myself did I truly appreciate that being embraced by mountains, albeit the smokey ones in upper East Tennessee cloaked in green or burnt orange depending upon the season, was as natural for him as being embraced by your mother? And he took to bluegrass music like a duck to water; little did I know at the time that the sawing on the fiddle, strumming the mandolin, plucking away a banjo, or crooning in those twangy, close-knit harmonies would evoke in my dad's mind's ear the distant strains of the three-stringed Cretan lyra, bowed with an entrancing, ecstatic frenzy, or perhaps a Greek bouzouki played lightning fast; or the voices of Greek island singers, what with their softly shrill, intertwined voices.

These may not have been identical to the first imprints stamped in his spirit, but for my dad, the local sights and sounds were close enough to satisfy a crevice in his soul and became as beloved to him as if he were an adopted child. He even wore a big ol' belt buckle with an old mountain fiddler; I don't know how it fits. And when my dad bought his first pickup truck, I'll bet he thought he had arrived! Perhaps this was the same sensation Hercules felt riding astride Pegasus, with his face peering through the helmet made from a lion's jaws. Both men were proud warriors to their cores. Although no native son, my father felt like a king when he finally sired a son, and this draws us to the final but foremost aspect of his identity: what it meant for him to be a man.

I don't pretend to know about my father's concept of being a man, but it certainly wasn't hard to see it was old-world and not American. He may not have been so barbaric to dismiss the second sex altogether in the way. For example, with his wayward niece, Antigone, King Creon would utter, "No woman shall be the master while I live." However, my dad's actions spoke loud and clear and rang: he would not play second fiddle to his wife. This typecast outlook cost him his marriage. We could take the battle of the sexes back to the Garden, whereby man's disobedience to God set up the subsequently fallen hierarchy that subordinated woman to man. My dad was a more complicated and liberated version than Adam. Let me explain. For my father, no achievement accomplished through the sweat of his brow eclipsed his becoming a father. However, the absolute zenith of being male (and father) was to sire a son and ensure the family's name lasted into perpetuity. Therefore, when I, the oldest of his daughters, who would have walked on hot coals to see her dad happy, overheard some local yokel tell him, "Well, Paul, you *finally* got it right!" when he learned that my dad had produced a son. It stung like acid rain and felt like hot lava poured over me. My dad just grinned. While I can appreciate that all men take pride in producing a namesake, in the American man, there may be some attempt to mask this favoritism in front of female family members, but not so for my dad; it was blatant and unabashed, and deny it he never tried.

On the day my mother came home from the hospital with our baby brother, we three girls and my grandmother hovered excitedly near the front door with balloons and homemade signs to welcome them, but instead, we got my father, who entered first. He shushed us with a dismissive wave and stalked protectively in front of them, practically hovering over his Madonna and child. Mom had a soft, snuggly blanket thrown over him as he lay against her chest. My dad acted as if she were cradling a bassinet filled with gold coins. Indeed, we four children were his most prized possessions, and here was his crown jewel! It began like that. My dad was so grateful for an heir that he suppressed whatever disappointment he may have felt in my mom's decision to rename him. At the time, that was small fry to him. You might think that the tradition and tendency of Greeks to name their children seems formulaic, formal, and fixed. The principle behind it is to honor one's parents or close relatives and, past that, to revere the saints who martyred their lives for their faith. And this system didn't die lightly in my dad; it just lay dormant. You'll see. For now, be mindful that for Greeks, naming one's child comes from a time-honored system whereby the past converges with the present in the swaddling infant. For the American, it seems weirdly curtailing, unimaginative, and uninspiring. Initially, my mom named my brother after the first Christian martyr, a respectable name among Greeks, but she didn't intend to appease them.

Then suddenly, on a whim justified by the fact that she disliked and would not want to hear the nickname "Stevie," she changed my brother's name to that of the Jewish shepherd boy who slayed a giant to become king. My parents sealed their incorrect deal by choosing to perform on my brother the modern hygienic rite (and Jewish covenantal ritual) that, I'm sure, increased my Greek grandparents' dismay. A glance in his diapers confirmed it for them. At least my dad got the consolation prize of naming his son's middle name after his father's first name, Giorgos. For the Greeks, Giorgos was another "glorious martyr of Christ, illustrious and courageous in battle"; he was beheaded in 296."[251] My dad bears the same first name as the greatest Christian missionary who ever lived; he, too, had an indomitable spirit. Though I'm sure it was hardly on my folks' minds, one's name and identity overlap in the saint after whom you're named. Think of it as a prototype for Greeks to jump-start their child on the righteous path (of a martyr, no less). Oh, and, of course, to *honor their mom and dad*, keeping up family traditions is on their mind. I mention this to you now because it will be relevant when you see how determined my father was to have his grandsons' names bear his (or his choice), but sadly for him, it was not to be.

Speaking of expectations and preferences, while my father sought validation, camaraderie, and acceptance from men, he *much* preferred the company of women. He had little interest in the activities or entertainment many men typically enjoy, like sports, hunting, or cars. He would rather have gossiped, shared recipes, or compared notes on the latest *"goings on"* of family members any day. So, while other men were drawn to the fairways playing golf in the spring or to the hills before dawn during deer season, *my dad was happiest at home with his family radiating about him in the icon of his mind.* But when my dad found himself with another male in the house, the battle of the sexes was on in our home, and when my dad wasn't around, we three girls tried our best to tip the scales in our favor. Our father involved himself in his child's activities for the first time, but he wasn't coolly masculine like the other dads; instead, he was more like a cheerleader or a hovering mother-hen. My brother was embarrassed by my dad's goofy, exuberant ways. Unlike the other fathers, my dad felt no need to bond with the other dads, who were proficient at the game of one-upmanship. That said, he was a busy man with a racing mind and visions of grandeur; he had numerous interests and several ongoing projects, but as far as that part of his identity that emanated rich masculine pride, *being the protector and provider for his wife and family were second to none.* Just as Hercules was a stalwart warrior in his community, my dad was a soldier of fortune for our family.

Like Hercules, my dad was both a simple and a complicated man; he attended only to his basic wants and needs: *family, food, and land* (and in that order). It always quenched him for us to be near or with him; no justification or words were necessary. He was the epitome of spontaneous combustion for being all-in if you hatched a plan for fun for the two of you to do together. And while one might dismiss him as sexist, I would be hard-pressed to find a man more supportive of his daughters. There was no implication that we ought to look to or for husbands to care for us. Daily, my dad spoke of our *"smarts,"* and *"many talents"* the way some men compliment girls for their appearance; our *"good looks"* were just an add-on bonus. He was a pusher for our education. We knew from grade school that graduating high school was just the beginning. My parents' active involvement in our studies showed us that this value and expectation to further ourselves was more than lip service; becoming the best version of ourselves was who we were. My dad would also be the first to tell you he was for equal pay, equal benefits, and a woman's right to do whatever she wanted with her mind, body, and life. Not only did my dad prefer the company of women to men, but women were drawn to him. Even if he was a smaller man by stature, he was a force of nature and bigger than life. No doubt, he possessed a magnetism in common with our mythical hero. On one of our last trips to Brooklyn, I recall my Uncle Kolya trying to get the best of my dad by hiring a belly dancer to entice him to at least blush as she snaked herself around him. Still, he sat as stoic as the Great Sphinx in Egypt to prove his fidelity and imperviousness to her provocative gyrations.

And yet, just as soon as I tell you this, I recall when my dad once was tasked with watching my younger brother at Busch Gardens on a family vacation while we girls were with my mom. My then six-year-old brother quickly slipped away undetected because my dad had become entranced by a group of Turkish belly dancers in one of the pavilions doing a mesmerizing performance. When we all met up, and my dad realized in horror that he had lost his son, he called in a brigade of the local police on top of the park's security solicited to help find him. I'm sure he would have commissioned the National Guard would that he could. While he was darting about yelling frantically, my mom spotted my happy brother contentedly riding astride an elephant in a nearby enclosed area; she calmly waved him down. As we progress in our story, you will observe that my dad's shepherding and use of volume to make his might right would become more pronounced in proportion to his intuition that his family was slipping away. Despite the opposite effect it produced, which he desired, he tried all the more to assert his bossy will and dominance in a growing void. And there's no doubt in my mind that when I was in high school, my dad's extra volatility was a hint of things to come. Now that we have uncovered key aspects of my dad's identity as a Greek man among Americans, I move on to the final theme my dad had in common with Hercules.

I save the best theme for last. Since my perspective is biased, to fill in the shades and gaps of my blind spots, I also consider the perception of others who knew my dad. Were they here, I do not doubt they would attest that his finest attribute was his endless wellspring of **hope**. Hope is also "the greatest theme within the play [of Hercules],"[252] I would also argue that this is the case in the preceding myth. Even though Hercules was a demigod, he had to contend *continuously* with Hera's treachery and wicked schemes to try and bring about his demise; the net effect was that he cultivated a reservoir of resilience. Hope and a steely strength of spirit were birthed in him. Yes, Hercules was a wily one in his own right, and he displayed a gutsy determination to survive her machinations and thrive. **What you have learned about what happened during the first decade of my dad's life and the fruitful years depicted in this chapter, taking him from twenty-five to forty-nine, surely confirm that he had that hope that springs eternal.**

His optimism made it seem like my dad had an extra lung that breathed possibility into brain and brawn and being. Was my dad charismatic? *Yes.* Passionate? *Check.* Optimistic? *To a fault.* Enthusiastic? *Without a doubt.* Energetic? *Positively.* When he talked of plans for our future, whether individually or corporately as a family, hope practically poured from his pores, and it spilled onto and into me. When I was a little girl, if I could tell I would get in trouble, I would use the power of suggestion with my parents and say, "Be nice to Anna." Years later, my dad used my quote on me if he discerned that I was not making a wise decision or if I were consorting with someone who did not have my best interest at heart.

Though my dad was ambitious, he was not competitive within our rank and file. His end-game focus was not whether or not he won or I lost, for example, at backgammon. He played like he was out for blood, but no one lost at the end of the day or the game because *we were on the same winning team*! This is not to say he coddled us or said things like "everyone wins, no matter what place." Oh, no! He celebrated our victories and mourned our losses as if they were his own. If I made a wrong move in life, he wouldn't just bark a critique; he would urge or entreat me in such a way that I knew he would be with me until we had this problem solved or conquered. We were in it *together*!

In addition to telling us all regularly that we could do *aaaanything* that we wanted to in life, the way he danced expressed his free spirit, a soul that said that life's possibilities were endless, so let's celebrate! He danced with the passion of a madman who dwelled in an endless Promised Land. Did he dance regularly? No, but when he did, believe you me, you could see a man in flight, suspended between earth and sky, lost and found in hope. Zorba had nothing on my dad. But when my dad's heart was breaking, his temper loosed from feeling torn asunder when his marriage fell apart. It turns out we, his children, provided him with the best medicine possible and a heap of hope for his soul.

On Father's Day, after he'd moved out of our home just a few months before, he invited us four children to dinner in his one-bedroom, plain-Jane apartment in the building he owned. He said he wanted to cook for us. With me home from college, the next two in high school, and my brother usually off riding his bike, it was hard to get all four of us together at any one time, but we managed and entered his shadowy, spartan bungalow. He had grilled chicken for us on his brand-new Hibachi grill and served us around his second-hand table with chairs that didn't match. As we hurried up and got ready to dive into our golden chicken and Greek salad, we noticed my dad sitting at the head of the table with no plate in front of him, and we all took a double-take! Incredulous, we asked him, "Why?" and "What's wrong?" He just shook his head and waved his hand to indicate he would have no words or discussion. Instead, he spoke softly and said he was "*happy just to watch us eat*" and that he could "*eat us up with his eyes*." Our look of love told him we understood. I now see that *we were his world, his everything*, and when he felt like he was standing on shaky ground, he fumed and stormed and raged, but there was never a doubt that he loved us more than life itself, more than himself.

Were Hercules a living and breathing man, I'm sure he would have felt and spoken like my dad. This chapter closes in 1984, the year before he turned fifty. And so, I end this precious section where I have given you my dad at his best, most authentic, raw, and real self before HD began to nibble away at him and take its toll. How could I not have taken my time to flesh out my father for you in this chapter? How else could you tell yourself that who he would become was a distortion of who you now know him to be? That time is not yet at hand; therefore, as a prelude and preparation for the breach you will soon witness in his mind, manner, and form, *I will now identify and familiarize you with the particular parts of the brain that become the most adversely affected by Huntington's Disease.* I feel like I've had this date with destiny for a long time coming, this probing into what happened where, so we will learn and journey together here and now, you and I. This exploration is intended for laypeople like us, so we will take baby steps into my dad's brain and work our way back to see what marched him into rack and ruin.

How Huntington's Disease Impacts the Brain: An Introduction

I have been looking forward to diving into this part of my father's journey since I was first struck with the idea of writing how HD afflicted my dad and intruded upon his life, and, in particular, how exactly this disease raided particular architectural structures within my dad's brain. Not only is it the brain's job to think, but it orchestrates a symphony of functions. Like a private detective looking for clues at the crime scene or a miner exploring tunnels and rooms that have collapsed, I have longed to explore the frontiers deep within my dad's brain that gave rise to what we all came to witness: my dad's subtle, but undeniably increasingly odd body movements, the (even more) bizarre workings of his thought processes — particularly his logic — as well as the tenor and expression of his emotions which got ever-more mercurial, moody, and manic.

Like the vast majority of you who are reading this book, I am no neurologist, but as one with a vested interest has arisen from my dealings with this disease, I wanted to look at the wreckage of those particular portions of the brain where the disease made its debut and left its indelible mark. Huntington's disease wreaks its havoc selectively; it punches no T.K.O.; this makes dealing with it all the more bewildering and confounding. You'll see. Through our last chapter's accounting of genetics, you already know how the disease came to be. The why is on God. Now it's time to learn the where and how. I wanted the precise coordinates of where HD strikes in the brain and how the impacted areas get corrupted. Let us begin our investigation together; I promise to focus only on the portions of the brain that are our key players.

When we can see the structural damage that is ever-so-slowly happening before our eyes, we can better appreciate the resultant debilitated functionality. If you are a neurologist, physician, or scientist with an advanced degree, I apologize in advance for my lack of precision, thoroughness, or maybe even inaccuracies, as noted from your perspective; this is no episode or chapter from *Gray's Anatomy*. There will be details I'll omit or abridge because this is no textbook; it's a story about my dad. For those of you like me who are fascinated with the brain, we will learn together. You'll realize that studying the various processes of the brain can be like chasing a rabbit down its rabbit hole: the starting point has us going from a single path to a spaghetti junction on an interstate in no time flat. Therefore, I'll keep blinders handy so we can concentrate on precisely what we need to know about a brain sideswiped by Huntington's disease. I promise to keep this mission at the forefront of my mind: I will not miss the forest for the trees. That said, I would be remiss if I did not expose bark and leaf and roots related to the whole of the blighted tree.

When we integrate the granular details into a reconstituted bigger picture, you'll see the version of who my dad would become. I plan to share a mental snapshot of a cross-section of portions of the brain impacted by HD. Then we will make our way and focus on four areas in the brain that get particularly ravaged: (1) the basal ganglia, which is the #1 worst-hit part, (2) the amygdala, (3) the hippocampus, and (4) the prefrontal cortex. Of course, since everything's connected, we'll also investigate the relationships between the basal ganglia and the other three portions. I'll draw mental pictures of these structures by comparing them to objects you're already familiar with. There will be specific and fascinating processes to tell you about. But I promise to keep the end in mind: what aberrant behavior or mystifying movement HD brings that can be observed.

Before we get started, we must be on the same page, so let's get familiarized with the most fundamental building block or cell in the brain: the neuron. The neuron is the cellphone tower's *signal* that gets sent to our "cellphones," that is, to the *different portions of our brain*. The HD brain came with a manufacturer's defect that is not apparent when you first bring it home. It contains a time-sensitive glitch that, in some unanticipated and indeterminable moment, will send out errant neuronal commands, resulting in fouled-up functions. The purpose of the nerve cell or neuron in the brain is to *communicate* with others like itself to transmit the *various instructions* for completing a plethora of multi-faceted tasks. Neurons communicate with one another by sending out *electrical impulses* like morse code.

Chemistry is *also* involved because various chemicals called neurotransmitters coat these electrical impulses, like cloaking a friendly ghost. In turn, they tell the receiving neuron either to get "excited" or to become "inhibited" about their upcoming task.[253] It makes me think of what happens when you hear a person say "hello" to you on the phone: you know by the tone of their voice whether it's going to be a stimulating, lively conversation or a downer and depressing one. You could think of it like facing a red light or green light moment; *HD puts you at a flashing yellow hazard light.* The "talking," that is, the transmission of neural information, occurs at the tip of the neuron among the synapses. Neurons have trumpet-like extensions that send signals and have a receiving end or receptor extending out. These tiny branches, called dendrites, "grab" the chemical messengers.

So far, I suspect much of this terminology is already vaguely familiar to you. Why is this communication process necessary to our study? This electrical firing of information that gets chemically transmitted throughout various parts of the normal *brain* — and then crisscrossed to send out messages to the rest of the *body* so that physical functions get completed in a smooth, seamless fashion, both voluntary and involuntary — *runs into significant roadblocks at particular intersections.* We bear witness to the wrecks that occur from these snags. In short, HD inserts a damaged cog in the wheel of the brain; thoughts and actions veer off-course from the directions pre-programmed to occur, and the outcome is that the person with HD will feel lost and get stuck or warbly. The damaged domino piece, which started the chain of events leading to unintended and adverse consequences, occurs in a part of the brain called the basal ganglia, and we will now rivet our attention to it.

The Basal Ganglia: An Overview

If you have read my two other books, you know I'm fascinated with etymology. I looked up "basal ganglia," of course, the first word refers to "base" or "foundational," but the word "ganglia" is the plural form of the Greek word "ganglion," which means "tumor under the skin."[254] However, since 1732, ganglia has come to mean "bundle of nerves," which is ironic, considering we use the phrase "bundle of nerves" as an idiom that means "jittery, nervous, anxious, or tense."[255] The HD-damaged basal ganglia turns fiction into fact. You may not know it, but the basal ganglia is the oldest structure in your brain; it has been "coordinating movement, motivation, and reward for all vertebrates some 560 million years."[256] The basal ganglia — not the amygdala — is the part of your reptilian brain, "the most primitive part of the brain <u>that governs *balance* and where your</u> <u>basic *instincts* reside</u>."[257]

While researching the brain, I found I had forty-eight tabs open in my search bar, a couple of books about HD on my desk with numerous pages marked, about a dozen pages of notes, including my rough sketches of the basal ganglia, and many a YouTube video saved in order even to begin to familiarize myself with how the basal ganglia functions, let alone explain it. For starters, just as seven islands make up the singular state of Hawaii, seven parts comprise the basal ganglia. We can't just sweep past this collection of nuclei without at least glancing at its kibbles and bits.

We will limit and concentrate our study by isolating the subparts and functions salient to HD, always bearing in mind the outcome of behavior. Like Newton's cradle in 3-D with interlocking operating systems, I confess it's hard to stop without looking at the next point of resultant impact. Our task in this section is fourfold: I will (1) tell the purpose of the basal ganglia; (2) describe where it is, what it looks like, and define the constituent parts that are specifically related to movement; (3) and explain how it operates and how HD damages it. Naturally, there are also subparts to our three tasks, but first things first. Let's examine the purpose of the basal ganglia.

Although we will also be looking at three other sections of the brain, no one part is more associated with HD and more impactful on the whole of the person than the basal ganglia because it doesn't just affect movement; it helps guide several other critical cognitive functions. I'll give you an overview in this paragraph. Concerning <u>movement</u>, the primary function of the basal ganglia is the "coordination and integration of body movements."[258] What I learned about how it works reminded me very much of how we used to control sound on an old stereo receiver: there were two knobs: one was for volume, which, in this case, is the amount and rate of movement that is voluntary, and the second was for tone, which in this case is any background or extraneous noise that needs to be toned down so that we don't hear any high-pitched feedback or excruciating tinny treble. What does this "background noise" or "audio feedback" look like in the person with HD? You will recognize it as any unintended, undesired, unplanned, unnecessary, involuntary, extraneous, and, might I add, quirky movement.

Once, I saw a homeless man with the same haunting, violent lurches of arm and leg similar to that my dad had, but upon rushing to speak to him, I learned that he had nerve damage as a result of getting shot; shrapnel had gotten lodged in his spine. The result looked the same. Consider the seamless and fluid movements of a ballet dancer or a basketball player. None of that would be remotely possible for the person with HD;

somebody would get hurt. Muscle memory gets trumped and tripped up by unimpeded and haywire extra movements; they look more like R2D2 malfunctioning erratically but not continuously. I'll get into more of this later.

Next, regarding cognition, the basal ganglia are involved in the "selection and activation of various cognitive, executive, and emotional programs that are stored in the prefrontal association cortex (the center of higher functions) and the limbic cortex,"[259] which, according to Oxford Languages, is concerned with our basic instincts like hunger, sex, dominance, and caring for your young and our most basic moods like fear, pleasure, and anger. When even a portion of the basal ganglia is damaged, the person will have difficulty forming new thoughts and following through with plans. Self-awareness and the ability to create (and recall) recent memories or learn new tasks will be shot. Let's break down these functions further. Decision-making and learning become problematic when the brain's executive function gets impaired.

In persons with HD, *connections to the cerebral cortex undergo deterioration,* and this is especially true of the *connections to the frontal lobes.* Add to that our damaged basal ganglia, which is *also* connected to the cortex, and you also get "poor judgment, personality changes, and aberrations of thinking and behavior."[260] The carnage is broad and sweeping. In Volume 2, I will provide many humorous and tragic examples of my dad's bungled logic and his difficulty in making the simplest either/or decisions for you. You first need to take a gander at what went wrong in the server room of his data bank. We wound up with a caricature of the man we knew and loved, but his most brutish aspects got amplified, making my dad's behavior as distorted as his countenance.

There are two more jobs the basal ganglia facilitate for us. One has to do with learning new tasks, and the other is the sense of reward we experience when a job is accomplished. The brain's way of promoting advantageous behaviors and thwarting those that are not beneficial is achieved through exposure to dopamine, and the basal ganglia circuitry is influenced heavily by dopamine.[261] Unusually high dopamine levels are thought to cause chorea, the involuntary jerking or twisting movements found in Huntington's patients.[262]

Just like the excess movements you can't help but notice, you'll also find the "volume" turned up in their emotions to the point that persons with HD quickly become irritable, agitated, and unhinged. Their emotional instability or volatility can sometimes lead to their becoming combative or explosive. They can get manic, and, at their worst, HD patients can become psychotic or delusional, spawning a host of ensuing troubles they can get into. Whatever social clues and rules we are expected to abide by or go by fly out the window, and all of those primal urges or thoughts we usually keep neatly tucked in or held in check come out, or, at least, get acted upon or verbalized. There is simply no governor to keep you minding your Ps and Qs. Therefore, since my dad typically didn't care what others thought about him, it didn't take much for him to abandon whatever little convention, decorum, or etiquette there was in him anyway. Thus, <u>disinhibition</u> became even more pronounced in him. It took no great leap but rather a short step to his being mal-mannered most of the time; over time, it got less amusing. Yet in some regard, like an innocent child would be unaware of doing anything wrong, his "transgressions," his faux pas, or social disgraces were never intentional or mean-spirited. My dad was rudely reactive at worst and boundlessly buoyant at best.

Had not my dad had to contend with another disease in old age, we would have witnessed a vacancy settle in him. In the most advanced stage of HD, the spinning top would have spun itself out, pockets of gray matter further erased, and he would have been bed-bound. How does this happen? Dopamine levels drop off even more, so movements continue to slacken, and mood further dampens. Since the basal ganglia become the most damaged in persons with HD, it becomes increasingly difficult for the brain to differentiate between essential and inconsequential information that needs to be recalled. Your brain is innovative because it is incredibly efficient: it shuts off when it becomes unable (or disabled) to properly take in new data, which it would now see as "irrelevant."[263]

That's why long-term memories remain astonishingly intact in person with HD, but the old dog can't learn new tricks. I don't know what in my dad prompted him to compensate for this inability to hold onto fresh, unfolding thoughts. However, he took to writing down things he didn't want to forget so much that he avoided reading and began obsessively scribbling mounds of hand-written notes. After he died, I sifted through reams of papers full of his jumbled thoughts. Thank goodness for his trusty clipboard! Now that you know the basic job description of the basal ganglia, I will shed light on what it looks like, that is, its physical structure, and this will include an introduction to its constituent components and what they each do. Again, I regulate the flow and volume of information concerning HD alone.

My first real glimpse at the physical assault HD does to the brain happened when I examined a cross-section (that is, a vertical slice) imaging of the normal brain in comparison to the brain with HD. The difference is striking; I was stunned. First, you'll notice a couple of broad, quasi-triangular darkened spaces, or ventricles, parallel to one another and toward the top of the skull. In the normal brain, they are conservative in size and more distinct in shape; their edges are soft. In the brain with HD, however, they are larger and more ghoulish looking, like the eyes of an agitated ghost. The ventricles are cavities within the brain that contain spinal fluid, which helps "keep the brain buoyant and cushioned."[264] The basal ganglia are housed on the *exterior* portion of each of these ventricles. We all have one pair of basal ganglia — that is, we have two basal ganglia.

At a glance, each looks like a solid rim that hugs alongside the hypotenuse (i.e., the long side) of the soft triangular-shaped nearby ventricle. In the normal brain, the basal ganglia remain thick; in the HD, they've become super-thin, like a slice of cheese that's dried out. Even when you glance at the complicated fabric-like rolls of the brain towards the top, you'll quickly notice that they have become smaller, tighter, compressed, and collapsed in the HD brain. Over time, the person with HD will have "a smaller brain because some of the neurons have degenerated over time," and the death of neurons "results in less brain tissue and a lower brain mass and volume."[265] When you hear that HD is a "rare and progressive neurodegenerative brain disorder,"[266] this boils down to *a disease that kills off neurons in pockets deep within the brain*; therefore, it's more accurate to say basal nuclei because they are a structure of neurons.

It's not surprising, yet still shocking, to see the brain diminished and so ravaged like a tinker-toy arrangement that got knocked down. Before I looked at the anatomy of the constituent parts of the basal ganglia, I also watched a YouTube video recording of a neurologist calmly slicing through the brain like it was a wet, crustless loaf of gelatinous white bread (or better, firm tofu). She carefully pointed out the parts of the basal ganglia in the Texas toast-sized slice she'd cut.[267] I already knew the grey was on the outer portion of the human brain and that the white was on the inside. Still, the coloration of the constituent basal ganglia parts was so similar. Everything was so close together I would have had an easier time picking out similar hues of off-white in a paint wheel, including bone white, antique white, or taupe, than I would have distinguishing its sub-sections. Therefore, I will describe the parts of the basal ganglia based on my observations of viewing a Basal Ganglia 3D Tour[268] and other illustrations that better deconstruct our dangling, gangling structure called the basal ganglia.

A Breakdown of the Basal Ganglia: Its Subparts [269]

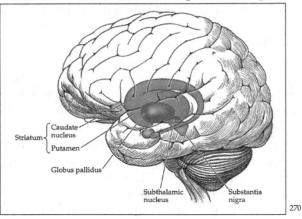

270

As I mentioned before, technically, there are seven parts to the **basal ganglia (BG)**; I will describe six because I'm focusing on the interplay between these since they impact *movement*, which ends up in HD's tell-tale, grotesque choreography. First, I want you to imagine the BG looking like a Bluetooth headset in the lower-middle pit of your brain. The part of the headset that goes around the back of your ear loops faces the backside of your skull, so the longer and thinner part that extends under your earlobe is oriented toward your mouth. The bulbous part of our "headset" is called the **putamen**, and the thin, long-ish extension that wraps around and projects off it is called the **caudate nucleus** (CN) or simply caudate; together, these two make the whole structure, which is called the **striatum**.

Fascinatingly (and as an aside and sneak preview), there is what looks like a pea or an ear stud attached to the tippy end of the caudate nucleus, and this is the amygdala! No, it is not a part of the basal ganglia; it is just a nearby neighbor, and I will discuss it later. If the striatum is the Bluetooth headset, then behind your earlobe, we would find the hippocampus, which is also not a part of the basal ganglia but another "neighbor" we shall meet later on as well. HD impacts the amygdala and hippocampus, but it is the striatum of the basal ganglia to which HD packs its biggest punch, particularly to its caudate. Why? Let's back up and review that huntingtin proteins are *everywhere* in the body but interact with other proteins found *only* in the brain.[271] Also, the abnormal protein produced by the genetic mutation in HD does not equally damage all areas of the brain. I emphasize that the hardest hit is the striatum's caudate nucleus because "it has within it a collection of spiny neurons that are particularly vulnerable to the huntingtin protein."[272] As a result, instead of the body being able to do its typical job of getting rid of and replacing living cells that break down, the bungled gene code within the huntingtin protein causes the CN to interact improperly with other nerve cells. How and in what manner? Again, I must quote what I couldn't say or know otherwise:

> HD causes the neurons [within the caudate] to become very sensitive to glutamate [which, as you know, is in excess in persons with HD]. This increased sensitivity leads to activating other proteins that cleave the huntingtin [protein] to [other] smaller fragments. These fragments then slip into the caudate nucleus and interfere with the normal production of other proteins. This interference causes cellular stress that leads to more huntingtin protein being broken into fragments, initiating a cycle that eventually leads to the death of the neuron.[273]

This is so dramatic! Our old friend, glutamate, "junks up" and kills nerve cells in the caudate, leaving a trail of trash in its wake. This pile of rubbish interferes with the caudate nucleus's regular job, including the operations it conducts with the rest of the basal ganglia. After naming the four other critical components of the basal ganglia, our brain's "Hawaii," or at least six of the seven islands, I'll explain this ripple effect and the final outcomes.

Inching our way further towards the center of the brain from the putamen is the globus pallidus (GP)or "pale globe."[274] You should also know that the GP is subdivided into the internal and external portions. From renderings and videos, you can see that the globus pallidus' proximity is so near that it touches the putamen. Like a chain letter that gets passed on, *the globus pallidus' job is to relay information from the putamen to the thalamus,*[275] which I'll tell you about in the next section. How does HD impact the globus pallidus, and what is the net result or impact? The GP external in the HD patient shows "a 54% overall volume decline, while the GP internal experiences a 38% reduction in overall volume. Decreasing GPe volumes... were associated with **poorer cognition and increasing motor impairments**, but *not* chorea [an abnormal involuntary movement disorder[276]].

In contrast, decreasing GPi volumes were associated with reduced irritability."[277] This differentiation in impact between these two portions is essential, but the bottom line is that HD causes both parts to shrink. Although, as I have said, the thalamus is not a part of the basal ganglia, it is a large-ish part sandwiched between our double "Bluetooth" headset and our pair of caudate nuclei. *Underneath* the thalamus, which looks like a pair of tiny beads, are the **subthalamic nuclei** (STN), which should make sense in that "sub" implies *under* the thalamus. Because of its location, the subthalamic nuclei play a crucial role in both motor selection and psychological processes, like "impulsivity, hyperactivity disorders or addictive behaviors."[278] Huntington's disease blockades "the neuronal activity in the subthalamic nuclei," causing a "dysfunction in the flow of information," with the final result seen in "**hyperkinetic [i.e., excessive] movement abnormalities**."[279] We now have two more parts of the basal ganglia to acquaint ourselves with.

Also, in the mid-brain and parallel to the subthalamic nuclei, but anterior (as opposed to further back or posterior) in orientation, we will find a pair of petite, crescent-shaped[280] streaks that look like fuzzy dashes. They are called the **Substantia Nigra** (SN), which is Latin for "black substance," since it is noticeable for there to be even a speck or whisp of pigmentation in the brain. This darkness is caused by a highly concentrated level of dopamine activity inside, and, as you know, dopamine is a critical neurotransmitter. The substantia nigra is a "distinct, deeply melanin-pigmented nucleus (i.e., neuromelanin) that is intimately involved in motor function."[281]

For starters, in [patients with] HD, "neuronal degeneration occurs in the substantia nigra"; here, too, we find "shrinkage" in neuronal number.[282] The SN "receives input from many other nerve cells,"[283] and it also plays a vital role in the brain's reward system (including motivation)."[284] Eye movement, sleep cycles, learning, and addiction become adversely impacted as well.[285] Next, a word about successful movement learning: the full grasp of acquired new information happens in the gestalt moment when one has progressed from learning to use the muscles to mastering a desired movement (or multiple ones). It's the point in time and space where muscle memory has been developed and takes over, and there is no longer any volitional thought needed to move; it has become automatic. Greek dancing, driving a stick shift, and playing soccer or the violin were deep in my dad's core of stored know-how, but later, he slipped, faltered, and fell despite his knowledge and best efforts. HD prevented neural dots from connecting, and commands became aborted midstream. This was not a significant issue since my dad was past the point of needing to learn new movements.

Meanwhile, plenty of other marred movements disrupted his everyday activities. In general, like the dampening pedal of a piano, the Susbtantia Nigra's primary function is to mollify, soften, or smooth out movements and make them seamless and fluid, not stilted and jerky. The

SN does this by using two neuroinhibitory chemicals: dopamine and another one, which is referred to as GABA.[286] Like the globus pallidus, the SN also has two sections to it. Interestingly, damage to one side of the Substantia Nigra, which delivers lower dopamine levels, is associated with Parkinson's Disease. The other portion relevant to HD is called the **Pars Reticulata** (or SNR for Susbtantia Nigra Reticulata), which is of relevance to us because it is part of the SN that contributes to movement problems associated with HD.

In the SNR of the Huntington's disease patient, we find "spiny neurons of the Pars Reticulata [which] are particularly susceptible to degeneration."[287] The primary inhibiting neurotransmitter on this side of the SN is GABA, and it streams into and works along with the Globus Pallidus. (I'll save the function of movement for our *next* section. There, I'll explain **the Direct and Indirect Pathways**, both of which get bungled in our person with HD.) Projections from Susbtantia Nigra Reticulata also modulate eye movement,[288] so checking the eyes is something a neurologist would know to observe in a person with HD. My dad had his eyes checked every time, and though not a word was said, the neurologist always scribbled fast and furiously in his chart. I just noticed a dullness in his gaze that wasn't present before, but it wasn't due to apathy or depression. Lesions on a portion of the SN negatively impact spatial learning[289] and navigating one's environment and location. HD patients grapple with the mechanics of their movement in dealing with the full spectrum of the space they occupy and move about in. It's painful to watch.

Even if a movement has long since become learned and automatic, the person with HD is still likely to stumble or falter. It's as if his inner grid or sense of balance has gotten shaken and stirred; then he'll get rattled. In real-time, this increases the likelihood of inadvertently bumping into people or, if operating a vehicle, colliding into objects. Accidents are almost a guarantee. Not only is this portion of the SN implicated in reward and pleasure, but it also impacts addictive behavior.[290] Since dopamine isn't delivered or received correctly, individuals with HD display varying degrees of difference in distorted personality features. For my dad, it was his innate aggression that got distorted as opposed to new traits appearing; *he was still him.* However, should HD proceed long enough in its progression, we would be able to point to decreased "nigral volume and receptor levels [which are] associated with certain specific neuropsychiatric disorders."[291]

I found it fascinating that "lesions of the SNR [that are present in HD patients], which cause hyposomnia and motor hyperactivity," indicate that the SNR plays a role in controlling sleep and motor activity.[292] My dad had always been energetic, but as his HD was chipping away at his brain, we saw that he became downright hyper — and, during stressful times, nearly frantic. There was no need to report his trouble sleeping; we all became aware that he was experiencing insomnia by the cockamamie emails he might send at any hour of the night. Speaking of motor activity, we are now at a good place to transition back to the Striatum (our "Bluetooth" headset comprised of the Caudate Nucleus plus the adjoining bulbous Putamen). Recall that the striatum of our basal ganglia is the Grand Central Station for how and where movement gets initiated and expressed; it is precisely where Huntington's Disease does its worst damage to the Basal Ganglia.

The Impact HD Makes on the Overall Functions of the Basal Ganglia

Now that I have introduced you to the individual components of the Basal Ganglia, the portion of the brain hardest hit by HD, I now want to get to the nitty-gritty of exactly what happens to the striatum such that all associated links in the chain of movements get altered and bumbled in the person with HD. Just as a refresher from the previous chapter's discussion on genetics, it is the brain's "over-production of the neurotransmitter glutamate which kills neurons in the basal ganglia."[293] Depending upon how high the CAG count is and how old the person with HD is, he or she will move like someone who has had electrical nodes randomly placed on different parts of his body so that these parts jerk or twitch randomly, unpredictably, and eerily, like the move is trying to roll itself out, frame by frame, and without haste. And because the precise places where these problems occur vary within each HD patient, *the expression and degree of such varies among them*! In Volume 2, I'll tell you more about variations I saw with my own eyes.

Suffice it to say, what HD does to movement is akin to Pablo Picasso's cubist painting entitled *The Weeping Woman*; both will leave you wanting to weep for ugliness caused by distortion and contortion. I will now do my due diligence and explain the two pathways to movement that occur within the Basal Ganglia, HD's locus primus. By now, you may be thinking that the person with HD is just one big wiggle or wriggle worm or that they are like a person with Parkinson's Disease with some bonus weird tics or maybe even like one with muscular dystrophy on steroids, but they are not. As neurodegenerative diseases go, PD and HD are categorically close, but definitely, no cigar. Most often, the involuntary, nearly continuous, and random movements in the person with HD occur in the arms and legs and, most tragically, in the face.[294] Why is it random? And in what manner is the movement unpredictable in its tenor or type? Again, I would be remiss if I did not quote what I could not have known. You will recall that chorea is an "uncontrollable, dance-like movement" common among people with HD. This short segue leads to a separate focus on the central purpose of the basal ganglia where movement is concerned. There are two parts to the BG's operation, including both the <u>direct and indirect pathways</u>. First, another word or two more about chorea and, in general, it relates to these two critical pathways:

> Choreiform movements are caused by the selective loss – meaning not all, but specific losses – of striatal neurons in the <u>indirect</u> pathway. Such means that the basal ganglia have a severely reduced <u>ability to inhibit unwanted motor plans</u> due to the shift in balance favoring the direct pathway. This enables thalamic neurons to be excited randomly, leading the motor cortex to <u>activate motor programs with no control of the individual</u>.[295] (Emphasis mine.)

In most academic scientific articles, specific and exact locations of the striatum are identified; I won't be doing this. However, I would like to conjecture that depending on precisely where the damage has occurred in/on any of the six (of the seven) particular portions of the BG, though we will witness a definite similarity in these haunting movement problems, they are still *uniquely expressed in each individual*, much, in the same way, snowflakes are concurrently alike, but dissimilar. Even though we are dealing with a minute area, infinitesimal points of contact exist where structural damage can occur; therefore, we find endless possibilities in how the damage will get expressed. Your po-ta-to is my po-tah-to, but we can't call the whole thing off.

Soon enough, we will get to the intellectual and psycho-emotional aspects of how HD makes its mark, but for now, let's return to our impaired Striatum. Think of a warped record that has a deep scratch in it. That's your Basal Ganglia. Now imagine that the scarred sound you hear is a marred movement you see. <u>Though not always the first sign to get manifested, motor symptoms are often the reason or impetus that prompts people who have undiagnosed HD to see a doctor.</u>[296] *The early psycho-emotional degenerative changes in the person with HD are the hardest to attribute definitively to this disease because the normal aging process is also nibbling away at our cognitive functions.* If you are around the person nearly daily, you won't notice as readily as if your visit were sporadic, but either way, the changes are more bizarre and sweeping than mere forgetfulness. We can't understate the import of the two pathways that control our movement.

To initiate movement and simultaneously keep undesired movements from occurring, the effect of which is producing fluid, facile, and coordinated movement, is something we all do without thought or effort because no portion of our basal ganglia is damaged. We aren't suffering from any unusual apoptosis, meaning programmed cell death.[297] For the person with HD, cellular homicide gets accelerated in the brain. Let's see exactly how this pans out into off-kilter movements.

Movement Problems and the Two Pathways of the Basal Ganglia

How we make conscious, voluntary movements — those fully executed without our inner volition — are divided into <u>direct and indirect pathways</u>. What usually occurs involves certain parts of the basal ganglia engaged in a delicate balancing act between (a) the "<u>excitation</u>" of the motor cortex (which is a part of the cerebral cortex) that gives the green light to make our muscles move the way we tell them to, and (b) the counter-balancing, suppressing, or "<u>inhibitory</u>" messages which are then sent back to the motor cortex to ensure that no extraneous (i.e., <u>un</u>called for) movements don't occur. The excitation occurs in one part of the BG, while the inhibition occurs in another (with the help of various neurotransmitters). If we pretend that all of the constituent parts of the BG are musical instruments, the net effect is that instead of well-tuned instruments playing a fine symphony of our choosing, ours will be a bad carnival song played out-of-tune on a clunky organ grinder. Everything that *should* occur, as described in the balancing act between (a) and (b) above, will play itself out in the *opposite* way in the person with HD. Let us proceed.

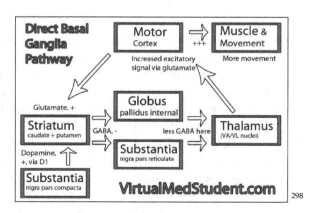

[298]

I will start with the **Direct Pathway** first since it has fewer steps, four to be precise. Its mission is to initiate directed movement (i.e., that of our choosing); HD will foil its outcome. Please allow me this disclaimer that the information I provide is nowhere near as in-depth as I would get from experts in the field; however, what you'll learn is also likely more than you've ever considered. I will try to maintain a balance between technical fidelity and no-nonsense facts. The easiest way to look at the steps of the direct pathway is to view them as a series of positives and negatives on the ends of a series of magnets coming together. The job of the direct pathway is to facilitate "the initiation and execution of <u>voluntary</u> movements."[299] There are just four steps involved. In step 1, we have the <u>motor cortex</u> giving a positive command. It sends its positive "excitatory" command to the first point of contact in our basal ganglia, the <u>Striatum</u> (which, as you know, is the Caudate and the Putamen). Incidentally, and right off the bat, our old friend Glutamate is the excitatory neurotransmitter here.

It's in Step 1 that the communication breakdown occurs because cells within the Striatum, we find "medium spiny neurons" that are "particularly damaged"[300] in the person with HD. Therefore, when the Striatum gets "excited" or stimulated, *it doesn't act as it should*. Think of it as our Bluetooth device with a dent in it. There'll be static – electronic glitches – interfering with the message. Step 2 is the <u>inhibitory</u> leg of the pathway. At this juncture, the (damaged) Striatum should send its inhibitory neurotransmitter, GABA, to our next player within the BG, the <u>Globus Pallidus Internal</u> (GPi). What ends up happening is that the GPi receives less of its expected transmitter; therefore, <u>it cannot adequately do its job, which is also inhibitory</u>. You need to know that the GPi works hand in hand with the <u>S</u>ubstantia <u>N</u>igra (and, again, the portion of the SN that is in use is called the Pars Reticulata). The notable function of the SN is that it pumps out dopamine, which, like GABA, is also inhibitory. (There are two types of dopamine, one for each pathway; bottom line, they both mollify.) Dopamine receptors "synapse onto cells in [both] the Substantia Nigra Pars Reticulata (SNpr) [as well as] the <u>i</u>nternal segment of the **Globus Pallidus** (GPi) which then projects [back up] to the Thalamus," eventually completing the loop or pathway.[301]

Recall, if you will, that in persons with HD, the SN is also a damaged player (just not as bad as the Striatum). Back to our GPi: since it gets fewer inhibitory signals from the Striatum than it should, it cannot do its job and relay the proper concentration of its message in our next step. Are you ready for step 3? Step 3 is also an **inhibitory** leg of our Direct Pathway, and this time, it takes us from the <u>GPi</u> (working together with the <u>SN</u>) back up to the **Thalamus**. However, since our GPi has had the brakes applied, it cannot reduce any of the tempering or inhibition that is supposed to occur between the GPi and the Thalamus. (Remember that the Thalamus, although not a part of the Basal Ganglia, is the weighty "middleman" between the Basal Ganglia and the motor cortex.) Since there's nothing to put the governor on this step's inhibitory ways, the net effect is a full-strength, full-throttle, and even more significant inhibition. Now our Thalamus has a choke-hold on it! This takes us back to our final phase, Step 4, which, as an excitatory "leg," will still deliver but in a much more dampened "positive." Here, we close the loop by having the Thalamus do its job of sending its now thwarted positive signal back up to the motor cortex. The net effect is that the Thalamus relays a fainter signal up to the motor cortex, which then sends its reduced message to the intended muscle; now, the muscle responds *more SLOWLY* than usual!

Now, let's take our middle-aged person with HD. When he sees traffic up ahead, his brain says it's time to hit the brakes, but his foot is too slow to respond, and likely, he hits the car in front of him. (You'll read about this in Volume 2 as it happened to my dad.) Because this step is not out-of-the-norm or odd-looking, your person with HD and others will likely chalk this up as a sheer coincidence or an accident. We know why his foot didn't hit its brake as quickly as the inner command he gave his muscles that split second before; oh, there's more than meets the eye as to what gets the leg moving yet suspended in a breath or second of lagging. This slowness of movement is called **bradykinesia,** again coming from the Greek "bradys," meaning "slow," and "kinesis," meaning "movement, motion."[302]

While I'm identifying and labeling this particular abridgment in movement, I just *"got reminded,"* as my dad would say, and can see my mind's eye yet another abnormal body movement of my dad's called **dystonia,** which is also a manifestation of the messed-up direct pathway in the person with HD. (In my dad, this transpired during the last three years of his life.) Its etymology is also Greek: "tonia" comes from "tonos," which in Greek means "tension," and this noun reaches back to "teinen," which means "to stretch."[303] The medical dictionary defines dystonia as "a syndrome of abnormal muscle contraction that produces repetitive, involuntary twisting movements and abnormal posturing of the neck, trunk, face, and extremities.'"[304] Double-check: my dad was full of tension, inside and out. Therefore, added to his diminished speed, dystonia will eventually produce a ghoulish twist or even slow-grind, writhing movement.

It is not a grand gesture, but it hurts to watch, and over time, I began to see Dad's facial muscles twist, like he was trying to get a fly to leave his nose. His eyes didn't have the fire and alertness in them as before, and his warbled voice that couldn't keep steady in its tone proved even his vocal cords were growing rigid. His Neanderthal-like penmanship betrayed the disease's assault on his fine motor skills. No, he wasn't chiseling words in stone like some ancient Greek artisan; HD crippled his agility and flexibility. Add to that the slo-mo, unplanned micro-rolling in his shoulder, or the unsure footing of his feet. And speaking of rolling, he'd get to where he'd mindlessly "pill-roll" his napkins at the table, massaging the napkin between thumb and index finger.[305] (This may be more usual in the person with PD, but as the problem has its root in the BG, it, too, manifested itself in my dad.)

Before we leave the Basal Ganglia and move on to the Hippocampus and Amygdala, it is time to turn our attention to the **Indirect Pathway**. Remember that the direct and indirect pathways work in tandem, like the gas and brake pedals do when we properly operate a car. Now that you have seen what happens to HD's "braking system," that it has gotten stiff and squeaky to the degree that the person's quickness of response has precipitously slowed down, it's time to check out the "acceleration system." Since we are dealing with the HD patient, you can anticipate that much of his movement will get further spurred, *but it is neither planned nor useful.* In short, it's all too much, too little, too late, *and* too bad.

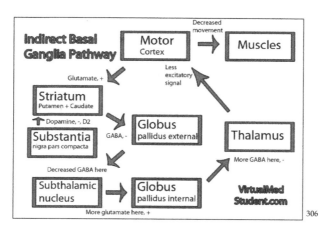

Unlike the Direct Pathway, the purpose of the Indirect pathway is to "suppress unwanted movement."[307] The net effect should be inhibitory, but we will not get our intended results in the neurological Ponzi scheme of HD. Like hearing that unmistakable high-pitched, ear-splitting feedback through a speaker when a speaker's microphone volume is too high or some electronic glitch has occurred, we will witness much the same with movement in the person with HD. It's off. Why? There is simply no margin for error during the interplay between neuron chemicals flowing between members of the basal ganglia when doing their appointed duty in the designated choreography. Damage done to even one component produces a toxic ripple effect. Recall that HD hits the Striatum of the Basal Ganglia particularly hard. Transcranial sonography can "detect abnormalities of the Caudate Nucleus and Substantia Nigra in Huntington's disease," and, fascinatingly, the degree to which they are impacted is, in part, associated with one's CAG repeat expansion number.[308] Ultimately, the imbalance of striatal output "contributes to the disruption of synaptic communication between the direct and indirect pathways," [309] meaning that if the blow has occurred in the Striatum, it ultimately contributes to motor dysfunction.

The Indirect Pathway has two more steps than the Direct Pathway, making a total of *six* steps; plus, *two additional sub-parts* of the Basal Ganglia get involved. Let's pivot and see what happens here. Step 1 is easy because it is the same as what we find in the Direct Pathway: the motor cortex sends its command (i.e., your willed instruction), which is an "excitatory" impulse, to the damaged Striatum (i.e., the Caudate Nucleus + Putamen combo). You will recall that since the Striatum is impaired, it can't do its job correctly. As with the Direct Pathway, everything that follows goes the *opposite* way that it should, like some bungled, backward domino effect. This time, in Step 2, we find that our now damaged "inhibitory" impulse will this time hit the Globus Pallidus external (GPe). This is an "inhibitory" leg of the pathway. However, since the GPe isn't receiving sufficient inhibitory GABA neurotransmitters, it can't curb or curtail the next point of contact in the pathway in the usual manner. Step 3 is also an inhibitory leg in the pathway, but since there's nothing to hold back or counter the GPe's inhibitory ways, the path between GPe and the Subthalamic Nuclei (STN) is now a wide-open floodgate of inhibitory neurotransmitters rushing through to the subsequent step.

Please note that, unlike the previous two steps, Step 4 is uniquely excitatory. At this juncture, we find neurons from the Subthalamic Nuclei now sending their axons back to our familiar Globus Pallidus internal (GPi),[310] which, as was the case in the Direct Pathway, works in tandem or is in groove with the Substantia Nigra (Pars Reticula), our dopamine maker. Since the Subthalamic Nuclei is now "more inhibited than usual, it will release fewer excitatory neurotransmitters." Meanwhile, the SNr gets nervous and sends more dopamine (but a different type than used in the Direct Pathway) back to the damaged Caudate, all to no avail. The usual job of the Subthalamic Nucleus is to stimulate the Globus Pallidus internal on this <u>excitatory</u> loop, but now, with it sending <u>fewer</u> neurotransmitters, the upcoming job in this pathway will also be botched.

Step 5 is familiar to us because now we are back to going from the Globus pallidus internal, which, as you remember, works together with our Substantia Nigra (Pars Reticula), the dopamine provider, to take us back up to the <u>Thalamus</u>. This is also an inhibitory leg. Since the thalamus receives fewer inhibitory neurotransmitters, the typical inhibitory effect has been canceled; we call this state <u>disinhibited</u>. (Think of it as a negative number times a negative, which yields a *positive*.) As with the Direct Pathway, what happens to the HD patient is the opposite of what should occur! The Thalamus now has no governor on it! You should know that the normal default state of the thalamus is one of <u>inhibition</u>, leaving our body in an efficient state of conservation and rest (not random fidgetiness).

Therefore, in our final Step 6, which is an <u>excitatory</u> step,[311] the Thalamus releases an excess of neurotransmitters back to the motor cortex, which then stimulates and gives a double green light to our muscles! **The result of the Indirect pathway is that the person with HD produces excessive, spontaneous, unpredictable, and erroneous movements, but not of their own accord**. Such is the tell-tale sign of a person afflicted with HD. In my imagination, I see a caricature or cartoon of a person who has touched an electric fence, whereby the unexpected overflow of electric "juice" has them jerkily shaking. In my memory, Dad was in a peculiar perpetual motion, inside and out. And because differentness is more striking than slowness, which is the byproduct of the Direct Pathway, this Indirect Pathway often gives us the first visible indication or clue to the person who doesn't know he has HD that something is eerily awry. Somethin' just ain't right. And there you have it! Zero for two on muscle speed and modulation.

Please know that there are additional pathways and a plurality of cortices involved, and as detailed as it is, I know for some, I did not do justice to explain the types and roles of the neurotransmitters. I did not want to miss the forest for the dendrites or get sidetracked by the fact that, for example, there are "horns" in our brains and fibers inside cerebral "peduncles," which, when I heard it described on a YouTube video, sounded like "pinochle." My focus was and remains on the parts of the brain adversely impacted by HD and how such gets manifested. I purposefully and first took on the most complicated portion, the basal ganglia, so our next three will be less taxing, though no less fascinating. I'll start with the amygdala, which, if you remember, looks like a tiny pea or caper at the tippy end of the "tail" of the Caudate nucleus "mouthpiece" on our "Bluetooth" Striatum.

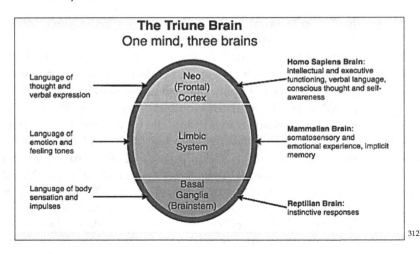

Before I proceed and shine a spotlight on the next part of the brain in our study, I want to have us stand back, take five, and reflect on the bigger picture inside our skull. Let's take a glance at the brain's major systems once more. (Please note I will not be examining the Neo (Frontal) Cortex at this point in our study.) A man by the name of Paul Maclean coined the term "Triune Brain,"[313] and in our discussion of the HD-damaged Basal Ganglia — our Rube Goldberg machine that went haywire — we learned that the Basal Ganglia is located or housed in the most primitive part of the brain. This is Square One or Ground Zero. Through the Basal Ganglia, the primitive or Primal Brain (sometimes called the Reptilian Brain) is where smooth and efficient movement is produced and balance is coordinated. Not only this, but the Basal Ganglia is also concerned with our basic survival.

Through biochemical motivation-and-reward feedback, this primitive part of the brain helps us to differentiate stimuli we encounter so we will make decisions that best benefit us, that is, those that keep us safe and sound and better ensure our survival.[314] This system stimulates our urge to eat and reproduce. Now that we know how and why movement gets initiated or launched, let's peek at how this part of the brain manifests itself in observable behavior. How might HD cloud one's perception of reality? In everyday interactions with others, we learn and recognize specific patterns of behavior, some of which are shaped by our particular culture, that let us know if we are in a state of war or peace. If we perceive a threat, our hackles get raised, and we are ready to fight, flee, or even freeze when it comes to the "defense of self, family, and personal property."[315] Non-verbal clues include "physical communication and socially-approved actions, such as handshakes, head nods, and bowing."[316] Volume 2 will spell this out loud and clear in my dad!

In the person with HD, <u>signals get crossed</u>; therefore, they become unable to accurately read the expression written on someone's face — something that the bulk of us do without a thought — to assess if that person means harm or good. The HD person assumes the worst, and anger may come out. <u>Mis</u>interpretations of another's bearing, demeanor, and behavior can lead to knee-jerk reactions of irrational or <u>un</u>-called-for expressions of "fear, aggression, territoriality, and dominance."[317] The person with HD increasingly cannot correctly assess <u>non</u>verbal clues, which spells t-r-o-u-b-l-e. This poor player must find himself in a frightening world and bewildering stage. No wonder my dad would complain daily about people who would *"harass and annoy"* him; likely, they did nothing.

Let us now proceed from the archipelago of the Basal Ganglia in the primitive part of the brain to the next layer, our "second" brain, the **Paleomammalian Complex**. It sends the warning, "Danger! Danger!" for us to do whatever it takes to keep us alive post haste! This older mammalian brain, called the Limbic System, "governs your emotions, social behavior, and some aspects of memory."[318] The reactive part of us initiates the "fight-or-flight" response to danger. As I mentioned earlier, the critical neurological structures of the brain for this system include the <u>Hippocampus</u>, the <u>Amygdala</u>, and the <u>Hypothalamus</u>. These parts "form a fast subconscious evaluation and response system designed to keep us safe in lightning speed."[319] One thing that impressed me in my study of the basal ganglion system is that *nothing works in isolation.*

This holds true for the Amygdala and Hippocampus. In fact, even their proximity to one another ensures their cooperative interplay. If the amygdala is the pea at the tippy end of our "Bluetooth" Striatum (but technically, not a part of it), then the directly behind our imaginary "ear lobe" where our "Bluetooth" set fits over, you'll find the Hippocampus. (It's situated in the lower half of where you'd rest a pencil, angled up behind your ear.) Thus, the Striatum and Hippocampus are next-door neighbors; the Hippocampus is but one micro step deeper in our brain. When combined, the Hippocampus and Striatum work together; their collective job deals primarily with "forming long-term memory, processing emotions, and determining how emotions are tied to memories."[320] Since HD packs a punch to the Hippocampus and the Amygdala within the limbic system, we will examine each in their own right.

The Amygdala

We are ready to focus on the <u>amygdala</u>, which in Greek is ἀμυγδαλή, and it means "almond."[321] We all have two of them, and I marvel at their proximity to the basal ganglia. These almond-shaped "clusters of nuclei are located deep and medially [in the middle] within the temporal lobes of the brain's cerebrum in complex vertebrates, including humans."[322] (The cerebrum is the largest part of the brain in <u>sub</u>cortical structures.) Interestingly, the amygdala is more prominent in males than females in human adults. What exactly does the amygdala do, how does it operate, and more to the point, what precisely does Huntington's disease do to tarnish its standard functionality? Anatomically, the amygdala can be further broken down into its subcomponents, but the overall function of the amygdala is of greater importance to us; my concentration will be selective. The amygdala is best known for its role in <u>fear processing</u>. When stimulated, it sends messages to the brain to prepare a split-second reflexive physiological response (e.g., increased heart rate and respiration and a rush of adrenalin) in response to whatever induced fear. All of this before we even have time to think about it.[323]

The amygdala makes "very fast, albeit not always accurate, evaluations." It has a direct pipeline from the thalamus. The thalamus provides the incoming "data," delivered directly into the amygdala, initiating a proper stress response "to forestall impending doom."[324] When we perceive a threat, the speed of the reaction surges at the expense of accuracy, so you can imagine how much worse the errancy of output from a damaged amygdala is! Plus, the amygdala's responses get directed to various other brain structures. One part is directed to subcortical structures "to mediate and process various... behavioral expressions of different emotional states,"[325] <u>especially fear and sadness</u>. Another duty of the amygdala is directed to the cerebral cortex, which "modulates cognitive processes such as <u>decision-making, attention, and memory</u>."[326] These are further divided into hemispheric roles, each with its own specialty, shaping "how we perceive and process emotion."[327] Our reward system also gets involved here so that the brain "learns" which primal memories to keep as a reference point for future response assessments to keep us safe and alive. These memories do not require conscious recall.

The problem is that even long after a threatening or traumatic incident has passed, "the amygdala can remain painfully sensitive and reactive, not only to our occasional memory of that prior trauma but to anything that even remotely resembles it, whether truly dangerous or not."[328] And if the amygdala is impaired, as is the case with HD, then when the amygdala alerts us to potential threats by noting the perceived similarity of some stimulus in our current environment to one or more "traumatically encoded" past experiences, *the HD-impaired amygdala will treat the new stimulus as if it is the same as the first one, but in actuality, it is not.* Oh, woe be he! PTSD is an actual phenomenon, and you have already discovered that my dad had cause for being psychologically scarred, having lived through wars, worries, and want. Can you imagine what would happen and how he would now feel when he witnessed what he perceived to be parallels from the direst pangs of his youth? He had to have experienced flashbacks, which tethered them to disconnected or unrelated current events!

As I ingest mountains of information about the amygdala, it takes no effort to recall my dad's bubbling aggravation about this and that, which didn't amount to a hill of beans. Mountains and molehills became the same. I can now deduce and point my finger at his amygdala, the culprit and captain of his cantankerousness. Since the amygdala is in charge of making our rapid-fire, instantaneous emotional responses, it pilots what is known as the "affective system"; it is responsible for many of our judgments, including discerning between good and bad, safe and threatening, and friend and foe."[329] By now, it should be apparent to you just how much everything is interrelated, and located deep in the midbrain is another section with which the amygdala works closely. The sum effect of this interplay has us dealing with impulsivity, something with which my poor dad would have considerable problems, and when combined with his aggression, it could lead to real trouble. How so, and in what manner?

To be honest, at times, we found Dad downright amusing because he might blurt out some blunt truth that we might have been privately thinking but would never say, and at other times, we prayed for clemency because he might have violated some basic code of civility or decency. It was a coin toss. What makes issues with the amygdala particularly and potentially problematic? When "stimulated, the amygdala appears to increase both sexual and aggressive behavior."[330] Recall also that the amygdala works closely with the mighty thalamus in our limbic system regarding the interpretation of emotional data, which, in turn, takes in from sensory input (even including olfactory stimuli). You already know what should happen; therefore, you might appreciate that a person with HD becomes his own worst enemy. Tragically, he can't tell friend from foe, as you'll observe more in Volume 2. I will give you a spoiler now: at one point in the throes of being his caretaker, my father considered me his public enemy #1. Swiftly, inexplicably, and for no reason you'll ever know, they can flip on a dime and get stuck in panic mode, activate aggression, or go stonewall silent and suspicious.

Take it from one who knows: this loss of ability to react in a manner appropriate to those they love and should trust, let alone with those they barely know, becomes a challenge with no perfect solution and a labor of love that requires the patience of Job. I even learned that a syndrome associated with it arises from alternations in the amygdala. It is characterized by features, among which include "the **loss of fear and inhibition,** causing risky behavior, disordered diet, and dysfunctional sexual activity, among others."[331] If you asked me if my dad displayed any of these characteristics, I could have checked in "Yes" to nearly all of those boxes, but there were two changes in particular that got pronounced in my dad: hypersexuality (a.k.a. promiscuity) — especially in the early years, that is, during the onset of his disease; and a **loss of inhibition** "which affects all spheres of personality."[332] I do not believe my dad had a syndrome on top of his disease, but the common denominator between the two is still the damaged amygdala.

How exactly does HD impair his amygdala, and what does this look like? Recall that unlike other neurodegenerative diseases, each of which has its hallmark features, the brain is impaired by HD, which presents its own quirky and haunting hints and evidences many expressions. The reason behind this degree of variation has to do with (1) the precise location(s) of degeneration (which, in turn, influences the resulting degree and manner of impairment) and (2) the all-important CAG count which determines the level of amplification and age of onset. These are the two ingredients in our crucible that produce the witches' brew of tangible trauma to specific parts of the brain, which then delivers the slo-mo death knell to our unsuspecting loved one. Meanwhile, at a glance, the casual observer and the unsuspecting family member will not be able to place their finger on precisely what is wrong with the HD-afflicted person, either in terms of changes in his behavior, irregular and involuntary movements, or both. But, oh, time will surely tell.

We need only look at concrete results from MRI studies to see proof-positive HD's dilatory impact on the amygdala and the wrack and ruin of the amygdala. In real time, we can witness the carnage in their brain through their transfigured behavior, particularly when there is a perceived threat. What the alternation looks like depends on the person's inherent personality: you will see an exaggeration of what already exists or is innate within them, shocking or ridiculous, though it may at first appear. One person may duck, run, and hide; the next, bow up and put up his dukes; my dad would be the latter. In general, we assess for danger in more ways than for those situations that prove life-threatening or harrowing. Our amygdala is constantly scanning and involving itself in the sophisticated interpretation of identifying facial expressions. For the person with HD, the ability to accurately assess gets jarred. One test conducted had HD patients and a control group observe angry faces to observe the amygdala response, which, as you now know, interprets facial expressions ultimately to discern friend from foe. The results were astonishing and revelatory, especially when I reflected on my dad's behavior. (You will discover more of his trends and tirades in the coming chapters.) The test results stated that "psychophysiological interaction analysis identified <u>reduced connectivity</u> between the left amygdala and right fusiform facial area in <u>pre</u>-manifest HD gene carriers compared to controls when viewing angry compared to neutral faces."[333] What this boils down to is that the corruption had started well before the HD made itself apparent!

Next, I read on and found further confirmation from such studies that our old friend, the Striatum of the Basal Ganglia, would have long since been defiled, spreading out like a bad ink stain: "Neuropathological changes can be detected *decades* before clinical signs emerge, beginning in the striatum and progressing to widespread brain atrophy."[334] I mention the Striatum again because this study wisely makes the critical point that we can't just look at the parts and pieces of the brain in isolation. Behavioral changes in the person with HD relate to the "disruption of the complex interactions between *multiple* brain circuits rather than as a result of distinct regional tissue degeneration."[335] And since these interactions are in progressive flux and flawed flow, they cannot be measured with finite authority by any singular MRI.

When HD becomes evident, we can find a positive correlation between noting discernable degenerated tissue and the person's misreading of others' surprise, disgust, anger, and fear. In particular, it is "anger recognition that is the most consistently reported impairment, closely followed by disgust and fear recognition in those with manifest HD."[336] That hit the nail on the head for my dad. Interestingly, I found another study examining oxygen levels in different brain regions to corroborate further how deterioration has blighted their brain. Let's return to our spotlight on the amygdala. We know that connectivity analysis indicates "abnormalities in the way that activity in the amygdala interacts with other brain regions."[337] What is the cause of this? Here, too, we can spot lesions on the amygdala.[338] I found no explanation describing how HD might bring about or be responsible for producing these particular lesions, but their debut marks the kiss of death. Literally. Cell death — also called "apoptosis" — is induced by a plethora of DNA-damaging agents, and lesions are one such type.[339] Remember that the mutated HD proteins kill only specific brain cells.[340]

Though science confirms it, as my dad would say, it is *"still a mystery"* why apoptosis occurs in the selective manner it does. One other study I read asserted that age, not just CAG length, has more of an effect on the rate of this disease's progression. This study also suggests that the amygdala is affected *early* in the course of HD, as in during the late pre-manifest stage. Changes in psychophysiological interaction (PPI) connectivity correlate with the disease onset.[341] As the disease progresses, the more pronounced the person with HD's inability to accurately read facial expressions (e.g., anger, disgust, fear, joy, sadness, and other neutral facial expressions),[342] leading to often bizarre, puzzling, or even ultimately vacant responses. My dad just seemed increasingly like a brat at worst or a cheerful and unaware child at best.

In addition to lesions, we find other phenomena that negatively impact the amygdala in our person with HD. Specifically, the connectivity "between the left amygdala, which is vulnerable to HD neuropathology, and the right FFA (fusiform face area) gets reduced... during emotional processing, facial emotional processing, reacting to fear, and social and emotional memory."[343] That is amazing! Technically, FFA stands for fusiform face area, but all we need to know is that it is a part of our vision system specializing in facial recognition.[344] Now we'll add insult to injury and return to the topic of lesions: when we consider that HD's abnormal huntingtin protein "gets bunched up into a huge ball of crud inside the (brain cell's) nucleus" and "gums up brain cells" such that "thick balls of the protein in the nuclei of cells within basal ganglia and cortex"[345] become evident, then it would be reasonable to deduce that ataxia, "the lack of muscle control or coordination of voluntary movements"[346] manifested as spots on the amygdala, *also* become collateral damage associated with HD. Without getting into any technical detail here, I would like to leave you with what the damaged amygdala looked like in my dad.

From about the age of fifty on and with a slowly creeping but intensifying degree, there came about a sometimes flustering, occasionally amusing, but often maddening lack of self-awareness. My father already had a robust and buoyant ego, but with increasing frequency in midlife, he would not acquiesce or accede that he might have done or said anything wrong or inappropriate. Not knowing what might have caused him to lose his cool or flip his lid, we chalked it off to his being Greek, but none of us could have disentangled his moment's madness to know which came first, the chicken or the egg. We didn't know then that the egg was cracked and the yolk was spoiled, that it would lead him to run around like a chicken with its head cut off. The emotional nadir in his life, his divorce, crossed paths and intersected at the very point in time when his middle-aged body was getting on with its aging process. His HD's destiny became manifest at this indeterminable but definite period in his life; however, to pinpoint the day or year his chorea *"kicked in,"* as he used to say, would be to separate "syllable from sound," as Emily Dickinson wrote in one of her poems, "The brain is just the weight of God."

No matter how hexed, vexed, or perplexed we who loved him could get over a peculiar movement or behavior, my dad remained nonplussed and unruffled over our concern or dismay. Even if he had noticed it, he couldn't do anything about it, and he was losing the capacity to care, which wouldn't have been strong anyway. Nature and nurture were compounding with reverse interest. Likely, he went from not caring to occasionally wondering and not noticing. Instead, his childlike tantrums inflated notions, delusions got stuck and remained in the forefront of his focus, and everybody within earshot heard all about his tiny woes. These "changes in empathy" became proof-positive demonstrations of an "impaired interpretation"[347] capability in our very own HD patient. It wasn't my dad's fault; nothing in his essential nature, healthy ego, extroverted personality, or Greek heritage decimated his ability to navigate the complex landscape of socio-emotional responses. From middle age on, awareness and empathy went down the tubes because HD had taken a toll on his amygdala. We shall now make our way to the third portion of the brain — the hippocampus — to our investigative work on how HD blunts the brain.

The Hippocampus

What is the hippocampus' unique role? In what manner does it interact with the damaged amygdala in the person with HD? When I introduced you to the amygdala, I mentioned that both the amygdala and hippocampus are part of the limbic system. Within the limbic system, the amygdala and hippocampus are located under the hypothalamus, another part of the limbic system near the left section of the thalamus.[348] When I peer at pictures of this part of the brain, which happens to be deep down and in the back center, I am ready to expand upon my previous analogy for you. The long-ish hippocampus is situated just behind the lower half of the ear of our person wearing the Bluetooth set (i.e., the Striatum of the Basal Ganglia), and it is adjacent to the "ball" at the tip of our "earlobe," the amygdala. Once again, the etymology is Greek. You can imagine my pleasant surprise when I learned that hippocampus comes from ἱππόκαμπος, which in Greek means "seahorse"[349] because of the similarity in shape, elongated with a "tail" and "head" of a similar sort. The two most influential hippocampal functions are related to space and memory.[350] The front portion or anterior of the hippocampus is connected to the amygdala and a portion of the frontal cortex. This anterior portion is thought to be involved in regulating emotion and stress. The back side (or posterior) portion of the hippocampus is connected to parietal cortices (i.e., near the side and top of the skull), and it is believed to be involved in cognitive and spatial processing.[351] These two parts deal primarily with "forming long-term memories, processing emotions, and determining how those emotions are tied to memories."[352]

Right out of the gate, I will tell you that persons with HD do not have nearly the damage done to the hippocampus as we find in patients with Alzheimer's Disease (AD). Therefore, long-term memories are *not* eradicated in HD patients, which is the case with AD patients. However, I would be remiss if I didn't briefly discuss the interactions between the two because of the intimate, synergistic relationship between the hippocampus and the amygdala, which HD has negatively impacted. Because so many people I have mentioned HD, which is largely unfamiliar to them, instinctively (albeit erroneously) try to associate it with AD. Unlike Alzheimer's, the pathology of which begins in the hippocampus and causes the infamous t.k.o. impact on one's memory (long-term and recent) and brings about "extensive confusion and disorientation,"[353] HD's impact on the hippocampus is i̲n̲direct and tangential. *That's why long-term memories in the person with HD remain impressively intact and unscathed; however, that's not to say that short-term memory-making isn't harmed. It is.* And I've seen my dad's confusion in space while yet not being disoriented in time. He just became disjointed. For example, he could readily recall detailed memories from when he was a boy in Greece but would fail the neurologist's quick, in-office cognitive test, not being able to retain the three words he was requested to memorize and recall some ten minutes later after an interlude of conversation in between.

While it is well-understood that "HD is associated with poor synaptic plasticity," the various deficits in the HD hippocampus are more likely to be "mediated by independently developing perturbations in a variety of combining signaling pathways [which] also contribute to HD hippocampal pathogenesis."[354] This is a fancy way of saying additional mitigating factors harm the hippocampal operations in the HD patient more than the genesis of organic damage done to it. What might such a mitigating factor be? You guessed it: glutamate. In a region essential for cognition, "excessive levels of the neurotransmitter glutamate [that] accumulate during neural activity" are detectable in the hippocampus of the patient with HD."[355] While required for rapid cellular communication, "too much glutamate impairs synapse strengthening and negatively impacts cellular health."[356]

The hippocampus does not function as effectively when it gets overwhelmed; thus, although we find no structural damage to the HD hippocampus, it does get overburdened by having to contend with excess glutamate. What is the significance of this? When the hippocampus is stressed — which, as you can imagine, living with HD progressively gnawing away at parts of the brain would do — the hippocampus reacts so that it "constantly logs things in the wrong place with incorrect information."[357] This is why memory of a traumatic time, say, for example, the Greek Civil War, can feel as though the original event is occurring again by way of "intrusive thoughts, flashbacks and re-experiencing hyperarousal symptoms."[358] In short, *any PTSD episode will get elevated in the person with HD.* My dad would experience this during the aftermath of 9/11. He must have bought a dozen first-responder police and firefighter ballcaps to pass out because he *"got reminded"* of the mayhem he experienced as a lad. We are now prepared to behold how the most sophisticated part of our reasoning mechanism, the prefrontal cortex, gets hijacked by HD.

The Prefrontal Cortex

Now that we have covered two of the three layers of the brain, that is, the so-called **reptilian brain**, which presents to us the particular piece of the brain that is the most jarred by HD, the **basal ganglia**, and the so-called **paleomammalian layer**, where we have analyzed the sophisticated dance between the amygdala and the hippocampus, we are finally ready to complete our focused sweep of the brain and gander a look at its most recent layer, the neocortex section, also known as the **neomammalian layer**; we refer to it as "the human brain."[359] Not only does it direct complex processes like "language, abstract thinking, advanced cognition, and planning,"[360] but it is associated with "concentration, decision-making, awareness, and our sense of wrong and right — pretty much everything we need to function in society and maintain our humanity."[361]

This part of the brain is *supposed* to calm our flight and flight response, to help us know to "maintain positive, rich, and healthy social connections," and to display a sense of "mindfulness."[362] Thus, to complete our investigation of how HD strikes the brain, I will transition from our discussion of the layers of the brain to one of its two hemispheres, the forebrain, the biggest part of the brain. The forebrain contains the **cerebral cortex**, which is the brain's outer surface; beneath it are various lobes.[363] I will spotlight only the particular lobe intimately connected with our damaged basal ganglia; you can't help but see that it, too, is adversely affected. Moving our way out and forward is our <u>frontal lobe</u>, which involves reasoning, motor control, emotion, and language.[364] Huntington's

Disease slowly but surely and progressively pummels the first three of the four of these functions.

Among other entities, the frontal lobe also contains both the **motor and prefrontal cortex**. Fascinatingly, the etymology of "cortex" is Latin, and it means "bark."[365] At this juncture, I would like to add that HD is *not* the same thing as dementia, but it does have many similarities to it. These include "lack of impulse control, agitation or apathy, and unexpected antisocial behaviors."[366] And of these characteristics, my dad lacked only apathy in later years. His already short fuse got blunted to the wick, often leaving him stuck in huff-and-puff. In the good old days, my dad had enough self-control to remain stoic in public if he got miffed. What proves mystifying is how and why specific behavioral characteristics are present in some HD persons, not at all in others, and amplified in still others. You can't predict the outcome perfectly because too many variables are in the mix. For example, my father's lack of impulse control was manifested in the way you would expect to see in one who has obsessive-compulsive disorder. When Dad got fixated on a particular thought or notion, he became like a mule or a bulldog, and his poor brain would go into clamp-down mode on some erroneous conclusion, farcical hypothesis, or outlandish idea. He had other compulsive behaviors, which I'll describe later.

Since we have already examined the part of the frontal cortex called the motor cortex, which is involved in planning and coordinating movement — and how HD causes the opposite of what is supposed to happen, let's move on to the part of the frontal lobe called the **prefrontal cortex**. Since the prefrontal cortex is responsible for higher cognitive functions, like reason, planning, concentrating, and the expression of our emotions,[367] any connections and interactions it has with the more afflicted parts of the HD brain — and, in particular, the damaged striatum (of the Basal Ganglia)— will undermine its task completions. It's like a messed-up 3-D version of falling dominoes gone rogue. Should you witness or have a loved one with HD, these bizarre changes will unfold before your very eyes and become hauntingly apparent. It's scary how HD strikes the prefrontal cortex, turning man back into beast.

As we take all of this information into account, there is a song that teaches children about the various bones of the body called "Dem Bones." When I arrived at our final frontier of the brain, its lyrics popped into my mind because the prefrontal cortex also works not in isolation but in concert with the other parts of the brain we have already investigated. To lighten our load and add a bit of humor, I remixed its lyrics to capture this interconnectedness. HD picking off and pummeling parts of the brain results in problems that ricochet off one another, exacerbating the whole of the person's not well-being exponentially and *ad nauseum*. There are way too many syllables for the song[368] to be sung with ease, but you'll get the idea:

> The basal ganglia is connected to the amygdala,
> The amygdala is connected to the hippocampus,
> The hippocampus is connected to the prefrontal cortex,
> And so, too, is the amygdala joined up to the prefrontal cortex
> And, yes, that striatum — it also talks to the cortex...
> Ezekiel cried, "Dat Brain, dat brain — HD's gonna bring it pain!"
> "Oh, hear the word of the Lord."

How do our other key players interface with the prefrontal cortex? We'll start with the relationship of the prefrontal lobe with the Basal Ganglia, specifically the Striatum. Because of the breakdown (i.e., death) and "loss of striatal dopamine receptors,"[369] we find an "early decline in working memory and executive function."[370] Working memory is processed in the prefrontal cortex, which has to do with the current/contemporary production of making new memories, *not* the recollection of long-term memories or identifying persons known for a lifetime. You already know this. Executive functions have to do with our decision-making apparatus, which we use all the livelong day. Therefore, with the gradual but decisive fraying and decaying of particular intracranial structures, it will be taxing for the person with HD to make even simple decisions. You will see them falter, hesitate, and get stuck in making choices you and I would not even give a thought to.

My dad would get to the point where he would ask me, *"What do you think?"*, as if he were taking a survey about all things great and (very) small that called for a decision to be made. This was hardly the father I grew up with, but his asking for input endeared him to me and made me feel all the more protective of him! If you recall, one other part of the basal ganglia is the caudate nucleus, and with connections between the caudate and the frontal lobes "severely disrupted" in HD,[371] we can also observe symptoms that are similar to those of the schizophrenic, including "complex delusions even auditory hallucinations."[372] My dad did *not* hear voices; he was loud enough. He was content unto himself while unknowingly being just beyond himself; it was *others* who were suspect. My dad did not become delusional but rather grandiose. To us who loved him, this seemed a comical yet also natural expansion of his already innate optimistic and confident self.

Before we leave this section, I'd like to mention how the prefrontal cortex (PFC) interacts not only with the BG but with other parts of the brain we've had reason to study. Prefrontal cortex dysfunction is common in patients with Huntington's disease, and the behavioral outcome, which is "significantly impaired...[is] fear expression."[373] Interestingly, this deficit in contextual fear conditioning is "likely due to impaired plasticity in the hippocampus."[374] Add that to the fact that the pre-frontal cortex–amygdala network "mediates expression and inhibition of fear responses,"[375] and the net effect will be that our person with HD will, without fail, express "anxiety and depressive symptoms"[376] if he perceives a stimulus to be a threat. I sure saw this. My dad would get to where he got agitated so easily, and not infrequently. It seemed as if he was a deranged soldier ready for combat. It got to the point where tip-toeing around his feelings didn't prevent friction or fraction on his part because it was anything that could get misconstrued as a threat, ironically all the more so if actions were meant to help him. Many of his eggshells were broken, emotional minefields got detonated, and he was left with a suspicious mind and an unsettled soul.

Studies suggest that "irritability in HD is related to impulsivity and aggression.[377] You don't say. Where does this come from? The amygdala and something called the medial orbito_frontal_ cortex (OFC) are key circuits involved in impulsive aggression.[378] (Focus on the "frontal" part.) When we factor in HD causing the amygdala to become dysfunctional, it's no wonder that the pre-frontal cortex-amygdala network — the normal job of which is to "mediate the expression and inhibition of fear responses," specifically in lowering levels of fear"[379] — also gets damaged and acts not as it ought. Biblically speaking, the expression of "a little yeast working through the whole batch of dough" (Gal. 5:9 NIV), means that one deleterious part has the power to bring about widespread damage, like a rankled ripple effect. Everything gets soiled.

Therefore, as I hope I've made abundantly clear, not only are there problems with movement, but reasoning gets rankled, and emotions get muddled in our beloved one with HD. We who are powerless but not helpless witness in shock and awe, angst and ire, their baffling misfit ways. Your person with HD can become moody and cranky or needful of affirmation and tenderness in the blink of an eye. And by the way, anti-social behavior is not a constant, just a distinct possibility. He lacks self-awareness and cannot curb himself from outbursts; on the underlying level, he feels threatened or scared. Yes, my dad always had a temper, but later, he reminded me of a child "full of sound and fury,"[380] having a tantrum over a whole lot of nothing. There is simply (and literally) little left to inhibit these fear responses. None of this cognitive decline happens overnight either; subtle behavioral and neuropsychological changes begin inexplicably and without cause or trigger; the changes proceed to vivify over time, like cancer invading your loved one's personality. That said, by the last year of his life, I became his "safe person" and was able to translate the world for him in a way that soothed and satisfied him.

What about the prefrontal cortex and the hippocampus? Does their interplay suffer deleterious consequences? The answer is undeniably *yes*, and in more than one way. Before we get to their networking, consider that, compared with the control group, patients with Huntington's Disease show "significantly impaired functional connectivity between anterior (front) and lateral (side) prefrontal regions in both hemispheres."[381] In my mind's eye, I see filaments and wires cut, frayed, and fried, and the electrical grid getting short-circuited and melting. By the time the person whose HD has progressed to the mid and later stages gets engaged in a multi-step task, "a loss of synchrony in activity between the prefrontal regions"[382] has already occurred, and it would be easy to "predict poor task performance." It doesn't get any better either, and you'll see how the networking between the prefrontal cortex and hippocampus also gets thwarted.

Usually, the symbiotic interplay between these two parts involves (a) retrieving memories that the hippocampus has established for any future context and (b) utilizing these memories to "flexibly switch" within any given context to complete specific tasks.[383] Since the prefrontal cortex is the weakest link between the two, its ability to retrieve and guide memories gets derailed, and the result is that, like a blind man, the prefrontal grabs at "conflicting information in its retrieval of … competing memories, [especially those needed for] solving spatial memory tasks."[384] What does this impaired cognitive flexibility look like in a person with HD? Confusion and an odd sense of evident puzzlement over, let's say, something as simple as tying one's shoelaces. Why? The (involuntary) retrieval of the memory as to how to do so, likely even just a portion of the task, gets lost, so the person with HD gets "stuck" and can't get the job done. My dad's announcing that he was *"sooooo frustrated"* still rings in my ears. Later, my dad went into an automatic and reflexive self-preservation mode and path of least resistance: he avoided said problem or task altogether. Case in point: he simply got to where he wouldn't even wear button-up shirts because they proved an insurmountable challenge to fumbling fingers and jumbled thoughts; therefore, he shunned them and donned his familiar and faded t-shirts. What exactly happened to the prefrontal cortex? Is the spoilage as bad as what has happened to the basal ganglia? No, but it has become corrupted nonetheless. Let's take a quick peek.

Although our now-familiar striatum [of the basal ganglia] has long been considered the cerebral area most dramatically, uniquely, and cripplingly involved in HD, recent reports have highlighted "widespread cortical and subcortical brain atrophy" and "progressive neuronal dysfunction" which create cortical brain changes even early on in the disease's course.[385] And just like the data suggests that the striatum experiences "massive inflammation in HD" even before symptoms appear, we can also observe "a similar expression observed in the prefrontal cortex."[386] Without delving deeper, it suffices to say that inflammation also contributes to brain degeneration.

When you look at scans of the brain of someone with HD in contrast to the normal brain, you will see that the cortex — the "highly twisted layer of the brain which controls thought, behavior, and memory"[387] — also gets ravaged. It looks like cauliflower that has shrunk, and its "flowers" have become more articulate with additional space in between. The "white matter" of our cauliflower stalks gets bolder yet more articulated and drawn up. Meanwhile, the "grey matter" that envelops them has also receded.[388] We could also compare it to a block of firm tofu with pockets of empty space waxing wider, indicating random pockets of the PFC that, for all intents and purposes, have gone MIA. Pieces of the puzzle go MIA without rhyme or reason, but you can still make out the whole that was and would have been.

Although scans indicate a "progressive loss of pyramidal neurons in cortical layers of HD patients and a decrease in the thickness of the respective cortical layers,"[389] this breakdown is selective, and not all areas are hit! It's hit or miss, and no one knows where the spinning wheel of reduced cognition will land; it's like pinning the tail on a moving donkey. To come back full circle, the decay of the cortical neurons occurs "principally [back] at the site of the primary degeneration in the caudate nuclei [of the basal ganglia]"! Do you see how specific HD is in its sneak attack? And yet, maddeningly, the resultant ripple effect impacts mind and mood and movement! Even though the aging process affects all of us in every aspect of our personhood, there is further evidence of additional desecration and looting of the HD brain, particularly as the aging process commences.

Aging and the HD Brain

If a person inherits HD and is born with it — juvenile HD withstanding — why does the disease take what seems like half a lifetime to present itself? As we age, cells die off; this accelerates in the middle years. We notice it more in HD patients because this also involves more neuron death, and as you now know, it is both precise in its location and rippling in its effect. In one particular abstract, I found proof that by examining MRI scans, patients with HD exhibited "cerebral volume changes" and "robust regional decreases in grey matter density."[390] What is the nature of these changes, and what is the outcome? Regardless of individual idiosyncratic displays, by and large, patients with Huntington's Disease

> "exhibit significant brain atrophy resulting from volume reductions in both cortical and subcortical grey matter. Atrophy of the cortex was relatively uniform, although the … temporal lobe structures were spared. The caudate nucleus and putamen were strikingly reduced [in size] in all cases, and this atrophy correlated with the severity of cortical atrophy."[391]

Once again, you will recall that the B.G.'s striatum (i.e., the caudate + putamen) is most adversely impaired, and one of its butterfly effects impacts the subcortex. What does this mean regarding how the brain functions on the cellular or neuronal level? In the cortical portion of the HD brain, "significantly less bursting" occurs in the "firing patterns," and there is a "loss of synchrony" between the brain's neuron pairs. What this translates to in terms of behavioral expression is a positive correlation between the reduced firing patterns, both with the progressively deteriorating motor impairment and with the level of "aggression expression" symptomatic in cognitive abnormalities.[392] Another study corroborated that ataxia in the prefrontal cortex of the HD patient made it possible to investigate "global disruptions."[393] When you factor in the progressive nature of this disease, what you can anticipate will be the unmistakable, mini monster-like movements, fidgety-ness, consternating behavioral changes, and cognitive decline. I lament and feel like a weeping prophet telling you this.

I found the "global disruptions" verbiage apt because my dad often seemed uncharacteristically lagging or suspended in his thought process, as if he got stopped at a cautionary flashing yellow light and had difficulty proceeding to Pass Go and collecting his $200. He also got to repeatedly asking me (and others), *"What do you think?"* over the most inane and inconsequential of things, as if, were he to collect enough tallies, he could help tip the scales in his favor, be it ordering food at a restaurant or collecting signatures from fellow residents at his assisted living home.

This never would have happened in the days when he was the head of the house, even if in his own mind. His word went. Period. My sister captured (and mocked) his healthy ego by giving him a Father's Day Card that depicted a mafiosi father surrounded by his family with him quipping out of the corner of his mouth, "If I want your opinion, I'll give it to you!" My dad loved it.

The further he got into middle age, the more trouble he would have in shaking off a wave of anger, frustration, or obsession that hit him; he would fight tooth and nail over a point or person. How exhausting and bewildering all this must have been for him! How terrifying. That part of his personality that had indelibly formed persistence in him and the discipline to promptly accomplish tasks as soon as they hit his mental plate, he retained with a vengeance until the day he died. It's just that the jobs got very small and frivolous. So, he kept his clipboard handy, chock-full of paper, ready to scrawl and scribble out his schemes and themes. Repeatedly.

We are almost done with the brain. I'll let my finishing up here with HD's effect on the outer "bark" of the brain, the cortex, by summing up how HD completes its holocaust. While it has not been my desire to overburden or swamp you with burdensome details, it has been incumbent upon me to share this rich information from varied sources that could not have originated from me. I'm following the advice I gave my students: it is better to have what seems like too much documentation than not enough, all the more so when you are wrapping your mind around so much new information to yourself. In short, I am no different than the mass of you reading this. I am pleased to have navigated and shared this weighty but fascinating background material with you because it sheds critical light on precisely what HD does to the architecture of particular brain regions. Oh, I wish I could have explained it to my dad. As a man of science, he would have been riveted. Even more, I wish there had been *no* reason to look up this disease in the first place, but since there was and is, I hope other families impacted can take note and comfort here.

Right now, I have a huge desire to thank you, dear reader. Not only have you covered the genetics behind HD, but you have also covered the basics of the brain as we have investigated HD's neurological impact on the mind. At times, it may have felt like you were going through a swamp, maze, or quicksand, but you won't be sorry! Now, you are prepared to watch and understand the erratic rollercoaster ride of my dad's mystifying descent and my herculean labors that accompanied them while I was helping him. It was like living through a Greek tragedy — and I don't mean a myth or play — this was real life with my heroic and halted father.

228

Before I could slay it with my pen, I had to look the monster in the eye from all angles.

The disease's accost of my father was complete — body, mind, and emotions were sullied; only his soul remained untouched. Out of respect for my dad, I wanted to take my time and explore what was happening to the motherboard of his central cerebral processing unit, scouring for what went haywire in the autumn of his life. Now that you have the back story of what was transpiring and devolving within my dad's brain, you are better prepared to understand what happened to him during his "the full catastrophe," as Zorba the Greek would say. You'll soon see as I'll mentally draw for you his uncontrolled movements and diminished intellectual faculties, echoed in a host of emotional and psychiatric problems.

It goes beyond the scope of our study to explore a potential way to intercept, blockade, and prevent this disease; furthermore, it simply hasn't been found *yet*. As is the case with other neurodegenerative diseases, while there do exist myriad ways to reduce the effects of HD, we have found no sure-proof cure. However, I will mention that in 2014, a UCLA team discovered that reducing the mutant huntingtin protein in the cortex partially improved the animals' symptoms. Even more impressively, completely cutting off and "shutting down the mutant huntingtin gene in both the cortical and striatal neurons... corrected every symptom measured in the mice, including motor and psychiatric-like behavioral impairment and brain atrophy."[394] Now, wouldn't that be an amazing and miraculous feat?!

However, that's still not preventing it from coming into existence in the first place. This is where genetic engineering might pioneer a total prevention, a circumvention altogether, but I'm sticking to my father's story, which is not fiction. When I meet God and Maker in Heaven, maybe I'll ask Him about the whys; perhaps by now, my dad already knows. Let's return to Hercules and momentarily fast-forward to his life after his well-known labors have been completed, but before he dies and is taken to Mount Olympus. I'll now march us straight to the edge of madness when my dad's disease had just begun to rear its ugly head when none of us knew what in the name of heaven was happening to him. It's when his tripping and trembles started that the whispers began.

My parents' wedding day, Christmas Day 1960.

My father in the early 1970s as I remember him best.

My parents in the late 1970s preparing Greek
goodies. This made the local paper.

Chapter 5

Coming Undone: 1985–1999

From "The Good Life"[395]
Mm, the good life lets you hide
All the sadness you feel...
It's the good life to be free
And explore the unknown
Like the heartaches when you learn
You must face them alone...
Well, just wake up
Kiss the good life, goodbye.
— "The Good Life," by Sasha Distel (1934), best known via the 1963
recording by Tony Bennet with lyrics by Jack Reardon[396]

"I count him braver who overcomes his desires than him who
conquers his enemies; for *the hardest victory is over self.*"
— Aristotle (384-382 BCE) (emphasis mine)

[3]*We also celebrate in our tribulations,* knowing that
tribulation brings about perseverance;
[4]and perseverance, proven character; and proven character, hope;
[5]and hope does not disappoint, *because the love of God has been poured out
within our hearts through the Holy Spirit who was given to us.*
— Romans 5:3–5 (emphasis mine)

"A person needs a little madness, or else they
never dare cut the rope and be free."
— from Nikos Kazantzakis (*Zorba the Greek*)

My dear reader, likely you are saying to yourself, "Well, possess my soul and body!" as you wonder when the "it" — my dad's Huntington's Disease — would begin to manifest itself in a way no one could deny *something* was off-kilter and going awry. *This* is the chapter that precedes my dad's official diagnosis we'll begin with in Volume 2. I was going to say it was the calm before the storm, but it's more like the storm brewing before we got swept in the eye of the tornado. Though we did have a relative lull, there were still wafts of "strong surface winds converging towards the center, [but not quite] reaching it."[397] We were marching towards the madness, his strange circumlocutions, the odd noises, mysterious commotions — in general, the *"goings on,"* as my dad would say. They would progress from occasional to frequent to commonplace before we would know it. Slowly but surely, my dad was being robbed of kibbles and bits of his wherewithal such that he was unable to recognize, let alone wonder *what*, *if* anything, was wrong with these new emissions of quirkiness. Truth be told, we were all getting used to his idiosyncrasies; they just seemed amped-up aspects of his indigenous self. I am referring to what appeared to be psycho-motor leakage, as in the tic-like movements that begin occurring and which his mind could not contain, let alone wrap itself around. I became familiar with the term "leakage" in college in a communications course that defined it as a form of non-verbal behavior that occurs when

> "a person verbalizes one thing, *but their body language indicates another.* Common forms *include facial movements and gestures.* [For those who] pick up any incongruity between verbal and non-verbal messages, [it] can be confusing and can cause cognitive dissonance."[398]

We watched on and were confused as we shook our heads, momentarily puzzled over what we were beginning to notice in our dad. I also learned that when an individual attempts to suppress this non-verbal leakage, "there exist some aspects that *are out of his voluntary control* and will *still* be expressed *despite any efforts to the contrary. . .especially* when trying to conceal a high-intensity emotion."[399] Eureka! My dad was loaded with "high-intensity emotions"! That *had* to be why my dad started displaying certain mannerisms and even making odd sounds. Life on his own without my mom and his family just had to have been the impetus for the micro eruptions transmitting themselves. It was apparent he had no control over them and didn't seem to be aware. Whether we liked it or not, we all were subconsciously coming to terms with the fact that *this was how it was going to be.* These randomly occurring "tics" weren't debilitating — just ghoulishly strange and weird was already the norm for my dad. But I get ahead of myself and how wrong I was.

In this chapter, we will spend time peering into the face and form of my dad *as* he was turning into our Hunchback of Notre Dame. No, he was no monster, but some aspects of him were becoming deranged or downright scandalous compared to his regular, unique self. We wrote off these oddities to his being Greek (and, thus, even foreign to us) as if this was how his frame and central force were responding to the trauma of divorce. It was clear that particular physiological quirks were starting up beyond his volition, like subconscious hiccups of mind and manner leftover from a quaking heart that could not accept his sense of abandonment. Again. This time, there was no escape or emigration; there was no way out but *through*. Yet because he was our father *and* an adult, we kids still expected him to act "right" and to keep the darker forces that could wreak havoc on others and mayhem on self tucked in.

While I was still in high school, I recall a couple in our church who were good friends of my parents, and when the wife left her husband, the husband had to be committed to the psychiatric hospital because he had a full-blown nervous breakdown; in fact, he fell out on the floor and had a seizure in church. I still remember my dad shaking his head in woeful sympathy, uttering something to the effect that he would have responded the same way if he had been in this man's shoes. What a foreboding premonition. However, my father's plight and demise would be of a very different nature; he did *not* have a nervous breakdown, but when my mother finally ended up calling it quits, none of us was surprised when we began to notice something aberrant and odd in our dad's central nervous system. We found him at once exasperating and consternating, puzzling but amusing, and through it all, remaining our tried-and-true, our one-and-only loving and loopy dad.

Now that you have become acquainted with relevant background on both my dad and the disease, it's time to buckle up and get ready to rumble and roll. The pace will pick up because we've crossed the peak, and his descent will begin. In this chapter, I will deconstruct the order of our framework to capture the reckless nature of his uncontainable and unstoppable decline. After I comment on this chapter's epigraphs, I will jump ahead to the time in Hercules's life *after* he completed his renowned labors. Since I will be the one performing the labors in *this* story — our focus for Volume 2 — for now, I will have us glimpse Hercules' *later* years when he had returned to some semblance of normalcy. However, for my father, this period here and now would be the final frontier of independence as he would know it. My dad's need for companionship and his pursuit of women will diverge from Hercules', but other commonalities exist. Instead of plowing into the next relevant phase of my dad's biography, we will investigate the textbook definition of the "early stage" signs of Huntington's Disease. Then, I will swing back around and show you how the disease first became noticeable in Dad. I find terms like "early," "middle," and "late-stage" not only inadequate and imprecise but also a little ludicrous as if we could cross a visible starting line where we could hear clearly in the near distance, "On your mark, get set, *go!*", complete with a pistol shot in the backdrop. There was no clear "mark," just broken chalk dust; none of us was "set" —least of all, my dad — and "go" amounted to "stumble" in every possible way.

That said, for clarity's sake, I will trace the lines of what one can expect to see at the onset of Huntington's Disease; then, I'll color in our drawing by fleshing in what was transpiring with my dad. As a caveat, because I was launching into the first decade of my life as an independent adult, I was not residing with my dad for the years I have slated to share with you. That said, I *did* visit him frequently, as in monthly; certainly, not more than six weeks passed, but one of us didn't visit the other. As it was, we only lived two hours' driving distance apart. Therefore, to corroborate what I noticed, I asked my brother to fill in some gaps here; after all, during this troubling decade and a half, my brother was either living with Dad or, if not, he saw him weekly. Combining our forces with parts of his letters to me will give you the most accurate account of how Huntington's disease made its mark on *our* story's not-at-all mythical hero. Let's prime the pump and review pertinent quotes first.

This Chapter's Epigraphs

The first time I heard Tony Bennet sing "The Good Life," I immediately thought of my dad; it happened while writing this chapter. I chose to include it because in the last twenty years of his life, his rock of Gibraltar cracked, and his happy home turned into a den of discord. My dad could have cared less if he lived in a cave so long as he had my mom and us around him. After the divorce, he moved into the house in which he would reside until the time I had him placed in an assisted living center. Unlike Hercules, my dad never got remarried. And although he loved the company of women, to his core, he was a one-woman man. Did my father achieve success and the "good life"? Without a doubt. After his wife left, did he "explore the unknown"? Yes, he surely did. However, when he re-entered the complicated web of dating, a world replete with even more unknown rules than in his marriage and complex games (that he would have approached like a Neanderthal), unbeknownst to him (and us), his Huntington's disease would have started "*kicking in,*" as later on, he would describe its onset.

Not only did he seek the company of women with a broken and longing heart, but he was making his way through midlife with a brain and body that was at odds with his will. You'll see. My dad's heartache was so seismic that it would seem he had no heart left to steal or hurt. That wasn't the case where his children were concerned, but HD would rob his perspective, self-awareness, and presence of mind. His moral compunction, modicum of decorum, and self-restraint were getting blunted. Did he come to care for certain women after the divorce? Yes, most certainly. I'm just letting you know that those who came after my mother became band-aids and comforters, albeit not all of equal strength or stature. The "good life" he'd known before got transformed into the life he would work hard to make good again, and, thanks to his indomitable spirit and a fresh desire to explore his adopted land *and* revisit his native soil, I believe he did achieve the good life. Again.

I can cover the rest of the quotes in a single paragraph. Time and again, we all saw in our dad a man who was both fierce and fearless and one who placed family over self. I do not think he ever achieved Aristotle's marker for success, that is, "victory over self." How could he? For self-realization to occur, a person must first have self-awareness and then turn the powers of critical analysis onto self so that actualization can occur. Indeed, in later years, my dad often said, *"We grow old too fast and wise too late,"* but I'm not sure if he could have told you how or even *if* he got "wise." I believe that somewhere deep inside, where there are no words, my dad could testify that it was no person but "The LORD [who] is my rock and my fortress and my savior. [It is] my God, my rock, in whom I take refuge" (Psalm 18:2). This passage from Psalms dovetails into the passage from Romans 5. Like his namesake, the Apostle Paul, my dad endured and surmounted trials and tribulations to a near-biblical degree. No, he received no lashes, nor was he jailed or beaten with rods for his defense of Christ, but I'll *bet* he felt shipwrecked.

There's no doubt that by the time he left Greece, he also would have experienced "dangers from rivers, dangers from robbers, dangers from countrymen, dangers from the Gentiles [i.e., in this case, the Germans and Italians], dangers in the city, dangers in the wilderness, dangers on the sea, dangers among false brethren [e.g., the "collaborators"]. [27]Furthermore, my dad had experienced labor and hardship, many sleepless nights, hunger and thirst, often without food, in cold and exposure (from 2 Corinthians 11:23–27). Heavens! Please don't equivocate my dad's hardship with what the Apostle Paul underwent; anyway, we oughtn't conflate anyone's capacity to endure as a source of intrinsic merit. To his credit, our dad never did lord over, brag about, or burden us with what he underwent—quite the opposite. Instead, what we witnessed in him was a miraculous and enduring hope and happiness he possessed; it was like the pitch from a pine tree that oozes from its trunk after it has been slashed, and the amber sap of his soul seemed in endless supply.

His confidence and gut trust gave him the fortitude and capacity to go through any Sisyphean task, including one no one anticipated. *His* Greek tragedy was that no matter how hard he tried, he missed the mark and never recaptured his wife's devotion, but tragedy did not end in defeat. I believe the Holy Spirit provisioned the scope of hope my dad possessed, and he guarded it with his life. To close these two introductory paragraphs, I'll end with a quote from Zorba the Greek. It seems appropriate because the "madness" of my father did *not* lie in his genetic pool, as some might expect me to say, but in his lust for life. From cutting the ropes and freeing himself from the constraints, curtailments, and expectations imposed on him by his parents, he became a free agent and married another renegade like himself. And as a man who was an optimist until his dying day, the world continued to hold endless possibilities and potential for him. Even in his last days, he often told me *he wanted to die a free man*, and there's a part of me that would have loved to have let him remain in Greece those final years and fade or fly away, like Icarus to the sun.

The adult in me would not throw caution to the wind to let chance gain the upper hand and bring harm to any. Although I would have my dad's tombstone engraved in both English and Greek, I could have copied the following phrase Kazantzakis requested for his epitaph, and my dad would've been pleased: "I hope for nothing. I fear nothing. I am free."[400] Let's return to our myth of Hercules and see what life was like for him *after* he'd unintentionally killed Megara. Again, please bear in mind that *this* chapter's slice of mythology will have us leap ahead just *after* Hercules completes his twelve labors and returns to live out the rest of his years. I will use this portion of the mythical Greek hero's life to bridge my dad's transitional years between 1985 and 1999, taking us from post-divorce to pre-diagnosis. For us on the close outside looking in, this era proved a mysterious grey zone of subtle changes. Unbeknownst to us, something was going awry with his gray matter; we just couldn't put our finger on what was slowly but surely unfolding before our very eyes. How could we? What was transpiring had yet to be identified, let alone *diagnosed*. Meanwhile, Hercules and my dad were uncoupled and wifeless, and while my dad did no*t* remarry, like Hercules, he did seek the companionship of women again.

Hercules and Women after Megara's Death

You have already learned of the life-altering tragedy that sent Hercules' life on a new trajectory, one that jumpstarted a reflex within him to atone for wrong-doings. You also know that Hercules was a simple-minded soul primarily led by baser emotions. These ways and means continued *past* the completion of the famous herculean labors, and that is where we will now momentarily rejoin Hercules and make our due comparisons to my father. Rather than murder, it would be *after* my parents' divorce, but *before* his disease presented itself to the degree that it was undeniable that something *had* to be done or figured out. For that, we would seek professional assessment to determine what was happening to our dad, but that moment is not current. Instead, we will tie the loose ends of the ends to what Hercules was up to *after* his renowned labors were done. In Volume 2, we will take the rollercoaster ride of reflecting on Hercules' labors while coalescing them to my laborious tasks while caretaking. It was my Call of Duty that would be no game.

Please remember that while Hercules is only a myth, several versions of his story exist that, <u>un</u>like my dad's woe, *never were true*. Hercules is the most famous of all the Greek heroes, and it ought to indicate that we will come in contact with worthy and transcendent ideals to which we all should aspire to emulate just like the iconic, albeit imperfect, mythical hero did. One of Hercules' fatal flaws was that, like his father, Zeus, he found that women were drawn to him, and he was restless where fidelity went. Though he had a stepfather, he had no "dad" from whom to seek counsel. My father would prove to be no different for all intents and purposes. Hercules' shenanigans led to all sorts of adventures that would plague him unto death. You may recall that as one account goes, Hercules "successively bed every one of the king's [of Thespiae] fifty daughters..."[401]

On the other hand, my dad would have been sheltered and retained his purity like any maiden of the day. This restlessness and rootlessness drove Hercules from one battle — or woman — to the next. Now, my dad and Hercules are similar because, during the marriage that brought each his most significant woman and the one who would bear them children, *they both remained devoted, faithful, and true.* After the pain each suffered from the loss of his wife — one to murder, the other, divorce — Hercules did remarry; however, my father would not. That said, both men had a series of relationships with women that are worth pointing out; the difference here is that my father's choice of partners revealed a man whose reasoning was dulled. I'll start with Hercules' resumption of normalcy after his life-altering loss.

Hercules would first fall in love with the Princess Iole of Oechalia. To win her hand in marriage, her father set up an archery contest; however, when Hercules won, the king refused to acknowledge this victory because he knew Hercules had murdered his first wife. He wasn't about to let anything like that happen to *his* daughter! Now, about this time, depending on which version you read, the king's horses were stolen or had wandered off, and one of the king's sons, Iphitus — the only one of whom who supported Hercules' right to his sister's hand in marriage — asked Hercules to help him rustle back the horses to his father. Hercules inclined and helped Iphitus, but wicked Hera, still bent on revenge for her husband's infidelity, bewitched Hercules and threw him into another mad fit, and — you guessed it — he murdered Iphitus, this time, by throwing him over a wall, where and when he would plunge to his death.

Hercules' anger was still piqued over King Eurytous' duplicity and the *rest* of his sons' backing, but more to the pressing matter at hand: Hercules again became filled with remorse. He had murdered again! He did *not* plead "not guilty" by reason of insanity. As was the norm of his day, he immediately sought the oracle's advice at Delphi on what he needed to do to atone for his latest egregious crime. Well, even the oracle wanted nothing to do with Hercules since he hadn't learned a thing from his past crime of passion. Hercules had a tantrum and stole the tripod given to this oracle by Apollo, which was part of her oracular "gear." Why did he do this? Desperate to pay his due penance, Hercules set up his stage with a tripod prop. Then, he became his *own* oracle, one who would guarantee the means of expiation. You have to admire him for his tenacity and ingenuity. Hercules got away with this farce of a trial because, meanwhile, Apollo was peeved, and he swiftly came after Hercules for this theft; in fact, the two of them got into a scuffle and wrestled over the tripod in question.

You'll see just how much Hercules was favored. In *deus ex machina* fashion, Zeus came to his son's rescue and broke up the fight by sending a dramatic thunderbolt. Through Zeus's prerogative and pressure, the *original* priestess relented and informed Hercules that he'd have to serve as a slave for a year to rectify this latest crime. Hercules gladly relented and made himself available for servitude. At this new "low" point, a certain queen named Omphale, from the foreign land of Lydia, bought Hercules to be her slave. During their three years together, Hercules led what can only be described as a bizarre life. Playwright and philosopher Sophocles tells us that Hercules would have felt "deep dishonor" at being forced into slavery."[402] Furthermore, slaves in Greek society often came from non-Greek regions, so the enslavement of Hercules by a barbarian queen would have seemed an "especially outrageous reversal to the Greeks."[403]

Speaking of reversal, that's just what they got into, and, for Queen Omphale's amusement, they dressed up in each other's clothing. Hercules even learned and took up specific "women's work," including knitting.

Though technically, Omphale liberated Hercules after one year's service, she turned around and married him, and they lived together for two more years before he finally extracted himself from this entanglement. There are other sundry exploits of his that are purported to have taken in the Peloponnesus after Hercules left his second wife; however, I will cut to the chase, which occurred when he rescued his next damsel in distress, Princes Deianeira. Together, they would eventually move and settle in another region in Greece. Although I read various accounts, Hercules and the beautiful Iole continued to have an off-again-on-again relationship, as you will see. My father did not have such a harrowing ordeal or engage in exploits, nor did he seek redress or reparation. However, my dad possessed a bold confidence, which showed in his own pursuits, as you will continue to observe in Hercules.

How did Hercules win the hand of Princess Deianeira of Chalkidon, who would become his third and final wife? If we keep to *Sophocles'* account of Deianeira, before her meeting Hercules, Deianeira was betrothed in marriage — apparently, against her will — to the river god Achelous. However, when Hercules arrived in Chalkidon, he met and fell in love with her. The feeling was mutual, but her hands were tied. In the end, he rescued her from having to marry Achelous by defeating this river god in (another) wrestling match.[404] Fate became their fortune, and Deianeira and Hercules wed. On their way to Trachis, they had to cross a broad river with a centaur named Nessos appointed as its ferryman.

As the story goes, when Nessos was transporting Deianeira across, he attempted to assault her, and upon hearing her screams, Hercules came to her aid.[405] Hercules shot the centaur in the heart with one of his arrows, the tips of which were poisoned with the blood of the monstrous Hydra Hercules had killed earlier.[406] While dying, Nessos whispered his final words to Deianeira. If she collected some of his blood and put it in a vial for safekeeping, she would be able to keep her husband's eyes from wandering and prevent him from ever desiring another woman. This sounded good to her, so she took the bait and the toxic blood for safekeeping, thinking she had obtained a magic love potion.[407] Hercules and Deianeira then settled in Trachus and had a son named Hyllos. Other children followed, but there was no happily ever after for them. My father also would not find a fairytale ending to the parade of women he later pursued.

The order of what happens next is less important than the result that it produces. Following some years of tranquility with his now third wife, Deianeira, Hercules decided to go back and exact revenge upon the double-crossing King Eurytous, not to mention the rest of his sons. Perhaps he also wanted to check on, if not rekindle, his affair with Iole, but in any event, he killed this king and his sons, destroyed the town of Oichalia, and took Iole as his "servant."[408] No fool to the amorous affections her husband still harbored towards Iole, Deianeira wasted no time. Through a servant, she sent her husband his battle cloak, onto which she carefully smeared some of the centaur's love potion so she was sure of its efficacy in keeping her husband's attentions for herself. Suffice it to say, the fluid did just what it was intended to do, and learning that she had been hoodwinked, Deianeira committed suicide out of exquisite remorse for what was to follow.

Meanwhile, Hercules donned the cloak and immediately felt a horrid burning sensation. Realizing he was meeting his demise, he instructed his son Hyllos to take him up to Mount Oeta[409], located in central Greece about four hours northwest of Athens. There "bellowing in agony," Hercules asked Hyllos and his friends to build a massive pile of wood on the top of this mountain, which would serve as his funeral pyre; he then laid himself upon the pyre and told his friends to light it.[410] What happens next? You'll have to wait and see until *after* we cover Hercules' twelve famous labors in Volume 2 to share what it took to care for *my* father. The *denouement* to this funeral is unlike any that transpired with any other Greek demigod. Meanwhile, wouldn't you like to see how my father, the *real* Hercules of *this* story, began to come unwound in mind and manner, form and function, with wine and women in *his* song of *his* life? I'll point out the warped parallels my father shares with Hercules regarding relationships with the women as a divorcée, specifically in a section dealing with his bungled social interactions.

As regards making an apt parallel with the myth, just as I briefly recounted Hercules' relationships with significant women *after* Megara's death, I will share my dad's hounding of women after the loss of his first wife to divorce. You've read several points where I've had to interrupt myself and say, "*But we have not reached that point.*" This chapter's helping of Huntington's disease will deal with the line in the sand known as the "onset" of this disease. Here, I will present an overview of the early stages of HD so that when you read the portion of my dad's biography that follows, you can tell beyond a shadow of a doubt that *we are there*. It has begun.

At the time, we who loved him were not infrequently amused, concerned, incredulous, bewildered, shocked, and puzzled because we had no earthly idea what was happening to him, that "it" was *in* and *of* him. Was this live or Memorex, fact or fiction, something or nothing? There's no that any of us — let alone and *especially* my dad — would have suspected that he had inherited neuro-degenerative disease already unfolding and unfurling itself upon his life. In a way, I find it ironic that as a boy who survived two wars, he would never guess that an invisible and treacherous enemy would invade his corpus. Let's see what the experts have chronicled as features we might expect before I go back and color in the lines with my dad's misadventures and manners.

The Latitude and Longitude of Huntington's Disease and One's CAG Count

Although I have no intention of rehashing what we covered in earlier chapters, it will serve us well to briefly review the CAG count and what this meant for my dad as he would begin to witness a metamorphosis in him that could not merely be chalked off to "his Greek nature." Let's quickly refresh our knowledge by examining the following two charts[411] I've provided. You can see that anything below a CAG count of 35 means that a person does not have HD. Then there's the murky zone between 36–39, where a person may or may not develop Huntington's Disease later in life; it seems unlikely or, at the very least, certainly not vividly. However, regardless of whether or not one becomes symptomatic, that person *will* be a carrier. In the case of my dad's parents, *we will never know for sure who the carrier might have been.* On the other hand, if the person inherits the *increased* CAG count whereby the count of CAG repeats has expanded to 40 or above, that person has ***definitely*** inherited the disease, which *will* manifest at some point in midlife. No question. It is an unvarnished and absolute fact.

CAG

10-26 Normal

27-35 Intermediate

36-39 Reduced penetrance

40+ Full penetrance

HD

Table C-2: Observed Age of Onset According to Number of CAG Repeats		
Number of CAG Repeats	Median Age of Onset *(Years)*	Range in Age of Onset (85% C.I.) *(Years)*
39	66	59-72
40	59	56-61
41	54	52-56
42	49	48-50
43	44	42-45
44	42	40-43
45	37	36-39
46	36	35-37
47	33	31-35
48	32	30-34
49	28	25-32
50	27	24-30

See Figure C-4 for corresponding graph.

Source: Brinkman et al., 1997

[412]

If, at genetic testing, the person comes to discover that he or she has a CAG count of, say, 50 or more, this would indicate he has Juvenile Huntington's, and, tragically, symptoms would begin appearing before the age of 21.[412] That said, "less than 10% of people with the faulty Huntington's gene have more than 50 CAG repeats, making Juvenile HD a very rare disease."[413] What does that mean for my dad when one might anticipate *his* age of onset? It is no spoiler for me to inform you that my dad's count was 41, so he fell within the 90th percentile of "normalcy," where those who inherit HD have a count within the range of 40–49. If you think about it, that's a very narrow range with very little wiggle room, so *a little bit can mean a lot about how and when its expression gets initiated*. The data shows an inverse relationship whereby the higher the CAG repeat score, the younger the person will be when their symptoms develop.[414]

There is nothing hard and fast to hang your hat on as to its presentation, and more than numbers are involved in predicting or discerning its debut. In short, you can't and won't know; it will slip up on you "like a thief in the night" (1 Thess. 5:2). Furthermore, when you consider the contributing factors that impact its onset, pace of progression, and degree of severity, you'll get a glimmer of the potential for the wide variability in its expression. What are these contributing factors, you ask? They include one's state of health and overall well-being, both physical and emotional; one's indigenous IQ; one's lifestyle, which encompasses self-care; the network of friends, co-workers, and family; and the degree to which the person with HD feels loved and supported. When it's all said and done, the age of onset varies little from the mean shown in the second chart shown above. Facts and figures withstanding, I contend we ought to transcend charts, diagrams, and figures and gently remind ourselves that, as was the case with the sorely tried Job, "all our days are determined, ...and [God] has set His limits ... [which] we cannot pass" (from Job 14:5).

My dad was no exception, and such was the draw of the cards for him. As it turned out, my dad was right on time. Conceived and born with a (previously unknown) CAG count of 41, the silent buzzer went off, "it" became apparent, and the sand in the hourglass began falling faster at around fifty years of age. Weirdly, he wasn't incorrect in saying he had "*mild HD,*" as if he had a moderate case of the common cold. I am suggesting that with his CAG count just over the dotted line from that of an asymptomatic carrier, it would manifest itself more slowly than, say, if his CAG count were 47. Every drop of infamy added up until its impact was visible and undeniable, loud and perversely proud.

Over the rest of his life, I heard many doctors mention something to the effect that since my dad had "a lot of gray matter" to start with, meaning he had a high IQ, the decline would precipitate more slowly, like whittling away at the thicker bark from a sequoia, now left blighted and vulnerable. It didn't seem like that to us because his usual weirdness only worsened when "it" started. Even though it launched at a time that might seem tardy, the disease would never retreat or abate, and there wasn't any "pesticide" to decimate this disease or blunt its rate. Even in later years, the "real" pre-HD man in my dad would pop up and present himself with stark clarity and awareness; however, such would increasingly become a fleeting occurrence. Let's now take a gander at what we could have expected to notice had we known what we were dealing with. I'd be willing to bet that none of Hercules' friends or family knew he had a bounty taken out on his life and that he had the deck stacked against him. Fate or destiny took no regard to the demigod's privilege or prowess, and the same was true for my father, except it was God who numbered his days in His book (Psalm 139:16)

Although HD starts its military campaign in the brain, it impacts the person *holistically*; every aspect of one's personhood falls prey to its harmful effects. Therefore, even with a high IQ, my dad wasn't afforded the luxury of extra time. Before I give an overview of HD's stages to settle in on the early stages for *this* chapter's slice of HD education, allow me to cut to the chase and tell you how long the disease *usually* takes to take a person out. In one source, I read that "people with Huntington's disease usually die within 15 to 20 years of their diagnosis."[415] This wasn't particularly helpful because denial may very well play a role such that you won't get a diagnosis in a timely manner to know when the so-called starting point is. In my estimation, the Mayo Clinic tells us more accurately, albeit vaguely, that "from the disease's emergence to death is often about 10 to 30 years."[416]

Looking back, if we go by my dad's *first* visible manifestation, the disease's invasion took 22 years to fully encroach upon his mind and manner, which then led to his passing away. My dad died a good decade to fifteen years *sooner* than either of his parents' passing. That said, and as I have intimated before, it was *not* HD but *another* intractable malady that stole my father's life before Huntington's Disease had a chance to commit its carnage fully. Hypothetically, my dad could have lingered on another three years or so before HD would have choked out his life. As odd as it sounds, when it came to my dad's dying time, we were all silently relieved that his final blow came earlier than a fate that seemed worse than death. What do I mean? By that time, we all had learned what *could* have happened had HD been the death of Dad; likely, it would have delivered death through pernicious pneumonia, an injury, or choking.[417] He probably would have become unable to eat because his swallowing mechanism would have stiffened. *That,* for my dad, would have been a fate worse than death!

Now that you have seen the would-be writing on the wall, let us proceed with what *actually* happened, you and I. I will enumerate the five stages of HD before we settle in on the early stages of *this* chapter. We'll click off its clinical features and then bring these facts to non-fiction light as we encounter my father in the earlier years *preceding* his diagnosis. Our span in this chapter takes us from 1985–1999, just shy of three years before we had him tested. Fortunately, for this chapter, I have a batch of old letters from my dad to me from which I'll selectively pick and choose and quote so you can hear him give unwitting testimony of a brain as it is coming unhinged. All the sources I investigated describe the changes in the person with HD in terms of (1 physical, (2) cognitive, and (3) behavioral/emotional aspects, but I will add one more: (4) spiritual, and by that I don't mean the religious dimension *per se*, but that which makes the person *who they are* and what brings existential meaning and delight to his person. I have yet to encounter any source that broaches this last category. Let us proceed since there's no actual start to our "once upon a time" without further ado.

The Five Stages of Huntington's Disease
within the Larger Frame of One's Life

Generally speaking, *any* disease can be divided into early, middle, and late stages, and HD is no exception. For *this* chapter, we will be focusing on the *early* stage. Still, by the time we finish it, we will have overlapped and stepped into the forefront of the middle stage because there are no clear-cut delineations, just a VIN diagram of intersecting areas, and these vary from person to person. Technically speaking, HD has five phases: (1) Preclinical stage, (2) Early stage, (3) Middle stage, (4) Late stage, and (5) End-of-life stage.[418] I will tell you right now that my dad passed away in the early portion of the Late stage. Sometimes, the preclinical stage is called the "prodromal phase,"[419] which is the period before the diagnosis. It could constitute quite a lot of years — especially if the person with HD in your family has had no known predecessors. Such was precisely the case for our family.

Technically, the so-called "prodromal" phase for my dad lasted seventeen-ish years and thereby subsumed both the early and early-middle stages. If one of his children had inherited the disease from my dad, then we already would have known to anticipate with greater accuracy these different stages, but as it was, we were shooting blind. In short, we will cover just over half the stages of HD with my dad, but I also won't leave you without knowing what might have been. In any event, unless one is

245

dealing with juvenile HD, where, sadly, contortions become apparent early on, *when* the afflicted person gets diagnosed typically depends on (or is associated with) some particular mitigating event or undeniable physical manifestation, either or both of which *compels* the person go to the doctor to solve the mystery causing the arising oddities or problem.

Likely, the person with HD will *not* be the one to initiate such an investigation. Why would he? There also will be some family members who will want to chalk off any peculiarity as a particular expression of *this* person's natural aging process. Others will deny or minimize the changes altogether, and still others will guess and gossip and gander, perhaps furtively doing online "research" to see what WebMD and the like might have to say. However, for us, this time was long before the days of the internet, so rationalizations, speculations, and sundry hypotheses circulated among us all in hushed tones, that is, until the outside world got involved, and we all had to face the music. And since symptoms of HD most commonly start between in middle age (i.e., between forty and sixty), technically, the "preclinical" or "prodromal" stage roughly amounts to *half* the person's life (again, unless we are dealing with juvenile HD).

When the aging process revs up in mid-life, the features expressed are likely to be so faint as to amount to no discernable difference in the person were he *not* born with the disease. But life marches on, and what was the debuting oddity merely hinting at HD will become a staid feature. To be sure, more symptoms will join in along the way. For clarity, even if at the expense of accuracy, I will draw a line in the sand and say that stage two was finishing up in the latter 1990s for my dad. It overlaps with the onset of and slow progression into stage three — the middle stage — into which we will tip-toe towards this chapter's close. Therefore, stage 3 does *not* stop just because this chapter ends. The main reason I'll turn the page and begin a new chapter starting with 2000 is that a significant event — a major car wreck (make that two) — would soon occur after that, which forced the moment to a crisis whereby *no one* could deny something extraordinary and darkly contributory was happening to our dad. I don't want to get too far out. Still, it would help to have a clearer picture of this fuzzy zone that gradually morphs from one stage to the next, spurred on by the individual's unique heredity, constitution, lifestyle, environment, and days portioned as the disease progresses. It is like the tolling of the death knell coming into sharper focus with each passing year, except here, it sounded more like a cracked gong.

As the disease progresses, a host of motor, emotional/behavioral, and cognitive symptoms are experienced, including "unsteadiness, trouble holding onto things, trouble walking, changes in sleeping patterns, delusions, and [possibly] hallucinations, intellectual decline, and memory loss."[420] We will track the early but inexorable, involuntary, and extraneous movements and subtle emotional changes, then shift gears whereby the more overt motor symptoms and behavioral issues come to the forestage. Clarifying the disease's progression is crucial to understanding the overall pathogenesis of HD, so let's see how the ball started rolling in my dad.

The Prodromal/Preclinical Stage 1: Shades of Gray in My Dad

I'm sure you've heard the question, "If a tree falls in the forest and no one is there to hear it, does it make a sound?" Regarding my dad for me, the answer is a definite *yes*. Looking back, one of the most frustrating things about my dad's disease was that since we did not know that dad had HD at the time — and again, there's no way we *would* have because there was no reason even to suspect its presence — we wouldn't have been able to differentiate between his genetically-sparked "madness" and some of the "insanity" he displayed during the dark days leading up to as well as the aftermath of their divorce. During the 1980s, a tremendous amount of our family's energy and angst precipitated from the storm of our parents' divorce. The disintegration, breakup, and aftermath took a particularly tough toll on my dad, who ignored the warning signs and was then left vulnerable to the elements. It was like our very own domestic war, and for *us*, it seemed as complex and protracted as the wars my father experienced as a boy. No, no one perished, but my dad would become scathed and suffer profound loss *again*.

My father would never have expected defection and desertion to be found in *his* camp on the literal home front. In short, he found himself living with a wife who would become for him Benedict Arnold. Yet, he *also* had a traitor within his constitution who would wage war and wreak havoc in ways incomprehensible and unsettling. This time, he would be dealing with this private and painful battle in public, and he dealt with the matter at the very time his disease would detonate like a silent, booby-trapped, dirty bomb. Its invisible shrapnel invaded and corrupted every aspect of his person. We just *thought* he was being extra Greek and extra angry. We were wrong. HD would pump up the volume of features already present and accounted for in his personality, then crank them up to a level of farce or force. There would be no truce, no peace treaty, and no "reunification" with my mom. There also would be no escape from the brute terrorist within. Meanwhile, my poor, ignorant dad quietly stepped into the first "real" stage of Huntington's Disease — Stage 2 — from which there would be no turning back and no way out.

Looking back from a vantage point of nearly forty years past this Time of Troubles, I still find it challenging to pinpoint what stage began when. Then again, as we all were just doing life, we experienced these changes alongside my dad, and we treated them as "aspects" of dad popping through like an organic midlife crisis, like his growing balder, only worse. It was impossible to identify or discern what was happening because we hardly knew what, let alone *to* look for as a sign or clue of this disease emerging in our dad. Therefore, to articulate when the disease *"kicked in,"* as my dad in later years would say, would be akin to looking for the proverbial needle in a haystack. It was like pinning the tail on a moving donkey or swinging at a piñata just beyond reach, and there were no goodies inside.

To be as accurate as possible for you taking this in, I read an abstract applicable to *our* case, which made conclusions based on surveys of over a thousand participants.[421] At the very least, this report narrowed down *involuntary movements* as a singular group identified as "the earliest reported symptom," so I chose *this* as my litmus test for our current hindsight. I've little doubt that mild symptoms were already presenting themselves at the end of the *last* chapter when my dad would have been forty-nine. But I see no need to go back and hypothesize since any deductions I made would amount to pure conjecture and mere speculation. Further, the "affected person is typically able to conduct all their day-to-day work and normal activities without requiring any assistance,"[422] which *was* undoubtedly the case for my dad.

I will wrap up the "prodromal" phase by acknowledging that none of us, least of all Dad, could disentangle his innate behavior and emotional expressions from the "mood problems" which appeared at this stage."[423] Surely, his HD-induced mercurialness was exacerbated by what was going on in his life. Oh, most certainly, he had *always* had a temper, but now his fuse seemed to be getting shorter, and his explosions louder and more frequent and over less and less. Up until he turned forty-nine, we saw no adverse motor symptoms and showed no problems with his executive or cognitive functions. Then again, his logic and mindset had never been what the rest of us would have called "average" compared to what we saw in *other* American men his age. Maybe he was just our own mad scientist mixed with Zorba the Greek. He seemed as fit as a fiddle and as active as they come; there seemed nothing he couldn't do! For expediency and clarity, I will limit *this* chapter's focus here and now to Stage Two. You will be glad.

I want to first prep you for four specific areas I'll showcase. I will also provide features of the clinical prototype and explain how HD instigates the brain's malfunctioning; then, I will share what this looked like in my dad. What are these four areas or aspects? To recap, the first will cover *physical* changes; the second will explore *cognitive* decline; the third focus will examine *psycho-emotional changes*; and finally, the fourth dimension will delve into the *spiritual* aspect of my dad. The gross sum or net effect of these four paradigms in my *dad* will look slightly different than how HD causes transmogrification in *your* person with HD. We have one disease with many familiar features but countless custom expressions. Therefore, let us cross the invisible dotted line and get into the nitty-gritty of *this* chapter's allotment of HD info., the *second* stage. Again, I would like to stress that although the marker for inheriting HD is stark black and white, precisely when and how it gets expressed will be distinctive, unique, and as colorful as the individual. Remember that because of HD's "broad impact," the overall effect on the person's functionality will be more holistic and sweeping than that of other neurodegenerative diseases.[424] Let the games begin, and our tragedy unfold.

Huntington's Disease: Generalities at Stage 2

Though this chapter here is regulated to Stage 2 (of 5), I cannot overstate enough that even at its dawn, HD chisels away at the afflicted person's physical, mental, *and* emotional abilities. Symptoms of HD will vary from person to person.[425] Over time, the disease's impact will get progressively stronger and worse, thus being described as "progressive."[426] I call it cruel. All persons with HD experience problems with thinking, behavior, and movements, albeit *each to different degrees*; my already one-of-a-kind dad was no exception. What exactly are the clinical features of Stage 2? How can we know if the person hasn't developed a tic or isn't stepping into the nascent stages of mild dementia? How can we tell that a person isn't fatigued or hasn't experienced some shock or trauma to his emotional system such that it gets manifested by an intermittent twitch here, an irregular quirk there, or some eccentricity of its own? After all, under the "right" circumstances, you and I might develop one or two of these, but certainly not the sweeping, all-encompassing holocaust caused by HD's knock-out punches to the basal ganglia.

The primary effect is seen in the unmistakable but irregular and grotesquely erratic movements in the arms and legs. It'll make you want to rub or blink your eyes to see if you haven't mis-seen something. You'll also witness unusual behaviors and thought patterns brought about by the blow to the amygdala, and the spotty, hit-or-miss memory issues, not to mention balance/spatial blunders, indicate that the hippocampus is off-kilter. In those early years, long before we knew what was up, our dad flew under the radar. The long and the short of it is that in this early stage, *life goes on pretty much as usual,* and daily activities like driving and doing one's work are carried out per norm. The person with early-stage HD can independently conduct his "finances, home responsibilities, and activities of daily living such as eating, dressing, and bathing"[427] with little to no fanfare. Troubles may be reported with eating and/or sleeping. Not *all* of these characteristics or markers will necessarily be expressed. They won't, but there will be enough hits such that the gestalt effect will be unmistakable.

Symptoms *will* worsen throughout 10 to 25 years.[428] Again, the course of my dad's disease ran approximately *twenty-two* years. The disease's rampage would have continued had it not been cut short by the saving grace of another unrelated disease; here might be the solitary case where one might say cancer was kind. Left to its own devices, the scope of HD's wake and scope is sweeping and broad enough, but since the slope and pitch of its descent are not neat or without variability, *its rate and presentation will be anybody's guess.* No, knowing when to expect HD's onset is like walking along the edge of a long, broad, sandy beach where calm waves kiss your toes. Then, as you tiptoe along the waves washing onto the ocean's shore, you find yourself knee-deep along its long shelf.

As you keep walking further and further out, perhaps stepping on an unexpected barnacled stone or even a shard of glass, before you are aware, suddenly, you can't touch the bottom anymore. You are dog paddling, and much too soon, you find yourself entirely at the waves' mercy. *You are no longer in control of what you never really were.* There's no swimming back to shore; you lose the ability to swim because it's as if your limbs go numb and stiff one by one. And there's your red flag: rip currents ahead. Still, you *do* have a lifeguard to see you through such a maelstrom. Psalm 41:3 promises that the Lord "sustains" us in our illness, but He cannot keep us from physical demise. What are the "classic features" of HD? According to Huntington's Diseases Society of America, HD's notable and prominent traits include:

> - Unsteady gait and involuntary movements [429]
> - Personality changes, mood swings, and/or depression
> - Forgetfulness and impaired judgment [Notice it does *not* say *loss* of memory.]
> - Slurred speech, difficulty in swallowing, and weight loss

These inset features will make their debut at their own pace and will; they did not rain down upon my dad suddenly, steadily, or even dramatically. It started like fog turning to drizzle and then grew into an afternoon storm, but, as I hinted before, our family never experienced the hail and damage some do. Early on, friends more than family, and family more than the patient will start to notice difficulties with "planning, remembering, and staying on task."[430] My dad had no problem with the first two, but for a man known for his powers of concentration, we would notice his thoughts becoming more haphazard, scattered, and focusing on the less consequential. That said, he *did* get monomaniacally obsessed with particular thoughts over others.

The person with HD may develop <u>mood changes</u> ranging from "depression and anxiety to irritability and/or anger."[431] I will elaborate on which of these beset my dad in the section on psycho-emotional well-being. As far as signs of *physical* changes, most people with HD become "fidgety" and develop flinch-like movements (a.k.a. "chorea") in the face and limbs, which they are *not* able to control.[432] Even before the disease peeked out and then eventually reared its ugly head, my dad never ceased to make us laugh, roll our eyes, or shake our heads. He never acted "right" according to our environment's social norms. He said it was his *"creative genius"* or his being a "fera-ner" (his imitation of "foreigner" in his ludicrous fake East Tennessee accent) that made him be and do as he was and did. He was his own man, and he never minded — or cared — what others thought. That would serve him as a benefit and loss as his circle of trusted ones dwindled quickly. Later, with no fanfare or seeming awareness, he made accommodations for himself to continue to make do on his own. It was as if instinct went into overdrive. In the upcoming section, we will dive into HD's impact on the *physical* frame, first in terms of what this looks like in *general* and then how it manifested in my father. Let's get physical!

Physical Changes in the Person with HD in Stage 2

You may be curious why I would start spotlighting the physical changes first when, in theory, if not actuality, other features were also making their debut. There's a reason. Yes, we can and do find conflicting reports indicating that, in some instances, emotional and cognitive symptoms *precede* the onset of motor symptoms, while others report as the presenting symptom. After all, emotionally, the person may very well grapple with depression, anxiety, or irritability in ways or to a degree he did not before. I find it worthwhile to share a survey I found, which was conducted by the National Huntington Disease Research Roster for Patients and Families on individuals with *symptomatic* HD and completed by a first-degree relative (like me). This survey included 1238 individuals who were asked to indicate if specific symptoms occurred and, if so, at what time during the disease they noticed them. This particular test's conclusions revealed that even though the *symptoms* of HD are relatively *well-characterized*, their *progression* — *especially in the early and middle stages* — *remains uncertain* (emphasis mine)."[433] The concerned person would look back but with <u>imprecise</u> recollection, have a natural tendency to start reading into this or that emotional expression, especially those more intense or "negative," and begin making *subjective* deductions, not knowing if they are accurate or not. In our case, it could have been my dad's over-the-top outbursts of fury or his extended bouts of silence coupled with that sneaking, suspicious dart of his eye that could have been our first clues, but we can't and won't ever know for sure.

Those emotions were not new or unique, just more striking. God only knows when it started; we frail ones tend to grasp at straws as we look back in hindsight with vision hardly 20-20. That said, without exception, we *all* recollected a new, previously unseen *physical* quirk my dad began manifesting: <u>his left shoulder would lightly pop up or singularly twitch up for no rhyme or reason</u>. Therefore, for our purposes, we will go with this physical "tic" as the first sign of his having HD. One more test I found clinched why we should desist from trying to figure out which comes first, the physical or behavioral symptom, and therefore *not* speculate whether this or that *emotional* expression was the definitive indicator that he had HD. This particular questionnaire polled 6,316 individuals and assessed eight symptoms: motor, cognitive, apathy, depression, obsessive behavior, irritability, aggressive behavior, and psychosis.[434] In its conclusions, I read a remark that made it *case-closed* as to which came first, the emotional outbursts or the physical twitches. (It bears reminding that one's CAG count impacts how early and *intensely* this disease gets expressed.) I again quote what I could neither know nor otherwise say; I underscore for emphasis:

> Psychiatric and cognitive symptoms are *common* and functionally *debilitating* in HD gene carriers. *They require recognition and targeting with clinical outcome measures...* However, <u>because it is impossible to distinguish confidently between nonmotor symptoms arising from HD and primary psychiatric disorders,</u> ... **non**motor symptoms should <u>*not*</u> be used to make a clinical diagnosis of HD.[435]

We are now ready to proceed with a checklist of general *physical* manifestations you can expect to *see*. As far as providing a timetable for my dad in this early portion of stage 2, knowing all the while that the disease's impact continues to get worse, please be cognizant that our guidepost for stage determination will primarily revolve around the degree to which one can live and function *independently*, staying relatively free from associated problems arising. We have already determined that the initial marker for <u>stage 2 starts when a person first experiences visible motor symptoms</u>, and this phase can begin and last up to eight years from the disease's otherwise pre-symptomatic onset.[436] Undoubtedly, the word "chorea" is *an* essential term to keep in the forefront of your mind because it is the hallmark feature of HD's manifestation in the physical frame. Chorea comes from the Greek word "χορεία," which means "dance," but it is unlike any choreography you've ever seen.

Technically, chorea is an "<u>involuntary movement disorder</u> from a group of neurological disorders called "**<u>dyskinesias</u>**," which itself is characterized by "involuntary muscle movements, which include movements *similar to tics* or … diminished voluntary movements" (emphasis mine).[437] Unlike voluntary movements, which we consciously initiate and accomplish smoothly and at lightning speed, these are obviously <u>in</u>voluntary, extraneous, excessive, and abnormal movements. They catch both the patient and observer off-guard. The earliest physical symptoms may include <u>twitches or odd [and non-repetitive] tics, especially in the hand or face</u>; this was the case for my dad. How can you spot or recognize chorea? It presents as "brief, semi-directed, irregular movements that are *not* repetitive or rhythmic, but appear to flow from one muscle to the next."[438]

I told you that the first physical sign for us was when his left shoulder would snap up as if he had received a mild, unexpected electrical jolt. At other times, his shoulder would awkwardly roll back, like he was trying to adjust a part of his shirt's collar. I used to hypothesize that this physical "leakage" I and others noticed was some quirky overflow expression of his emotions spilling out onto his body mechanics. Whenever my dad's shoulder jerked up, and, again, it was random and infrequent enough to make you take a double take. It looked as if this unpremeditated and unscripted movement was a response to a conversation he might have been having with himself, like an involuntary gesture he was making in reply to some inward comment that might have him shrugging his shoulder as if to say, "Who knows?", "So what?" or even "Get away from me." It turns out that none of these phantom prompts were the cause; it was just the corrupted basal ganglia showing its dying self to the world.

When chorea becomes more serious, these slight movements can become "thrashing motions."[439]

We can also blanket our ubiquitously present chorea under *another* broader term called **hyperkinesia**, which, by deducing from its prefix, "hyper, one can surmise it refers to an "increase in muscular activity resulting in either excessive abnormal *or* normal movements or a combination of both."[440] Lovely. Again, because the basal ganglia were damaged (at conception) and do not function as they should, yet another term we should familiarize ourselves with is **bradykinesia**, which denotes "slow movement."[441] (The etymology of the word breaks down to *"brady"* for "slow" and *"kinesia"* for "movement.") *Bradykinesia* refers to the *"decreased velocity"* with which a movement is performed.[442] So, rather than a hammer to *initiating* a movement, bradykinesia describes a *slowness in the complete execution of movement.*[443] My dad's shoulder "popping" or rolling up and back was neither fast nor particularly slow. The errant and ghoulish movement occurred spontaneously, unexpectedly, and rather jerkily, but its overall enactment was *not* swift. One might easily anticipate that ambulation would also become problematic and that we might *also* see "odd postures and leg movements."[444] My dad couldn't stand still, let alone be in one position, to save his life. As it turns out, he was more than merely hyper. Did we know any of the terms above? No, of course not. He didn't get diagnosed until January of 2003. However, using these clinical terms will be more efficient than merely going by my jagged descriptions. There are additional terms related to movement that will be beneficial to share, but we have enough for now.

All this notwithstanding, Huntington's chorea is *not* present over the *entirety* of one's frame; the movement is typically more regulated to the *limbs and facial movements.*[445] Why? The motor cortex directs its misfired cues to the hands, feet, and face, including the eyes.[446] Our person with HD is *not* going to appear as if his whole body is experiencing mild tremors as, sadly, one can observe in a person having an epileptic seizure or even Parkinson's disease. You will see random flickers as opposed to minor quivering. However, because of the near-perpetual motion caused by chorea, over time, a person with HD may also experience significant weight loss without intending to. The caloric expenditure of a person with HD may require anywhere from 3500 to 5000 *additional* calories per day just to maintain weight because of these excessive movements.[447] "We move"[448] is not just a cheery slogan! Movement issues may also extend to the person having trouble walking, balancing, and moving about safely.

For my dad, problems with his balance impacted his ability to negotiate his surroundings without sporadic accidents occurring, *especially* where operating a motor vehicle was concerned. These problems with balance and coordination became more readily apparent towards the middle and latter part of this stage, that is, right around when he turned 60. Approximately two to five years after the onset of HD, affected individuals may also experience changes in sleeping patterns, sexual problems, and worsening motor control and clumsiness.[449] My dad was three for three in exhibiting these symptoms—more on these in a bit and their own category. Nothing tells a story better than when it comes straight from the horse's mouth. Since I have handwritten letters from my dad from 1985 to the late '90s, I will selectively quote him to provide proof of the changes *as they were transpiring*. To be fair, between 1985 and 1999, I was in college, graduate school, traveling abroad, or in the first decade of a demanding career; I was *not* living with my father. However, during these fourteen years, there wasn't more than a month to six weeks between our visits, so I *did* have *regular* face-to-face contact with him. To compensate for any first-hand details I might not have noticed had I been living under the same roof as my father, I recently asked my brother to fill in the gaps with his recollections because within a couple of years after the divorce, my brother moved in and lived with our dad for several years. Even when he moved out, my brother lived within thirty minutes of our dad and visited or stayed with him at least twice a week. I tell you this so you know that our anecdotes and observations are close, primary ones.

Physical Changes in My Father during Stage 2 and Problems Associated Therewith

As I muse and press myself to recollect those early days when I first spotted Dad's odd shoulder roll, I remember that it happened right after he and I had met in the parking lot of his work, and he had turned to walk back into a building. The soft flicker of his shoulder took me by surprise, and as I looked back, I did a quick double-take. He and I had been discussing some unpleasantry that had to do with the divorce, and my first thought when I spotted his errant and puzzling shoulder roll was that he was trying to shrug off something in his mind he wished he could expel. I dismissed it and gave it no more thought until my brother and I talked, and he confided that *he'd* noticed it, too. And more than just that once. I must stress that because my dad was only just middle-aged and *his* parents had lived well into their eighties, thoughts of something impacting his longevity, as in what *we* considered premature mortality, was the furthest thought from our minds. Still, *there was this "thing"*… There are two other matters I cannot stress enough: the first one is that while HD patients can remain "highly functional" in the *first* years of the disease, "independence gives way as symptoms get worse."[450]

During this focus of this chapter, my dad would remain independent, although you *will* see problems crop up. Secondly, if you are currently one who knows that your loved one already has HD and what I am describing here is different from what *you* have observed, don't let that jar, bewilder, or even concern you. I have seen more than several persons with HD with my own eyes, and though the overall impact is unmistakable, the variation of expression is wide. Part of this is due to how far along their disease has progressed, another to how high their CAG count in that normal but fluid range between 40 and 50 (recall that my dad's was 41), and yet another to how much the brain may have already physically deteriorated and become dysfunctional due to ataxia (i.e., "death") in the particular structures of the brain which I discussed in the previous chapter. Stanford University confirms that each person has a different disease course, and people with HD begin the disease at various ages.[451] Some individuals pass through the stages of HD more slowly, others more quickly, and symptoms may arise at different times for different people.[452] Also, "the *sequence* of motor impairment is not well characterized." In short, the *progression* of symptoms in HD is *not* well understood. My dad's words echo in my inner recesses: *"It's still a mystery..."*

Now that I have underscored the variability of how, when, and where this disease manifests, it will be easier for us to proceed. Incidentally, none of us directly confronted or asked dad about his "twitch" in those early days. To be honest, we even started to joke about it behind his back, and my brother got really good at imitating him and his increasingly bizarre gait. I do not judge or fault him for this; in those early days, we all snickered. Perhaps it was our attempt to alleviate some of the stress from dealing with his behavioral quirks and moodiness, so we tried to levitate the situation and make light of what we saw. Our dad became our very own Marx brother. Suddenly, it seemed like he had become one of the Three Stooges. Nonetheless, even our father was noticing something was awry in his system.

The experts say that "involuntary movements were grouped alone as the earliest reported symptom,"[453] but my dad would report *pain* in the afflicted areas and then proceed to conjecture as to why he felt such. On November 15, 1985, my dad wrote me — and I quote, *"I 'doodled' on the violin 2x already — hard& painful on the left arm."* One month later, on December 11, 1986, he wrote me, *"my left arm (between shoulder & elbow) is very, very sore due to twist–stress I guess? Out of condition no doubt."* Doesn't this sound like the beginnings of arthritis? I am unsure if my dad *saw* or noticed these movements in himself. Indeed, it turns out that many patients are *not* aware of the movements."[454] I am sharing with you his private thoughts because they show that he was experiencing discomfiture as to what was happening to him. My dad was merely trying to "problem solve" — one of his favorite and often-said expressions — as to *why* he was *sensing* what he did.

After this first shoulder-rolling incident, the following physical mis-movement we all noticed was his gait becoming <u>disjointed and all over the map</u>. At random times, his right hip might pop up as he walked, which might or might not be accompanied by his left shoulder roll. The hip going up caused his lower leg to come up too, and correspondingly, his left elbow and forearm might barely kick out, again with neither rhyme nor reason and without any reliable predictability. It *was* apparent that he was *not* doing this on purpose. In educated hindsight, my dad was right on time and on cue. The jerky and unintentional movements a person with HD develops "tend to worsen *during walking*, leading to <u>a wide-based gait called 'hyperkinetic gait.'</u>"[455] ("Hyperkinetic" refers to excessive movement in one's walk.) This gait is unmistakable in its being both easy and painful to identify. No one in their right mind would walk that way unless he'd had a disfiguring car accident or maybe a stroke or, as we now know, had inherited HD. Putting two and two together, recall that the reason for this errant movement's transpiring is because the damaged basal ganglia causes the motor cortex to send a convoluted, mish-mash message such that the resultant effect is

> "a slow motion with involuntary flexion of the knee and raising of the leg. Movements are often jerky and may be accompanied by other extraneous movements of the upper or lower body."[456]

This clinical description fit my dad's movement to a tee, but bear in mind that all this was unfolding ever so slowly before us. It's not like the light went from red to green; the flashing yellow continued for a long time. As I have indicated, and which all of us bystanders of my dad would agree, "the progression of symptoms in HD is *not well understood*."[457] As in, *not at all*. His random shoulder twitch and that weird, wobbly walk were slowly increasing in frequency and intensity, and even though some of us occasionally might quietly remark about it, we also were getting used to it without being aware of it; *that's* how slowly it evolved. When I was a child, I was given a toy called a "lumberjack dancing doll."[458] When I think back, I realize its crude, mechanical movements seem eerily similar to my dad's. Looking back with a hindsight of 20/20 and an arsenal of medical journals, my dad was right on cue and on time. His symptoms were consistent with other cases of HD and how others' early symptoms presented themselves. He may have been special to me, but where HD was concerned, he was hardly unique. Even if neither he nor we knew what was going on, my dad's adult-onset HD was exhibiting all the classic signs of onset through involuntary motor abnormalities: "mild chorea, brisk muscle stretch reflexes, and diminished rapid alternating movements."[459] Check, check, and check.

Speaking of stretching, when our family would take our long-distance vacations to see family, and my dad would stop to "gas up," he always took the opportunity to do some stretches (by the gas pump), which included touching his toes or doing deep knee bends while extending his arms straight out in front of him. The latter was more of a strengthening and balancing exercise. However, with his disease having now arrived and presenting its visible "attributes," he could no longer do any of his stretches without standing near a wall or poll to serve as a safety prop. He made no announcement; he just instinctively and quietly made the needed accommodation by positioning himself near his chosen support. Other than that, as far as independent functioning, our dad was "normal." He stopped wearing ties because he said that he didn't like to feel like he was being "choked," but there is a possibility it may have been starting to be a bit cumbersome for him to reckon with. Less than a decade later, he would avoid wearing button-up shirts altogether since getting the button in its proper hole proved nearly impossible, or if he *did* succeed, he might (or might not) have discovered that he'd misbuttoned altogether. He also sought slip-on or Velcro-strapped shoes where no tying was needed. Let us continue our steady keel ahead.

Over time, as we approached the midpoint in stage 2, these "involuntary **choreiform** [i.e., the jerking movements caused by chorea] movements decreased while [at the same time] rigidity and bradykinesia [i.e., its slowing] increased."[460] I'll now introduce you to one more term because it overlaps with others in my dad; eventually, it would become more prominent than even his curious gait, and that was **dystonia**. If you were guessing by "dys" and "stone," you might deduce that it has something akin to being dysfunctionally "stone-like." You wouldn't be entirely wrong. It is when the muscles "contract involuntarily, causing repetitive or *twisting* movements."[461] Were it not for his haphazard movements *not* being relegated to one side, judging by the way my dad walked, you might have wondered if he had had an accident causing nerve damage. On the *macro* level, it looked more like a type of writhing, but on the micro level, depending on the activity, it just panned out as plain clumsiness.

Speaking of clumsiness, another tell-tale sign of something running amok was the change in his penmanship. When I look back at his organic chemistry notebook, which I saved from his graduate school days, I see line after line filled with chock-full of chemistry equations in neat and dense penmanship, deftly making the most of the available space. The change would have made me wonder if poor eyesight was prompting him to write larger. That didn't explain the irregularity in the letters' size or oddness in formation, as if he had taken to writing with frozen claws. Likely because he was focusing on me *and* letting me know how much he loved me, my name on the envelope was always more prominent than the rest of the words. However, over this timespan, it got grotesquely large, as in at least four times the size of the rest of his letters; both would have been gargantuan compared to his penmanship from two decades earlier. Again, it all seemed laughable, like some cosmic hoax my dad didn't get, but we sure did. It was dramatic irony at its worst: my dad was out of the loop and the target of our joke. My confession of disrespect does not mean that I disregarded him or didn't still adore him. I did. That the mind and body are connected is not just some medical platitude, and this fact alarmingly came to life because it was *apparent* that his dystonia definitely "got worse with stress, fatigue or anxiety."[462]

Over time, bit by piece by chunk, HD robbed him — and us — of more of him. To be sure, the more agitated *or* tired my dad became, the worse his clumsiness *and* sharper his jerky movements. Dad had one more symptom that troubled him. Like an overtired child, my dad got to where he would get tired but had difficulty falling asleep. Maybe it was the racing thoughts he was experiencing, but more likely, it would have been the same snatches of a few thoughts on a repeat loop cycle with no off switch. Occasional insomnia is an often reported symptom seen in the early stages of HD.[463] Indeed, my dad began telling me about this problem because it was new to him and uncharacteristic. Usually, my dad could not only fall asleep on a dime, but snoring would soon follow; therefore, problems with sleeping would have been an anomaly and notable even to him. On February 22, 1987, he wrote, *"Last night I did not sleep much at all! Have been going around like a zombie today."* Being tired and experiencing sleeplessness *had* to have been a contributing factor to muscle fatigue, and this also could have exacerbated both his bradykinesia and dystonia since both of these conditions involve a deceleration in one's movements. That didn't mean my dad was lethargic or didn't keep up with his jogging.

Seven months later that same year, on 14 Sept. 14, 1987, he reported that he *"did 10 mile run yesterday... Arms (elbows down) were very tired."* There were other ways this debilitating combo of stiffness plus queer movements got rendered in my dad.

Poor penmanship and sleepless nights hardly caused grief or genuine concern, but when his *legs* would get stiff, accidents would and did occur. Did his teeter-tottering interfere with his daily living? Not initially, but over time, it indeed did, to the point where intervention was the prudent and right thing to do. But in the meanwhile, my dad was just doing life with occasional oddball things happening. Without a doubt, his chorea impaired his *voluntary* movement, like walking. In those days, some faint, uncontrollable facial twitches or the glassy look in his eyes had not yet begun. However, the "jerky limb movements, clumsiness, and [the reduction] of coordination and balance"[464] were all present and accounted for. As time went by, the muscles in his legs got more rigid, and he started to have an "abnormal posture" and the slightest hint of what was never to be — "writhing movements fully."[465] Why? He would not live to see these wrack his frame.

His idiosyncratic-laden gait would haunt and contribute to his becoming increasingly accident-prone. In what manner? Recall that "as motor symptoms *progress* ... voluntary movement abnormalities, and motor deficits [will] *naturally interfere with the activities of daily living."*[466] My father's cases in point follow, but not necessarily in chronological order. On February 8, 1987, Dad wrote me the following:

> Dearest ANNA —Hi. I miss you so VERY MUCH... I slipped at bottom of staircase & hit my lower left side. Must have gotten a rib fracture. I was healing & the following Fr. I had a sudden caugh & the strain refractured. I had to wear that old corset for 4 days... Take the very best care of *ANNA* [in red sharpie in humongous letters] for I LOVE HER a lot.
> Dad

Other mishaps occurred that likely would not have happened in earlier days. They did not raise any red flags because they weren't severe enough to warrant attention, let alone require outside action. Another time in the mid-eighties, when I came home from college, Dad greeted me at the door, and I immediately noticed he had a small but recently-made gash on the top of his bald pate. He had not only *not* cleaned the wound, but there were tufts of dark shavings from the now-dried blood. "What *is* that stuff?" were my first words to him. Without blinking an eye, he proudly informed me that he had packed the 2-inch gash with dried oregano, as if I should know. When I asked him to explain, he clarified, nonplussed, like this was the obvious course of action. *"Back in the village, we did this to close the wound."* His reports as to *how* the accident occurred, however, were conflicting. It reminds me of various accounts of Hercules' exploits, but in this case, it was about my dad's not wanting to share his bungles; maybe he "forgot."

During this particular visit, he explained he had been dusting a chandelier and inadvertently knocked one of the bulbs too hard, and it broke off, the shattered parts hitting his head. Later, he reported he had *"walked into the chandelier"* over his kitchen table and that his head knocked into a bulb, breaking it. I am inclined to believe this version. Yet somehow, I *also* recall his saying that he had stood on a rocking chair to reach the chandelier in the dining room, and he lost his balance, inadvertently whacking the chandelier and causing some of the crystal pendeloques to break on his head. I tell you this because my dad would increasingly distort the truth like a child who didn't want to get in trouble, but his fibs were far-fetched and easy to spot. It was sad but easy to imagine my dad misnavigating his surroundings and not being able to stop in time before his noggin hit that glass head-on, leading to the glass rupturing the skin's surface of his forehead. He used to have a small soft knob projecting ever-so-slightly on the upper part of his forehead, nearly indiscernible, but enough such that my sister would jokingly wonder aloud if he were turning into a unicorn. Maybe *that* bump got in the way or took the lead in the accident. I jest, but there's more.

In the early eighties, my dad had another bad accident in the industrial garage he rented to mix and store his coolants in 55-gallon drums. This particular mishap could have left him blinded. In pouring one of the concentrated solvents into one of these drums, he hadn't kept the flow rate slow or steady enough; in so doing, he caused some of the acid to slosh into his eye. Driving with the injured eye shut, he drove himself to the nearest ER. Although he had already begun flushing it out on his own, cocking his head to one side and letting water from the faucet pour over and onto his burned retina, they did much the same at the hospital. My dad insisted that he remain there so that they could continue flushing his eyes with water, and he stayed another half an hour. I can see him wobble while pouring, and the uneven flow quickly turns into a splatter. He may not have been able to *prevent* these accidents, but at least he still had the presence of mind to tend to himself adequately. He was still quick enough to think on his feet and on the fly, which God knows how many times enabled him to live independently for as long as he did, even by creative ways and unorthodox means.

The 1990s

As we move on to the decade of the nineties, I can recall another accident that *never* would have occurred in earlier years. One time, around 1994, my dad visited me so we could go to the local annual Greek Fest together. He would inhale the spirit of song and dance as much as he would devour pastries, souvlaki, and any and everything else they had. His desiccated soul longed for the old country and the release the bouzoukis playing would deliver. At every Greek Fest, there is a generous stage set up for dancing, both for the performers and the audience, when the floor is opened up for all to join in. My dad instinctively went up when he heard the tell-tale initial strains of "Zorba" starting. I watched on, happy for his soul to take flight in dance. He'd even found someone to give him the handkerchief to hold onto and link him to the other Greek dancers. He'd been given the okay to lead! However, *this* time, as he was coming down from his valiant attempt to launch himself up for a high leap and then slap the side of his ankle mid-air, instead of popping up to make a square landing, he plopped over and fell from his bungled bound. Immediately, he became disconnected from his human chain and got stuck in his crumpled little heap. I rushed over to take his arm and help him up, yet also, oddly, he wasn't embarrassed. It was as if it hadn't happened at all! He took my hand, and then *we* joined the rest of the dancing human chain, but this time, we were its *tail*, leaving my dad plenty of room for nothing. He kept a close watch on his feet as if they were doing some foreign dance with which he wasn't familiar. He also held onto my hand like a child with a vice grip. Afterward, we likely went for more "goodies" — Greek desserts — before we went inside to sit together in the church sanctuary, where he may have said silent prayers in a place that felt like home. On our way back to my house, not a word was spoken about his accident.

Recently, I read about other symptoms that my dad had *not* exhibited or ones that were so mild that it took us a while to notice them. One that was *not* apparent to us early on was abnormal "extraocular movements."[467] It makes sense that the eye muscles would be affected because these in the eye are so exquisitely fine and sensitive. Plus, their structures are close to the brain, so it's no wonder that eye movement would be impacted. One might easily anticipate the eventual "slowing of and abnormal eye movements, [where] the eyes move up and down or around in a circle." That said, as this section focuses on physical manifestations, for those of us on the outside looking in, changes in his eyes' gaze were not readily discernible to our purview. It's only by looking back on photos taken from this time that one can start to detect a slowing down, if not a slight glassy, stare-like quality, to his gaze, but this did not happen until the late nineties. Perhaps the ocular muscles were losing their subtle reflex flexibility. The second symptom I recently read about that we did *not* see in my dad at *any* stage of his HD was tremors I've read about, which are more common in juveniles with HD,[468] though not exclusively so. A final symptom that we did *not* see early on but *would* eventually become hauntingly evident from 2000 on would be changes in the tonality of his facial expressions; however, I'll save that for later.

Our dad's problems with coordination were evident not only by the slow but steady changes in his walking but also by the difficulty he had with the coordination of his hand movements. He couldn't sequence and select seamlessly with what *we* use — muscle memory — to perform any automated action, be it drive stick shift, dance, or fold your hands in your lap. It was as if someone had hit "random" in his brain's command station. Regardless of the possible symptoms, I scoured articles to corroborate my hunches and to help me double-check what I might have theorized — or dismissed — as a sign. I remind us here that the greater truth is that "the *progression* of symptoms in HD is [still] not well understood."[469] When problems are getting real, other people begin noticing, and a few start asking. My brother recalled that in the late '90s, a friend and co-worker of my dad's for some twenty years and one who sat across from him at work confided in my brother that "something is changing in your dad." He mentioned this out of evident care and concern for our father. Even secretaries dealing with my dad over the years knew him well enough to realize this mannerism or that behavior wasn't a fluke. They began to wonder and whisper about his odd movements.

I have told you that his chorea was present and ongoing but not continuous or continual. In the early days, where his *next* mis-movement might pop up was anyone's guess, but once we recognized which body part of his *would* twitch or lurch or roll —his shoulder — we *still* couldn't have described it as perfectly modulated or precisely the same as the just-prior jolt. I believe the reason that, long ago, HD was described as "*dancelike*" is that its "unpredictable involuntary movements 'flow' from one body part to another."[470] In my opinion, the phrasing "flow" is a generous description. Someone who didn't know my dad *well* but was sufficiently acquainted with him such that they were familiar with his abundant energy, drive, focus, and willpower might have confused his movement as a natural restlessness, fidgetiness, or even some fleeting moment of agitation. Following the roll, jerk, or twitch of his left shoulder, we next noticed that his left heel would begin to pop. My brother said that as he'd watched my dad drive during the mid-nineties, he began to notice that *our dad couldn't keep his left heal on the floorboard,* that "if one were to count to ten, you'd be sure to see that left heal kick up." I doubt my brother would have commented on it to my dad because it was already obvious my dad had neither control nor awareness of this. If he did, he certainly wasn't concerned. If you didn't know any better, you'd think he might have been dealing with planter fasciitis or that it somehow comforted him to "adjust" his foot; neither was the case.

By the *late* nineties, I believe falling was becoming more of an issue than any of us could guess or appreciate because my dad continued to live and function independently without any severe or debilitating problems cropping up. You can't put the cart before the horse and report any *likely* accident that hasn't happened *yet*, even if the horse is hobbling and the cart is getting too heavy. However, I did get a clue about how problematic going *down* steps was becoming when I took him to a Klezmer Concert in Atlanta; it starred one of his violin *"heroes,"* Itzhak Perlman. Though my dad was slow and careful to use the handrail going up, he practically clutched it going down, and I could tell it took all his powers of concentration to order his wayward foot to plant itself solidly on the step. Further, his trunk and frame were stiff, and as he made his way down these concrete steps, it was as if he were trying to will away some pain we could not see. Quietly, I put my arm around him and watched him like a hawk, ready to catch or be his crutch. I was getting another performance that evening, and I recognized descending these steep steps as a small miracle and a big victory for my dad. I said nothing to him, but then I gently and unobtrusively took his arm in mine, and we walked side his side, father and daughter, out of the music hall. His broad grin was my reward.

What adds to the complexity of this disease is that in the early stages, when early symptoms are beginning to make their debut, at times, the HD patient *can* mollify, dampen, or even suppress these excessive movements. Still, he cannot *prevent* or thwart them. Therefore, by the time he can no longer contain himself, *the disease is further along than you think,* so the downward spiral will seem to accelerate more. You have only just noticed the *visible* tip of the iceberg, except this one moves. No medicine or personal effort can prevent the neural cells from dying.[471] Some medications can merely mute its effects. Another unpredictable and random movement in the mid-to-late nineties was *not* in what we saw but in what we *heard*. We began to overhear Dad issue forth sounds like Scooby Doo makes when he's confused, but it was when he was in the privacy of his own company. It was as if his voice finally relaxed and soothed itself and him by releasing these falsetto-like soundbites from a tangled vocal cord. He wasn't upset, but it was as if his voice had a mind of its own, and *it* decided to erupt octave-high, humming notes fluttering lightly apart. They were short, sing-song sounds made with neither rhyme nor reason; it was a tune in name only. The first time we heard these odd sounds, we would have been watching TV in his living room while he was doing the dishes in the calm of the evening after some feast of a meal my brother or I had prepared. Under the hum of the fluorescent light over his bright orange kitchen sink, there was no mistaking; we heard him in the near distance. We might have stopped to glance at one another to double-check and see if the other had heard this almost inhuman utterance. My brother recalled asking our dad if he was alright and telling him we'd heard him make his soft, nonsensical humming. In response, my dad might momentarily desist from making his wee warbles and nod in the affirmative that all was okay. After my brother left the kitchen, he would resume, as if this were a private, happy tune he enjoyed "humming" to soothe himself.

Speaking of sounds, according to many sources, I read that the rate of speech in the person with HD gets *slower*, which is an early form of dystonia, which, as you know, is the stiffening of muscles. Increasingly, my dad would say — as if it were news to us — that he was not a native speaker of English. Unlike his next older brother, my dad admitted he *"never had a way with words."* As his speech rate was neither remarkably fast nor slow, I myself did *not* notice my dad's speech getting slower in this early time frame. The exception may have been his Greek *"Ehhhhhh...,"* which is analogous to its English counterpart, "Uh..." when he was between this or that thought. It became more prolonged and pronounced as if this syllable had gotten stuck. Again, I want to remind you that HD is progressive, and there will be more to tell you about his speech and other oral issues later.

During the time frame I've chosen to aim at the moving target and pinpoint when his symptoms began, I reiterate that "psycho_motor_ abilities show the most significant and consistent decline across disease progression."[472] This amounts to saying that matters can and will get worse even if they start out mild or scant or faint such that, unbeknownst to you, the sound person, *you are also getting used to them.* And before you know it, you've got a deconstructed form of what — and still *is* — your loved one. Initially, the changes add up and are assessed as a mild and harmless eccentricity. It's easy to get used to and dismiss the weird movements because they begin so faintly and are not debilitating or problematic. In what manner might these excessive, mildly spastic movements and clumsiness evidence themselves in a way that *does* lead to actual accidents? You guessed it: car wrecks and many a fender-bender.

Now, mind you, when we moved to Tennessee, my mother wryly quipped that she knew the police in Tennessee *had* to be laxer because my father wasn't being cited as often for an infraction or traffic violation as he had been the case in *other* states where they'd lived. He never had been a good driver; the destination was more important than how he drove to get there. Simply put, the rules didn't apply to him, especially if they seemed picayune, picky, or pesky. He wasn't overtly arrogant or prideful; he merely willfully ignored the existence of certain societal norms and laws. We always chalked it off to his being Greek, but that was *our* rationalization, not his, let alone the truth.

Beginning in the late '90s, my dad's problems with driving were not confined to passing on double yellow lines or routinely parking in the loading zone as if he had his own VIP parking spot. Recently, my brother reminded me that around this time frame, my dad rear-ended someone at a local restaurant called the Mountaineer; he was in his white Jetta. No, no one was hurt; in fact, this minor incident might well be considered an isolated incident, but it would not be his last accident or the most severe collision. There were more to come. Not only that, but we can't write off this accident because his car was stick shift or he needed a break job. He was neither speeding nor driving during poor weather, let alone at night. Nope, this happened in broad daylight, with little to no traffic, and he was going at a turtle's pace. In my mind, his foot slipped from the break to the accelerator. For all we know, that afflicted left heal may have popped and brought his left foot up enough to tap on the accelerator.

In rounding the corner of this section on the initial outward changes I saw in my dad, starting from the disease's onset to year fourteen, please bear in mind that the physical symptoms first appear to vary significantly from person to person. Some features may have more of a prominent effect in one person than in someone else; however, since HD is a *progressive* disease, the degree to which these movement aberrations manifest themselves can vary but *will* intensify throughout the disease's complete arc. There's simply no turning back. Most of the physical changes transpire slowly over an expanse of *years*. Likely, you may not notice (or accept) the changes until the middle or even advanced stages of the disease when the impact has intensified enough such that it is undeniable how much the disease has wreaked havoc on both body and brain. The corruption of one leads to the debilitation of the other, and yet our Heavenly Father would continue to provide for my dad. Oh, we all are more important than the birds of the sky (Matthew 6:26)! I pray you discover the disease earlier than we did so you can better help your loved one navigate his world with greater ease and dignity. Whereas changes to the physical motor skills of affected patients may be challenging to pick up on, this is not the only area over which you'll experience consternation. Like a tree that's gotten a blight, HD also tarnishes the person's interior resources, not just the outer form. In the next section, I'll focus on intellectual decline, including, among other features, errors in logic, the inability to maintain focus, and fragmentary memory lapses.

Cognitive Changes in the Person with HD in Stage 2
A. Memory Problems

As we enter the realm of the unseen, deep where decisions are made and logic is employed, I still remind myself that we are God's pinnacle creation. In Genesis, we can read that we were created in His image, so in this case, the image is what's on the inside — our imagination, reasoning, conscience, and spirit — all beautifully suffused within our *brain*. What happened when the Fall got played out in my dad? The *possibility* for the mind to get marred and mired by the mud of Huntington's disease got spurred and spun into existence. There's nothing he or anyone in his family did other than to be human in an imperfect world where spontaneous mutation brought this into his being. For better or for worse, we *all* struggle with various frailties and infirmities. At the moment, while we are reckoning with what HD is doing to my dad's brain, may I remind you that on the grander scale, our soul, our essence, is housed in an imperfect, frail, albeit miraculous body, which the Apostle Paul refers to as

> "our earthly tent, which is our house [i.e., the *body* that is being] torn down. We have a building from God, a house *not* made by hands, eternal in the heavens. ² For indeed, <u>in this tent we groan, longing to be clothed with our dwelling from heaven,</u> ³ since, in fact, after putting it on, *we will not be found naked.*" (2 Cor. 5:1–3)

I take "naked" to mean vulnerable to the diseases and infirmities of life. Later, at the resurrection of the dead, I believe my dad will go from being "sown a natural body [to] raised a spiritual body" (1 Cor 15:44 HCS). He will be in the "presence of the Lord" (2 Cor. 5:8 NKJV) and will not squirm, wriggle, or wallow. Although we cannot know for sure what God has in mind for what our physical bodies will look like, the Apostle John supernaturally foretold believers — which would include my father — that they "will walk with [God] in white, for they are worthy.⁵ He who overcomes will thus be clothed in white garments" (from Rev. 3:4–5). So, you see, I am compelled to insert the good news to come during our seeming tragedy. I already know and am told that my dad will overcome and be victorious, basking in the glory of our maker and His Lord! But I digress.

In the previous chapter, you learned about the parts of the brain that get impaired; now, you will see how this damage gets played out in the *behavior* of the middle-aged person whose HD has become manifest. It's like in fall, when the leaves turn from green to golden to bronze, only in this scenario, the unfurling of the disease leads to apoptosis, the dying of our brain cells. What does the damaged thinking mechanism in the HD brain look like, and how is it different from dementia or any of the other more commonly known neurodegenerative diseases like Parkinson's, Alzheimer's, or even Muscular Dystrophy? You have noticed I refer back to this other, more familiar disease, but it is only for a point of reference, differentiation, and additional clarity. There are three distinct ways HD impairs a person's cognition. First, we will look at the damage to the brain's <u>executive</u> function, <u>memory</u> problems, and decline in <u>self-awareness</u>. Then, I will show you how it manifested in my dad, and it was not pretty.

The brain's "executive function" includes a sweep of tasks that it performs for us daily and that we don't even think about. And just as you will notice physical symptoms like chorea in the person with HD, you also can't miss the mental symptoms, including problems with logic and memory. I'll start with memory. You would be right in wondering how HD is any different than, say, dementia, which is "a *syndrome* associated with memory deterioration and thinking…a memory disorder"[473]; however, unlike HD, dementia is *not* a *hereditary disease*. That said, Huntington's disease does present "similar symptoms [to those] of the patients of dementia."[474] After all, both HD and dementia are progressive, and neither has any known cure. Other neurodegenerative disorders, such as AD, can *lead to* dementia, which, at its basis, is "the progressive and irreversible loss of neurons." We used to call it "old age." As I have said, there does exist an overlap between HD and dementia as to particular *symptoms* that are exhibited. The most prominent is memory loss, but we would also notice problems with "communicating, difficulty in completing familiar tasks, disorientation, problems with abstract thinking, and even mood changes."[475] As the old Ronco commercial used to say, "But *wait*! There's *more!*" In addition to movement problems, HD displays similar symptoms with dementia, except that *everything* worsens — body and mind, albeit uniquely, erratically, and individualistically. Dementia's trademark feature remains memory loss and problems that spiral from such forgetfulness; HD's blow to the memory is nowhere near as severe. In one particular article, I read that the decline in short-term memory for the HD patient "typically appears before any motor function symptoms,"[476] but, as I've argued, I contend that since *chorea* is the definitive hallmark characteristic of HD because you *can* see it, then it — not memory loss — ought to be the sign you go by as the forewarning indicator that your person has something *other* than dementia.

As I covered in the previous chapter's section on the portions of the brain damaged by HD, how the hippocampus gets impaired uniquely impacts the HD brain regarding memory; likewise, the altered prefrontal cortex gets involved and miscommunicates with other parts of the HD brain. In short, since *both* the hippocampus and prefrontal cortex are intertwined in their functions *and* are both sullied by HD, memory will misfunction in a manner and measure *differently* than what we see in patients with (just) dementia. In what way? Persons with HD in the early stages "may find they have difficulty recalling information [which] may make them appear forgetful,"[477] and they will also show "working memory problems."[478] From what I saw with my father, he corroborated a tendency towards memory decline, particularly *short-term* memory.[479]

Unlike AD, where memory loss can lead to a near TKO such that those persons nearest and dearest to you whom you've known over half your life you might not be able to come to recognize (and vice versa from their loss/ lack of mental presence), HD will eradicate random pockets and patches of memories while leaving others unmolested and secure. There is neither rhyme nor reason to the disease's selective nibbling away of the cheese. From what I beheld in my dad, I would go so far as to say that with the erasure of some *short*-term memories, certain particularly vivid, *long*-term memories will pop up sporadically, even more powerfully, and crystal clear. It is astonishing. It's as if now that the outer curtain of more recent memories has been taken down, light now falls on the older memories further back. Perhaps these long-term memories, now resurrected, had been ones suppressed. Maybe his capacity to make associations and recall his older memories planted in his younger, more agile brain became easier to access since the more recent, fringe thoughts never went past being short-term or working memories. I pause to differentiate these terms so you can better appreciate how HD uniquely impacts memory. It will leave you amazed over what *can* be recalled and frustrated over what falls through, as readily as sand through a sieve. Before I proceed with an example from my dad, I quote several terms that I otherwise would not fully know; I italicize for emphasis specific salient points:

The term **working memory** is often used interchangeably with short-term memory; however, working memory technically refers to <u>the whole framework of structures</u> and processes used for the *temporary* storage and manipulation of information, *of which* <u>short-term memory is just one component</u>. **Short-term memory** is specifically for temporary recall of the information being processed at any point in time, and this information will quickly disappear forever unless we consciously try *to retain it*. The transfer of information to **long-term memory** can be facilitated or improved by *mental repetition* of the information or by *associating* it with other previously acquired knowledge. *Motivation is also a consideration in that information relating to a subject of* <u>vital interest</u> *to a person* [e.g., in my dad's case, all things related to family and Greece are more likely to be retained in long-term memory.[480]

During the broken years in the mid-1980s when my dad was running, on the eve of one marathon in particular, as he was feasting on a mound of spaghetti before the "big day," out of nowhere, he started to tell me about every one of his Greek relatives that he knew from boyhood. These personages included an aunt living in Tripoli, his closest cousin with whom he played in the village, and his recollection of desperate days when he said his mom would hide things in the yard before they'd head for the hills. The details of these stories don't matter here as much as he talked about this *for over an hour and a half, like a cassette tape with no end*. I don't think I blinked or moved a muscle other than asking questions to keep the flow going. At the time, I thought he was telling me this because the crisis of divorce had cracked loose, something that allowed the deeper memories to bubble to the surface; now, I know differently. Clearly, these long-term memories fell under the category of those with a "strong interest."

Let me remind you that HD proves detrimental to the prefrontal cortex, so it should be no surprise that the most recently acquired information in the HD patient will come and go quite quickly. After all, the central part of the prefrontal cortex at the front of the brain appears to play a fundamental role in short-term and working memory.[481] Perhaps this is one reason my dad would increasingly come to taking notes, sometimes frantically, but always in that heavy-handed, loopy, and increasingly enlarged script information which *he* deemed vital. Starting in the mid-1980s, I have scads of my dad's scribble pads, spiral notebooks (of various sizes), folders full of his notes, and telephone contact books he used to in order keep this most recently acquired information in some semblance of order. We memorized phone numbers back then, but all bets were off for him, yet somehow, he must have subconsciously discerned it. I have no reason to believe that Dad was mindful or aware he had a problem; nonetheless, he had some gut reflex of more profound insight, which "knew" he needed to etch down information he might need to recall later. I will deal with his other short-term memory problems when I cover the troubles he would have at work.

You will recall the damage in the HD brain occurs mainly in the striatum [of the basal ganglia], which helps the "inner subcortical and prefrontal cortex parts of the brain to communicate," the final and negative effect of which it impacts is on memory."[482] As HD progresses, memory deficits range from short- *and* long-term difficulties to the far-reaching conclusion of dementia. For those HD patients who live to reach the latter stages, other extenuating problems with memory crop up. These problems won't necessarily terminate into full-blown dementia because other factors come into play. The HD brain gets accosted on several fronts. My dad never got to the most advanced stages of HD; therefore, I cannot speak to the loss of long-term memories that I've read, which can occur in some who bear out its latter stages. Still, unlike AD, in HD patients, we do *not* typically see a vacancy or the inability to recognize loved ones. In a sense, their presence of mind and self-awareness make this disease's impact all the more tragic because mindfulness of loved ones and their predicament or plight adds up to a shared grief.

These cognitive deficits further corrupted his already imperfect command of the English language, and his comic blunders occurred most often if he was put on the spot to have to recall some new term or piece of information on the fly. I'll never forget those days when I visited and we'd rent a VCR movie from Blockbuster. He was game and all in and might propose that we rent a flick from *"Blackbuster."* Similarly, Betty Crocker became Betty *"Cracker,"* what with her *"Snappy"* ("Snack") cake he was fond of. That he never *formally* learned Greek but could still read and write in a crude, rudimentary form also got churned up in a reconstituted memory. On September 8, 1987, he wrote me a letter in which he confided, *"I wrote yiayia [in Greek] and Vivian last week, I had to stop (really) & grope for the GK words – amazing how one forgets when don't use much. Very surprised, too, that it cam back to me after much memory groping!!"* You never knew what prompt might trigger a tangential memory where he would *"get reminded."*

Years later, in 1995, when for the first time he returned to Greece with my brother and me, memories blossomed richly, and he not only recalled memories, but he retained the ability to spatially navigate and find places he had long-since frequented — as in four decades. Such is a clear indication that his long-term memories remained unsullied. As time went by and HD was making its dark mark more strikingly on my dad when he might recollect those bygone days of Greece, it would haunt us both like a ghost, but one we welcomed despite its being bittersweet. I could give more examples that deal with memory, but to be honest, because my dad's memory problems were less of an issue than other more pressing cognitive concerns, I'll shift gears and now have us move on to the *second* tier of what is negatively-impacted in the HD brain: the *executive* function. Primarily, to differentiate it from dementia in AD, I started with memory, but memory problems do not prove to be the most challenging aspect of HD by any stretch of the imagination.

Cognitive Changes in the Person with HD in Stage 2:
B. The Executive Function

Having just touched upon one cognitive symptom of HD's blow — memory — what are *other* problems instigated? How else can we tell the thinking apparatus is becoming botched? As you know, Huntington's disease impairs important structures and pathways in the brain, and this damage causes more problems than those with movement. We'll look at early signs of other diminished intellectual functioning, but the proof is in the pudding: you'll see such manifested in my dad's behavior. The biggie we all noticed was "a regression of reasoning/rationale."[483] Losses in cognitive capabilities further burden HD patients with "frustration, anger, and grief," not to mention "other psychiatric symptoms" that may spring up from the illness.[484] (I'll focus on the tainted emotional expressions in the following chapters.)

My jagged feelings are the natural precipitation of dealing with a cloudy mind. One of the most troublesome things that happens to your person with HD is that their logic begins to fly out the window bit by bit, and simple things become harrowing. They will show increasing difficulty in making everyday decisions we take for granted. They can and will get confused, leading to their being consumed by anger or frustration. *They can't understand what is happening* and why the world seems to be turning upside down or even against them. Why would they be vexed over what color shirt to wear or which shoe to put on first? You are already familiar with the ravaged parts of the brain and the constituent neurons that are dying. We will probe into how this breakdown hampers normal thought processes, mainly where decisions and deductions are made. All this new dead weight will be incorporated within the brain's executive functioning, which concerns "planning, organization and sequencing, and cognitive flexibility."[485] The scratch in the record will be heard in the song. What this translates to in the HD patient will be a reduction in...

"one's speed of thinking, poor planning, skewed prioritizing, haphazard or frazzled organizing, lackluster concentration, a waffling decision-making apparatus, lack of flexibility, and/or diminished creativity.[486]

Add to this a reduced performance on verbal fluency tasks.[487] Although I would be remiss if I hadn't started by listing typical clinical features here, do not think that at the time, we were checking in boxes of these symptoms readily or all at once. Oh, no. Please recall that we still didn't know that Dad had HD. We were *all* boggled. These features are not exhibited concurrently, and there is no predictable consistency or regularity. Slowly but surely, faintly then inexorably, the breakdown and decay within the HD brain will stain and sully your person's ways and means. The afflicted person *and* their family will become frustrated, bewildered, saddened, and exasperated. You will feel like you dwell in the house of Job, and as you deal with your baffling one, you may feel as though *you* are the wacky one. Do not forget: the bizarre way HD adversely affects movement is mirrored in the person's way of cogitating, so the impact is doubly jarring.

In contrast to the next volume of *A Labor of Love*, where in about *half* the time, Dad's HD seemed to *double* in its rate of declension, the current rate at which my dad's HD was progressing, which this chapter covers in roughly fifteen years, would be much *slower*. I have no data or graphs; it's just my troubled soul that can corroborate this. I did discover that as time goes by, "more and more neurons dying causes brain shrinkage or cerebral atrophy [at an] increasingly faster rate."[488] He had no control over the changes; his hands and heart were clean of his *faux pas* and fumblings. Now that I've listed the clinical features of cognitive impairment in the person with HD, let's look at its impact on how my dad dealt with living on his own and independently for the first time in his adult life, right as his disease was burgeoning.

When my mother left my dad, and they split, we assumed dad's mismanagement of his affairs was because he was grief-stricken, blinded with rage, or in a state of denial. It turns out that it was all about the above *and more.* That my dad was smack dab in the center of middle age meant that HD was manifesting itself right on time and cue. Not to give HD all of the credit, but you should also know that it had always been our *mom's* job to balance the checking book and do their taxes. My dad rarely shopped except for "emergency" groceries in the morning. Therefore, it should come as no surprise when I tell you the first snafu that happened was when he let his car insurance lapse. He simply didn't pay the bill; likely, he hadn't even opened it and ignored all notifications warning him of impending cancelation. Therefore, when he got pulled over for God-knows-what, it was only *then* that he discovered he no longer possessed auto insurance.

Likely, he was incredulous and began his huffing and puffing. He thought he could just cut a check, and all would be forgiven, but he learned the hard way there were penalties to pay. He got placed in a lower tier with a higher premium through a subsidiary branch of his now former insurance company. Interestingly, sandwiched in among the papers, I found an envelope dated June of 1984 in his folder crudely labeled "DIVORCE + STUFF." Still, when I opened it, I discovered an "Operator's License Reinstatement Form," which amounted to a bill because his driver's license had been revoked for failing to pay a fine of $25.00 for a speeding ticket issued in December of 1984. In the summer of 1985, he was delinquent in paying a doctor's bill, and the letter he got was to inform him they were getting ready to report him to the credit bureau. Until then, my dad had never paid for a haircut because my mom had always done this for him. Never one to put stock or store or care in his appearance, after the divorce, my dad started to look like a disheveled, unshaven homeless man. It was my *brother* who, at the age of fourteen, got him to go a bonafide barber to get his first haircut, and it was also my *brother* who found the house my dad would purchase, and after my dad's stint at the apartments, they both moved in.

Without formally labeling it such, I would consider my brother's promptings as the first glimpse at caretaking; in the not-too-distant future, I would be at the helm, and the responsibilities and burdens would skyrocket. It was as if the red pop-up indicator in the turkey silently burst out, but no one knew it was there or he had one. These may seem relatively small, but every complication or issue that cropped up (or persisted) made it increasingly difficult for my father to handle them. Like a juggler being thrown more balls or pins, but one with one arm tied behind his back, my dad fumbled, faltered, and failed. Another area that shows my dad was getting snowed under and overwhelmed was the mounting *stacks* of litigation related to the aftermath of the divorce. He never got rid of them, and I have been sifting through them now. Was his heart broken? *Yes*? Did he lose hope for a "reunification"? *Never*. His repeated pleas to solicit my help in his quest to get my mom back went on for five years. Could we have separated and differentiated the first signs of HD from the usual effects of aging or even heightened ones due to stress and loss? No, not *then*, no more than anyone could correctly answer which comes first, the chicken or the egg, but I will attempt to do so now.

The first time my dad was summoned to court was for their divorce proceedings on March 21, 1983, but a judgment by default was taken on

July 1, 1983; I can only assume he failed to show up. Four months later, that July, my dad took his first legal action after being served: he changed his will to remove my mom from it; as his eldest, I was then designated as his POA and executrix. My role was sealed. By December of that same year, my parents had their first property settlement agreement; I use the term "agreement" loosely; it turned out to be a <u>dis</u>agreement, and soon, all accords were off. The following year was pock-marked with further actions my mom took and ignored by my dad. On <u>January 6, 1984, their divorce was finalized</u> and submitted as a public record. Then the games really began; there would be no détente.

It is neither my point nor my focus to rehash their legal battles. Still, I can tell you that in 1985 alone, I have before me eight pieces of mail from attorneys to my dad that dealt with notices and motions, custody details, mortgage payments, and other "indebtedness" (i.e., unpaid bills), "reneging" of payments, medical and insurance bills, child support criteria, written reminders of certain divorce decrees, requests for reimbursement for repairs, and finally, moneys "to be used to pay for college education" for my sisters. At the cusp of a disease's invasion of my dad's brain and being, this onslaught of legal action must have felt like an avalanche. It's easy to see why he reacted like Godzilla. The two pieces of writing I have from my dad to his attorneys are simple hand-written lists of accounting he kept pertaining to expenditures he made and hoped to use to offset the money he owed my mom. I found no proof that his lists or figures were taken seriously or acknowledged. His math was sound, but half the "losses" he counted had nothing to do with anything (e.g., his bills and expenses related to his new house purchase).

From 1986 alone, I have nine pieces of mail from the divorce attorneys to my father that also likely went unanswered. By far, the most telling pieces of evidence that my dad was coming unhinged was that for a man who placed education and family above all, the fact that my second sister had to sue him to get her guaranteed student loan paid for was beyond ludicrous; it was unthinkable, but not for my dad who was losing his faculties and running on fumes. He was cutting off his daughter's nose to spite his ex-wife's face, but it was everybody who got hurt. Ultimately, he had no contest or rebuttal; he simply didn't show up. Among this three-inch stack of documents, I found one letter my sister wrote in mid-November 1986 that accompanied her suit and GSL bill. In it, she wryly quipped, "I've learned a lot more than education + grades, thanks to you. My financial independence will be the greatest achievement of my life." Her hurt still stings.

Conversely, my youngest sister handled the delicate matter of getting blood from our turnip quite differently. Rather than strategize when would be the most advantageous time to strike and ask my father for a fat check for school, by the end of her first year, she had fallen into depression, then she fell in love, and finally, she flew the coop — out of college *and* the country. Who would want to haggle with my ogre dad about what constituted an education? Was it tuition alone? Room and board? What about books and food? Each semester, we'd have to present our case to my dad. With foretaste of eventual victory, the prize for our endurance, we'd wait until *after* he'd eaten to make our request. Then we endured the shaking of his head, the dramatic sighs, the likely yelling and gesticulating, and the wondering and waiting. It was all a part of a game and routine my youngest sister refused to play. Two years later, when she returned home to the States, in part to complete her undergraduate degree, she did so with the help of a PELL grant, *not* her pop. When she received this lump sum, my dad sent her a spray of a dozen roses. I've no doubt they went straight into the trash. In mid-November of 1986, I also discovered that my dad had furtively visited our then-for-sale home and pilfered insulation from the attic. It was the last thing he'd bought, and he felt entitled to it even if he had no use for it. This brought a swift response and demand for restitution by my mom's attorney. She was playing chess to his checkers. I also hold four more pieces of unopened mail from his attorney, and *not one was opened*! (I opened one and saw it was a bill.)

The more overwhelmed my dad got, the less he did, as if he had gone on strike, and nowhere is this more apparent than failing to open letters from his attorney. I counted six from 1986 alone, and from 1987–1989, I found *another* seven letters from attorneys to my dad, two of which were unopened. Limbo land became his comfort zone, and denial was his auto-reply. To my surprise, he *still* had unpaid bills dealing with my second sister's education; this time, these payments in arrears were to the school's credit union. The point is that the nightmare continued. When my brother moved in with my mom to attend a better high school for his last two years, now my dad had to pay child support for one he would never have thought would leave; not only that, the amount had increased. What was particularly noteworthy to me was a letter my dad had typed and copied in *sextuplicate* to his attorney. In it, he justified the reason for being in contempt of court. He was a year late and dollars short. He explained that since he had *verbally* agreed to my sister that he would take care of this bill, he saw no need to appear in court. You can hear the exasperation in his tone at no one "*bothering to notify [him] of the change of plans.*" I now see he let his mail pile up. He refused to pay any amount over the standard four years of college tuition but said he would pay her three extra quarters for food. His "logic" had no consistency, as the *opposite* had been the case for me. He paid for two additional quarters of tuition (beyond the four years), yet he was delinquent on my final food bill, and my diploma was held hostage until it was paid. Ultimately, he acquiesced, but the installments were his choice in timing and amount.

Why do I cover matters related to the aftermath of the divorce? They reveal a mind and man on the brink of a precipitous fall. He was just then beginning to spin like a top, like a whirling dervish, like the Tasmanian devil, full of vim, vigor, and fury, *sooo* frustrated in his confounding plight. If he had gotten agitated to the point where he would tack on an ironic mock address by adding "Mister" or "Miss" in front of our names, we knew where we stood. We were sadly amused when he meant to indicate his disdain and disrespect. It could be argued that since he was more of the "absent-minded professor" type, he was seemingly incapable of dealing with mundane tasks like handling daily affairs and keeping one's financial house in order. However, I contend that although there is weight to these arguments, my dad's failings were *not* isolated events or singularly connected to the legal entanglements he found himself in.

In my estimation, the mounting difficulty he was having in keeping up with his bills and obligations was the direct result of his brain's inability to think and process swiftly, let alone prioritize and adjust to life's curve balls deftly. Others might say that pride and prejudice led to his fall or that his cognitive inflexibility — a.k.a. stubbornness — turned him into his own worst enemy. Hindsight, education, and time have given me positive proof that HD was turning certain executive functions of his to stone. Why? My father may have started in shock and awe, but his disease *also* played a role and added to the snowball effect of the advent of decay. My dad was reactive and regressive; in his mind, every "provocation" was met with an attack, and he struck with blunt force. No one was in his corner; therefore, he often exploded or lashed out like a wounded animal. In a way, he was; we just didn't know it. Sure, a bill lapsing here or there and some ongoing issues stemming from disagreements about their divorce might not be remarkable were it not for the fact that his cognitive deficits brought on *additional* problems, and this leads us to the *next* feature of how HD adversely impacted his brain.

Not only were organizing, prioritizing, and flexibility steadily whittled away, but so was his ability to multi-task as we all do daily. There is neuropsychological evidence that shows "problems in [maintaining] attention in both automatic and dual-tasks… [which] healthy individuals would consider relatively undemanding… *require more conscious attention in people with HD* (emphasis mine)."[489] How could this *not* be taxing and exhausting? Children of all ages become the crankiest or most cantankerous when overtired. Where might this be seen? I have already touched upon driving in the last section and will return to these problems in the next chapter. For now, I can tell you that as time went by and whenever we were together with Dad, my brother and I would take over and drive for him more and more. In the eighties, this wouldn't have been a thought for us; now, it was a harrowing experience to be a passenger in his car. For now, I'll turn to the next piece of evidence that indicates his mind wasn't doing what it needed to.

Another sign of cognitive decline is a <u>lack of impulse control</u> that can spawn any number of additional expressions, including "outbursts, acting without thinking, and sexual promiscuity."[490] Before I get into his problem with promiscuity, let's take a gander at additional issues he had that deal with multitasking. My dad was already as volatile as a jerry-rigged, homemade pipe bomb, and even though he could get increasingly stuck on an idea and perseverate, it was his outbursts over frustrations from finding himself needing to deal with life's usual hiccups and speedbumps that rocked his — and our— world. In hindsight, we would have given Dad the benefit of our doubts by guessing that he was no mere Mediterranean man with his hackles raised. The Mayo Clinic tells us that cognitive impairments associated with HD also "lead to particularly sensitive issues [not only like] unsafe driving [but] *declining work performance.*"[491] These issues are "sensitive" because our autonomy gets threatened.

We will now shift our attention to my dad's problems at work. My dad began getting in trouble at work, all during the very time when he should have been coasting towards the golden years of retirement. Instead, near the end of his career, my dad was put on notice at work in the mid-nineties when his HD began to rear its ugly head. When I asked my brother *why* he'd gotten in trouble, he said he thought it had been "for something verbal" – that dad had "probably called somebody out [because he] couldn't tolerate pompousness in upper management." His outburst is a clear example of his increasing lack of impulse control; you don't call out upper-level management, especially not in front of others, without expecting reprisal. Well into his third decade, a man in his early sixties would know this well. For punishment, he was tasked with "homework," as he would put it. He had to do detailed (and likely irrelevant) computations at home as a passive-aggressive form of "payment" for his offensive remark. The management's strategy was simple: give him enough rope to hang himself. What might have taken a man of his mental caliber and education a few evenings took my dad *weeks* to complete. He was required to do exacting computations and keep a ledger of all of his work details, the sheer volume of which would have stressed out even a sound man. My dad was clearly overwhelmed.

I remember visiting him these days, and he didn't even come to the door when I arrived. Instead, I would find him sitting in one of the old director's chairs or sunk low in his recliner with his feet extended out onto another chair as a footrest and near a window with plenty of natural light. He made himself a makeshift lap desk made of a piece of plyboard. Atop this, he'd plunk a long clipboard thick with paper and the 17-inch spreadsheet with all sorts of figures and scratchings. I'd come in, and there he'd be sitting, wriggling his toes, snapping his big toe to his next, as he always did, only more than usual. His hips were squirmy, and while one hand grasped a pen, the other would be plunking away at his Texas Instruments calculator. Talk about multi-tasking! There he'd sit as I made dinner or until such a point where, in frustration, he'd throw in the towel from having not come up with the same answer twice and would get up to push his trusty grill out onto the gravel driveway to grill us salmon.

For all I know, his fingers just couldn't and didn't hit the intended numerical pads, or perhaps one wiggle caused him to get abstracted and lose his concentration, and he'd have to start his Sisyphean task all over again. Though none of us ever thought to ask my dad to pat his head and rub his tummy, what he had to do for work proved as tricky. Through sheer willpower, he persisted until he completed his assignment so he was not fired or "let go." For us on the outside looking in, it was bewildering to see him lose his cool and composure at the workplace. It seemed he was aging at an accelerated pace, but I have no evidence, just my gut's reaction to his graying and groaning. Though we may have hoped to overlook his "eccentricities" (even for him), it was clear it was becoming challenging for our dad to abide by the safety and work protocol he had known, but which he now seemed ready to dismiss, [492] as if safety had become superfluous and came in last, not first. During this time of slow release, he never forgot the names of his chums, the organic elements, and certain polysyllabic compounds; they were etched in his long-term account.

While these troubles continued to mount in his world, my brother and I were sweating behind the scenes. What in the world was happening to our dad? Had we known then that my dad had HD, we might have been able to see that he was having difficulty "thinking through complex problems and finding the best solutions,"[493] but as it was, we tended to smirk, gossip, and chide rather than to lament, sympathize, or help. We were in the dark as much as he was at a growing loss. Had we been aware, we would have known that, sadly, his cognitive losses would continue to the point where he would "develop [further] global impairments in the later stages." HD will stump you with its hit-or-miss assaults. Meanwhile, long-term "memory, language, and conceptual ability" remained relatively unscathed, albeit at "limited output."[494] This was *not* the case because none of us knew. Although they say ignorance is bliss, for both my father and us, such blindness led to heated confrontations, my dad's outbursts, and ultimately, a longing and heartache that could not be quenched. That said, *had* my father been capable of appreciating the fact that he had *inherited* this disease, I still don't think he would have *accepted* it because for him to have or to have spun out damaged or defective genes would be unthinkable.

In any event, it wasn't until 1993 that it was even possible to do genetic testing for HD,[495] so we would do well not to engage in futile "what if" speculations. During the early nineties, my father was just Dad doing normal activities after work like jogging, gardening, making coolant, cooking, and grilling or making Greek dishes like stuffed peppers. On the weekends, you might find him heading off to hear bluegrass music in Hilton, VA, or going to his local parish. During a good portion of the early half of the 1990s, he would live with my brother and *his* young daughter, whom my dad cherished and adored. Being a "papou" or grandfather gratified him greatly and suited him to a tee. Taking care of his home, visiting me, or taking a business trip here and there to various parts of the country contented him. He was still our goofy, lovable dad, but when and for what reason his emotions would flare and gruff words would fly, it was increasingly becoming a game of Russian roulette.

The final area of impaired cognition, which I believe is further evidence that HD was wracking and ruining its mental apparatus, was a growing lack of awareness and difficulty in processing new information, both of which are symptoms of cognitive decline in persons with HD.[496] When you combine these two features with his lack of impulse control and flexibility, particularly his tendency to get fixated or stuck on a thought, we have a near picture-perfect broken image of my dad at the time. We just didn't know it. I want to delve into the feature of lack of awareness; its polar opposite is empathy, and my dad ran out of this early, hard, and fast. How one considers his behavior vis-à-vis his world is critical to the person's being a moral and ethical citizen. Self-awareness is such a vital aspect of maturing cogence! Without it, we have no way of evaluating ourselves and the manner and measure we impact the world. The less one is aware of self, the less he is concerned with how he regards or treats others. Truth becomes relative based upon what the *self* wants; right or wrong gets evaluated through the lens of personal contentment.

In my dad's tainted state, he blurted out all thoughts and feelings; his social filter was diaphanous, so what came out might be blunt but true, or it might be baseless and frivolous; it was a coin toss. In better days, I would be hard-pressed to tell you of anyone in my life who was more aware and supportive of us kids than my dad. To his core, he was a natural encourager, and after five minutes of his singing praises to *you* or listing all the ways *you* were talented, you would think that nothing was beyond your reach, that there was nothing you couldn't do if you put your mind and energies to it. My dad had always been a "touchy" and naturally affectionate man, one sensitive to the unique needs of his precious ones. It was as if he became grounded by physical contact or, as time went by, just being near us. Through close proximity, it was as if we could sense each other's feelings through our familial sonar.

For me, his eldest, his energy knew no bounds because we matched each other's passion, intensity, and joy. My youngest sister, who was sensitive, shy, and introverted, showed a particular tenderness and sweetness. With my brother, the only other billy goat in our fold, my dad was on-call and ready to make any dream my brother conceived come true. For my next sister and me, trips abroad were made possible; for my brother, dirt bikes were bought, and scouting extravaganzas occurred. He was game and ready to fulfill our wishes and even whims, that is, until he wasn't, and the outward arc of his energy and focus began inverting until, eventually, the world revolved around himself and his petty demands.

What better way to appreciate the person's mindset with HD than to get the message straight from the horse or donkey's mouth? I've sifted through my dad's letters to me from this time and picked out gems that speak louder than a thousand of my words. In the early days, they indicate a man who had awareness; when I proceed to the second half, you'll note a very apparent lapse in meta-cognition; impulse control would prove daunting and elusive. His behavior would bear witness to a man increasingly returning to the state of a child, and we didn't know if he'd be a brat or a bull. However, he was still *ours*, yes, even if he would increasingly manifest "inappropriate behaviors"[497] like outbursts, tantrums, and, as I've hinted at earlier, bouts of sexual promiscuity.[498] My poor, single dad, who had been faithful to my mother for the entirety of their marriage, seemed to be making up for lost time and lack of affection.

What's the worst that could have happened, you may ask? Misconduct without misgiving, honesty without integrity, and haunting loneliness without despair. I will show what I tell because *it didn't start that way*: during the messy aftermath of the divorce, initially, my dad was sensitive to the impact his behavior had on us, his kids. You will see by how he addressed me that he never stopped showering me with terms of endearment. Over time, even though he was drawn to us like a magnate, his sphere of those trusted would grow smaller and smaller. Following are some examples of his salutations and closings to me. I've attempted to render their size and spacing, and his spelling has *not* been corrected. Interestingly, his final signature, "Dad," would *always* be in a smaller font and way off to the side, as if he didn't want the spotlight or was his own afterthought. We will cover seven years here in chronological order:

- Love **YOU** [5 x bigger] always   me   your dad
                                                                            (Oct. 24, 1985)
- Dearest Darling ANNA   (Nov. 11, 1985)
- Take care of yourself precious Anna   Dad   (Oct. 12, 1986)
- ANNA – *AΓAΠH MOY* ["MY LOVE" in Greek]   (Dec. 11, 1986)
- Dearest ANNA —Hi. I miss you so VERY MUCH. . .
  Take the very best care of **ANNA for I LOVE HER** (ADA) a lot (← in red sharpie] Dad   (Sept. 21, 1987)
- Dearest, Dearest SWEET ANNA ... PS I'm trying to adjust to loness without Stephen. For me little harder than some others.
                                                                            (June 22, 1990)
- YOU'RE SO BRILLIANT & SO VERY, VERY TALENTED IN WRITIG. I'M PROUD OF YOU.   (Feb. 7 1993)
- Inside a Valentine's Day card: unsigned and with nothing written/blank card. On the front of the envelope:

  MS. ANNA [at least 5x larger]   (Feb. 1993)
- Very glad & proud of your recent LIFE rearrangements! They are great. Keep it up.

      LOVE   dad   (Mar. 11, 1993)

We'll now delve further and look at other examples that reveal his decline.

Since self-awareness and the capacity to show empathy are signs of a mentally healthy adult, my dad would increasingly have difficulty thinking beyond self, which was Nature's way of giving us clues. Still, we weren't on this clue train. Let this serve as my gift of gentle warning to you. In this in-between period of transition and decline, his index of compassion would increasingly shrink as his public displays of friction would rise. You'll be able to see the writing on your wall for yourself. In an early letter written on September 12, 1985, my dad wrote me,

> *"I'm sorry I was in such a rotten mood, but having to bear all the costs of the most critical part of the life cycle without any help from a partner is hard to bear. It is hard for me because I*

want to do all I can & not go 'American Style' like some of your friends' parents..."

His apology segued and devolved into self-pity. I'm not sure if you are aware, but there used to be a TV show called *Love American Style*, and it reflected the "Me Generation" of the '70s by exploring fluid boundaries in marriage. My dad would have been appalled by this, but at the time, no doubt he kept his composure by remaining quiet as a pall; now, his resentment and disgust found vent and outlet in his letter. Oh, he *still* felt like a foreigner in a strange land! In this same letter, he gave me the go-ahead to sign his name for some document I needed at school, saying, "Go ahead and forge my signature." Expediency trumped ethics; that wasn't new to us, but now it went unchecked. During this year, my dad got arrested for shoplifting, but what was as remarkable as his crime was his response: he showed zero remorse or compunction. He had neither; maybe it was no different than helping himself to life's all-you-can-eat salad bar, except that someone minded, and he got caught red-handed. There's no hint of his wrongdoing; it was like an incidental finding. One month later, on Oct. 24, 1985, Dad reported what transpired in a postscript to me, which I now highlight:

> P.S. This morning 10 AM had a court hearing on PGA's Hills [Dept. Store] shoplifting incident on 9/29/85, 11:55 AM. I was acquitted & the case dismissed. I had [old friends] as character witnesses, The power/influence of good, solid friends, like above, is unimaginable! Next time I see you I'll tell you all about it. After court this morning I went by the house & thoroughly enjoyed reading your card.

Can you tell how unaffected he is by the affair without acknowledging his petty crime?

Among his "solid friends" was a couple who had been my parents' friends since the days of Clemson, and the man in particular knew, understood, and loved my dad. I'm sure they testified that my dad was an educated man, albeit currently one bereft and acting out of the norm; that would be the truth insofar as they could know it. Another aspect of my dad's mindset and focus in keeping with his character and core values — *family unity* —would become an obsession. No matter what followed in life, I don't think my dad ever gave up hope that my mother would return to him, and he solicited my help whenever he could. Three years after their divorce, on November 11, 1985, he wrote, *"If there was a way to reunite OUR FAMILY, I would give it my best shot. By definition I'm human & therefore imperfect like the rest of those other imperfect humans on this globe!"* I suppose this sweeping "confession" of his not being perfect was sufficient for wiping the slate clean in his mind.

Only once did I hear him express dejection, as you can see from this line written on November 15, 1986: *"I'm too beat, numb, & tired to worry about anybody/anything else but myself & seeing Stephen through."* Conceding defeat and giving up were foreign thoughts to my father, and even when the chips were down or he momentarily felt down and out, he still held hopes high, even in times of quiet desperation. One year later, on February 22, 1987, we find him singing his own praises, minimizing my mom's feelings, and placing the blame squarely on her for her failure to communicate in a way familiar and effective to him but repugnant and unnatural to her (e.g., yelling). You'll easily be able to tell that his underlying motive for writing me was so that I would come to his emotional rescue *and* his defense in the case of my mom versus him. There was no statute of limitations for his heart. Notice his primitive style, truncation of thought, and ellipsis of unnecessary words:

> My TEC job was a peak accomplishment & really did not need to have done anything else. A lot of these other – points in [his ex/my mother's] mind were really NOTHING. She should have shook me, talked 9strongly & aggressively) to me or something to wake me up & ~~possibly~~ still be together... Please be my advocate in no matter what comes up – especially in exchanges with [her].

Like many men, my dad based his merit on his *professional* accomplishments, not his homefront contributions; by that, I do not mean mere *material* provision. Having known my mom for over twenty-five years, he ought to have understood that she was reserved and would never have expressed her needs and wants "strongly and aggressively." He resorted to indirect means of diplomacy and "triangularization," whereby he appointed me, his unwitting ambassador, as their courier and translator in one fell swoop. He thought I had a Midas's golden touch, and I felt as if I were the cadet Christian to his being Cyrano de Bergerac, except that my dad liked his nose and fully expected her to see *his* light. I failed, and she fled. Like Hercules, my dad never had a problem tooting his own horn, but he never realized that a man who boasts about himself has an audience of one; the subjective claim is no proof of objective reality. He truly believed that if he could find one more unturned stone and unsung virtue, all could return to normal, but neither would live as he knew it, nor he ever would.

My final example of the *early*-stage HD mindset also came straight from the horse's mouth and was penned on March 9, 1987, less than a couple of weeks after the note above. My dad would have been fifty-two, well within the expected range where HD is making its public appearance. Here, he wrote what I would consider his only acknowledgment of how his actions adversely impacted his children, *"his most priceless treasures,"* which is such a poignant Greek way of looking at us. As time marched on, there would be far less reaction to other's feelings. Almost immediately after this fleeting moment of sympathy, please notice that his mind jumps back to self-justification in the following paragraph. He lists his socially acceptable grounds for grievance, none leaving room for his wife's pain or line of reasoning. In this early phase of HD, charity still resided in my father's breast; "forgiveness" was not a term with which our family was familiar. Such a possibility would have come from my dad's religious upbringing, which was still deeply rooted in him.

Now we know that not only was this response less likely to be sifted off, but apparently, his moral schemata were returning to their default settings from childhood. At the very time he was trying to get what he wanted, he mocked psychoanalysis for its inflated self-serving. I admire his longed-for goal of *"reunification,"* as if they were one country that had gotten torn asunder and could be stitched back together even after their civil war. However, like all the kings' horses and men couldn't put Humpty Dumpty together again, my father found no algorithm, no clue, no formula, no recipe, no breadcrumb to help him figure out this crumbled Rubix cube of their marriage, let alone the greater misdirection in his own life. I contend that his just-hatching HD tipped the scales of a mindset that previously was more or less balanced between logic and feeling to one that was now weighted in favor of gut and gall. The following letter is gold in that you can nearly watch the decline as your eyes snap down the lines of the page. In mere paragraphs, we'll bound from his sympathy to antipathy to bathos.

Subject: PGA'S APPOLOGIES

MY DEAREST CHILDREN: MY MOST PRICELESS LIFE TREASURES. I
WANT TO APPOLOGIZE AND ASK YOUR FORGIVENESS FOR MY SELFISH
ATTITUDE AND ACTIONS FOR THE LAST 3 YEARS!... SUCH A BURDEN IT
MUST HAVE BEEN ON ALL OF YOU TO HAVE TO HEAR THE SAME OLD
ENDLESS RECORD... YOU NEEDED SOMEONE TO TURN TO & LEAN ON
WITHOUT FEAR OF THORNING.

PGA'S MINUS POINTS, AS A RESULT OF FEEDBACK FROM YOU 4 AS WELL
AS *** [←*my mother's initials*], SEEM INCONSEQUENTIAL COMPARED
TO AN ALCOHOLIC, DRUG ADDICT, PHYSICAL ABUSER, A PHYSICAL
HANDICAP[PED OR EVEN DEATH!

EVEN THE MOST PERFECT COUPLE CAN SHOW IMPERFECTIONS IF
ANALYTICALLY NIT-PICKED BY EITHER CLOSE OBSERVERS OR "PARLOR
FREUDIANS." ... I FOR GOT AND FORGAVE SHA GRIEVANCES WITH SHA
& TO THIS LETTER WOULD ENJOY NOTHING MORE IN THE WORLD BUT
A REUNIFICATION...TO THIS LETTER IF SOMEBODY SHOWED ME A WAY,
I WOULD CERTAINLY IMPLEMENT IT.

His "minus points" were not "inconsequential, and there would be no "somebody" to show him the way to achieve his coveted peace accords. Shifting gears from the cognitive to the emotional will serve us well as we broach the third category and explore the psycho-emotional problems that beset the person with HD, including behavioral manifestations spawning from a mind running amuck. I'll leave you with a few final odds-and-ends and observations from this section dealing with cognitive decline. They spring from my *brother's* recollections. My uncle told me he had quit speaking to my dad because he *never paid him back*. My brother confirmed what my dad had told me earlier. He justified his reneging (and basic theft) by snarling the excuse that *"Kolya didn't need the money — he got everything!"* Were my father a sound man, I do not think he would have robbed his brother to pay back his father, even for feeling wronged.

During the first decade of his marriage to my mom, to keep the peace, my father suppressed a lot. Even at the beginning, he never blinked an eye as my mom was rolling hers when my dad asked her if they could also be wed in the Greek Orthodox Church in Chicago after they married in Florida. Who knew he wanted God to be their witness, not a non-Christian Unitarian clergyman? Ten years later, my mother renamed their son, my brother, "Stephen." Though my dad did not protest, it rankled, and such came out when it came time for naming his grandsons; he had no voice that counted here either. I applaud my dad because he did not let himself idle in self-pity or linger in loneliness. On November 11, 1985, he wrote, *"Between work, all the necessary chores & all my interests, there is no time for boredom. Too many things to conquer & do in LIFE for boredom to set in."* I love that he used the word "conquer"; it shows me how much vigor and passion he had. Eight years later, on Jan. 14, 1993, he gave *me* similar advice, *"Keep busy& active in the meantime until you're over the initial aloneness..."* The next section shows how heedlessness and recklessness began to rear their ugly heads in his behavior.

Although we have meandered in this chapter's chronology, do know that when my father retired in 1998, things really began to break loose. After all, he'd suddenly gotten out of a 28-year routine that had imposed its own daily routine and regularity. Now that there were no rules or set schedule, all bets were off. He followed no one's expectations or regimen regarding how to operate appropriately, particularly where personal conduct, diet, and hygiene were concerned. He was a free-wheeling agent! No one knew to realize that the parts of our father's brain were getting cracked and crinkled and were being destroyed as the disease marched on its unsteady pace and rate. Its effects — be it his odd gait and increasingly eccentric thought processes — we all would notice. Who among us could not recall his janky sweatband made from a rubber band and sponge, which he situated on the center of his forehead to mop up his sweaty brow when he'd jog? None. And, my, he was proud that he was a *"sweat monster — it is soooo healthy!"* Who among us could forget when he quit using the drier and would lay out clothing on beds to dry or let his hole-ly tube socks, well-worn underwear, and Funfest t-shirts flutter in the breeze on a makeshift clothesline out on his back porch? None. HD was darkening his emotional landscape, what with it revving up his already explosive temper; now, it would increase in frequency. You've also a picture of his distorted amble in your mind. Let's now look at the various psychoses the HD patient may experience, and I'll let you in on what my dad had.

Psychological Changes in the Person with HD in Stage 2

Eventually, my dad would have to have a psychological evaluation and cognitive assessment performed to check his intellectual ability, memory, judgment, and reasoning,[499] and by the time this would take place, he would fare poorly. How did he get from A to Z? Were there also signs that abnormalities were encroaching upon and creeping into his psychological state as his movement issues got more vivid? Oh, yes, for sure. In tandem with his stirred mind and body were disturbances within his emotions and the convoluted manner in which they were expressed. How did the impaired striatum of the basal ganglia and eroding amygdala present themselves in my dad's emotional palette? As HD chips away at the stone (of the brain), many manifestations begin to surface, some of which will eventually become permanent features of your person with HD. Most likely, you'll notice a gross exaggeration of ways and means that before had been "normal," but you may also observe a reduction of other familiar aspects; the net result will be a unique cocktail, tinted and tinged by the poison of HD.

As HD progressed in my dad, though we could not *see* that the connections between the caudate nucleus to his frontal lobes were becoming frayed, we would bear witness to amped-up emotions that no longer had a way of turning themselves down, a service which the typically healthy frontal lobes provide. With the HD patient's frontal lobes now short-circuited and frazzled, emotions run amuck, and our loved one finds himself in a tailspin or whirlwind; it gives us whiplash watching.[500] There exist a host of psychiatric problems common in HD patients, which can be challenging for patients and families, so it's important to remember that these problems are *"caused by the illness* and *not* by the person who has Huntington's disease."[501] I tell you this because when you are facing these problems and quandaries in real-time, your patience will be tried by your person with HD, who seems to be acting out willfully as if his m.o. is to be contrary, come what may. You cannot shake your fist at the disease, so there will be times, as was the case with me, when I lost my temper and my cool. Unfortunately, although we had many a clue, we were all still in the dark.

Speaking of darkness, I can tell you that people with HD may suffer from depression as well as other conditions found in the general population, including "mania, obsessive-compulsive disorder, or various forms of psychosis."[502] My dad's ego and a strong sense of self kept him buoyed against depression and its worst effect, suicidal tendencies. That said, almost all people with HD — and that would include my dad — will manifest "disease-specific personality and behavioral changes"[503] as part of what might be termed "a hypofrontal [i.e., decreased blood flow in the prefrontal cortex] or dysexecutive syndrome, [which is] characterized by (a) irritability, (b) impulsivity, and (c) obsessionality."[504] Check, check, and (d) double-check *all* these boxes for my dad. These disorders of HD ought not to be considered in complete isolation, and they certainly do not pop up immediately. That said, unfortunately, psychiatric symptoms have long been understood to be "a common and inherent part of Huntington's disease."[505] My dad would have to contend with this afflicting disease in the same way that

Hercules dealt with tragedy after tragedy instigated by Hera, who was bent on exacting revenge on him since birth and for life.

Let me tell you about peculiar emotional displays which got hyped up in my dad before we move on to bonafide *psychological* problems that would also eventually burgeon. Though tell-tale commonalities exist and overlap, my father's HD will not present itself precisely the same as it does for your person with HD. I do not intend to be vague or evasive; it's just that when we're looking at the person's *behavior*, HD spins itself particularly uniquely. How could it not? There are countless areas to be degraded on several parts of the brain, each having its individualistic nuances. Behavioral symptoms cropping up serve as additional proof of the disease's broad-spectrum impact on the brain, and what you may start to notice will be more than a movement disorder.

What behaviors are you likely to notice that won't remain the same as when they started? The first will be <u>extra volatility or agitation</u>, like a child on the verge of a tantrum. HD cranked up select emotional features that were in keeping with his indigenous personality. This revved-up norm makes it hard to tell when things really start since you're already used to his ways and means, even if they're getting bolder. It's like watching a carnival vendor turn up the volume of random parts of the quirky aspects of your loved one's personality. You just don't know how loud or screechy the volume can get. My dad was loud, but yours may be sullen; inane things will have them bowing up. Over time, darker emotions can develop into a bonafide psychosis. The brain can't repair the damage done to itself and will continue to decay. According to the Huntington's Outreach Project at Stanford University, some of the "specific and predictable behavioral changes" to look for may include any combination of the following: "apathy, depression, aggression, disinhibition, repetition, anxiety, denial, hallucinations and mania, and altered sexuality."[506]

Of these, only depression and hallucinations would my father be spared. And just like those jarring *movements*, the person with HD has no control over making (or curtailing) psychiatric problems that arise just as swiftly and mysteriously. In fact, "almost all patients with Huntington's disease will have at least one psychiatric symptom during their lives, and *most patients will have multiple symptoms* (emphasis mine)."[507] Such was certainly the case for our dad. When it rains, it pours. However, none of us on the outside looking in were in the loop, so it's no wonder my father would become increasingly frothy, cranky, or hot around the collar when we lost patience and got cross with him. He bore his burden alone. Ultimately, we need to get our loved ones tested so that the future caretaker can be better prepared and equipped to make their environment safe and tranquil, making it less likely to trigger their ire and confounding behaviors. They need your kindness and all the prayers you can muster because they will feel lost or at their wit's end. They are. At this time, although the tottering had started, my dad was still a free and independent agent.

Starting in the late 1980s, I recall that it got more challenging for him to take down his Christmas tree, and the Christmas cards he received might have remained on his long stone mantle, nestled among family photos, well past Valentine's Day. Like many American men, my dad loved to hop on his riding lawn mower and attend to his lawn, and his garage was chockfull of odds-and-ends chemicals, wood, tools, the canoe, and my brother's skeletal Camaro and its engine parts. His activities would be relegated to gardening, feeding loaves of day-old bread to the horses on his property he'd rented out to a friend, and tending to the spring, which provided water to his heat pump. I don't know if it's because physical survival trumped *all*, but hygiene came in at a distant second. Yes, he "cleaned up good," but it was my mom who had bought his clothes and often picked out what he would wear to work; such was of little consequence to him. My brother became our father's personal attendant and groomer when he was in his fifties and living independently; after Dad retired, it would be my turn. My dad did not notice the changing of the guard.

When the daily grind came to a screeching halt at retirement, it got easier for my dad to neglect his cleanliness. For years, he had the same crusty bar of olive oil soap, a faded bottle of Head & Shoulders shampoo, and a calcified washcloth in his grimy shower. At that time, I hadn't taken the time to help him clean *yet*. What made my dad different than other retirees in this same boat is that he justified his sporadic bathing by announcing that *"germs bounce off me."* I'm serious. And more and more, when he *did* shower, because of his movement problems, it sounded like there was a circus tromping about in his bathtub. When he'd get out, he'd leave his towel on the floor to absorb all the water that had sloshed out while he'd bathed. Like a chimpanzee picking at fleas and whatnot on his partner, I ended up doing this for my dad while he patiently sat like a king, and he soaked up this primitive form of physical touch.

Shifting gears from apathy to <u>depression</u>, I do not think my father was depressed in the clinical sense of feeling hopeless or withdrawn; he was too much of an egoist or Hercules for that! That said, I have reason to believe that sadness can exude or get expressed in the form of <u>anger</u>, and my dad would repeat that he was "*soooooo* frustrated." Later on, frequently, he would fume that he was "depressed like a jail," but that was because of the constraints we imposed upon him for his safety, which crimped his spirit and cramped his style. Like a pocket watch overwound, another expression seen in HD patients is mania, and we would all become familiar with this mode in my dad. Still, he never got to the point where he was having hallucinations, at least none that we could tell.

In the fifteen years that this chapter covers, on top of my father losing his wife, finding himself embroiled in ongoing legal entanglements, and ending a nearly thirty-year career in less-than-ideal circumstances— any one of which would challenge any person in my dad's place, my father found himself dealing with a disease he knew not that he had, let alone that it existed, or that it was overpowering him. Who knew his caudate was deteriorating and his frontal lobes were not working properly,[508] to the point that my dad would become as incapable of suppressing his addled emotions and rattled psyche as he would his extraneous movements? Certainly, neither we nor he! Since I've dispensed with the three *least*-prominent features of behavioral changes in my dad, it's time to take a closer look at the ones that would become more prominent.

First and foremost, **agitation** became one of his most frequent garments. In general, everyday life could quickly seem "*wild and wooly*" — a phrase my dad was fond of even on good days —without anything extraordinary occurring. It turns out that chaos is also in the eye of the beholder. **Irritability and poor temper control** are among the most troublesome behaviors exhibited in HD[509], and my dad already had a quick temper to begin with. Such a personality feature that is so prominent in HD patients would have been challenging to differentiate as anything unique in him. It's just that now my dad would combust over more and more trivial matters, and sometimes even we who knew him best would scratch our heads, puzzled as to his train of thought or reason the molehill had become a mountain. And while *how* we express our anger *is* a learned behavior, in the case of one with HD, since neural messages are not being carried out wholly or efficiently[510] — or in some cases, not at *all* — the impetus that tells us *why* we got mad, etc. and what we might do about it might not reach the frontal lobe. Therefore, it's no wonder my dad felt left in a lurch but with no real reason, cause, or provocation, just the irritating stimulus and his hyped-up frustration and dismay. How does the message get misdelivered? An undamaged caudate in the basal ganglia would lead to mild frustration or irritation; however, in the case of a person with the *damaged* caudate, "*too much of the 'anger signal' is sent, and the [affected] individual may have a temper tantrum.*"[511]

In retrospect, when Dad felt like he was being opposed or challenged, what came out were not words but actions louder than words, as if he very core were demanding to know, "*Where was I? Can't you see I'm fuming because you haven't obeyed me; therefore, I will repeat myself without end or fail until I get my way!*" He became the bull in our China shop. Recall that starting in the mid-eighties, our family would often keep him in the dark so as not to rile him, leading to his flying off the handle. Right or wrong, we buoyed and buffered him, so now that he was living on his own and HD was slowly bringing about the rack and ruin of his brain, his volatility went unchecked, and his bouts of fury were doubly off the chain. It is understandable why he felt what he did: the things he used to have control over were moving further from his reach; he grasped at straws. We never saw how he might have acted as a well man because HD hijacked and took over his emotional feedback system.

Through it all, though, I never doubted my dad's love for me and us. As his world got smaller, we became more valuable to him, so if he perceived we were not *on his side,* he believed we were against him. He might have treated us like traitors or marauders, even when we knew *deep down* that he loved us not only with blood, sweat, and tears but with all his gall and bone and heart. Once, when he thought I was *"brainwashed"* and not sympathetic towards him in his plight with my mother, uncharacteristically, he left me high and dry when he dropped me off at graduate school. Although I already knew he would not be paying for school, there wouldn't have been thought that he would help me with food, even if but a single trip to the grocery store or us enjoying a final meal together before he left. This time, however, he deposited my luggage and me in the parking lot and speedily whisked off without glancing back. That was *not* my dad!

In the end, my dad was never *formally* diagnosed with any psychosis or disorder. Still, for us who knew him, his compulsions became obsessions, and his usual energetic and driven self turned into a manic man who was on edge and got hot under the collar over matters that didn't add up to a pile of beans. In Volume 2, you'll see his mania up close and personal, for example, in his sweeping attempts to snatch up his dying brother's life insurance policies. While he already tended to be bullish about accomplishing his goals, his fixations *and* inflexibility intensified to such a degree that even for us who knew him, it was growing hard to justify his behavior as just par for his course. Perhaps he was combatting an inner chaos he *had* to have felt but was left shadowboxing alone. Also, in the next section, we will take a closer look at how his mania fed upon itself to the point where likely he *did* suffer from OCD, certainly grandiosity. It was as if the racetrack in the halls of his brain had become his very own Indy 500, and his defective car was going nowhere fast. What other psychological features can we note changed?

I would never have described my dad as one suffering from <u>anxiety</u>, in that he was not a "worry-wort" and not plagued with inner doubts or anguishes, but he could get restless. If he set his mind on some goal or task, he would not relax or rest until he had done all he could to finish. Thus, although there had never been a procrastinating bone in his body, he was now a steam engine with no off switch. His <u>moods</u> became even more mercurial and would shift like wind rushing through a wildfire. If he did get anxious, he alleviated this sense by trying to get a handle on the situation — or the person — on the spot. As time went by, he went from assertive to <u>aggressive</u>, but not in any overtly or intentionally harmful way. What do I mean? In one regard, my dad would become what I can only describe as increasingly touchy, and by that, I mean if he wanted to impress his opinion upon you, he tended to reach out and touch your forearm, hand, or knee in conversation. Greeks do this anyway, so now, looking back, my father was returning to his root means of non-verbal communication. (It's just that it hadn't been like this as much in the early days when *I* was a child.) He gesticulated more, and if he were walking with you, it would not be uncommon for him to lean into your walk to involve or assert his will, not to mention the direction he might want you to take. Was this frequent? No. Was it new or odd? Yes. However, I got comfortable and at ease with his touching of my forearm or whatever of me was handy, and it happened as naturally as breathing while we were conversing, eating together, or playing backgammon. In the early days of his HD blooming, back when we were all ignorant, these touches most often occurred when he was calm, happy, and comfortable. Perhaps this was a mild and innocuous form of <u>disinhibition</u> that spilled out from a place of love: he *liked* being connected to his closest ones. Literally. That said, I readily concede that this touchiness could get ugly if mixed with the right amount of perturbation. And although he was not in the habit of swearing, hitting, or hurting anyone, I've heard many a door slam, and when "*provoked*," his yelling could come nearer bellowing.

Also, in the mid-to-late nineties, we began to notice in our dad another new, recurrent, and quirky *behavior* that overlapped with his odd *movements*. I recently read that HD patients will engage in <u>repetitive mannerisms</u>, which are a subconscious means of "reducing inner discomfort."[512] An extraneous quirk here or there would have been in keeping with my dad's underlying restlessness. Looking back, it was as if he didn't know how to act in his newly-forming HD skin. This particular mannerism he adopted served as a means of self-soothing, like a child who fingers his favorite blanket. Dad started to do something called "<u>pill-rolling</u>" with his napkins. In between heaping bites or perhaps stopping to turn to listen to you, he would clasp his folded-over napkin between his straight thumb and forefinger and roll it over and over until the now diaphanous napkin became flimsy. How could we have possibly known that my dad *wasn't* just oddly enjoying the tactile sensation of his napkin, likely swiped from "Micky D's." In actuality, by definition, "pill-rolling" is a tremor named for how it appears, which, in this case, is the phenomenon whereby

> "*it looks like you are trying to roll a pill or another small object between your thumb and index finger.* [And while it is] the most common tremor associated with Parkinson's disease, [this type of tremor] is caused by problems in the parts of the brain that control movement, including the cerebellum, frontal lobe, and *basal ganglia*."[513]

It used to be a pleasure to sit across the table from him and watch him eat something or a meal that brought him no end of delight. He would make his soft, happy, guttural sounds, sometimes with his eyes and eyebrows raised from deep satisfaction, and he'd erupt a compliment from a place of primal joy: "*Sooooo tasty!*" It was like he was the first of the five thousand in line to get the bread and fish, and he was ever grateful. However, when he ate, now he would often *not* close his mouth while chewing, and he might raise a hip to make it easier to flatulate — with no "excuse me," let alone acknowledgment of his indecorum. I began to sit *next* to him so as not to watch him eat, but I never could take my eyes off his pill-rolling, busy fingers.

Speaking of touch, tics, and temper, I will proceed to my dad's final psycho-behavioral issues. I will also connect my dad to the dose of Hercules' dispensed at the beginning of this chapter; it concerns my dad's love life. As for Hercules, none compared to his first wife, Megara, the mother of his children; my mother, for my dad, was his everything. And even though, in general, my dad preferred the company of women to men, on October 12, 1986, some three years after their divorce, my dad wrote me, "*Sometimes I think that I will never get committed to a woman other than the woman of my children!!!*" As it turned out, gradually, then with seeming reckless abandon, my dad *did* get involved with other women, but because of his HD munching away at the grand central control station for impulse control, some became the objects of his base desire. To a select few, he gave the piece of his heart he had left; however, for many women who got swept away by his passion — or their pity — his words above proved prophetic and true: *he never did remarry.*

That said, as was the case with Hercules, my dad got involved with multiple women after the divorce. Hercules' days of sowing wild oats in youth contrast with three marriages after becoming a widow. My dad's case was the inverse: purity in youth, devotion in marriage, and haphazard companionship as a divorced man. When he *did* start dating, it seemed as if he either was making up for lost time or filling a collapsed vacuum in dire need of affection in the same way a man with a collapsed lung resuscitates with oxygen. He sought to perish the reality of abandonment with conquests and intimacies. No, my dad did not attain the company of a younger woman, as did Hercules with Iole, and, thankfully, my dad didn't get attached to any mal-intentioned Omphale who would use him. He acquired no jealous Deianeira, who would prove to be the end of him. Instead, in matters of the heart and love, sickness and health, my dad would be his worst enemy, the villain in his tragedy. And where my dad's HD-induced impulsivity and disinhibition converged with aggression, we find one more problem area for my dad that, as it turns out, shares with many HD patients, and that is a term called "altered sexuality."[514] Let's explore what this puzzling terminology means regarding my dad.

Reflecting on my dad's issues with women whom he dated after the divorce and after his HD had begun to break ground, I ingested several articles to determine if my dad's case was an anomaly; it was *not*. As the disease progresses, one of the many behavioral symptoms to arise is "sexual problems."[515] One reason this phrasing is vague and broad is that, depending upon the person's level of decline, another affiliated problem that can arise due to changes in body dynamics would be the resultant inability, lack of ease, or awkwardness during closeness "due to the new, interferant, and erratic movements."[516] Such would *not* be the case for *our* hero. His lust and lack of self-awareness knew no bounds. Maybe his aggressiveness increased when intimacy he'd enjoyed in marriage came to a halt, and with his brain getting blotted in the precise area that *ought* to inhibit our indiscretions, improprieties, or even harm, he became all the more avaricious, if not a little predatory.

Add to this fact, HD causes changes in the "delicate balance of hormone levels, sometimes resulting in a decreased sex drive."[517] However, though less frequently occurring, HD may also cause an increase in sex drive and, often with it, inappropriate sexual behavior.[518] This was the case for *our* little Hercules. Disinhibition is "due to damage to the caudate nucleus, a deep area of the brain that controls behavior."[519] Now, if you were like us, who at the time were ignorant of his disease, you might rightly have said, "I thought your dad was a one-woman man who attempted to get back together with your mom for *years*. What about *that*?" You would have been correct, but loneliness trumped hopes faltering, and he gave himself over to opportunism without entirely giving himself away. As the 1990s were passing us by, his frequent and clumsy attempts to *"find [and be with] a woman,"* as if a woman were something to pick up at the local market, made him seem like a caveman on the prowl as if he were our very own goat-footed Pan. The truth is not found in mythology but in neurology.

By now, you know that the HD shows "significantly impairs functional connectivity of the prefrontal regions in both hemispheres."[520]And though *typically*, the brain's neuroplasticity gives it the resiliency to try to fix itself or to become amenable to behavior modification methods[521] used to <u>re</u>-teach necessary parameters, in the case of the HD brain, since these delicate structures are <u>atrophying</u>,[522] *there will be no fixing their problematic behaviors*. They get stuck or stymied. We corrected, cajoled, and scolded our dad, but none of us understood the futility of our fuming, least of all, our dad. This boiled down to my dad's interactions with women often spelled double trouble.

Maybe it was my dad's birth order as the youngest that drew in caretaker types; maybe it's the fact that women who were sensitive to those *not* well felt compassion for *him*. Regardless, three of the eight women he was intimate with were nurses before things really started to go downhill. My brother reminded me that also during the late '80s, my dad got a case of scabies, and it grossed everyone out but my dad. He used to joke about *"finding a woman"* at the long-since shut down Click's Hotel, an establishment known among the locals for its scurrilous goings-on. My dad's puffed-up braggadocio amounted to carnal longings and a lot of hot air. That said, his behavior *did* comport with what I also read, which is that "some [HD] patients may be more likely to engage in risky sexual behavior, such as one-night stands."[523]I should thank my lucky stars I don't have more to report.

<u>Disinhibition</u> in my dad at this time and in this arena *did* lead to sexual misconduct. According to my brother, who was living with my dad in the late '80s and into the early '90s, there was a girl — and by "girl," I am implying one who is over sixteen but under twenty-one — who worked in the Kroger deli whom dad talked into coming home with him during her break. He was attempting to have his way with her, but she escaped his clutches, went back to work, and reported it to her mother. The next thing you know, my brother —also a minor at the time — found himself talking

to this girl's mother on the phone. She was ready to have files charged against my dad, but my brother "talked her off the ledge." However, not all matters related to my dad's "love life" were worrisome or unwholesome. In the late '80s, my dad met a lawyer who, for some time, genuinely cared for Dad and he for her. She became possessive of this quirky, loveable Greek man. In fact, she encouraged him to fulfill one of his unrealized dreams: to plant a vineyard to produce grapes for his *own* wine. And so, sow he did. Happy was this little man with a rototiller, stakes, nets, and fresh clusters of his homeland's fruit to plant and tend to his homeland's fruit. (I recently found the order form from where he got these grapes.) I'm not sure what came of this endeavor, but it was salvific in his last decade of relative wellness and independence.

As my dad's world was closing in, those he chose to have in his inner circle dwindled to a handful, and he closed more doors than he opened. Loyalty was his love language. So, when this attorney girlfriend criticized one of his children — a cardinal sin for my father— he dropped her like a hot potato. That breakup gave us all mild whiplash. The next thing we knew, he was dating another woman, but she was stranger than he was, and she was one of those "cat people" who lived with more cats than she had relatives. My dad couldn't fake interest in her for long. Next was a shy and demure Greek lady from Knoxville, who, although pitied him and understood his ways, would report odd things my dad revealed to her from his past that bore no relevance to their relationship, and no context was provided. She, too, faded into history with no fanfare. By the very late '90s into 2001, my dad saw a widow who was the sister of someone he'd worked with, and this woman was a generous soul and compassionate person. He visited her several times in her home in Maryland. Still, with her family issues and financial problems mounting and coming more to light, I will jump the gun and tell you that my dad got a feeling of desperation during his last visit, and he suddenly decided to drive back home right then and there without a word of explanation to anyone. I don't know which came first, the thought to come back to Tennessee or the fact that he had hit a car in her driveway. He just bumblingly vanished. Such is the reader's digest condensed version of this erratic, hit-and-run accident in the final episode of my dad's HD-impacted amorous life. Perhaps, thankfully, "inappropriate sexual behavior can be *secondary to disinhibition*,"[524] so as time went by and his libido and seeking *"companionship"* waned, what remained was disinhibition, like a stubborn ring around his collar. The final domain I'll conclude this chapter with will be my dad's *spiritual* changes, and by that, I am referring to his religiosity as his core identity, *not* his religion.

Spiritual Changes in the Person with HD in Stage 2

[11]When I was a child, I used to speak like a child,
think like a child, reason like a child;
when I became a <u>middle-aged</u> man <u>with HD</u>, I
<u>could not</u> do away with childish things.
[12]For now, we see in a <u>cracked</u> mirror dimly, but then <u>I
will get to see myself</u> as I was and would be face to face
<u>with my Maker</u>; now I no longer even know in part,
but then I will know fully, just as I also have been fully known."
— a personal remix of 1 Cor. 13:11–12, underscoring/modifications mine

While I am well aware that one ought not to add or take anything away from Scripture, I offer up this well-known Scripture edited if but to suggest that what *ought* to happen in our adult years becomes <u>un</u>done with the Huntington's patient: he not only *doesn't* put away childish things; in some ways, he will *return* to them and in a quasi-like state of childhood. If the middle-aged man with HD in some sense, is returning to his childhood at the very time he is entering what *should* be his golden years, we must evaluate his life through his prism of a *cracked* glass. This will prove both salty and sweet. Thus far, I have shed light on what was happening to my dad in terms of his physical, intellectual, and emotional impairment, but I remind you that at that time, we had *no diagnosis*. No one considered having him checked for a disease that wasn't on our minds, lips, or radar. Why, Huntington was the name of the town my mom was from, *not* the disease my dad had! For the most part, he was still lucid, compelling, and *himself*, even if he could get a little too hot under the collar at times or make one of his quirky movements here and there.

During the mid-80s through the late '90s, we excused his random tics, extra irritability, preoccupations, and lack of self-awareness to the residual after-effect, bi-product, or scratchy consequences from the divorce, all shrouded and colored by his unique Greekness and banged-up baggage from his youth. We weren't looking for "signs and symptoms." In this chapter, we have cogitated on one troubling feature after another, each compounding with interest over the years. In Volume 2, we will find and face the music, that is, the stark *diagnosis* of a disease he'd been born with. In *this* portion of our current chapter, I am going to describe a genial, dare I say, *positive* consequence of my dad's having HD. I can assure you you'll not find a category like this elsewhere! Do you recall my telling you earlier that my dad's wartime experiences as a boy in Greece brought about a psychological hibernation and a shut-down where conversations about his youth in Greece went? It would have taken little effort to recall and imagine horrific images he had shut in the vault of his memory, including deprivation of both food and father during these years.

It is my speculation that as HD is carving away at parts of the brain such that we begin to notice the Frankenstein-like movements, concurrently being pared away is the mantle of our sensibility and control over what we think *and* react to. I believe that for my father, all the hurt and pain as well as the love and familiarity he felt for his homeland, his beautiful and bitter Greece, came back with a vengeance, like a torrent with ever-increasing velocity and force or like a fire hydrant that had an air pocket blocked in its subterranean pipe causing the water to burst forth when released. Somewhere beyond words and wisdom, when he finally agreed to return to Greece in 1995 — the first time since he left in 1947— my father's spirit leapt for joy. He left a scared boy of eleven, not to return until nearly a half-century later when he was a scarred man of sixty, but he was ripe for revival.

Considering his past, I had doubts about whether my dad would follow through and purchase his airline ticket, so, to my surprise and wild delight, not only did he agree, but he proposed that my brother and I also come, and he bought *all* our plane tickets! My brother could only take a week off, so he joined us for the first half of this two-week sojourn. While it is not my intent to give a travelogue or diary account, there are things that happened that summer that were precious to me then and golden to me now because although my dad's HD invaded his genetic framework before he was born and was just now beginning to blight his mind and manner, it still left the *core* of who he was intact and unscathed. It was as if his HD was also scorching away the scars so he could return home. *It was time!*

I'll share a few salient memories by having us shadow my dad through my memory. First, he bought the rock-bottom cheapest airline tickets he could find, so I believe we went via Air Tunisia if I'm not mistaken. One of the funniest memories I have is that at the airline counter in the airport when they were checking in our luggage, the attendant asked us if we had *anything of value.* Lickety-split, my dad unzipped his duffle bag, whipped out a brand-new, unopened 10-pack of Fruit-of-the-Loom briefs, and exclaimed, *"I just bought these!"* The attendant looked at me incredulously and wordlessly asked, "How am I supposed to react to *this*?!?" At the time, I was as surprised as she, but I just stared at him while holding back suppressed laughter, not that he would have noticed or cared whether I had guffawed. When my brother arrived, we rented a car, and it was my brother who drove us around Athens to our relatives, then over to the beach house where my dad's oldest brother would *not* let us stay. However, we *did* stop there, and with encouragement from our dad, my brother and I scaled the low iron gate fence and then proceeded to reach over to a fruit tree just within its confines. That way, at least, we could feel like we'd touched the earth and property our grandfather had staked claim to and built his house and garden on. And that plucked apricot was so juicy and sweet!

After this, we made our way down through the easternmost finger of the Peloponnesus, stopping whenever the mood struck us or we felt like exploring a remote cove, and then we snaked our way over to his hometown and port of Gythio. My dad's Greek often got muddled, and he misunderstood directions; my brother's innate sense of direction proved far more reliable than my dad's recall of some locale. Once, while making our way down a street in Athens, we had stopped at a red light, and my brother looked over at me, grinned, and said, "Watch this." As we had anticipated, every red light offered my dad the opportunity to lower his window and ask some passersby for directions to where we were going. Looking back, it occurred to me that HD negatively impacted his ability to make a definitive decision and worsened his already poor sense of direction. By now, he'd probably asked half a dozen people; therefore, my brother decided to lock the back window, so when my dad pushed the magic button to lower it, nothing happened, and he couldn't figure out why it wouldn't work. Big success! He just kept mashing the button harder. Now, he would *have* to desist from taking his survey of directions. My brother and I burst out laughing as my dad, still confused, frothed and swore. While in Athens, we stayed in a spacious apartment my grandparents owned, and two of its four sides had those classic broad baloneys. We all would have been content to camp on its cool marble floors. At the time, my dad's self-awareness was intact enough such that when the weekly flea market came to a nearby street, he asked me *not* to stand near him because my likely scolding or scowling would have blown his haggling methods.

The main focus of our trip was to head down through the Corinthian Canal and make our way down the right-most "finger" to and then past Nafplio, down to Monemvasia, and over to settle in his hometown of Gythio. This was not just a road trip but an odyssey back home; we were with our own Odysseus. Instead of taking ten years to get home, it took my dad five decades, and in one week, we drove down the craggy coastline in our rental car as we made our beeline for this port. My dad was not interested in famous historical sites or ancient ruins. Oh, no. He resisted these sites — tourist traps — and called the ruins "*a pile of rocks.*" No, it was sea and sun and souvlaki, his family, and the feeling of freedom he would feast on while we were in Greece. My dad's soul was resuscitating, and it was like the part of him that had been at times mystifying to us at home now made total sense, as if we had found the puzzle's frame into which his piece fit. He was a fish in its own tank, a player back on his own turf, and the expression on his face was complete contentment, pure peace, and utter joy shining through; no words were necessary. His body, height, and complexion looked like everyone's here: that nose, those lips, those softly hairy arms, but, oh, *not* that gait.

At times, he could be extravagant and would spend money on a meal like a king at a banquet; at others, he was back to being a clever boy, and he'd go from one restaurant to the next to ferret out which had the rock-bottom, lowest price and most gregarious chef inside, happy and willing to talk to him. A few times, his quest took us past the point of famished to fuming. We finally arrived and got settled in our hotel rooms. Ah, they were those old-fashioned, lofty, and airy ones but with the now-familiar, small, hard beds as if for the eighth dwarf. Invariably, we dropped our luggage and, like Greek lemmings, made our way to sit out on our respective balconies, side by side. We gazed out onto the harbor and boardwalk like we'd lived there like natives, just choosing to check out *this* angle. My brother and I glanced over at our father, who was taking in the sea with his eyes as he wriggled and snapped his happy toes resting on the balcony's railing. Earlier that day, he showed my brother and me the section of town and the very street he'd lived on as a boy. Why, that used to be where their house was, he'd point out to us. And here's where he'd get bread that was still warm in the mornings. There was some scaffolding on the façade of this building, and an old pickup truck was parked in front of it; in its bed were barrels of feta cheese. The vendor was standing by his truck, and since my dad had asked, the man gladly obliged and cut us a thick slice of the soft sheep's milk cheese, still tangy from dwelling in that salty brine. It was like no feta I'd ever tasted, and I looked over at my dad, still munching in quiet ecstasy, and was already holding out his hand for another piece.

The next day, Dad wanted to take us up to the village in the mountains where they had hidden during the worst of the war, but honestly, with his poor sense of direction, we weren't so sure we could find it. My dad was positive he could, and he was right. As we drove up, up, and up, and around, around, and *more* around, we finally arrived in the sleepy little square of Agios Nicholas and parked our car. We didn't see a soul, but our dad opened his car door and started to make a beeline towards a house on a hillside with a distant tower in the near background; he made his way through a narrow alleyway as if he were in an open-eyed, somnambulatory state. Oh, but this time, he knew *exactly* where he was going, and my brother and I were tagging along, following him as if we

301

were following a man in a memory-induced trance heading straight for Atlantis *found*. He walked up the external flight of steps of a two-story building and knocked at the door. Finally, after a few minutes, an elderly man with disheveled hair wearing a rumpled pair of shorts and an ill-fitting guinea tee creaked open the door. My brother and I realized we'd arrived at Greek siesta or Nap Time — a serious affair!

The look of recognition spread over his face like a glorious sunrise! He nearly jumped for joy and bound to take my father up in his arms as if my dad was still the little boy who had left. He indicated for my dad down in the kitchen with us, his children flanking him. He quickly dialed someone on the phone and then sat in front of my dad while both men drank in each other with their whole beings. Within three shakes of a lamb's tail, a neighbor by a relative by a friend came up those stairs and into the house to witness this modern-day miracle. My dad always did say the story of Lazarus was his favorite story in the Bible, and now my dad was he! The old man's wife had put fresh grapes and other Greek delectables on the table. Before you knew it, the room was aswirl with a crowd of Greeks my brother and I had never seen before, all animated, gesticulating, and loudly speaking, not a word did we understand. Our dad was smack dab in the middle, nearly reeling from radiant wonder. So many questions were flying at him that it became apparent to us he was overwhelmed with emotion and could not understand all that was being asked of him concurrently. No one minded or cared because *their boy had come home*; he was safe, and it was good. There were more adventures and mishaps on this particular trip, but it was the one that broke the ice and got the ball rolling that enabled him to come back to Greece five more times, each visit for a longer block of time. For me, it is one of the sweetest, most sacred times my brother and I got to spend with our father because *we got to go home with him* and understand that a part of his nature that had been a mystery to us before Nature itself would take him away from us.

Why do I mention this? I believe that my father's spirit resurrected itself unto itself *and* relinquished itself from that scary time and place — *not* despite his disease but even in part *because* of it! Had it *not* chipped away at the stone such that he would become more willing to risk and unthinkingly open Pandora's box of dark memories, he might have likely kept that cold case closed. HD shaved away just enough of some cranial portion such that there no longer existed the reason or excuse that prevented his coming back. It was time to go home! I believe that Freud had it right when he said it is the *id* that houses our most primal impulses and primitive desires that pulse the strongest within us. Even though our *ego* — the Greek word for the first-person singular pronoun, "I" — makes the call as to whether or not to indulge in the *id*'s demands or to bow to conventions, norms, and social mores, our *super-ego* esteems and judges the choice.

For a person like my dad with HD, when the more recently-acquired outer "layer" housing the rules and regulations of "civilized society," which acts as a restraint, gets scotched by HD's damaging touch, the primal id rushes forth unimpeded, and at full throttle to get *its* demands met. Self over other, beast over man, Hades *and* high water. Beyond volition, thought, or intent, *my dad let go of his past* and became enabled to pursue his heart's desire: a return *to* home. Whatever reasons he clung to for *not* going simply vanished or didn't matter. He got a healing to boot. I'm grateful to have been the catalyst for his decision to go and that my brother and I shared this with him. This trip also broke the ice and set a new direction because he and his next brother began to communicate regularly about family history and relations, past and present. Though not the eloquent writer his brother was, my dad's exclamation points abound, caps were kept on, and vigorous bouts of analysis as to what went awry with their mother and oldest brother which kept them connected by an invisible umbilical cord of their shared and painful past.

Although his brother did the lion's share of writing, it was clear to me that they had a love-hate relationship: my dad's return to Greece garnered him respect from his brother, but his lack of restraint and janky judgment came out in words that bit. As I mentioned, this would *not* be my dad's last trip to Greece. Two years later, in the fall of 1997, he and my brother went, and they expanded their journey to include several Greek Islands, including Spetses, Hydra, Santorini, and Crete, my dad's favorite. Since you have only my testimony, I cannot speak to my brother's experience with my dad, but suffice it to say it became a sweet and unforgettable time for him, too, and his memories are as crystal clear as if they happened yesterday. My dad returned the following year by himself, the summer of his retirement in 1998, but this time, he would join his parents and oldest brother. He relaxed in their beach house and accompanied them on daily jaunts to their favorite coffee shops and restaurants, but being ever more curious and adventuresome, my dad expanded his outreach, rented a car, and headed for new places (to him) like Volos, its beach he would describe to me as if he were still there, entranced and enthralled, cooing that it was "*soooooo quiet!*" Of course, he would join his parents at Kamena Vourla, what with its hot mineral baths; after all, *his* father swore its curative effects on arthritis.

Later, in ignorance and denial, my dad would return here himself in hopes that these radioactive waters would remedy the pain he felt in those unsteady joints of his. Meanwhile, during this visit in '98, like some Homeric homing pigeon, Dad headed back to his southern roots in the Peloponnesus. Do I know whether or not my dad would have returned to Greece anyway, that is, had he *not* HD? No, I do not, but I *am* suggesting that my dad benefitted from the loss in this singular respect with its soft erasure of certain cognitive strongholds like reason and logic. It led to a gain. There was no viable excuse *not* to go back to Greece anymore. Literally. The end result was a lifting of his spirits and a resuscitation of his core — his very *identity* — that had gotten disjointed when he *had* to leave and then fermented over the years.

We have reached the turning point of Volume 1 of *A Labor of Love*. When you figuratively turn the page, it will be like going from the Old Testament to the New. However, there will be no resurrection; instead, there will be a great reversal when the child becomes the parent. I am that child. A great deal of effort had gone into building the man who would soon have his life snatched from him — seemingly before his time — by a disease that was like a ticking time bomb and one he had been born with. Up to now, I have used the platform of Hercules's story to animate my father's unknown and anonymous life; after all, who hasn't heard of the most renowned hero of all Greek mythology? You've gotten more than you bargained for because now you are equipped with an arsenal of background information on Huntington's disease. You know its clinical features, genetic background, and the tragic impact on key players in the brain. My deepest longing is that by investing your time and interest in this part of our journey, *you have come to love my father and appreciate his complicated, tangled past, which haunted him like a ghost.*

In the next volume, I am going to have us switch seats and drivers and stories: it is time for us to embark on Hercules' famous labors, only now it will be I, his eldest, doing the appointed herculean labors for my "patera," my HD-damaged dad. You'll get more than either of us could have imagined, so when you take up and start reading Volume 2, know that *it is my heart's desire to help you, too, should you find yourself the caretaker of your aging or infirm parent* as he "struts and frets his [last] hour upon the stage."[525] My father's story is no tale of or told by a fool. Macbeth had it all wrong! And although my father could be full of sound and fury, strutting and fretting about during his final hours, _his life bore great significance_. I pray that in the days of their final frontier, when your parents need honoring most, you will help them off life's stage. Won't you join me now as we continue? *Let's go!*

Afterword: A Segue to
A Labor of Love, Volume 2: Caring for Hercules

As we enter my dad's life in **Volume 2**, the disease's impact on him will have become manifest and evident. <u>Each chapter will be devoted to a singular mythical Herculean labor to which I will connect my herculean caretaking role for my father</u>. You have already learned a *ton* in Volume 1 and have truly gotten to know my dad. We have spanned the disease from the macrocosmic level down to the cellular level regarding my father's nature *and* nurture. That said, as fascinating as my father's foundational background has been, next, <u>my primary focus will be on the intense stint when I became his caretaker during those final unlucky seven or so years of his life</u>. Building up to these labors has been my way of nurturing *your* investment in his story. *Hopefully, you, too, have come to love my father.* Without a doubt, you now understand what HD is! The book is now ready to take its turn when my father's life bobbed upside down, so I trust you are now all-in in this one-of-a-kind tale that is no myth.

The fork in the road at which Huntington's disease begins adversely impacting my father's life takes us to <u>Volume 2</u> of this book. Here, I will home the final decade of his life — and in particular, *the final three years*. I will be performing the herculean labors for my father — <u>my</u> Hercules — when his overall health began precipitously declining. **In short, my father and I swap out and exchange parts in this tragic but heroic story, except that I am no hero, just a daughter who said "Yes" to serving when he needed it most.** Thus, <u>I will perform the herculean labors for *him*</u>, but this is no play. Volume 2 recounts all the twelve familiar labors; each chapter will start with an abbreviated account of a singular herculean labor that you'll come to see resembles a portion of my caretaking responsibilities. In Volume 1, my dad is Hercules; <u>he's never not *my* Hercules</u>. In Volume 2, I switch the role of Hercules as well as the *nominal* part of speech: Here, I'll apply the *adjective* associated with this famous Greek hero to capture the relatively brief, albeit incredibly intense, and thus **herculean** stint of tending to my father when he was in the throes of Huntington's disease.

You may well ask why I bring Hercules into the next volume of our story. What does Hercules have to do with my *father*? With *me*? <u>I want you to see my dad's life as triumphant, not tragic</u>, so I decided to tell his story with a unique spin. There will be "labors" involved, but there's *so* much more. *Everyone* has heard of Hercules; *no* one knows my father, so I chose this ancient Greek hero to tell you my father's tale. <u>The myth serves as the</u>

<u>platform for telling my dad's tale</u>. We have already made parallels between Hercules' upbringing and roots and my father's background. As we now proceed, I will deconstruct the myth of Hercules as I move my dad's plot forward. Thus, I have saved the subsequent punishment the demigod took on for Volume 2.

A deeper motive comes from my seeking to remind you that <u>all</u> of us will have to deal with the dying and death of our parent or parents; it is just a matter of time. Should it be that they do need care, each of us will be impacted, be it directly or indirectly, depending upon our level of involvement and the nature of our relationship should it be another person. Therefore, I'm going to invert what you *may* have thought God's fifth commandment meant and look at it from the rear-view mirror: let's see how we can honor our mother and father at their life's end *now*! My experience as a caretaker and as a daughter who adored her father will serve as a bridge to share a sympathetic bond with *you*, should you be in this position someday, if you aren't already. I aim for this revelation to become a guide, inspiration, and beacon. My father's life story is merely the vehicle. Ultimately, as a follower of Jesus Christ, I aim to steer you to the greatest strength and source of love you can *ever* hope to know; in fact, He will accompany us along our way. My tale of woe and wonder is not for the fainthearted, squeamish, or disinterested! You and I have already established a bond and traveled *decades* here together, so now, *let's continue*! I believe you have the grit and grace to peer into this story from a woman who loved her father unto death. As the twenty-third psalm tells us, you'll find that *goodness and mercy will surely follow.*

My father with his running buddies from work.
He would run several marathons over the course of three years.

My father at Gerolimano in the Peloponnesus part of Greece in 1995.
This was his first time back to Greece since having left as a boy.

My brother, father, and I standing outside St.Fotoni
Church in Oropos, Greece, also in 1995.

My father's official retirement picture in 1998.

Endnotes

1   "How Many People Have Huntington Disease?" *HD Insights*, huntingtonstudygroup.org/hd-insights/how-many-people-have-huntington-disease/. Accessed 09 Apr. 2024.

2   NHS Choices, NHS, www.nhs.uk/conditions/huntingtons-disease/. Accessed 08 Apr. 2024.

3   Nervous, nervous-system.emedtv.com/huntington%27s-disease/huntington%27s-disease-statistics.html. Accessed 09 Apr. 2024.

4   "Chorea." *Wikipedia*, Wikimedia Foundation, 19 Feb. 2024, en.wikipedia.org/wiki/Chorea. Accessed 09 Apr. 2024.

5   Thomas Bird, *Can You Help Me?: Inside the Turbulent World of Huntington Disease*. Oxford University Press, 2019. 11.

6   Robert Graves. *The Greek Myths*. Penguin Books Ltd., 2011, 445.

7   Robert Graves. *The Greek Myths*. Penguin Books Ltd., 2011, 446.

8   "George I of Greece." *Wikipedia*, Wikimedia Foundation, 21 Feb. 2024, en.wikipedia.org/wiki/George_I_of_Greece. Accessed 09 Apr. 2024.

9   "Eleftherios Venizelos." *Wikipedia*, Wikimedia Foundation, 23 Mar. 2024, en.wikipedia.org/wiki/Eleftherios_Venizelos. Accessed 09 Apr. 2024.

10 "Eleftherios Venizelos Car Exhibition in His House in CHALEPA, Chania." *Crete Gazette*, 20 Oct. 2014, www.cretegazette.com/2009-10/eleftherios-venizelos-car.php. Accessed 09 Apr. 2024.

11 Greek Royal Family." *Wikipedia*, Wikimedia Foundation, 22 Mar. 2024, en.wikipedia.org/wiki/Greek_royal_family#History. Accessed 09 Apr. 2024.

12 Kennedy Hickman. "World War II: Battle of Greece." *ThoughtCo*, 16 Apr. 2018, www.thoughtco.com/world-war-ii-battle-of-greece-2361485. Accessed 09 Apr. 2024.

13 *Metaxas Project*, 23 June 2020, metaxas-project.com/book-burnings-under-metaxas-rule/. Accessed 09 Apr. 2024.

14 *Strong's Greek: 1085. Γένος (Genos) -- Family, Offspring*, biblehub.com/greek/1085.htm. Accessed 09 Apr. 2024.

15 *Chronic Pain and Chronic Stress: Two Sides of the Same Coin? - Chadi G Abdallah, Paul Geha*, 2017, journals.sagepub.com/doi/full/10.1177/2470547017704763. Accessed 09 Apr. 2024.

16 Chadi G. Abdallah and Paul Geha, "Chronic Pain and Chronic Stress: Two Sides of the Same Coin?" *Chronic Stress* (Thousand Oaks, Calif.), *U.S. National Library of Medicine*, Feb. 2017, www.ncbi.nlm.nih.gov/pmc/articles/PMC5546756/. Accessed 09 Apr. 2024.

17 Stephanie Liou and Stephanie Liou. "Glucocorticoids." *HOPES Huntington's Disease*, 11 Oct. 2015, hopes.stanford.edu/glucocorticoids/. Accessed 09 Apr. 2024.

18 Ibid.

19 Ewen Callaway and *Nature* magazine. "Older Fathers Pass on More Mutations to Children." *Scientific American*, 20 Feb. 2024, www.scientificamerican.com/article/older-fathers-pass-on-mor/. Accessed 09 Apr. 2024.

20 "Huntington Disease - Causes, Symptoms, Diagnosis, Treatment & Pathology." *YouTube*, 7 May 2019, youtu.be/nJoS5MOqmH4. Accessed 09 Apr. 2024.

21 Harri Daniel. "Benefits of Mutations." 3 Dec. 2011, benefitof.net/benefits-of-mutations/. Accessed 09 Apr. 2024.

22 "Medlineplus: Genetics." *U.S. National Library of Medicine*, National Institutes of Health, ghr.nlm.nih.gov/primer/mutationsanddisorders/genemutation. Accessed 09 Apr. 2024.

23 FamilyEducation Editorial Staff, et al. "The Role of Genes and Inheritance from Mother and Father to Baby." *FamilyEducation*, 24 June 2010, www.familyeducation.com/pregnancy/genetics-pregnancy/role-genes-inheritance. Accessed 09 Apr. 2024.

24 Marta Figueiredo, PhD. "Huntington's Alters Brain Development in Fetal Stages, Study Shows." *Huntington's Disease News*, 1 Sept. 2020, huntingtonsdiseasenews.com/2020/09/01/huntingtons-alters-brain-development-before-birth-study-shows/. Accessed 09 Apr. 2024.

25   "Stem Cell Program." *Stem Cell Program Research | Boston Children's Hospital,* stemcell. childrenshospital.org/about-stem-cells/adult-somatic-stem-cells-101/what-are-progenitor-cells/. Accessed 09 Apr. 2024.

26   Marta Figueiredo, PhD.

27   "One Species, Living Worldwide." *The Smithsonian Institution's Human Origins Program,* 3 Jan. 2024, humanorigins.si.edu/evidence/genetics/one-species-living-worldwide#:~:text=We%20are%2C%20in%20fact%2C%20remarkably%20similar.%20The%20DNA,years%20to%20the%20evolutionof%20the%C2%A0earliest%C2%A0human%20species%20in%20Africa. Accessed 09 Apr. 2024.

28   "Colossus of Rhodes." *Wikipedia,* Wikimedia Foundation, 2 Apr. 2024, en.wikipedia.org/wiki/Colossus_of_Rhodes. Accessed 09 Apr. 2024.

29   Ibid.

30   "Statue of Liberty - Height, Location & Timeline." *History.Com,* A&E Television Networks, www.history.com/topics/landmarks/statue-of-liberty. Accessed 09 Apr. 2024.

31   Joshua J. Mark, "The Life of Hercules in Myth & Legend." *Ancient History Encyclopedia,* 21 Feb. 2023, www.ancient.eu/article/733/the-life-of-hercules-in-myth--legend/. Accessed 09 Apr. 2024.

32   Robert Graves, *The Greek Myths.* Penguin, 2012, 450.

33   Edith Hamilton, *Mythology.* Little, Brown and Company, 2013, 228.

34   Joshua J. Mark, "The Life of Hercules in Myth & Legend." *Ancient History Encyclopedia,* 21 Feb. 2023, www.ancient.eu/article/733/the-life-of-hercules-in-myth--legend/. Accessed 09 Apr. 2024.

35   Richard G. Buxton, *The Complete World of Greek Mythology.* Thames & Hudson, 2004, 114.

36   Robert Graves, *The Greek Myths.* Penguin, 2012, 452.

37   "Birth & Childhood of Herakles." *The Birth and Childhood of Herakles,* www.greecetravel.com/greekmyths/argos6.htm. Accessed 09 Apr. 2024.

38   Richard G. Buxton, *The Complete World of Greek Mythology.* Thames & Hudson, 2004, 115.

39   *Winston Churchill - Russia Is a Riddle Wrapped in a...,* www.brainyquote.com/quotes/winston_churchill_156896. Accessed 09 Apr. 2024.

40   Edith Hamilton. *Mythology.* Little, Brown and Company, 2013, 226.

41   Madeleine. "Who Trained Hercules." *THEOI GREEK MYTHOLOGY - Exploring Mythology in Classical Literature & Art,* 17 Sept. 2019, www.theoi.com/articles/who-trained-hercules/. Accessed 09 Apr. 2024.

42   C. M. Woodhouse, *Modern Greece: A Short History.* Faber, 1998, 227-228.

43   Costas Stassinopoulos, *Modern Greeks Greece in World War II, the German Occupation and National Resistance, the Civil War.* American Hellenic Inst. Foundation, 1997, 81.

44   C. M. Woodhouse, *Modern Greece: A Short History.* Faber, 1998, 230.

45   *The Greek Labour Movement and Greek Politics,* www.ocnus.net/artman2/publish/Editorial_10/The%20Greek%20Labour%20Movement%20And%20Greek%20Politics_printer.shtml. Accessed 09 Apr. 2024.

46   Saul Mcleod, "Freud's Stages of Human Development: 5 Psychosexual Stages." *Simply Psychology,* 16 Jan. 2024, www.simplypsychology.org/psychosexual.html. Accessed 09 Apr. 2024.

47   "Ioannis Metaxas." *Wikipedia,* Wikimedia Foundation, 15 Mar. 2024, en.wikipedia.org/wiki/Ioannis_Metaxas. Accessed 09 Apr. 2024.

48   "George II of Greece." Wikipedia, Wikimedia Foundation, 4 Apr. 2024, en.wikipedia.org/wiki/George_II_of_Greece. Accessed 09 Apr. 2024.

49   Harry Cliadakis, "The Political and Diplomatic Background to the Metaxas Dictatorship, 1935-36." Journal of Contemporary History, vol. 14, no. 1, Jan. 1979, pp. 117–138, doi:10.1177/002200947901400106.

50   "George II of Greece."

51 Harry Cliadakis, "The Political and Diplomatic Background to the Metaxas Dictatorship, 1935-36." *Journal of Contemporary History*, vol. 14, no. 1, Jan. 1979, pp. 117–138, doi:10.1177/002200947901400106.

52 "Ioannis Metaxas." *Wikipedia*, Wikimedia Foundation, 15 Mar. 2024, en.wikipedia.org/wiki/Ioannis_Metaxas. Accessed 09 Apr. 2024.

53 C. M. Woodhouse, *Modern Greece: A Short History.* Faber, 1998, 233.

54 Thomas W. Gallant, *Modern Greece: From the War of Independence to the Present.* Bloomsbury Academic, 2016, 218.

55 Woodhouse, 232.

56 C. M. Woodhouse, Modern Greece: A Short History. Faber, 1998, 236.

57 Thomas W. Gallant, Modern Greece: From the War of Independence to the Present. Bloomsbury Academic, 2016, 221.

58 Tiara Dennis, "February Symbolism: Focusing on New Life." Sun Signs, 28 Sept. 2023, www.sunsigns.org/february-meaning-symbolism/. Accessed 09 Apr. 2024.

59 "Map of Greece 1941 Invasion from Italy." Yahoo! Images.search.yahoo.com. Accessed 09 Apr. 2024.

60 "The Balkans 1941: Invasion of Yugoslavia and Greece, April 1941." Yahoo! Images.search.yahoo.com/. Accessed 09 Apr. 2024.

61 "Axis Occupation of Greece." Wikipedia, Wikimedia Foundation, 2 Apr. 2024, en.wikipedia.org/wiki/Axis_occupation_of_Greece. Accessed 09 Apr. 2024.

62 Thomas W. Gallant, Modern Greece: From the War of Independence to the Present. Bloomsbury Academic, 2016, 227.

63 Philip Chrysopoulos, "Kalavryta: The Bloodiest Nazi Massacre in Greece." *GreekReporter.com*, 13 Dec. 2023, greece.greekreporter.com/2019/12/13/kalavryta-the-bloodiest-nazi-massacre-in-greece/. Accessed 09 Apr. 2024.

64 "World War II." *Wikipedia*, Wikimedia Foundation, 6 Apr. 2024, en.wikipedia.org/wiki/World_War_II. Accessed 09 Apr. 2024.

65 Stathis N. Kalyvas, *Modern Greece: What Everyone Needs to Know.* Oxford University Press, 2015, 84.

66 "Battle of Greece." *Wikipedia*, Wikimedia Foundation, 17 Sept. 2021, en.wikipedia.org/wiki/Battle_of_Greece. Accessed 09 Apr. 2024.

67 Costas Stassinopoulos, *Modern Greeks Greece in World War II, the German Occupation and National Resistance, the Civil War.* American Hellenic Inst. Foundation, 1997, 85.

68 "Alexandros Koryzis." *Wikipedia*, Wikimedia Foundation, 4 Mar. 2024, en.wikipedia.org/wiki/Alexandros_Koryzis. Accessed 09 Apr. 2024.

69 "German-Occupied Europe." *Wikipedia*, Wikimedia Foundation, 31 Mar. 2024, en.wikipedia.org/wiki/German-occupied_Europe#Occupied_countries. Accessed 09 Apr. 2024.

70 "Holocaust in Thessaloniki: The Tragedy of Greek Jews." *Maksym Chorny's Personal Blog on WWII, WAR-DOCUMENTARY.INFO*, 18 Dec. 2023, war-documentary.info/holocaust-in-salonica/. Accessed 09 Apr. 2024.

71 United States Holocaust Memorial Museum, *newspapers.ushmm.org/events/german-law-authorizes-sterilization-for-prevention-of-hereditary-diseases*. Accessed 09 Apr. 2024.

72 United States Holocaust Memorial Museum.

73 "German Troops Raising the Swastika over the Acropolis, 1941." *Rare Historical Photos*, 21 Nov. 2021, rarehistoricalphotos.com/nazi-raising-swastika-acropolis-1941/. Accessed 09 Apr. 2024.

74 Thomas W. Gallant, *Modern Greece: From the War of Independence to the Present.* Bloomsbury Academic, 2016, 224.

75 "Holocaust in Thessaloniki: The Tragedy of Greek Jews."

76 Gallant, 227.

77 "WWII German Reparations to Greece." *WW-II German Reparations*, 1 Oct. 2011, www.greece.org/blogs/wwii/?page_id=220. Accessed 09 Apr. 2024.

311

78   Leni Riefenstahl, *Leni Riefenstahl: A Memoir*. Picador, 1987, *295*.

79   "WWII German Reparations to Greece."

80   Skatharaki, et al. "By Whom and When Was Said the Quote, 'Hence You Will Not Say That Greeks Fight like Heroes but That Heroes Fight like Greeks'?" 13 Sept. 2016, www.funtrivia.com/askft/Question115404.html. Accessed 10 Apr. 2024.

81   "WWII German Reparations to Greece."

82   "Greek Civil War." *Wikipedia*, Wikimedia Foundation, 6 Apr. 2024, en.wikipedia.org/wiki/Greek_Civil_War. Accessed 10 Apr. 2024.

83   "The Greek Civil War, 1944-1949: The National WWII Museum: New Orleans." *The National WWII Museum* | New Orleans, www.nationalww2museum.org/war/articles/greek-civil-war-1944-1949. Accessed 10 Apr. 2024.

84   Thomas W. Gallant, *Modern Greece: From the War of Independence to the Present*. Bloomsbury Academic, 2016, 243.

85   "Percentages Agreement." *Wikipedia*, Wikimedia Foundation, 1 Apr. 2024, en.wikipedia.org/wiki/Percentages_agreement. Accessed 10 Apr. 2024.

86   The Greek Civil War, 1944-1949: The National WWII Museum: New Orleans." *The National WWII Museum* | New Orleans, www.nationalww2museum.org/war/articles/greek-civil-war-1944-1949. Accessed 10 Apr. 2024.

87   Stassinopoulos, 215.

88   "The Greek Civil War, 1944-1949:..."

89   Ibid.

90   Ibid.

91   "Greece and the Marshall Plan - the George C. Marshall Foundation." The George C. Marshall Foundation - Explore the Life and Achievements of George C. Marshall - a True American Hero. *Discover Our Research Library, Digital Resources, and Educational Programs*, 31 July 2015, www.marshallfoundation.org/blog/greece-and-the-marshall-plan/. Accessed 10 Apr. 2024.

92   Vetsopoulos, A. "The Economic Dimensions of the Marshall Plan in Greece, 1947-1952." *UCL Discovery - UCL Discovery*, University of London, 1 Jan. 1970, discovery.ucl.ac.uk/id/eprint/1317677/. Accessed 10 Apr. 2024.

93   C. M. Woodhouse, *Modern Greece: A Short History*. Faber, 1998, 255.

94   "Great Famine (Greece)." *Wikipedia*, Wikimedia Foundation, 4 Apr. 2024, en.wikipedia.org/wiki/Great_Famine_(Greece)#:~:text=The%20nutritional%20situation%20became%20critical%20in%20the%20summer,reached%20a%20climax%20and%20a%20famine%20was%20unavoidable. Accessed 10 Apr. 2024.

95   Ibid

96   Thomas W. Gallant, *Modern Greece: From the War of Independence to the Present*. Bloomsbury Academic, 2016, 228.

97   Gallant, p. 231.

98   "Great Famine (Greece)." *Wikipedia*, Wikimedia Foundation, 4 Apr. 2024, en.wikipedia.org/wiki/Great_Famine_(Greece)#:~:text=The%20nutritional%20situation%20became%20critical%20in%20the%20summer,reached%20a%20climax%20and%20a%20famine%20was%20unavoidable. Accessed 10 Apr. 2024.

99   Ibid.

100   "Kalimavkion." *Wikipedia*, Wikimedia Foundation, 7 Jan. 2024, en.wikipedia.org/wiki/Kalimavkion. Accessed 10 Apr. 2024.

101   "Course Hero." *Introduction to Psychology* || *Course Hero*, courses.lumenlearning.com/wsu-sandbox/chapter/freud-and-the-psychodynamic-perspective/. Accessed 10 Apr. 2024.

102   "Post-Traumatic Stress Disorder." *Wikipedia*, Wikimedia Foundation, 2 Apr. 2024, en.wikipedia.org/wiki/Post-traumatic_stress_disorder. Accessed 10 Apr. 2024.

103   Plants & Flowers of Greek Myth 1, *www.theoi.com/Flora1.html*. Accessed 10 Apr. 2024.

104   Hagen, Linda. "Prickly Pear: How to Grow and Care for Opuntia Cactus - Garden Design." *GardenDesign.Com, Garden Design Magazine*, 20 Oct. 2023, www.gardendesign.com/succulents/prickly-pear.html. Accessed 10 Apr. 2024.

105   Henein, Maryam. "6 Things You Didn't Know about Bees in Greece." *HoneyColony*, 8 Feb. 2020, www.honeycolony.com/article/6-things-you-didnt-know-about-bees-in-greece/. Accessed 10 Apr. 2024.

106   "The Greek Civil War, 1944-1949: *The National WWII Museum*: New Orleans." The National WWII Museum | New Orleans, www.nationalww2museum.org/war/articles/greek-civil-war-1944-1949#:~:text=In%20Athens%2C%20Greece%2C%20the%20bloody%20events%20of%20Sunday%2C,in%20a%20city%20rife%20with%20suffering%20and%20discontent. Accessed 10 Apr. 2024.

107   "Greek Civil War." *Encyclopædia Britannica*, Encyclopædia Britannica, Inc., www.britannica.com/event/Greek-Civil-War. Accessed 10 Apr. 2024.

108   "Greek Americans." *Wikipedia*, Wikimedia Foundation, 10 Apr. 2024, en.wikipedia.org/wiki/Greek_Americans#:~:text=Greeks%20again%20began%20to%20arrive%20in%20large%20numbers,approximately%20211%2C000%20Greeks%20emigrated%20to%20the%20United%20States. Accessed 10 Apr. 2024.

109   "Greek Civil War." *Encyclopædia Britannica*, Encyclopædia Britannica, Inc., www.britannica.com/event/Greek-Civil-War. Accessed 10 Apr. 2024.

110   Charalambos Kasimis, Chryssa Kassimi. "Greece: A History of Migration." *Migrationpolicy.Org*, 2 Mar. 2017, www.migrationpolicy.org/article/greece-history-migration/. Accessed 10 Apr. 2024.

111   Charalambos Kasimis, "Greece: Illegal Immigration in the Midst of Crisis." *Migrationpolicy.Org*, 27 Aug. 2021, www.migrationpolicy.org/article/greece-illegal-immigration-midst-crisis/#:~:text=More%20than%201%20million%20Greeks%20migrated%20in%20this,1967-1974%20period%20of%20military%20junta%20rule%20that%20followed. Accessed 10 Apr. 2024.

112   *Gripsholm*, www.salship.se/grip2.php#:~:text=The%20Gripsholm%20made%20the%20first%20cruise%20in%20Swedish,of%20321%2C213%20transatlantic%20passengers%20and%2023%2C551%20cruise%20pasengers. Accessed 10 Apr. 2024.

113   *Gripsholm*, www.salship.se/grip2.php. Accessed 10 Apr. 2024.

114   "The Gripsholm WWII Exchanges." *The Gripsholm WWII Exchanges | Densho Encyclopedia*, encyclopedia.densho.org/The%20Gripsholm%20WWII%20Exchanges/. Accessed 10 Apr. 2024.

115   "The Gripsholm WWII Exchanges." *The Gripsholm WWII Exchanges | Densho Encyclopedia*, encyclopedia.densho.org/The%20Gripsholm%20WWII%20Exchanges/#:~:text=Built%20in%201925%2C%20the%20M.S.%20Gripsholm%20was%20the,S.S.%20Drottningholm%20%2C%20to%20use%20as%20repatriation%20vessels. Accessed 10 Apr. 2024.

116   Ibid.

117   "Why Are the Tummies of Malnourished Children Bloated?" *Science ABC*, 19 Oct. 2023, www.scienceabc.com/eyeopeners/tummies-malnourished-children-bloated.html. Accessed 10 Apr. 2024.

118   "Why Are the Tummies of Malnourished Children Bloated?"

119   Archives, Gjenvick-Gjønvik Archives - GG. "New York (Ellis Island) Passenger Lists 1930-1939." *New York (Ellis Island) Passenger Lists 1930-1939 | GG Archives*, www.gjenvick.com/Passengers/Ports/NewYork-PassengerLists09.html. Accessed 10 Apr. 2024.

120   "Laconia." *Wikipedia*, Wikimedia Foundation, 23 Mar. 2024, en.wikipedia.org/wiki/Laconia#Ancient_history. Accessed 10 Apr. 2024.

121   "The Mani Page 1." *Peloponnese Guide: The Mani in Laconia Prefecture P1*, greeceathensaegeaninfo.com/p_laconia_mani.htm. Accessed 10 Apr. 2024.

122 Archives, Gjenvick-Gjønvik Archives - GG. "SS Gripsholm Passenger List - 18 June 1946." *SS Gripsholm Passenger List - 18 June 1946 | GG Archives*, www.gjenvick.com/Passengers/ SwedishAmericanLine/Gripsholm-PassengerList-1946-06-18.html. Accessed 10 Apr. 2024.

123 *SS Gripsholm Passenger List - 18 June 1946 | GG Archives*

124 "Religion in Greece & the Islands: Greeka." *Greekacom*, +greekacom, www.greeka.com/ greece-culture/religion/. Accessed 10 Apr. 2024.

125 "Live Services." *Annunciation Greek Orthodox Church*, www.goann.net/. Accessed 10 Apr. 2024.

126 Sterlin, Svetlana. "Lost in Translation: 11 Best Quotes." *Our Culture*, 21 Oct. 2020, ourculturemag.com/2020/10/21/lost-in-translation-11-best-quotes/. Accessed 10 Apr. 2024.

127 M, Emelda. "Difference between Citizenship and Naturalization." *Difference Between*, 6 Feb. 2011, www.differencebetween.net/miscellaneous/politics/difference-between-citizenship-and-naturalization/. Accessed 10 Apr. 2024.

128 "Eudora Welty, a Worn Path.Pdf." *Google Drive*, Google, docs.google.com/file/ d/0Byq6h70zkproWGFLc3BwOUFvMUk/edit. Accessed 10 Apr. 2024.

129 *The Social Psychology of Immigration: The Greek American Experience*, www. alexandermakedon.com/articles/GreekAmerican.html. Accessed 10 Apr. 2024.

130 *Tomorrow-Lyrics.Pdf*, www.hmdt.org.uk/hmdtmusic/satprogonline/wp-content/uploads/ sites/14/2020/06/Tomorrow-Lyrics.pdf. Accessed 10 Apr. 2024.

131 *The Social Psychology of Immigration: The Greek American Experience*, www. alexandermakedon.com/articles/GreekAmerican.html#(8). Accessed 10 Apr. 2024.

132 *The Social Psychology of Immigration: The Greek American Experience.*

133 "The Great Gatsby: Chapter 8 -- 'the Holocaust Was Complete.'" *Conrad at OEHS*, conradoehs. weebly.com/blog/the-great-gatsby-chapter-8-the-holocaust-was-complete. Accessed 10 Apr. 2024.

134 *The Social Psychology of Immigration: The Greek American Experience*, www. alexandermakedon.com/articles/GreekAmerican.html#(8). Accessed 10 Apr. 2024.

135 "The Nobel Prize in Chemistry 1954." *NobelPrize.Org*, www.nobelprize.org/prizes/ chemistry/1954/pauling/facts/. Accessed 10 Apr. 2024.

136 "Vitamin C and the Common Cold (Book)." *Wikipedia*, Wikimedia Foundation, 10 Jan. 2022, en.wikipedia.org/wiki/Vitamin_C_and_the_Common_Cold_(book). Accessed 10 Apr. 2024.

137 "Home." *Famous Scientists*, www.famousscientists.org/linus-pauling/. Accessed 10 Apr. 2024.

138 *Linus Pauling: Discovering Protein*, www.sas.upenn.edu/~upshaw/chemproject.pdf. Accessed 10 Apr. 2024.

139 "How Did It Happen That so Many Diners Have Greek Owners?" *Quora*, www.quora.com/ How-did-it-happen-that-so-many-diners-have-Greek-owners. Accessed 10 Apr. 2024.

140 "How Did It Happen That so Many Diners Have Greek Owners?" *Quora*, www.quora.com/ How-did-it-happen-that-so-many-diners-have-Greek-owners. Accessed 10 Apr. 2024.

141 Philip Chrysopoulos, "The Ancient Greek Ideals That Inspired American Independence." *GreekReporter.Com*, 25 Jan. 2021, greekreporter.com/2020/07/04/the-ancient-greek-ideals-of-democracy-that-inspired-american-independence/. Accessed 10 Apr. 2024.

142 Eliot, T. S. "The Love Song of j. Alfred Prufrock by T. S. Eliot." *Poetry Foundation*, www. poetryfoundation.org/poetrymagazine/poems/44212/the-love-song-of-j-alfred-prufrock. Accessed 10 Apr. 2024.

143 "Misty." *Ella Fitzgerald - Misty Lyrics | Lyrics.Com*, www.lyrics.com/lyric/1844677/ Ella+Fitzgerald/Misty. Accessed 10 Apr. 2024.

144 *Emily Dickinson the Complete Poems.Pdf*, edisciplinas.usp.br/pluginfile.php/3985124/mod_ resource/content/1/EMILY DICKINSON THE COMPLETE POEMS.pdf. Accessed 10 Apr. 2024.

145 "Our Wedding Ceremony." *Our Wedding Ceremony and Its Symbolism*, web.mit.edu/manoli/ www/wedding/ceremony.html. Accessed 10 Apr. 2024.

146   "Overview of Huntington's Disease - Huntington's Disease Society of America." *Huntington's Disease Society of America - Family Is Everything*, 6 Nov. 2020, hdsa.org/what-is-hd/overview-of-huntingtons-disease/#:~:text=In%20the%20huntingtin%20gene%2C%20most%20people%20have%20around,children%20has%20a%2050%25%20chance%20of-%20developing%20HD. Accessed 10 Apr. 2024.

147   "History of Huntington's Disease - Huntington's Disease Society of America." *Huntington's Disease Society of America - Family Is Everything*, 20 Mar. 2019, hdsa.org/what-is-hd/history-and-genetics-of-huntingtons-disease/history-of-huntingtons-disease/. Accessed 10 Apr. 2024.

148   "Huntington's Disease: Advocacy Driving Science." *Annual Review of Medicine*, U.S. National Library of Medicine, pubmed.ncbi.nlm.nih.gov/22248319/. Accessed 10 Apr. 2024.

149   Ridley, Matt. Genome: *The Autobiography of a Species in 23 Chapters*. New York, 1999, 58.

150   *Genetic Testing*, nya.hdsa.org/genetic-testing#:~:text=Genetic%20Testing%20In%201993%2C%20scientists%20discovered%20exactly%20where,to%20have%20what%20is%20called%20a%20%27predictive%20test%27. Accessed 10 Apr. 2024.

151   "Deoxyribonucleic Acid (DNA) Fact Sheet." *Genome.Gov*, www.genome.gov/about-genomics/fact-sheets/Deoxyribonucleic-Acid-Fact-Sheet#:~:text=What%20does%20DNA%20do%3F%20DNA%20contains%20the%20instructions,do%20most%20of%20the%20work%20in%20our%20bodies. Accessed 10 Apr. 2024.

152   Dhruv Khullar, "Faith, Science, and Francis Collins." *The New Yorker*, 7 Apr. 2022, www.newyorker.com/news/persons-of-interest/faith-science-and-francis-collins. Accessed 10 Apr. 2024.

153   "Where Are Genes Located?" *Reference*, IAC Publishing, www.reference.com/science/genes-located-cac7a3c405d18fbd. Accessed 10 Apr. 2024.

154   *Etymology of the Word Gene, Latin Genus, Ancient Greek Genea, Uralic, Indo-European, Turkish, Egyptian Ankh, Sumerian Language Comparisons*, sumerianturks.org/gene-latin-genus-etymology-turkish-ugan.htm. Accessed 10 Apr. 2024.

155   Dr.Samanthi. "Difference between Amino Acid and Nucleotide." *Compare the Difference Between Similar Terms, Differencebetween.Com*, 14 Oct. 2019, www.differencebetween.com/difference-between-amino-acid-and-vs-nucleotide/. Accessed 10 Apr. 2024.

156   Madhu. "Difference between Amino Acid and Nucleic Acid." *Compare the Difference Between Similar Terms*, Differencebetween.Com, 10 Dec. 2018, www.differencebetween.com/difference-between-amino-acid-and-vs-nucleic-acid/. Accessed 10 Apr. 2024.

157   Stephanie Liou. "The Basics of Huntington's Disease (Text and Audio)." *HOPES Huntington's Disease*, 29 Oct. 2014, hopes.stanford.edu/the-basics-of-huntingtons-disease-text-and-audio/. Accessed 10 Apr. 2024.

158   National Center for Biotechnology Information (US). "Huntington Disease." *National Center for Biotechnology Information*, U.S. National Library of Medicine, 1 Jan. 1998, www.ncbi.nlm.nih.gov/books/NBK22226/?report=reader. Accessed 10 Apr. 2024.

159   Ibid.

160   S. Arrasate and M. Finkbeiner. "Protein Aggregates in Huntington's Disease." *Experimental Neurology*, U.S. National Library of Medicine, pubmed.ncbi.nlm.nih.gov/22200539/. Accessed 10 Apr. 2024.

161   "Huntingtin." *Wikipedia*, Wikimedia Foundation, 6 Sept. 2023, en.wikipedia.org/wiki/Huntingtin. Accessed 10 Apr. 2024.

162   *Nature News*, Nature Publishing Group, www.nature.com/scitable/topicpage/gene-expression-14121669/#:~:text=Genes%20encode%20proteins%20and%20proteins%20dictate%20cell%20function.&text=Moreover%2C%20each%20step%20in%20t-he,type%20of%20proteins%20it%20manufactures. Accessed 10 Apr. 2024.

163   Ananya Mandal, "What Is Chromosome 4?" *News*, 17 June 2023, www.news-medical.net/health/What-is-Chromosome-4.aspx. Accessed 10 Apr. 2024.

164   "Chromosome 4: Medlineplus Genetics." *MedlinePlus*, U.S. National Library of Medicine, medlineplus.gov/genetics/chromosome/4/. Accessed 10 Apr. 2024.

165   Mandal.

166   Regina Bailey, "How Chromosome Mutations Occur." *ThoughtCo*, 13 Apr. 2019, www.thoughtco.com/chromosome-mutation-373448. Accessed 10 Apr. 2024.

167   "Htt Gene: Medlineplus Genetics." *MedlinePlus*, U.S. National Library of Medicine, medlineplus.gov/genetics/gene/htt/. Accessed 10 Apr. 2024.

168   "RNA." *Wikipedia*, Wikimedia Foundation, 8 Apr. 2024, en.wikipedia.org/wiki/RNA. Accessed 10 Apr. 2024.

169   "Controlling Element of Huntington's Disease Discovered: Molecular Troika Regulates Production of Harmful Protein." *ScienceDaily*, 26 Feb. 2013, www.sciencedaily.com/releases/2013/02/130226113826.htm. Accessed 10 Apr. 2024.

170   "Genetic Code." *Wikipedia*, Wikimedia Foundation, 15 Mar. 2024, en.wikipedia.org/wiki/Genetic_code. Accessed 10 Apr. 2024.

171   Karl Leif Bates. "Neuroscientists Find New Roles for Huntington's Protein." *Duke Today*, today.duke.edu/2020/01/neuroscientists-find-new-roles-huntington%E2%80%99s-protein. Accessed 10 Apr. 2024.

172   "Huntington's Disease: Medlineplus Genetics." *MedlinePlus*, U.S. National Library of Medicine, medlineplus.gov/genetics/condition/huntington-disease/#causes. Accessed 10 Apr. 2024.

173   "Controlling Element of Huntington's Disease Discovered: Molecular Troika Regulates Production of Harmful Protein." *ScienceDaily*, 26 Feb. 2013, www.sciencedaily.com/releases/2013/02/130226113826.htm. Accessed 10 Apr. 2024.

174   *Huntingtin Protein and Protein Aggregation – Hopes Huntington's Disease*, hopes.stanford.edu/huntingtin-protein-and-protein-aggregation/. Accessed 10 Apr. 2024.

175   "Huntington's Disease: Medlineplus Genetics." *MedlinePlus*, U.S. National Library of Medicine, medlineplus.gov/genetics/condition/huntington-disease/#causes. Accessed 10 Apr. 2024.

176   Mhedlin and Mhedlin. "Genetic Modifiers of Huntington's Disease." *HOPES Huntington's Disease*, 11 Oct. 2015, hopes.stanford.edu/genetic-modifiers-of-huntingtons-disease/. Accessed 10 Apr. 2024.

177   Stefanie Rich, et al, "Counting CAG Repeats in the Huntington's Disease Gene by Restriction Endonuclease ECO P15i Cleavage." *OUP Academic*, Oxford University Press, 15 Aug. 2002, academic.oup.com/nar/article/30/16/e83/2380405#. Accessed 10 Apr. 2024.

178   "Exon." *Wikipedia*, Wikimedia Foundation, 2 Apr. 2024, en.wikipedia.org/wiki/Exon. Accessed 10 Apr. 2024.

179   Rich.

180   "Overview of Huntington's Disease - Huntington's Disease Society of America." *Huntington's Disease Society of America - Family Is Everything*, 6 Nov. 2020, hdsa.org/what-is-hd/overview-of-huntingtons-disease/#:~:text=In%20the%20huntingtin%20gene%2C%20most%20people%20have%20around,children%20has%20a%2050%25%20chance%20of-%20developing%20HD. Accessed 10 Apr. 2024.

181   Mhedlin. "Genetic Modifiers of Huntington's Disease." HOPES Huntington's Disease, 11 Oct. 2015, hopes.stanford.edu/genetic-modifiers-of-huntingtons-disease/. Accessed 10 Apr. 2024.

182   Ridley, 60.

183   S. Arrasate and M. Finkbeiner. "Protein Aggregates in Huntington's Disease." *Experimental Neurology*, U.S. National Library of Medicine, pubmed.ncbi.nlm.nih.gov/22200539/. Accessed 10 Apr. 2024.

184   Ridley, 59.

185 "Neurodegenerative Diseases." *National Institute of Environmental Health Sciences*, U.S. Department of Health and Human Services, www.niehs.nih.gov/research/supported/health/neurodegenerative/index.cfm. Accessed 10 Apr. 2024.

186 Stephanie Liou, "Huntingtin Protein and Protein Aggregation." *HOPES Huntington's Disease*, 18 Nov. 2014, hopes.stanford.edu/huntingtin-protein-and-protein-aggregation/#the-huntington-gene. Accessed 10 Apr. 2024.

187 Ibid.

188 Steven Finkbeiner, "Huntington's Disease." *Cold Spring Harbor Perspectives in Biology*, U.S. National Library of Medicine, 1 June 2011, www.ncbi.nlm.nih.gov/pmc/articles/PMC3098678/. Accessed 10 Apr. 2024.

189 Liou.

190 "Apoptosis." *Encyclopædia Britannica*, Encyclopædia Britannica, Inc., 4 Apr. 2024, www.britannica.com/science/apoptosis. Accessed 10 Apr. 2024.

191 "Overview of Huntington's Disease - Huntington's Disease Society of America." *Huntington's Disease Society of America - Family Is Everything*, 6 Nov. 2020, hdsa.org/what-is-hd/overview-of-huntingtons-disease/. Accessed 12 Apr. 2024.

192 HealthPrep Staff. "Huntington's Disease Causes and Diagnosis." HealthPrep.Com, healthprep.com/articles/conditions/huntington-disease-causes-diagnosis/. Accessed 12 Apr. 2024.

193 RFC Editor, *www.rfc-editor.org*/info/rfc824. Accessed 12 Apr. 2024.

194 HealthPrep Staff. "Huntington's Disease Causes and Diagnosis."

195 "Autosomal Dominant Disorder." *Genome.Gov*, www.genome.gov/genetics-glossary/Autosomal-Dominant. Accessed 12 Apr. 2024.

196 Juvenile Huntington's Disease (Text and Audio) – Hopes Huntington's Disease, *hopes.stanford.edu*/juvenile-huntingtons-disease-text-and-audio/. Accessed 12 Apr. 2024.

197 Esther Heerema, MSW. "Explore the Treatment Options for Juvenile Huntington's Disease." Verywell Health, 2 Mar. 2022, www.verywellhealth.com/juvenile-huntingtons-disease-4154704. Accessed 12 Apr. 2024.

198 Juvenile Huntington's Disease (Text and Audio) – Hopes Huntington's Disease.

199 "Huntington's Disease." *National Institute of Neurological Disorders and Stroke*, U.S. Department of Health and Human Services, www.ninds.nih.gov/Disorders/Patient-Caregiver-Education/Hope-Through-Research/Huntingtons-Disease-Hope-Through. Accessed 12 Apr. 2024.

200 Ridley, 59.

201 Finkbeiner, S. "Huntington's Disease." *Cold Spring Harbor Perspectives in Biology*, U.S. National Library of Medicine, pubmed.ncbi.nlm.nih.gov/21441583/. Accessed 12 Apr. 2024.

202 "Worry Beads." *Wikipedia*, Wikimedia Foundation, 31 Mar. 2024, en.wikipedia.org/wiki/Worry_beads. Accessed 12 Apr. 2024.

203 Mark, Joshua J. "Megara (Wife of Hercules)." *Ancient History Encyclopedia*, 21 Feb. 2023, www.ancient.eu/Megara_(Wife_of_Hercules)/#:~:text=Megara%20was%20the%20first%20wife%20of%20the%20Greek,in%20winning%20back%20Creon%27s%20kingdom%20from%20the%20Minyans. Accessed 12 Apr. 2024.

204 Madeleine. "Who Was Hercules Wife in Greek Mythology?" *THEOI GREEK MYTHOLOGY - Exploring Mythology in Classical Literature & Art*, 3 Dec. 2019, www.theoi.com/articles/who-was-hercules-wife-in-greek-mythology. Accessed 12 Apr. 2024.

205 Robert Graves, *The Greek Myths*. Penguin, 2012, 460.

206 *Larousse Encyclopedia of Mythology*. Batchwork Press Limited, 1960, p. 194.

207 Edith Hamilton, *Mythology*. Little, Brown, and Company, 1942, 229.

208 Graves, 460.

209 Hamilton, 230.

210 Mark Cartwright, "Delphi." *Ancient History Encyclopedia*, 11 Apr. 2024, www.ancient.eu/delphi/. Accessed 12 Apr. 2024.

211 Hamilton, 230.

212 Madeleine. "Who Was Hercules Wife in Greek Mythology?"

213 *Hercules: The Spiritual Emphasis in Euripides - Digital Commons* ..., digitalcommons.brockport. edu/cgi/viewcontent.cgi?article=1003&context=spectrum. Accessed 12 Apr. 2024.

214 Ibid.

215 Ibid.

216 Donald Robertson, *The Choice of Hercules in Stoicism*, 9 Dec. 2013, donaldrobertson. name/2013/03/25/the-choice-of-hercules-in-stoicism/. Accessed 12 Apr. 2024.

217 Ibid.

218 Ibid.

219 Brett & Kate McKay, "Manvotional: The Choice of Hercules." *The Art of Manliness*, 3 June 2021, www.artofmanliness.com/articles/manvotional-the-choice-of-hercules/. Accessed 12 Apr. 2024.

220 Alex Barrientos, "The Mandalorian Way and Stoicism." *Classical Wisdom Weekly*, 8 Feb. 2020, classicalwisdom.com/philosophy/the-mandalorian-way-and-stoicism/. Accessed 12 Apr. 2024.

221 "Passion (n.)." *Etymology*, www.etymonline.com/word/passion. Accessed 12 Apr. 2024.

222 Salzgeber, Jonas. "The Story of Hercules – Life Is Supposed to Be Hard." *NJlifehacks*, 25 Sept. 2019, www.njlifehacks.com/story-of-hercules-life-is-supposed-to-be-hard/. Accessed 12 Apr. 2024.

223 Donald Robertson, *The Choice of Hercules in Stoicism*, 9 Dec. 2013, donaldrobertson. name/2013/03/25/the-choice-of-hercules-in-stoicism/. Accessed 12 Apr. 2024.

224 Alex Barrientos, "The Mandalorian Way and Stoicism." *Classical Wisdom Weekly*, 8 Feb. 2020, classicalwisdom.com/philosophy/the-mandalorian-way-and-stoicism/. Accessed 12 Apr. 2024.

225 "The Mighty Hercules Theme Song and Lyrics." *Theme Song*, 19 Aug. 2023, themesong.info/ the-mighty-hercules-theme-song-and-lyrics/. Accessed 12 Apr. 2024.

226 "Herakles (Euripides)." *Wikipedia*, Wikimedia Foundation, 7 Mar. 2024, en.wikipedia.org/ wiki/Herakles_(Euripides). Accessed 12 Apr. 2024.

227 "7 Health Benefits of Bitter Gourd (Karela) Juice." *NDTV Food*, 27 June 2016, food.ndtv. com/food-drinks/7-health-benefits-of-bitter-gourd-karela-juice-1423896. Accessed 12 Apr. 2024.

228 Ibid.

229 Holland, Kimberly. "10 Leading Causes of Death in the United States." *Healthline*, Healthline Media, 25 Sept. 2023, www.healthline.com/health/leading-causes-of-death. Accessed 12 Apr. 2024.

230 "Grave of Nikos Kazantzakis: Iraklio, Greece: Attractions." *Lonely Planet*, www.lonelyplanet. com/greece/crete/iraklio/attractions/grave-of-nikos-kazantzakis/a/poi-sig/446295/359430. Accessed 12 Apr. 2024.

231 "Parish History." *Christ the Savior Greek Orthodox Church*, christthesaviororthodox.org/ about/parish-history. Accessed 12 Apr. 2024.

232 "Cor." *The Latin Dictionary*, latindictionary.wikidot.com/noun:cor. Accessed 12 Apr. 2024.

233 John Davis, "The Scarcity Mindset, the Abundance Mindset, and the Impact on Public Policy." *Guide for Loan & Credit Card Reviews*, 2 Feb. 2024, www.hullfinancialplanning.com/ the-scarcity-mindset-the-abundance-mindset-and-the-impact-on-public-policy/. Accessed 12 Apr. 2024.

234 "Seahorse Fathers Take Reins in Childbirth," 14 June 2002, *www.nationalgeographic.com/ pages/article/seahorse-fathers-take-reins-in-childbirth. Accessed 12 Apr. 2024.*

235 "Betta Fish Bubble Nests (Every Question Answered)." *Betta Care Fish Guide*, www. bettacarefishguide.com/betta-fish-bubble-nests/. Accessed 12 Apr. 2024.

236 "Male Betta Fish," home.adelphi.edu/~ve21375/Male%20Betta%20Fish.html. Accessed 12 Apr. 2024.

237 "Degassing Homemade Wine." *Wine Making and Beer Brewing Blog - Adventures in Homebrewing*, 27 July 2022, blog.homebrewing.org/degassing-homemade-wine/#:~:text=At%20the%20very%20center%20of%20wine%20making%20is,both%20alcohol%20and%20CO2%20gas%20by%20the%20fermentation. Accessed 12 Apr. 2024.

238 "17 Health Benefits of Green Tea: 11. Anti-Cancer." *Very Healthy Life*, 15 July 2021, veryhealthy.life/17-health-benefits-green-tea/11/. Accessed 12 Apr. 2024.

239 "Grandfather Mountain Marathon, 09 Jul 2022." *World's Marathons*, worldsmarathons.com/marathon/grandfather-mountain-marathon. Accessed 12 Apr. 2024.

240 "Herakles (Euripides)." *Wikipedia*, Wikimedia Foundation, 7 Mar. 2024, en.wikipedia.org/wiki/Herakles_(Euripides). Accessed 12 Apr. 2024.

241 Christos F. Kleisiaris, et al. "Health Care Practices in Ancient Greece: The Hippocratic Ideal." *Journal of Medical Ethics and History of Medicine*, U.S. National Library of Medicine, 15 Mar. 2014, www.ncbi.nlm.nih.gov/pmc/articles/PMC4263393/. Accessed 12 Apr. 2024.

242 "Herakles (Euripides)." *Wikipedia*, Wikimedia Foundation, 7 Mar. 2024, en.wikipedia.org/wiki/Herakles_(Euripides). Accessed 12 Apr. 2024.

243 "Quasimodo Character Analysis," *www.litcharts.com*/lit/the-hunchback-of-notre-dame/characters/quasimodo. Accessed 12 Apr. 2024.

244 "It's a Thin Line between Love and Hate." *Psychology Today*, Sussex Publishers, www.psychologytoday.com/us/blog/the-mysteries-love/201803/it-s-thin-line-between-love-and-hate. Accessed 12 Apr. 2024.

245 Ibid.

246 "'And That's The Way It Is': Walter Cronkite's Final Sign Off." *CBS News*, CBS Interactive, 18 Mar. 2021, www.cbsnews.com/video/and-thats-the-way-it-is-walter-cronkites-final-sign-off/. Accessed 12 Apr. 2024.

247 "What Is the Greek Orthodox Memorial Service?" *iCal*, 10 June 2020, www.greekboston.com/religion/memorial-service/. Accessed 12 Apr. 2024.

248 "Koliva." *Wikipedia*, Wikimedia Foundation, 17 Feb. 2024, en.wikipedia.org/wiki/Koliva. Accessed 12 Apr. 2024.

249 "1st Saturday of Great Lent: The Miracle of the Boiled Wheat." *Orthodox Church in America*, www.oca.org/saints/lives/2021/03/20/9-1st-saturday-of-great-lent-the-miracle-of-the-boiled-wheat. Accessed 12 Apr. 2024.

250 "Russian Americans in New York City." *Wikipedia*, Wikimedia Foundation, 28 Feb. 2024, en.wikipedia.org/wiki/Russian_Americans_in_New_York_City. Accessed 12 Apr. 2024.

251 "George the Great Martyr and Triumphant - Greek Orthodox Archdiocese of America - Orthodox Church." *Greek Orthodox Archdiocese of America*, www.goarch.org/chapel/saints?contentid=29. Accessed 12 Apr. 2024.

252 "Herakles (Euripides)." *Wikipedia*, Wikimedia Foundation, 7 Mar. 2024, en.wikipedia.org/wiki/Herakles_(Euripides). Accessed 12 Apr. 2024.

253 Liou, Stephanie. "The Basic Neurobiology of Huntington's Disease (Text and Audio)." *HOPES Huntington's Disease*, 28 July 2016, hopes.stanford.edu/the-basic-neurobiology-of-huntingtons-disease-text-and-audio/#what-parts-of-the-brain-are-most-affected-in-hd-patients. Accessed 12 Apr. 2024.

254 "Ganglion (n.)." *Etymology*, www.etymonline.com/word/ganglion. Accessed 12 Apr. 2024.

255 "Bundle of Nerves." *The Free Dictionary*, Farlex, idioms.thefreedictionary.com/bundle+of+nerves#:~:text=a%20bag%2Fbundle%20of%20%CB%88nerves%20%28informal%29%20a%20person%20who,a%20break.%20See%20also%3A%20bag%2C%20bundle%2C%20nerve%2C%20of. Accessed 12 Apr. 2024.

256 Foster, Jasmine. "Basal Ganglia: Definition, Function, Location & Anatomy." *SelfHacked*, 25 Aug. 2020, selfhacked.com/blog/basal-ganglia-your-reptilian-brain/. Accessed 12 Apr. 2024.

257 Ibid.

258 Thomas Byrd, *Can You Help Me?: Inside the Turbulent World of Huntington Disease*. Oxford University Press, 2019, 7.

259   "Basal Ganglia: Functions, Anatomy, Disorders & Pathways." *Brain Made Simple*, 20 May 2022, brainmadesimple.com/basal-ganglia/#:~:text=You%20can%20begin%20to%20 infer%20the%20relative%20location,exercise%20caution%2C%20however%2C%20is%20 with%20the%20term%20%E2%80%9Cganglia.%E2%80%9D. Accessed 12 Apr. 2024.

260   Byrd, 7.

261   "Basal Ganglia." *Kenhub*, www.kenhub.com/en/library/anatomy/basal-ganglia. Accessed 12 Apr. 2024.

262   Sarah Neidler, "Antidopaminergic Agents." *Huntington's Disease News*, 20 July 2018, huntingtonsdiseasenews.com/antidopaminergic-agents/. Accessed 12 Apr. 2024.

263   Foster.

264   "Brain Ventricles." *Mayo Clinic*, Mayo Foundation for Medical Education and Research, *www.mayoclinic.org*/diseases-conditions/hydrocephalus/multimedia/brain-ventricles/img-20007652. Accessed 12 Apr. 2024.

265   *Healthtap Online Doctor*. What Parts of the Brain Are Most Commonly Affected by Huntington's Disease?, www.healthtap.com/questions/22502-what-parts-of-the-brain-are-most-commonly-affected-by-huntington-s-disease/. Accessed 12 Apr. 2024.

266   Alex Rice, "Huntington's Disease - Brain Disorder - Genetic Disorder." *Familydoctor.Org*, 1 Mar. 2021, familydoctor.org/condition/huntingtons-disease/. Accessed 12 Apr. 2024.

267   "Neuroanatomy S1 E7: Basal Ganglia #neuroanatomy #ubcmedicine." *YouTube*, 1 Mar. 2014, www.youtube.com/watch?v=InJByqg1x-0&t=75s. Accessed 12 Apr. 2024.

268   "Basal Ganglia 3D Tour." *YouTube*, 6 Jan. 2018, www.youtube.com/watch?v=s-6sOscx8-E. Accessed 12 Apr. 2024.

269   "Basal Ganglia: Group of Structures in the Brain." *Brain Made Simple*, 20 May 2022, brainmadesimple.com/basal-ganglia-structure/. Accessed 12 Apr. 2024.

270   Melinda T. Owens and Kimberly D.Tanner, "Teaching as Brain Changing: Exploring Connections between Neuroscience and Innovative Teaching." *CBE Life Sciences Education, U.S. National Library of Medicine*, 2017, www.ncbi.nlm.nih.gov/pmc/articles/PMC5459260/. Accessed 12 Apr. 2024.

271   Stephanie Liou, "Huntingtin Protein and Protein Aggregation." *HOPES Huntington's Disease*, 18 Nov. 2014, hopes.stanford.edu/huntingtin-protein-and-protein-aggregation/#:~:text=Although%20researchers%20are%20still%20investigating%20 huntingtin%20protein%20%E2%80%99s,even%20though%20it%20is%20found%20 throughout%20the%20body. Accessed 12 Apr. 2024.

272   Thomas Byrd, *Can You Help Me?: Inside the Turbulent World of Huntington Disease*. Oxford University Press, 2019, 6.

273   *The Basic Neurobiology of Huntington's Disease (Text and Audio) – Hopes Huntington's Disease*, hopes.stanford.edu/the-basic-neurobiology-of-huntingtons-disease-text-and-audio/. Accessed 12 Apr. 2024.

274   "Globus Pallidus." *Wikipedia*, Wikimedia Foundation, 4 Apr. 2024, en.wikipedia.org/wiki/Globus_pallidus. Accessed 12 Apr. 2024.

275   Ivan Suarez Robles, "Globus Pallidus." *HOPES Huntington's Disease*, 7 Feb. 1970, hopes.stanford.edu/glossary/globus-pallidus/. Accessed 12 Apr. 2024.

276   *Chorea Information Page | National Institute of Neurological Disorders and Stroke, www.ninds.nih.gov*/Disorders/All-Disorders/Chorea-Information-Page. Accessed 12 Apr. 2024.

277   "Globus Pallidus Degeneration and Clinicopathological Features of Huntington Disease." *Annals of Neurology*, U.S. National Library of Medicine, pubmed.ncbi.nlm.nih.gov/27255697/. Accessed 12 Apr. 2024.

278   The Healthline Editoria Team. "Subthalmic Nucleus Anatomy, Function & Diagram | Body Maps." *Healthline*, Healthline Media, 20 Jan. 2018, www.healthline.com/human-body-maps/subthalmic-nucleus#1. Accessed 12 Apr. 2024.

279   Ed, Callahan. "Age-Dependent Alterations in the Cortical Entrainment of Subthalamic Nucleus Neurons in the YAC128 Mouse Model of Huntington's Disease."

Neurobiology of Disease, U.S. National Library of Medicine, pubmed.ncbi.nlm.nih.gov/25772440/#:~:text=Huntington%27s%20disease%20%28HD%29%20is%20an%20autosomal%20dominant%20neurodegenerative,in%20hyperkinetic%20movement%20abnormalities%2C%20similar%20to%20the%20. Accessed 12 Apr. 2024.

280 "Substantia Nigra." *The Free Dictionary*, Farlex, medical-dictionary.thefreedictionary.com/substantia+nigra#:~:text=The%20substantia%20nigra%20is%20involved%20in%20the%20metabolic,midbrain%20and%20receives%20fibres%20from%20the%20BASAL%-20GANGLIA. Accessed 12 Apr. 2024.

281 "Substantia Nigra." Substantia Nigra - an Overview | ScienceDirect Topics, *www.sciencedirect.com*/topics/veterinary-science-and-veterinary-medicine/substantia-nigra. Accessed 12 Apr. 2024.

282 *A Quantitative Investigation of the Substantia Nigra In ...*, onlinelibrary.wiley.com/doi/abs/10.1002/ana.410260103. Accessed 12 Apr. 2024.

283 Ivan Suarez Robles, "Substantia Nigra." *HOPES Huntington's Disease*, 15 Nov. 1970, hopes.stanford.edu/glossary/substantia-nigra/. Accessed 12 Apr. 2024.

284 "Substantia Nigra." *Wikipedia*, Wikimedia Foundation, 22 Mar. 2024, en.wikipedia.org/wiki/Substantia_nigra. Accessed 12 Apr. 2024.

285 Ibid.

286 Michelle Pugle, "GABA: What It Is, Functions, and Disorders." *Verywell Health*, 27 Nov. 2023, www.verywellhealth.com/gaba-5095143. Accessed 12 Apr. 2024.

287 W.R.G. Gibb, "Neuropathology of the Substantia Nigra." Karger Publishers, S. Karger AG, 20 Feb. 2008, www.karger.com/Article/PDF/116721. Accessed 12 Apr. 2024.

288 "Huntington's Disease." *Mayo Clinic*, Mayo Foundation for Medical Education and Research, 17 May 2022, www.mayoclinic.org/diseases-conditions/huntingtons-disease/symptoms-causes/syc-20356117#:~:text=The%20movement%20disorders%20associated%20with%20Huntington%27s%20disease%20can,muscle%20contracture%20%28dystonia%29%20Slow%20or%20abnormal%20eye%20movements. Accessed 12 Apr. 2024.

289 "Substantia Nigra." *Wikipedia*, Wikimedia Foundation, 22 Mar. 2024, en.wikipedia.org/wiki/Substantia_nigra. Accessed 12 Apr. 2024.

290 Ibid.

291 "Substantia Nigra." Substantia Nigra - an Overview | *ScienceDirect Topics*, www.sciencedirect.com/topics/neuroscience/substantia-nigra#:~:text=The%20basal%20ganglia%20inhibit%20the%20rapid%20firing%20of,the%20increase%20in%20tremors%20through%20lack%20of%20inhibition. Accessed 12 Apr. 2024.

292 Yuan-Yang Lai, "Substantia Nigra Pars Reticulata-Mediated Sleep and Motor Activity Regulation." *OUP Academic, Oxford University Press*, 18 Aug. 2020, academic.oup.com/sleep/article/44/1/zsaa151/5893883#:~:text=The%20substantia%20nigra%20pars%20reticulata%20%28SNR%29%20is%20a,in%20the%20control%20of%20sleep%20and%20motor%20activity. Accessed 12 Apr. 2024.

293 *Brain Basics: The Life and Death of a Neuron | National Institute of Neurological Disorders and Stroke*, www.ninds.nih.gov/Disorders/Patient-Caregiver-Education/Life-and-Death-Neuron. Accessed 12 Apr. 2024.

294 "Basal Ganglia: Functions, Anatomy, Disorders & Pathways." *Brain Made Simple*, 20 May 2022, brainmadesimple.com/basal-ganglia/#:~:text=You%20can%20begin%20to%20infer%20the%20relative%20location,exercise%20caution%2C%20however%2C%20is%20with%20the%20term%20%E2%80%9Cganglia.%E2%80%9D. Accessed 12 Apr. 2024.

295 Ibid.

296 Stephanie Liou, "The Motor Symptoms of Huntington's Disease." *HOPES Huntington's Disease*, 26 July 2016, hopes.stanford.edu/motor-symptoms/. Accessed 12 Apr. 2024.

297 "Apoptosis." *Wikipedia*, Wikimedia Foundation, 6 Mar. 2024, en.wikipedia.org/wiki/Apoptosis. Accessed 12 Apr. 2024.

298 "The Direct Basal Ganglia Pathway." *VirtualMedStudent.Com* - Life, Liberty, and the Pursuit of Health, 15 Mar. 2023, www.virtualmedstudent.com/links/anatomy/basal_ganglia_direct_pathway. Accessed 12 Apr. 2024.

299 "Direct Pathway." *Wikipedia*, Wikimedia Foundation, 15 June 2023, en.wikipedia.org/wiki/Direct_pathway. Accessed 12 Apr. 2024.

300 Oliver Quarrell, *Huntington's Disease* / Oliver Quarrell. Oxford University Press, 2008, 102.

301 "Nigrostriatal Pathway." *Wikipedia*, Wikimedia Foundation, 31 Dec. 2023, en.wikipedia.org/wiki/Nigrostriatal_pathway. Accessed 12 Apr. 2024.

302 "Brady-." *Etymology*, www.etymonline.com/word/brady-#:~:text=medical%20word-forming%20element%20meaning%20%22slow%2C%20delayed%2C%20tardy%2C%22%20from,Greek%20kin%C4%93sis%22movement%2C%20motion%3B%22%20bradypnea%2C%20with%20Greek%20pneo%2Fpnein%22to%20breathe.%22. Accessed 12 Apr. 2024.

303 "Dystonia Definition & Meaning." *Dictionary.Com*, www.dictionary.com/browse/dystonia. Accessed 12 Apr. 2024.

304 "Dystonia." *The Free Dictionary*, Farlex, medical-dictionary.thefreedictionary.com/dystonia. Accessed 12 Apr. 2024.

305 "Pill-Rolling Tremor: Causes, Treatment, and More." *Medical News Today*, MediLexicon International, www.medicalnewstoday.com/articles/pill-rolling-tremor#symptoms. Accessed 12 Apr. 2024.

306 "The Indirect Basal Ganglia Pathway." *VirtualMedStudent.Com* - Life, Liberty, and the Pursuit of Health, 15 Mar. 2023, www.virtualmedstudent.com/links/anatomy/basal_ganglia_indirect_pathway.html. Accessed 12 Apr. 2024.

307 "Nigrostriatal Pathway." *Wikipedia*, Wikimedia Foundation, 31 Dec. 2023, en.wikipedia.org/wiki/Nigrostriatal_pathway. Accessed 12 Apr. 2024.

308 T. Postert, B. Lack, et al, "Basal Ganglia Alterations and Brain Atrophy in Huntington's Disease Depicted by Transcranial Real Time Sonography." *Journal of Neurology, Neurosurgery & Psychiatry*, BMJ Publishing Group Ltd, 1 Oct. 1999, jnnp.bmj.com/content/67/4/457. Accessed 12 Apr. 2024.

309 Barry Joshua, et al, "Striatal Direct and Indirect Pathway Output Structures Are Differentially Altered in Mouse Models of Huntington's Disease." *The Journal of Neuroscience: The Official Journal of the Society for Neuroscience*, U.S. National Library of Medicine, pubmed.ncbi.nlm.nih.gov/29691329/. Accessed 12 Apr. 2024.

310 "Basal Ganglia." *Kenhub*, www.kenhub.com/en/library/anatomy/basal-ganglia. Accessed 12 Apr. 2024.

311 "Basal Ganglia Direct and Indirect Pathways - #usmle Neuroanatomy Animations." *YouTube*, 5 July 2020, www.youtube.com/watch?v=UtacLPnoa28. Accessed 12 Apr. 2024.

312 "The Concept of the 'Triune Brain.'" *The Interaction Design Foundation, Interaction Design Foundation*, 12 Apr. 2024, www.interaction-design.org/literature/article/the-concept-of-the-triune-brain. Accessed 12 Apr. 2024.

313 Foster, Jasmine. "Basal Ganglia: Definition, Function, Location & Anatomy." *SelfHacked*, 25 Aug. 2020, selfhacked.com/blog/basal-ganglia-your-reptilian-brain/. Accessed 12 Apr. 2024.

314 "Know Your Brain: Reward System." *@neurochallenged*, www.neuroscientificallychallenged.com/blog/know-your-brain-reward-system. Accessed 12 Apr. 2024.

315 "Our Three Brains - the Reptilian Brain." *The Interaction Design Foundation*, Interaction Design Foundation, 12 Apr. 2024, www.interaction-design.org/literature/article/our-three-brains-the-reptilian-brain. Accessed 12 Apr. 2024.

316 Ibid.

317 "Our Three Brains - the Reptilian Brain." *The Interaction Design Foundation, Interaction Design Foundation*, 12 Apr. 2024, www.interaction-design.org/literature/article/our-three-brains-the-reptilian-brain. Accessed 12 Apr. 2024.

318 Jasmine Foster, "Basal Ganglia: Definition, Function, Location & Anatomy." SelfHacked, 25 Aug. 2020, selfhacked.com/blog/basal-ganglia-your-reptilian-brain/. Accessed 12 Apr. 2024.

319 *The Triune Brain - the Science of Psychotherapy*, www.thescienceofpsychotherapy.com/the-triune-brain/. Accessed 12 Apr. 2024.

320 Jennifer Long, "What Is the Relationship between the Amygdala and Hippocampus?" The Health Board, TheHealthBoard, 3 Mar. 2024, www.infobloom.com/what-is-the-relationship-between-the-amygdala-and-hippocampus.htm#:~:text=The%20hippocampus%20and%20amygdala%20are%20both%20located%20under,determining%20how%20those%20emotions%20are%20tied%20to%20memories. Accessed 12 Apr. 2024.

321 "Amygdala." *Wikipedia*, Wikimedia Foundation, 30 Mar. 2024, en.wikipedia.org/wiki/Amygdala. Accessed 12 Apr. 2024.

322 Ibid.

323 *Know Your Brain: Amygdala - Neuroscientifically Challenged*, www.neuroscientifically challenged.com/blog/know-your-brain-amygdala. Accessed 12 Apr. 2024.

324 *Paleomammalian Complex - The Science of Psychotherapy*, www.thescienceofpsychotherapy.com/glossary/paleomammalian-complex/. Accessed 12 Apr. 2024.

325 "Amygdala." *Encyclopædia Britannica*, Encyclopædia Britannica, Inc., www.britannica.com/science/amygdala. Accessed 12 Apr. 2024.

326 Ibid.

327 Ibid

328 "A Quick Look under the Hood: The Amygdala, Hippocampus and Traumatic Memories." *Applied Metapsychology International*, 23 July 2020, www.appliedmetapsychology.org/research-publications/articles/mygdala-hippocampus-and-traumatic-memories/#:~:text=A%20Quick%20Look%20Under%20the%20Hood%3A%20The%20Amygdala%2C,we%20often%20say%20the%20hippocampus%20is%20in%20control. Accessed 12 Apr. 2024.

329 "Our Three Brains - the Emotional Brain." *The Interaction Design Foundation*, Interaction Design Foundation, 12 Apr. 2024, www.interaction-design.org/literature/article/our-three-brains-the-emotional-brain. Accessed 12 Apr. 2024.

330 "Amygdala." *Wikipedia*, Wikimedia Foundation, 30 Mar. 2024, en.wikipedia.org/wiki/Amygdala. Accessed 12 Apr. 2024.

331 "Klüver–Bucy Syndrome: The Loss of Fear." *Exploring Your Mind*, 17 June 2020, exploringyourmind.com/kluver-bucy-syndrome-the-loss-of-fear/. Accessed 12 Apr. 2024.

332 "Huntington's Disease: Medlineplus Genetics." *MedlinePlus*, U.S. National Library of Medicine, medlineplus.gov/genetics/condition/huntington-disease/. Accessed 12 Apr. 2024.

333 "The Role of the Amygdala during Emotional Processing in Huntington's Disease: From Pre-Manifest to Late Stage Disease." *Neuropsychologia*, Pergamon, 17 Feb. 2015, www.sciencedirect.com/science/article/pii/S0028393215000780. Accessed 12 Apr. 2024.

334 Ibid

335 Jane S. Paulsen, "Functional Imaging in Huntington's Disease." *Experimental Neurology*, U.S. National Library of Medicine, Apr. 2009, www.ncbi.nlm.nih.gov/pmc/articles/PMC3810959/. Accessed 12 Apr. 2024.

336 "The Role of the Amygdala during Emotional Processing in Huntington's Disease: From Pre-Manifest to Late Stage Disease." *Neuropsychologia*, Pergamon, 17 Feb. 2015, www.sciencedirect.com/science/article/pii/S0028393215000780. Accessed 15 Apr. 2024.

337 Ibid.

338 V.E. Stone, et al. "Acquired Theory of Mind Impairments in Individuals with Bilateral Amygdala Lesions." *Neuropsychologia*, U.S. National Library of Medicine, pubmed.ncbi.nlm.nih.gov/12459219/. Accessed 15 Apr. 2024.

339 "DNA Damage-Induced Cell Death: From Specific DNA Lesions to the DNA Damage Response and Apoptosis." *Cancer Letters*, Elsevier, 16 Jan. 2012, www.sciencedirect.com/science/article/abs/pii/S0304383512000328. Accessed 15 Apr. 2024.

340 Sandra Blakeslee, "Scientists Find Cause of Death of Brain Cells." *The New York Times*, 8 Aug. 1997, www.nytimes.com/1997/08/08/us/scientists-find-cause-of-death-of-brain-cells.html. Accessed 15 Apr. 2024.

341 *Europe PMC*, europepmc.org/article/MED/25700742. Accessed 15 Apr. 2024.

342 "Dynamic Changes in Amygdala Psychophysiological Connectivity Reveal Distinct Neural Networks for Facial Expressions of Basic Emotions." *Nature News*, Nature Publishing Group, 27 Mar. 2017, www.nature.com/articles/srep45260. Accessed 15 Apr. 2024.

343 "The Role of the Amygdala during Emotional Processing in Huntington's Disease: From Pre-Manifest to Late Stage Disease." *Neuropsychologia*, Pergamon, 17 Feb. 2015, www.sciencedirect.com/science/article/pii/S0028393215000780#bib63. Accessed 15 Apr. 2024.

344 "Fusiform Face Area." *Wikipedia*, Wikimedia Foundation, 9 Nov. 2023, en.wikipedia.org/wiki/Fusiform_face_area#:~:text=The%20fusiform%20face%20area%20%28FFA%29%20is%20a%20part,the%20FFA%20is%20evolutionary%20purposed%20for%20face%20perception. Accessed 15 Apr. 2024.

345 Sandra Blakeslee. "Scientists Find Cause of Death of Brain Cells." *The New York Times*, 8 Aug. 1997, www.nytimes.com/1997/08/08/us/scientists-find-cause-of-death-of-brain-cells.html. Accessed 15 Apr. 2024.

346 "Ataxia." *Mayo Clinic*, Mayo Foundation for Medical Education and Research, 30 Jan. 2024, www.mayoclinic.org/diseases-conditions/ataxia/symptoms-causes/syc-20355652. Accessed 15 Apr. 2024.

347 "The Role of the Amygdala during Emotional Processing in Huntington's Disease: From Pre-Manifest to Late Stage Disease." *Neuropsychologia*, Pergamon, 17 Feb. 2015, www.sciencedirect.com/science/article/pii/S0028393215000780. Accessed 15 Apr. 2024.

348 "Hippocampus." *Encyclopædia Britannica*, Encyclopædia Britannica, Inc., 2 Apr. 2024, www.britannica.com/science/hippocampus. Accessed 15 Apr. 2024.

349 "Hippocampus." *Wikipedia*, Wikimedia Foundation, 6 Apr. 2024, en.wikipedia.org/wiki/Hippocampus. Accessed 15 Apr. 2024.

350 "Hippocampus." *Encyclopædia Britannica*, Encyclopædia Britannica, Inc., 2 Apr. 2024, www.britannica.com/science/hippocampus. Accessed 15 Apr. 2024.

351 Ibid.

352 Long, Jennifer. "What Is the Relationship between the Amygdala and Hippocampus?" *The Health Board*, TheHealthBoard, 3 Mar. 2024, www.infobloom.com/what-is-the-relationship-between-the-amygdala-and-hippocampus.htm#:~:text=The%20hippocampus%20and%20amygdala%20are%20both%20located%20under,determining%20how%20those%20emotions%20are%20tied%20to%20memories. Accessed 15 Apr. 2024.

353 Thomas Byrd, *Can You Help Me?: Inside the Turbulent World of Huntington Disease*. Oxford University Press, 2019, 14.

354 Jade G. Quirion and Matthew P. Parsons. "The Onset and Progression of Hippocampal Synaptic Plasticity Deficits in the Q175FDN Mouse Model of Huntington Disease." *Frontiers*, 3 July 2019, www.frontiersin.org/articles/10.3389/fncel.2019.00326/full. Accessed 15 Apr. 2024.

355 Crystal M. Wilkie, et al. "Hippocampal Synaptic Dysfunction in a Mouse Model of Huntington Disease Is Not Alleviated by Ceftriaxone Treatment." *eNeuro*, Society for Neuroscience, 1 May 2020, www.eneuro.org/content/7/3/ENEURO.0440-19.2020. Accessed 15 Apr. 2024.

356 Ibid.

357 "Amygdala, Hippocampus, Prefrontal Cortex." *Mental Wealth Hub*, 3 Apr. 2018, www.mentalwealthhub.com/police-wellbeing/policing-and-the-stress-response/amygdala-hippocampus-prefrontal-cortex/. Accessed 15 Apr. 2024.

358 Ibid.

359 Jasmine Foster, "Basal Ganglia: Definition, Function, Location & Anatomy." *SelfHacked*, 25 Aug. 2020, selfhacked.com/blog/basal-ganglia-your-reptilian-brain/. Accessed 15 Apr. 2024.

360 Ibid.

361 "Amygdala, Hippocampus, Prefrontal Cortex."

362 Ibid.

363 Lumen Learning, "Introduction to Psychology." *Lumen*, courses.lumenlearning.com/waymaker-psychology/chapter/reading-parts-of-the-brain/. Accessed 15 Apr. 2024.

364 Ibid.

365 *Google Search*, Google, www.google.com/search?q=cortex%2Betymology&sxsrf=ALe Kk03zjQ9o7ZHcYn3jJ8dAckExt-93_A%3A1620638974301&source=hp&ei=_vyYYO iFEKjm_QbG2r-oDw&iflsig=AINFCbYAAAAAYJkLDmWkKNa_ZzRaEfl_Tizt2Id9KKa K&oq=&gs_lcp=Cgdnd3Mtd2l6EAEYADIHCCMQ6gIQJzIHCCMQ6gIQJzIHCCMQ6g IQJzIHCCMQ6gIQJzIHCCMQ6gIQJzIHCCMQ6gIQJzIHCCMQ6gIQJzIHCCMQ6gIQJ zIHCCMQ6gIQJzIHCCMQ6gIQJ1AAWABggCRoAXAAeACAAAQCIAQCSAQCYAQ CqAQ dnd3Mtd2l6sAEK&sclient=gws-wiz. Accessed 15 Apr. 2024.

366 Thomas Byrd, *Can You Help Me?: Inside the Turbulent World of Huntington Disease*. Oxford University Press, 2019, 15.

367 "What Is the Difference between the Prefrontal Cortex and Frontal Lobe?: Socratic." *Socratic. Org*, 23 Jan. 2016, socratic.org/questions/what-is-the-difference-between-the-prefrontal-cortex-and-frontal-lobe. Accessed 15 Apr. 2024.

368 "Dry Bones Song and Lyrics from Kididdles." *Kididdles*, www.kididdles.com/lyrics/d009. html. Accessed 15 Apr. 2024.

369 "Impaired Long-Term Potentiation in the Prefrontal Cortex of Huntington's Disease Mouse Models: Rescue by D1 Dopamine Receptor Activation." *Neuro-Degenerative Diseases*, U.S. National Library of Medicine, pubmed.ncbi.nlm.nih.gov/21282937/. Accessed 15 Apr. 2024.

370 Ibid.

371 Thomas Byrd, *Can You Help Me?: Inside the Turbulent World of Huntington Disease*. Oxford University Press, 2019, 231.

372 Ibid.

373 Adam G. Walker, et al. "Reduced Expression of Conditioned Fear in the R6/2 Mouse Model of Huntington's Disease Is Related to Abnormal Activity in Prelimbic Cortex." *Neurobiology of Disease*, U.S. National Library of Medicine, Aug. 2011, www.ncbi.nlm.nih.gov/pmc/articles/PMC3114205/. Accessed 15 Apr. 2024.

374 Ibid.

375 Ibid.

376 "Development of White Matter Microstructure and Intrinsic Functional Connectivity between the Amygdala and Ventromedial Prefrontal Cortex: Associations with Anxiety and Depression." *Biological Psychiatry*, U.S. National Library of Medicine, pubmed.ncbi.nlm. nih.gov/28274468/. Accessed 15 Apr. 2024.

377 D. Craufurd, et al., "Behavioral changes in Huntington disease." *Neuropsychiatry, Neuropsychology, and Behavioral Neurology*, 14 (2001), pp. 219-226

378 "Irritability in Pre-Clinical Huntington's Disease." *Neuropsychologia*, Pergamon, 28 Oct. 2009, www.sciencedirect.com/science/article/pii/S0028393209004199. Accessed 15 Apr. 2024.

379 Adam G. Walker, "Reduced Expression of Conditioned Fear in the R6/2 Mouse Model of Huntington's Disease Is Related to Abnormal Activity in Prelimbic Cortex." *Neurobiology of Disease*, U.S. National Library of Medicine, Aug. 2011, Www.ncbi.nlm.nih.gov/pmc/articles/PMC3114205/#:~:text=Prefrontal%20cortex%20%28PFC%29%20dysfunction%20is%20 common%20in%20patients,PFC%20of%20the%20R6%2F2%20mouse%20model%20 of%20HD. https://www.poetryfoundation.org/poems/56964/speech-tomorrow-and-tomorrow-and-tomorrow.Accessed 23 Apr. 2024.

380 William Shakespeare, "Speech: "Tomorrow, and Tomorrow, and Tomorrow" by..." *Poetry Foundation*, www.poetryfoundation.org/poems/56964/speech-tomorrow-and-tomorrow-and-tomorrow#:~:text=The%20way%20to%20dusty%20death,Out%2C%20out%2C%20

brief%20candle!&text=Told%20by%20an%20idiot%2C%20full,Signifying%20nothng.
Accessed 23 Apr. 2024.

381　D. R.Thiruvady, et al, "Functional Connectivity of the Prefrontal Cortex in Huntington's Disease." *Journal of Neurology*, Neurosurgery & Psychiatry, BMJ Publishing Group Ltd, 1 Feb. 2007, jnnp.bmj.com/content/78/2/127. Accessed 23 Apr. 2024.

382　Ibid.

383　"Interplay of Hippocampus and Prefrontal Cortex in Memory." *Current Biology*, Cell Press, 9 Sept. 2013, www.sciencedirect.com/science/article/pii/S0960982213006362. Accessed 23 Apr. 2024.

384　Ibid.

385　Andrea Ciarmiello, "Brain White-Matter Volume Loss and Glucose Hypometabolism Precede the Clinical Symptoms of Huntington's Disease." *Journal of Nuclear Medicine*, Society of Nuclear Medicine, 1 Feb. 2006, jnm.snmjournals.org/content/47/2/215. Accessed 23 Apr. 2024.

386　Ana Pena, PhD. "Huntington's Marked by Inflammation and Changes in Brain's..." *Huntington's Disease News*, 29 Oct. 2019, huntingtonsdiseasenews.com/2019/10/29/inflammation-changes-in-brain-striatum-evidet-present-symptoms-study-says/. Accessed 23 Apr. 2024.

387　"Structure and Function of the Brain: Boundless Psychology." *Collegesidekick*, courses. lumenlearning.com/boundless-psychology/chapter/structure-and-function-of-the-brain/. Accessed 23 Apr. 2024.

388　Psychology, MY. "Adapted from Https://Image.Slidesharecdn.Com/." *Flickr*, Yahoo!, 23 Apr. 2024, www.flickr.com/photos/142700890@N07/32853700890. Accessed 23 Apr. 2024.

389　"Morphometric Analysis of the Prefrontal Cortex in Huntington's Disease." *Neurology*, U.S. National Library of Medicine, pubmed.ncbi.nlm.nih.gov/1829794/. Accessed 23 Apr. 2024.

390　J. Kassubek, "Topography of Cerebral Atrophy in Early Huntington's Disease: A Voxel Based Morphometric MRI Study." *Journal of Neurology*, Neurosurgery, and Psychiatry, U.S. National Library of Medicine, Feb. 2004, www.ncbi.nlm.nih.gov/pmc/articles/PMC1738932/. Accessed 23 Apr. 2024.

391　"Regional Specificity of Brain Atrophy in Huntington's Disease." *Experimental Neurology*, U.S. National Library of Medicine, pubmed.ncbi.nlm.nih.gov/9878201/. Accessed 23 Apr. 2024.

392　"Altered Information Processing in the Prefrontal Cortex of Huntington's Disease Mouse Models." *The Journal of Neuroscience*: The Official Journal of the Society for Neuroscience, U.S. National Library of Medicine, pubmed.ncbi.nlm.nih.gov/18768691/. Accessed 23 Apr. 2024.

393　"Common Dysregulation Network in the Human Prefrontal Cortex Underlies Two Neurodegenerative Diseases." *Molecular Systems Biology*, U.S. National Library of Medicine, pubmed.ncbi.nlm.nih.gov/25080494/. Accessed 23 Apr. 2024.

394　Elaine Schmidt. "UCLA Scientists Hunt down Origin of Huntington's Disease in the Brain." *UCLA*, 21 May 2014, newsroom.ucla.edu/releases/ucla-scientists-hunt-down-origin-of-huntington-s-disease-in-the-brain. Accessed 23 Apr. 2024.

395　"Tony Bennett – the Good Life." *Genius*, genius.com/Tony-bennett-the-good-life-lyrics. Accessed 23 Apr. 2024.

396　"The Good Life (1962 Song)." *Wikipedia*, Wikimedia Foundation, 14 Feb. 2024, en.wikipedia. org/wiki/The_Good_Life_(1962_song). Accessed 23 Apr. 2024.

397　The Eye: The Center of the Storm, ww2010.atmos.uiuc.edu/(Gh)/guides/mtr/hurr/stages/cane/eye.rxml. Accessed 23 Apr. 2024.

398　"Non-Verbal Leakage." *Wikipedia*, Wikimedia Foundation, 18 Feb. 2024, en.wikipedia.org/wiki/Non-verbal_leakage. Accessed 23 Apr. 2024.

399   Stephen Porter, "Secrets and Lies: Involuntary Leakage in Deceptive Facial Expressions as a Function of Emotional Intensity." *Journal of Nonverbal Behavior*, vol. 36, no. 1, 9 Oct. 2011, pp. 23–37, doi:10.1007/s10919-011-0120-7.

400   +Greekacom. "Kazantzakis Tomb in Heraklion, Greece: Greeka." *Greekacom*, +greekacom, www.greeka.com/crete/heraklion/sightseeing/tomb-kazantzakis/. Accessed 23 Apr. 2024.

401   Richard Buxton, *The Complete World of Greek Mythology*. Thames & Hudson, 2004, 122.

402   *Omphale*, www.perseus.tufts.edu/Herakles/omphale.html. Accessed 23 Apr. 2024.

403   Ibid.

404   "Deianira." *Wikipedia*, Wikimedia Foundation, 12 Dec. 2023, en.wikipedia.org/wiki/Deianira. Accessed 23 Apr. 2024.

405   *Deianira, Hercules' Second Wife*, www.perseus.tufts.edu/Herakles/deianira.html. Accessed 23 Apr. 2024.

406   "Arrow Poison." *Wikipedia*, Wikimedia Foundation, 17 Apr. 2024, en.wikipedia.org/wiki/Arrow_poison. Accessed 23 Apr. 2024.

407   Madeleine. "Who Was Hercules Wife in Greek Mythology?" *THEOI GREEK MYTHOLOGY - Exploring Mythology in Classical Literature & Art*, 3 Dec. 2019, www.theoi.com/articles/who-was-hercules-wife-in-greek-mythology/. Accessed 23 Apr. 2024.

408   Cartwright, Mark. "Hercules." *World History Encyclopedia*, Https://Www.Worldhistory.Org#organization, 21 Feb. 2023, www.worldhistory.org/hercules/. Accessed 23 Apr. 2024.

409   Mark Cartwright, "Hercules." *World History Encyclopedia*, Https://Www.Worldhistory.Org#organization, 21 Feb. 2023, www.worldhistory.org/hercules/. Accessed 23 Apr. 2024.

410   *The Life and Times of Hercules*, www.perseus.tufts.edu/Herakles/bio.html. Accessed 23 Apr. 2024.

411   *What Does My CAG Number Tell Me?*, insidehd.com/the-in-between-years-part-5-1786644b0eac. Accessed 23 Apr. 2024.

412   *Department of Neurology UC Davis Health*, "The Huntington Gene." UC Davis Health, health.ucdavis.edu/huntingtons/genetic-change.html. Accessed 23 Apr. 2024.

413   Ibid.

414   *What Does My CAG Number Tell Me?*, insidehd.com/the-in-between-years-part-5-1786644b0eac. Accessed 23 Apr. 2024.

415   Staff, Familydoctor.org Editorial and Alex Rice. "Huntington's Disease - Brain Disorder - Genetic Disorder." *Familydoctor.Org*, 1 Mar. 2021, familydoctor.org/condition/huntingtons disease/#:~:text=A%20trusted%20advisor%20can%20help%20with%20important%20 decisions,related%20to%20falls.%20Questions%20to%20ask%20your%20doct   or. Accessed 23 Apr. 2024.

416   "Huntington's Disease." *Mayo Clinic*, Mayo Foundation for Medical Education and Research, 17 May 2022, www.mayoclinic.org/diseases-conditions/huntingtons-disease/symptoms-causes/syc-20356117. Accessed 23 Apr. 2024.

417   Ibid.

418   Dr. Jasmine Shaikh, MD. "What Are the 5 Stages of Huntington's Disease (HD)?" *MedicineNet*, 22 July 2022, www.medicinenet.com/what_are_the_5_stages_of_huntingtons_disease/article.htm. Accessed 23 Apr. 2024.

419   *Stages of Huntington's Disease – Hopes Huntington's Disease*, hopes.stanford.edu/stages-of-huntingtons-disease/. Accessed 23 Apr. 2024.

420   Ibid.

421   "Progression of Symptoms in the Early and Middle Stages of Huntington Disease." *Archives of Neurology*, U.S. National Library of Medicine, pubmed.ncbi.nlm.nih.gov/11176966/. Accessed 23 Apr. 2024.

422   "What Are the 5 Stages of Huntington's Disease (HD)?" *MedicineNet*, 22 July 2022, www.medicinenet.com/what_are_the_5_stages_of_huntingtons_disease/article.htm. Accessed 23 Apr. 2024.

423   Ibid.

424 "Huntington's Disease." *Mayo Clinic*, Mayo Foundation for Medical Education and Research, 17 May 2022, www.mayoclinic.org/diseases-conditions/huntingtons-disease/symptoms-causes/syc-20356117. Accessed 23 Apr. 2024.

425 "Overview of Huntington's Disease - Huntington's Disease Society of America." *Huntington's Disease Society of America - Family Is Everything*, 6 Nov. 2020, hdsa.org/what-is-hd/overview-of-huntingtons-disease/. Accessed 23 Apr. 2024.

426 "Huntington's Disease." *Mayo Clinic*.

427 BioNews Staff, "Stages of Huntington's Disease (HD)." *Huntington's Disease News*, 18 Oct. 2021, huntingtonsdiseasenews.com/stages-of-huntingtons-disease/. Accessed 23 Apr. 2024.

428 "Overview of Huntington's Disease - Huntington's Disease Society of America." *Huntington's Disease Society of America - Family Is Everything*, 6 Nov. 2020, hdsa.org/what-is-hd/overview-of-huntingtons-disease/. Accessed 23 Apr. 2024.

429 Ibid.

430 Ibid.

431 "What Are the 5 Stages of Huntington's Disease (HD)?" *MedicineNet*, 22 July 2022, www.medicinenet.com/what_are_the_5_stages_of_huntingtons_disease/article.htm. Accessed 23 Apr. 2024.

432 "Overview of Huntington's Disease - Huntington's Disease Society of America." *Huntington's Disease Society of America - Family Is Everything*, 6 Nov. 2020, hdsa.org/what-is-hd/overview-of-huntingtons-disease/. Accessed 23 Apr. 2024.

433 "Progression of Symptoms in the Early and Middle Stages of Huntington Disease." *Archives of Neurology*, JAMA Network, 1 Feb. 2001, jamanetwork.com/journals/jamaneurology/fullarticle/778574. Accessed 23 Apr. 2024.

434 "Timing and Impact of Psychiatric, Cognitive, and Motor Abnormalities in Huntington Disease." *Neurology*, U.S. National Library of Medicine, pubmed.ncbi.nlm.nih.gov/33766994/. Accessed 23 Apr. 2024.

435 Ibid.

436 BioNews Staff, "Stages of Huntington's Disease (HD)." *Huntington's Disease News*, 18 Oct. 2021, huntingtonsdiseasenews.com/stages-of-huntingtons-disease/. Accessed 23 Apr. 2024.

437 "Dyskinesia." *Wikipedia*, Wikimedia Foundation, 26 Nov. 2023, en.wikipedia.org/wiki/Dyskinesia. Accessed 23 Apr. 2024.

438 "Chorea." *Wikipedia*, Wikimedia Foundation, 19 Feb. 2024, en.wikipedia.org/wiki/Chorea#:~:text=Chorea%20%28or%20choreia%2C%20occasionally%29%20is%20an%20abnormal%20involuntary,the%20feet%20or%20hands%20are%20comparable%20to%20dancing. Accessed 23 Apr. 2024.

439 "Chorea." *Wikipedia*, Wikimedia Foundation, 19 Feb. 2024, en.wikipedia.org/wiki/Chorea#:~:text=Chorea%20%28or%20choreia%2C%20occasionally%29%20is%20an%20abnormal%20involuntary,the%20feet%20or%20hands%20are%20comparable%20to%20dancing. Accessed 23 Apr. 2024.

440 "Hyperkinesia." *Wikipedia*, Wikimedia Foundation, 15 Feb. 2024, en.wikipedia.org/wiki/Hyperkinesia. Accessed 23 Apr. 2024.

441 "Bradykinesia (Slowed Movements)." *ParkinsonsDisease.Net*, parkinsonsdisease.net/symptoms/bradykinesia-slowed-movement#:~:text=Bradykinesia%2C%20which%20means%20slow%20movement%2C%20is%20one%20of,in%20facial%20expressions%20and%20a%20chronic%2C%20abnormal%20stillness. Accessed 23 Apr. 2024.

442 "Bradykinesia." *Bradykinesia - an Overview | ScienceDirect Topics*, www.sciencedirect.com/topics/neuroscience/bradykinesia. Accessed 23 Apr. 2024.

443 "Bradykinesia." *Psychology Wiki*, Fandom, Inc., psychology.wikia.org/wiki/Bradykinesia#:~:text=In%20medicine%20%28%20neurology%20%29%2C%20bradykinesia%20

denotes%20%22slow,describes%20a%20slowness%20in%20the%20execution%20of%20 movement. Accessed 23 Apr. 2024.

444 "Chorea." *Wikipedia*, Wikimedia Foundation.

445 "Huntington's Disease - Symptoms, Causes, Treatment: Nord." National Organization for Rare Disorders, 20 Nov. 2023, rarediseases.org/rare-diseases/huntingtons-disease/. Accessed 23 Apr. 2024.

446 Ibid.

447 *Nutrition and HD*, health.ucdavis.edu/huntingtons/files/Nutrition_and_HD%5B1%5D.pdf. Accessed 23 Apr. 2024.

448 *A Caregiver's Guide to HD - Huntington's Disease Society Of ...*, hdsa.org/wp-content/ uploads/2015/03/A-Caregivers-Guide-to-HD.pdf. Accessed 23 Apr. 2024.

449 Sandra Close Kirkwood, PhD. "Progression of Symptoms in the Early and Middle Stages of Huntington Disease." *Archives of Neurology*, JAMA Network, 1 Feb. 2001, jamanetwork.com/ journals/jamaneurology/fullarticle/778574. Accessed 23 Apr. 2024.

450 *Stages of Huntington's Disease – Hopes Huntington's Disease*, hopes.stanford.edu/stages-of- huntingtons-disease/. Accessed 23 Apr. 2024.

451 Kirkwood.

452 *Stages of Huntington's Disease – Hopes Huntington's Disease*.

453 Kirkwood.

454 *Stages of Huntingtons Disease and Treatment - Stanford ...*, aemstage.med.stanford.edu/ content/dam/sm/neurology/documents/md/MD-HD%20Stages%20Talk.pdf. Accessed 23 Apr. 2024.

455 *10 Symptoms of Huntington's Disease - Facty Health*, facty.com/conditions/huntingtons- disease/10-symptoms-of-huntingtons-disease/. Accessed 23 Apr. 2024.

456 Ibid.

457 "Depression and Stages of Huntington's Disease." *The Journal of Neuropsychiatry and Clinical Neurosciences*, 1 Nov. 2005, neuro.psychiatryonline.org/doi/10.1176/jnp.17.4.496. Accessed 23 Apr. 2024.

458 "Limberjack Dancing Doll - Etsy Canada." *Limberjack Dancing Doll - Etsy Canada*, www.etsy. com/ca/listing/64150362/limberjack-dancing-doll. Accessed 23 Apr. 2024.

459 "Progression of Symptoms in the Early and Middle Stages of Huntington Disease." *Archives of Neurology*, JAMA Network, 1 Feb. 2001, jamanetwork.com/journals/jamaneurology/ fullarticle/778574. Accessed 23 Apr. 2024.

460 "Depression and Stages of Huntington's Disease." *The Journal of Neuropsychiatry and Clinical Neurosciences*, 1 Nov. 2005, neuro.psychiatryonline.org/doi/10.1176/jnp.17.4.496. Accessed 23 Apr. 2024.

461 "Dystonia." *Mayo Clinic*, Mayo Foundation for Medical Education and Research, 18 June 2022, www.mayoclinic.org/diseases-conditions/dystonia/symptoms-causes/syc-20350480. Accessed 23 Apr. 2024.

462 "Dystonia." *Mayo Clinic*, Mayo Foundation for Medical Education and Research, 18 June 2022, www.mayoclinic.org/diseases-conditions/dystonia/symptoms-causes/syc-20350480. Accessed 24 Apr. 2024.

463 "14 Early Warning Signs of Blindness." *SimplyHealth.Today*, 8 Apr. 2021, simplyhealth. today/14-early-warning-signs-of-blindness/. Accessed 24 Apr. 2024.

464 "Huntington's Disease." *Mayo Clinic*, Mayo Foundation for Medical Education and Research, 17 May 2022, www.mayoclinic.org/diseases-conditions/huntingtons-disease/symptoms- causes/syc-20356117. Accessed 24 Apr. 2024.

465 Ibid.

466 Sandra Kirkwood, "Progression of Symptoms in the Early and Middle Stages of Huntington Disease." *Archives of Neurology*, JAMA Network, 1 Feb. 2001, jamanetwork.com/journals/ jamaneurology/fullarticle/778574. Accessed 24 Apr. 2024.

467   Sandra Kirkwood, "Progression of Symptoms in the Early and Middle Stages of Huntington Disease." *Archives of Neurology*, JAMA Network, 1 Feb. 2001, jamanetwork.com/journals/jamaneurology/fullarticle/778574. Accessed 24 Apr. 2024.

468   "14 Early Warning Signs of Blindness." *SimplyHealth.Today*, 8 Apr. 2021, simplyhealth.today/14-early-warning-signs-of-blindness/. Accessed 24 Apr. 2024.

469   Jane S. Paulsen, "Depression and Stages of Huntington's Disease." *The Journal of Neuropsychiatry and Clinical Neurosciences*, 1 Nov. 2005, neuro.psychiatryonline.org/doi/10.1176/jnp.17.4.496. Accessed 24 Apr. 2024.

470   *Stanford*, med.stanford.edu/content/dam/sm/neurology/documents/md/MD-HD%20Stages%20Talk.pdf. Accessed 24 Apr. 2024.

471   Oliver Quarrell, *Huntington's Disease / Oliver Quarrell*. Oxford, 2008, 13.

472   Jane S Paulsen, et al, "Depression and Stages of Huntington's Disease." *The Journal of Neuropsychiatry and Clinical Neurosciences*, 1 Nov. 2005, neuro.psychiatryonline.org/doi/10.1176/jnp.17.4.496. Accessed 24 Apr. 2024.

473   "Dementia: Disorder, Symptoms, Causes, Illness & Condition." *The Human Memory*, 20 May 2022, human-memory.net/dementia/. Accessed 24 Apr. 2024.

474   Ibid.

475   Ibid.

476   Tracy@kidskonnect.com. "Huntington's Disease: Symptoms, Causes, Illness & Condition." *The Human Memory*, 20 May 2022, human-memory.net/huntingtons-disease/. Accessed 24 Apr. 2024.

477   BioNews Staff, "Stages of Huntington's Disease (HD)." *Huntington's Disease News*, 18 Oct. 2021, huntingtonsdiseasenews.com/stages-of-huntingtons-disease/. Accessed 24 Apr. 2024.

478   *Stanford*, med.stanford.edu/content/dam/sm/neurology/documents/md/MD-HD%20Stages%20Talk.pdf. Accessed 24 Apr. 2024.

479   Tracy@kidskonnect.com. "Huntington's Disease: Symptoms, Causes, Illness & Condition." *The Human Memory*, 20 May 2022, human-memory.net/huntingtons-disease/. Accessed 24 Apr. 2024.

480   Tracy@kidskonnect.com. "Short-Term Memory & Working Memory: Definition, Duration & Capacity." *The Human Memory*, 20 May 2022, human-memory.net/short-term-working-memory/. Accessed 24 Apr. 2024.

481   Ibid.

482   Tracy@kidskonnect.com. "Huntington's Disease: Symptoms, Causes, Illness & Condition." *The Human Memory*, 20 May 2022, human-memory.net/huntingtons-disease/. Accessed 24 Apr. 2024.

483   "Dementia Due to Huntington Disease." *DoveMed*, www.dovemed.com/diseases-conditions/dementia-due-to-huntington-disease-hd/. Accessed 24 Apr. 2024.

484   *Challenging Behaviors in Huntington's Disease: Strategies* ..., health.ucdavis.edu/huntingtons/images/Challenging Behaviors in HD - Kocsis.pdf. Accessed 24 Apr. 2024.

485   "Cognitive Symptoms - Huntington's Disease Society of America." *Huntington's Disease Society of America - Family Is Everything*, 19 Mar. 2019, hdsa.org/what-is-hd/cognitive-symptoms/. Accessed 24 Apr. 2024.

486   *Challenging Behaviors in Huntington's Disease: Strategies* ..., health.ucdavis.edu/huntingtons/images/Challenging Behaviors in HD - Kocsis.pdf. Accessed 24 Apr. 2024.

487   Julie S. Snowden, "The Neuropsychology of Huntington's Disease." *OUP Academic*, Oxford University Press, 18 Sept. 2017, academic.oup.com/acn/article/32/7/876/4161107. Accessed 24 Apr. 2024.

488   "Dementia Due to Huntington Disease." *DoveMed*, www.dovemed.com/diseases-conditions/dementia-due-to-huntington-disease-hd/. Accessed 24 Apr. 2024.

489 Julie S. Snowden, "The Neuropsychology of Huntington's Disease." *OUP Academic*, Oxford University Press, 18 Sept. 2017, academic.oup.com/acn/article/32/7/876/4161107. Accessed 24 Apr. 2024.

490 "Huntington's Disease." *Mayo Clinic*, Mayo Foundation for Medical Education and Research, 17 May 2022, www.mayoclinic.org/diseases-conditions/huntingtons-disease/symptoms-causes/syc-20356117. Accessed 24 Apr. 2024.

491 Ibid.

492 "A Simple Way to Get Seen Get Healthy Get Rewardedget Seen." *Simplyhealth*, www.simplyhealth.co.uk/. Accessed 24 Apr. 2024.

493 "Cognitive Symptoms - Huntington's Disease Society of America." *Huntington's Disease Society of America - Family Is Everything*, 19 Mar. 2019, hdsa.org/what-is-hd/cognitive-symptoms/. Accessed 24 Apr. 2024.

494 Ibid.

495 "About Huntington's Disease and Related Disorders." *Johns Hopkins Medicine*, www.hopkinsmedicine.org/psychiatry/specialty_areas/huntingtons_disease/patient_family_resources/education_whatis.html. Accessed 24 Apr. 2024.

496 "Huntington's Disease." *Mayo Clinic*, Mayo Foundation for Medical Education and Research, 17 May 2022, www.mayoclinic.org/diseases-conditions/huntingtons-disease/symptoms-causes/syc-20356117. Accessed 24 Apr. 2024.

497 *Challenging Behaviors in Huntington's Disease: Strategies ...*, health.ucdavis.edu/huntingtons/images/Challenging Behaviors in HD - Kocsis.pdf. Accessed 24 Apr. 2024.

498 "Huntington's Disease." *Mayo Clinic*, Mayo Foundation for Medical Education and Research, 17 May 2022, www.mayoclinic.org/diseases-conditions/huntingtons-disease/symptoms-causes/syc-20356117. Accessed 24 Apr. 2024.

499 "Dementia Due to Huntington Disease." *DoveMed*, www.dovemed.com/diseases-conditions/dementia-due-to-huntington-disease-hd/. Accessed 24 Apr. 2024.

500 *The Behavioral Symptoms of Huntington's Disease – Hopes Huntington's Disease*, hopes.stanford.edu/the-behavioral-symptoms-of-huntingtons-disease/. Accessed 24 Apr. 2024.

501 *Challenging Behaviors in Huntington's Disease: Strategies ...*, health.ucdavis.edu/huntingtons/images/Challenging Behaviors in HD - Kocsis.pdf. Accessed 24 Apr. 2024.

502 "Behavioral / Psychiatric Symptoms - Huntington's Disease Society of America." Huntington's Disease Society of America - Family Is Everything, 20 Mar. 2019, hdsa.org/what-is-hd/behavioral-psychiatric-symptoms/. Accessed 24 Apr. 2024.

503 "Behavioral / Psychiatric Symptoms - Huntington's Disease Society of America." *Huntington's Disease Society of America - Family Is Everything*, 20 Mar. 2019, hdsa.org/what-is-hd/behavioral-psychiatric-symptoms/. Accessed 24 Apr. 2024.

504 Ibid.

505 Ibid.

506 *The Behavioral Symptoms of Huntington's Disease – Hopes Huntington's Disease*, hopes.stanford.edu/the-behavioral-symptoms-of-huntingtons-disease/. Accessed 24 Apr. 2024.

507 *Challenging Behaviors in Huntington's Disease: Strategies ...*, health.ucdavis.edu/huntingtons/images/Challenging Behaviors in HD - Kocsis.pdf. Accessed 24 Apr. 2024.

508 *The Behavioral Symptoms of Huntington's Disease – Hopes Huntington's Disease*, hopes.stanford.edu/the-behavioral-symptoms-of-huntingtons-disease/. Accessed 24 Apr. 2024.

509 Julie S. Snowden, "The Neuropsychology of Huntington's Disease." *OUP Academic*, Oxford University Press, 18 Sept. 2017, academic.oup.com/acn/article/32/7/876/4161107. Accessed 24 Apr. 2024.

510 *The Behavioral Symptoms of Huntington's Disease – Hopes Huntington's Disease.*

511 Ibid.

512 *Challenging Behaviors in Huntington's Disease: Strategies ...*, health.ucdavis.edu/huntingtons/images/Challenging Behaviors in HD - Kocsis.pdf. Accessed 24 Apr. 2024.

513 Erica Hersh, "Pill Rolling Tremor: Parkinson's, Motion, and More." *Healthline*, Healthline Media, 29 Sept. 2023, www.healthline.com/health/parkinsons/pill-rolling-tremor#outlook-and-prevention. Accessed 24 Apr. 2024.

514 *The Behavioral Symptoms of Huntington's Disease – Hopes Huntington's Disease*, hopes. stanford.edu/the-behavioral-symptoms-of-huntingtons-disease/. Accessed 24 Apr. 2024.

515 "Progression of Symptoms in the Early and Middle Stages of Huntington Disease." *Archives of Neurology*, U.S. National Library of Medicine, pubmed.ncbi.nlm.nih.gov/11176966/. Accessed 24 Apr. 2024.

516 "Huntington's Disease." *Mayo Clinic*, Mayo Foundation for Medical Education and Research, 17 May 2022, www.mayoclinic.org/diseases-conditions/huntingtons-disease/symptoms-causes/syc-20356117. Accessed 24 Apr. 2024.

517 *The Behavioral Symptoms of Huntington's Disease – Hopes Huntington's Disease.*

518 "Progression of Symptoms in the Early and Middle Stages of Huntington Disease."

519 Victoria Tan, "Sexual Problems in Huntington's Disease." *Huntington's Disease News*, 1 May 2018, huntingtonsdiseasenews.com/sexual-problems-huntingtons-disease/#:~:text=Less%20frequently%2C%20Huntington%E2%80%99s%20disease%20may%20also%20cause%20an,deep%20area%20of%20the%20brain%20that%20controls%20behavior. Accessed 24 Apr. 2024.

520 D. R.Thiruvady, "Functional Connectivity of the Prefrontal Cortex in Huntington's Disease." *Journal of Neurology*, Neurosurgery, and Psychiatry, U.S. National Library of Medicine, Feb. 2007, www.ncbi.nlm.nih.gov/pmc/articles/PMC2077648/#:~:text=A%20direct%20comparison%20of%20prefrontal,prefrontal%20regions%20in%20each%20hemisphere. Accessed 24 Apr. 2024.

521 Kendra Cherry, MSEd. "How Brain Neurons Change over Time from Life Experience." *Verywell Mind*, www.verywellmind.com/what-is-brain-plasticity-2794886. Accessed 24 Apr. 2024.

522 Alonso Montoya, "Brain Imaging and Cognitive Dysfunctions in Huntington's Disease." *Journal of Psychiatry & Neuroscience*: JPN, U.S. National Library of Medicine, Jan. 2006, www.ncbi.nlm.nih.gov/pmc/articles/PMC1325063/. Accessed 24 Apr. 2024.

523 "Progression of Symptoms in the Early and Middle Stages of Huntington Disease." *Archives of Neurology*, U.S. National Library of Medicine, pubmed.ncbi.nlm.nih.gov/11176966/. Accessed 24 Apr. 2024.

524 *The Behavioral Symptoms of Huntington's Disease – Hopes Huntington's Disease*, hopes. stanford.edu/the-behavioral-symptoms-of-huntingtons-disease/. Accessed 24 Apr. 2024.

525 Shakespeare, William. "Speech: "Tomorrow, and Tomorrow, and Tomorrow" by... *Poetry Foundation*, www.poetryfoundation.org/poems/56964/speech-tomorrow-and-tomorrow-and-tomorrow. Accessed 24 Apr. 2024.

Printed in the United States
by Baker & Taylor Publisher Services